PLOTS AND CHARACTERS
IN MAJOR RUSSIAN FICTION

Volume II
Gogol', Goncharov, Dostoevskii

Thomas E. Berry

Archon Books
Dawson

First published in 1978

Archon Books, The Shoe String Press Inc.
995 Sherman Avenue, Hamden, Connecticut 06514 USA

Wm Dawson & Sons Ltd, Cannon House
Folkestone, Kent, England

Library of Congress Cataloging in Publication Data

Plots and characters in major Russian fiction.

(The Plots and characters series)
CONTENTS: v. 1. Pushkin, Lermontov, Turgenev,
Tolstoi.—v. 2. Gogol', Goncharov, Dostoevskii.
1. Russian fiction—Stories, plots, etc.
2. Characters and characteristics in literature.
I. Title.
PG3095.B4   891.7'3'03   76-58458

Archon ISBN 0-208-01601-5 (v. 2)
Dawson ISBN 0 7129 0760 2 (v. 2)

PLOTS AND CHARACTERS
IN MAJOR RUSSIAN FICTION

THE PLOTS AND CHARACTERS SERIES

Robert L. Gale
General Editor

To my Parents on their
Fiftieth Wedding Anniversary

CONTENTS

PREFACE

This Volume II on Gogol', Goncharov, and Dostoevskii is designed like Volume I on Pushkin, Lermontov, Turgenev, and Tolstoy to help and encourage the reading of Russian literature.

As a reference book or reader's guide, this book has various functions:

1. Part I, the plots, can serve to recall plots and themes in famous Russian novels. Character lists are given after each plot: last names only for historical personages; full names for fictional characters.

2. Part II, the characters, is an index to fictional and historical characters in Russian literature. Biographical information (dates, etc.) is given for historical personages to assist the reader in seeking additional information in other sources. If a reader is looking for a particular historical personage or cannot remember where the figure appeared in a particular novel, he can find the information in the character section: for instance, Napoleon is listed in *The Brothers Karamazov* (4, 10, 6) which means Part 4, Book 10, Chapter 6. Another example would be the German philosopher Schiller, who is listed in *Crime and Punishment* (1, 4), meaning Part 1, Chapter 4.

3. Part II can help a reader identify the multitudinous generals, statesmen, and mythological references that abound in Russian literature. If a reader is not acquainted with Russian names, he is advised to read the following explanation of names in this book.

Russian Names

Russians have three names: first name, patronymic, and surname: for instance, Ivan Ivanovich Ivanov. The patronymic has the ending "ich" (son of) if it is a male name and "ovna" (daughter of) if it is a female. In alphabetizing, if a Russian has no surname, his name will be alphabetized by the first name. The patronymic will be given with the first name, but it does not affect the alphabetizing. Consequently, Ol'ga Ivanovna willl appear in the "O" section, not the "I" section.

The Library of Congress transcription system is used for the names in this volume. It should be pointed out that the system is different for French, German, Italian, English, and Russian names. For instance,

PREFACE

Peter in English is spelled Petr in the Russian system. Alexander is
Aleksandr. The spelling will depend on the country the name is from.
A reader should have no trouble, but some common names are given
under both spellings with cross references to avoid any confusion.

Acknowledgements

I wish to thank the outstanding scholar Dr. Charles A. Moser for
recommending me for this series.

I am grateful to Dr. Robert L. Gale, the General Editor of the Plots
and Characters Series, for his help, kindness, and encouragement
during the creation of these volumes.

I am indebted to my mother–in–law, Mrs. V. A. Kalichevsky, for her
careful checking of this manuscript against the hundreds of cards I
wrote out during my work on this project.

I used the following editions of Soviet publications during the
preparation of this work:

Gogol', N.V., *Sobranie sochinenii v semi tomakh.* (Moskva: Izdatel'stvo
"Khudozhestvennaia Literatura," 1966).

Goncharov, I.A., *Sobranie sochinenii v shesti tomakh*(Moskdv:
Izdatel'ctvo "Pravda", 1972).

Dostoevskii, F.M., *Polnoe Sobranie sochinenii v tridtsati tomakh.*
(Leningrad: Izdatel'stvo "Nauka," 1972).

I also wish to thank the librarians of the McKeldin Library of the
University of Maryland for their assistance during my work on this
volume.

Thomas E. Berry

Slavic Department
University of Maryland

CHRONOLOGY

Nicolai Vasil'evich Gogol', 1809-1852
Ivan Aleksandrovich Goncharov, 1812-1891
Fedor Mikhailovich Dostoevskii, 1821-1881

1809   N. V. Gogol' born at Sorochintsy, Poltava Province, in a family of Ukrainian Cossack gentry.

1812   I.A. Goncharov born in Simbirsk in a wealthy merchant family.

1820   Gogol' entered a provincial grammar school and remained until 1828.

1821   F. M. Dostoevskii born in Moscow, where his father was a doctor in a public hospital.

1828   Gogol' went to St. Petersburg and published a lengthy poem entitled *Hanz Kuchelgarten* at his own expense under the name V. Alov. Critical derision caused him to buy up available copies and destroy them.

1831   Gogol' published *Evenings on a Farm near Dikan'ka*. From its success he met members of the literary aristocracy: Pushkin, Zhukovskii, and Pletnev.

1832   Gogol' published second volume of "evenings."

1834   Gogol' made Professor of History at University of St. Petersburg but was not successful.

1835   Gogol' published *Mirgorod* and *Arabesques*.

1836   Gogol's famous comic-drama *Revizor (The Inspector General)* created.

1836-48   Gogol' lived abroad, mainly in Rome, returning to Russia for short visits.

1837   Dostoeskii attended Military Engineers' School in St. Petersburg.

1841   Dostoevskii commissioned but remained in school one more year. Received a post in Engineering Department.

1842   Gogol' published *Dead Souls*.

1844   Dostoevskii resigned his commission in the military, having completed his two-year obligatory term.

1846   Dostoevskii published *Poor Folk* and was greatly acclaimed. Published second novel *The Double* and was criticized.

1847   Goncharov published *A Common Story*. Gogol's *Selected Passages from a Correspondence with Friends* completed.

1849   Doestoevskii arrested as a member of the Petrashevskii circle, a group of zealous young intellectuals who discussed socialism. Sentenced to be shot, Dostoevskii was spared as he waited in line to be executed. Exiled to Siberia.

1850-54 Dostoevskii served term of penal servitude at Omsk convict prison.

1852   Gogol' died.

1855-57 Goncharov's notes about his travels in the Far East appeared under the title *Frigate "Pallada."*

1856   Dostoevskii's commission restored to him.

1857   Dostoevskii married Isaeva, a widow, while staying at Kuznetsk.

1859   Goncharov published *Oblomov*, which had immense success. Dostoevskii's *Village of Stepanchikogo* written and the author allowed to return to European Russia.

1861   Dostoevskii started the review *Vremia* (Time) with brother Mikhail. *Notes from a Dead House* appeared in it. Suppressed in 1863.

1863   Dostoevskii wrote *Winter Notes and Summer Impressions* after his trip to Europe.

1864   Dostoevskii began the journal *The Epoch*, but it was not as popular as his previous tabloid. His wife died and journal closed. Dostoevskii's *The Underground Man* published.

1866   *Crime and Punishment* and *The Gambler* completed.

1867   Dostoevskii married his secretary Anna Grigorievna Snitkina.

1868   *The Idiot* published.

1869   Goncharov finished his lengthy work *The Precipice*.

1870   Dostoevskii's *The Eternal Husband* published.

1873   Dostoevskii became editor of the gazette *The Citizen*. Published *The Devils (The Possessed)*.

1876   Dostoevskii published *An Author's Diary*.

1880   *The Brothers Karamazov* completed. Dostoevskii delivered his famous *Pushkin Speech* in Moscow.

1881   Dostoevskii died.

1891   Goncharov died.

PLOTS

The Adolescent (A Raw Youth), F. M. Dostoevskii, 1875.

Arkadii Andreevich Dolgorukii, the twenty-one-year-old narrator of the story of his family's history, was going home. He had been educated in distant schools and had seen his parents only once or twice in the past nine years. He had been sent away because he was the illegitimate son of Andrei Petrovich Versilov, a landowner who had squandered his fortune and who had lived for twenty years with Sofia Dolgorukaia, the wife of one of his serfs and the mother of Arkadii. Versilov had paid Makar Dolgorukii three thousand roubles after seducing his wife. Arkadii was returning to Versilov's estate with an ulterior motive: he wanted to establish a close relationship with his true father and then break it off forever. His greater aim was to achieve money and power, because they provide liberty.

At the estate, Arkadii soon realized that his parents had little in common, save for their physical bond. Versilov soon sent his son to old Prince Sokolskii, for whom the young man became a secretary and companion. Their most frequent topics of conversation were women and the existence of God.

Arkadii began visiting some old school friends at the home of Dergachev. The group was political in nature, but was vague about their aims. Arkadii rejected their ideas on communal dormitories, atheism, and communal wives. He felt that his love of humanity was ten times greater than theirs. Kraft, a newcomer to the group, asked to speak with Arkadii alone. The stranger revealed a letter which would settle a lawsuit Versilov was involved in with Prince Sergei Sokolskii, a relative of the old prince. The document supported Prince Sergei. Kraft also informed Arkadii about a past liaison between Versilov and Katerina Akhmakova, the daughter of old Prince Sokolskii. When that relationship had finished, Versilov proposed to Katerina's step-daughter Lidia, who was pregnant at the time by Prince Sergei Sokolskii. Katerina opposed the marriage, but Lidia died from self-inflicted sulfur poisoning before the wedding could take place. Lidia's daughter lived and was cared for by Versilov. Some thought that he was her father, but it was not true. Kraft also revealed to Arkadii knowledge about a letter which Katerina had written to a lawyer, inquiring whether she could stop her old father, Prince Sokolskii, from spending so much money during a trip through Europe for convalescence. Katerina was fearful that the letter would fall into the hands of her father and that he would write her out of his will. Arkadii already had possession of Katerina's letter, having been given it by Mar'ia, the wife of his former schoolmaster, but he did not tell Kraft that he had the letter sewed into his coat lining. Later Kraft shot himself, and Arkadii had the opportunity to read the deceased's diary. He learned that Kraft felt that Russians were inferior people; so he killed himself.

Arkadii gave the letter which he had received from Kraft about the legal affairs to Versilov, who turned it over to Prince Sergei. Winning the lawsuit, Prince Sergei insisted that Versilov take some of the money that came with the victory. Instead, Versilov challenged Prince Sergei to a duel because of a slap the prince had given him years before. However, they were able to talk things out peacefully and Arkadii was impressed by his father's behavior. They became closer.

Arkadii decided to work on his idea of depriving himself in order to build up his capital on the way to riches. He lived as frugally as possible, sometimes eating only bread and water. When he had convinced himself that he was capable of attaining any goal, he suddenly forsook his idea and began to waste money. He ate well, bought the best clothes, and started gambling.

Arkadii heard two rumors: Prince Sergei had proposed to Anna, Arkadii's half-sister, in the hope of obtaining her money so that he could pay off a debt he owed to the gambler Stebelkov; and Katerina was going to marry the Baron Bjoring. Arkadii decided to investigate both reports. When he went to Prutkova's, he thought that he was alone with Katerina, who was visiting there. He expressed his feelings for her and revealed that he had torn up her letter about her father. She then confessed that she was seeing him only because she knew he had the letter. Later Arkadii found out that Prutkova had been in the house. She and Katerina had been having a joke at his expense. When he went to Versilov, he learned that Anna was going to marry old Prince Nikolai Sokolskii instead of Prince Sergei. Arkadii was dumbfounded. Versilov had found out about the marriage plans because Anna had asked him if he planned to marry Katerina. Since the Russian church did not allow two men to marry each other's daughters and then be each other's sons-in-law, it was important for Anna, being Versilov's daughter, that he not marry Katerina, Prince Nikolai's daughter.

Gambling, Arkadii lost a considerable amount and was forced to borrow three hundred roubles from Prince Sergei. While the latter needed the money himself, he loaned it to Arkadii. The young man again went gambling but this time won heavily. When he met Prince Sergei, the aristocrat treated him unkindly. Later Arkadii learned that the reason the prince had given him the money was that he was responsible for Arkadii's sister Liza's pregnancy. Prince Sergei had assumed that Arkadii knew about his sister's predicament and was demanding the money as payment for his family's honor. But Arkadii had known nothing about Liza's situation and convinced Prince Sergei of his innocence. The latter begged for forgiveness and became closer to Arkadii, telling him the following story about his involvement with Liza. After resigning from the service because of an unethical incident, he had gone to Luga and met Liza. He was very depressed and contemplated suicide. Liza talked him out of his depression and they fell in love. However, he decided to deceive Liza and marry Anna; but when he asked her, she refused. Prince Sergei also confessed to Arkadii that he was involved in a forgery ring. Stebelkov had once given him three thousand roubles to write a letter of introduction for him to Naschokin, a professional forger. Prince Sergei was then an accomplice in the crime the two committed. Stebelkov gave the letter of introduction to a man named Zhibelskii, who began blackmailing Prince Sergei for eight thousand roubles. Arkadii suggested that the prince borrow ten thousand roubles from Prince Nikolai. Sergei reluctantly agreed; but when he learned that Prince Nikolai was going to marry Anna, he refused to approach the prince for money.

Arkadii went to Stebelkov, asking him to go persuade Prince Sergei to go to Prince Nikolai for his debt. Stebelkov, however, asked Arkadii for a letter of introduction to Dergachev. Arkadii refused but informed Vassin that Stebelkov knew about the group. Then Arkadii went to Prince Nikolai, who admitted that he was going to marry Anna. He told Arkadii that Katerina knew about the marriage and approved. Suddenly Katerina entered the room but quickly left when she saw Arkadii. He ran after her, but she was with Baron Bjoring. Arkadii followed them outside to their carriage, but the baron pushed Arkadii down into the snow when he reached the vehicle. Arkadii was humiliated. Arkadii found out that Katerina was cold toward him because Versilov had written her a letter asking her to quit seducing his son. Versilov's motive was his hatred for Katerina. When Arkadii went to his father, he found Baron Bjoring there. Versilov provoked the baron, who left in a rage. Arkadii demanded to know why his father had written such a letter, causing his son such anguish. Versilov only laughed, and Arkadii realized that the proud aristocrat had used his son as a means of vengeance on Katerina.

Arkadii returned to Prince Sergei, and the two decided on gambling for the ten thousand they needed. Arkadii became embroiled in a fight at the roulette wheel and was accused of stealing three hundred roubles. He was thrown out. Totally disgraced, he wandered around town and accidentally fell, losing consciousness. He was awakened at the home of Versilov, who informed him that the money he was accused of stealing had been found and a public apology made. The casino sent Arkadii the money he had won that night.

Makar Dolgorukii became seriously ill and came to live with Versilov and Sof'ia. Arkadii was drawn to the old man and spent much time listening to his stories and exchanging philosophical thought.

Arkadii found out that it was Lambert who had found him unconscious in the street. During his ravings, Arkadii had told Lambert about Katerina's letter concerning her father's money. Lambert thought up a devious plot: he would steal the letter and offer it to Anna for thirty thousand roubles and then actually sell it to Katerina for more. However, Anna went directly to Arkadii when she learned of the letter, and he informed her that he had torn it up. Lambert's plans were pointless.

Prince Sergei decided to marry Liza. However, when he found out that she was a friend of Vassin, he reported to the authorities about the Dergachev group. They were arrested, and Liza was furious at the prince.

Makar Dolgorukii died, and Sof'ia and Versilov planned to marry. When Arkadii went to Prutkova's, he met Katerina. She forgave Versilov for the letter and wished to be left in peace. When Arkadii went to Versilov, the father showed his son a letter from Katerina in which she told him of her impending marriage to Baron Bjoring. Versilov forgave her the past and sent a message of blessing. He no longer hated her and urged Arkadii to destroy Katerina's letter about her father.

Arkadii decided to return the letter to Katerina through Prutkova. Lambert stole the letter out of Arkadii's coat lining, substituting paper for it. Arkadii found out that Anna was planning to marry old Prince Sokolskii and go abroad with him and Katerina. There the two women would have the old man declared insane and take his money. Katerina, however, decided that she could not participate in the plan. Finding out that Katerina's letter still existed, Anna decided to obtain it and show it to the old prince in the hope of shocking him into an early grave. When Arkadii would not surrender the letter, Anna decided to tell the old prince anyway and then confront Arkadii about it in the prince's presence. Anna brought the old prince to Versilov's, but Arkadii refused to acknowledge the existence of the letter.

When Versilov and Arkadii went to Prutkova's, Lambert was there pointing a gun at Katerina and demanding that she buy her letter for thirty thousand roubles. The men rushed Lambert and took the gun, knocking him unconscious. Katerina fainted, and Versilov picked her up, still holding Lambert's gun. Arkadii tried to take the gun from his father because he noticed that Versilov was holding it at Katerina's head. Versilov kissed the unconscious woman, but before he could shoot her, Arkadii tore the gun from his hand. In the shuffle, Arkadii accidentally shot Versilov in the shoulder, and he dropped to the floor beside Lambert.

Time passed. Versilov became devoted to Sof'ia. The old prince died and left Katerina much wealth. She went abroad and never married. Prince Sergei died in prison, where he went in punishment of his past unlawful activities. Liza lost his child in a miscarriage and suffered permament damage to her health. Prutkova encouraged Arkadii to continue his studies in the university.

Arkadii sent his manuscript to a former tutor for evaluation. The teacher approved it. He told Arkadii that he was a member of an exceptional family and that one day his manuscript would be famous.

Acis, Aferdov, Agafia, Agrafena, Akhmakov, Katerina Akhmakova, Lidia Akhmakova, Tsar Aleksei, Alphonsine, Ancheia, Andreev, Nikolai Semenovich Andronikov, Anikiia, Anna, Anton, Arina, Arkasha, Averianov, Avistage, Balle, Barbara,· Bashutskii, Belinskii, de Berry, Bismarch, Bjoring, Charlemagne, Chatskii, Chernyshev, Cherviakov, Copernicus, Dar'ia, Daria Onisimovna, Aleskei Darzau, David, Dergachev, Desdemona, Dickens, Liza Makarovna Dolgorukaia, Sof'ia Andreevna Dolgorukaia, Arkadii Andreevich Dolgorukii, Makar Ivanovich Dolgorukii, Dubasov, Eliseev, Fanariotova, Faust, Ferzing, Filipp, Foma, Galatea, Galileo, Gogol', Anton Goremyka, Granz, Gregorii, Gretchen, Gubonin, Harpagon, Hecuba, Hertzen, Horatius, Hugo, Iago, Kilian, King of Sweden, Kock, Kokorev, Korovkin, Kraft, Krylov, Kudriumov, Maurice Lambert, Lavrorskii, Law, Lebrecht, Lichten, Litvinov, Lorrain, Lucia, St. Luke, Lukeria, Machiavelli, Mahomet, Savin Makarov, Malgasov, Mar'ia, Mars, St. Matthew, Matvei, Militrisa, Minerva, Abbess Mitrofania,

Molière, Modier de Mongeot, Montferrant, Napoleon I, Ippolit
Nashchokin, Nastas'ia, Nekrasov, Nikolai Ivanych, Nikolai Se-
menovich, Ol'ga Onisimovna, Olympiada, Othello, Petr, Petr
Stepanovich, Petr Valerianovich, Philip, Pontius Pilate, Piron,
Pliushkin, Poliakov, Polinka, Tat'iana Pavlovna Prutkova, Push-
kin, R---, Abbé Rigaud, Romeo, Rothschild, Rousseau, Poliuka
Sachs, Safronov, Anfisa Sapozhkova, Schiller, Semen, Shake-
speare, Aleksandra Sinitskaia, Sistine Madonna, Maksim Skoto-
boinikov, von Sohn, Nikolai Sokolskii, Sergei Petrovich Sokolskii,
Solomon, Stebelkov, Stepanov, Stolbeev, Anna Stolbeeva,
Suvorov, Talleyrand-Périgord, Tat'iana, Tikhomirov, Touchard,
Trishatov, Turgenev, Prince V---, Valoniev, Vasin, Verigina,
Versilov, Andrei Petrovich Versilov, Anna Andreevna Versilova,
Aleksandra Vitovtova, Zavialov, Zershikov, Zhibelskii, Zhileiko,
Efim Zverev.

Arabesques, N. V. Gogol', 1835.
"Nevskii Prospect"
A street as distinct and awe-inspiring as the Nevskii Prospect has a
personality all its own. In the earliest morning, it is empty save for the
smell of fresh baked bread and the hordes of old ragged women on the
way to church. Gradually working people move through the street
and peasants on errands run about. Up to twelve o'clock, the Nevskii
Prospect is not the goal of any man but simply the means of reaching
it. At noon tutors of all nationalities descend on the avenue. By two
o'clock, clerks on special duties and customers in fine clothes fill the
area. By three o'clock, government clerks are everywhere; but they
disappear by four, when the street is almost empty. As dusk falls, a
mysterious time approaches and young men are on their way to
parties.

Once the artist Piskarev and a Lieutenant Pirogov met on the great
avenue. They were detracted by young beauties. Pirogov went after a
striking blonde, while Piskarev followed a beauty who held him in a
trance. When they came to an apartment building, she turned and
motioned for him to follow. What would have awakened base
thoughts in a dissolute man became a source of holiness in him. He
was sure some mysterious and important circumstance was causing
the young lady to want to share a confidence with him. On the fourth
floor, he followed her into a room where three female figures were
lying around. One was playing cards, another played a piano, and the
third was combing her hair. The room was filthy. Piskarev was taken

aback. Why did such a heavenly creature live in such a place? As he looked at her beauty, her lips suddenly opened and vile, vulgar words came to his ear. Instead of accepting her favors, he dashed to the street and returned to his room, despondent. Later a footman in gorgeous livery entered his room and informed him that the lady he had just visited had sent a carriage for him. Piskarev ran down the steps of his building and entered the carriage, which took him to an elegant ballroom. As he made his way through the crowd, he came upon the beautiful woman. She took him aside and asked him to listen to her secret. He agreed. Just as she was about to reveal it, they were interrupted by a man speaking a strange language. She left with the stranger, telling Piskarev to wait. He did for a long time and then looked for the beauty, who had disappeared. Suddenly, he awoke. It had all been a dream. Piskarev began to live for his dreams so that he could see the beauty. His health began to fail. Wishing to invoke more dreams, he sought opium. A Persian gave him some for a painting the artist had been assigned to paint. His life became an eternal battle between dream and reality. He thought of nothing but the beauty and even gave up eating. Finally, he decided to marry her and save her from a life of shame. He went to the house where he had followed her, but she rebuked his proposal, refusing to be poor for love. It was more than the artist could bear, and he went home and cut his throat. His passion for beauty had destroyed him.

Lieutenant Pirogov also had an unusual experience after following the blonde. He entered her house but was confronted by two drunken Germans, the ironmonger Schiller and the bootmaker Hoffman. They chased him away. When he went to Schiller's shop the next day, the blonde waited on him but resisted his advances. She called her hus band Schiller. Pirogov asked the German to make a set of special spurs for him. Schiller asked a ridiculous price, but Pirogov accepted and squeezed the blonde's arm in leaving. When he returned for the spurs, he admired the workmanship and ordered a sheath for a dagger he owned. Schiller wanted to refuse, but his pride made him accept. However, he was stupefied when Pirogov kissed the blonde on the lips as he left the store. When the stupid blonde told Pirogov that her husband was not home on Sundays, the eager young man appeared at her door that day. The blonde wife appeared frightened but was soon dancing with the officer. As he was showering her with kisses, Schiller and his drinking companions came in. What a beating they gave Pirogov! He went home planning to lodge a complaint; but after eating cream puffs and dancing a fine mazurka in a restaurant, he changed his mind. How fate plays with us! No one receives what he expects. But the strangest things happen on the Nevskii Prospect. The devil himself lights the street lamps.

   Bianco of Perugino, Bulgarin, Dmitrii Donskoi, Filatka, Hoffmann, Hoffmann, Kuntz, Orlov, Pirogov, Piskarev, Pushkin, Schiller, Schiller, William Tell.

"The Notes of a Madman"
Waking late, Aksentii Ivanovich Poprishchin rushed to his office even though he did not want to go. The chief of his division had been tormenting him lately, and he was depressed. Near a store he heard two dogs talking about their correspondence with each other, but he was not surprised. After all, the world has had many similar occurrences. In England a fish said three words, and scientists have yet to untangle them. He had also read an article in which two cows went into a store and asked for a pound of tea. Yet the dogs attracted him, and he followed the owner of one of the mutts home.

   At one time the director's daughter came into the office and Poprishchin was transformed. He saw a celestial image in white with the voice of a canary. He thought of a forbidden subject. Later the divisional chief accused Poprishchin of trailing the director's daughter Sof'ia and made fun of his presumptions. However, Poprishchin knew that he would do well in the world. After all, he went to the theater, which, in his opinion, set him above other civil servants. One actress reminded him of a forbidden subject. He also thought of "it" when he once looked into the director's quarters. He imagined Sof'ia's boudoir and envisioned her leg, a most roguish thought, he concluded.

   Poprishchin decided that he must obtain the letters exchanged between the two dogs he overheard talking. He went to the apartment of one dog's owner and knocked. When a maid asked what he wanted, he replied that he wished to talk with her dog. The animal itself came running and barking. It bit Poprishchin, but he went straight to its basket and took some papers from under the straw. He left the startled maid and went home to read. As he suspected, the dogs wrote to each other some revealing news: Sof'ia was in love with an officer, and she made fun of a clerk in her father's office, Poprishchin himself. He was stunned by the news. Sof'ia even said that his hair was like straw. He tore the paper into shreds. They contained only lies, he concluded, just like the absurdity that he was a clerk when he was probably a count or a general. But things were confused all over. Poprishchin read that in Spain they were having trouble choosing an heir to the throne. After a dinner during which his servant Mavra reminded him of his absent-mindedness, he went to bed to consider the Spanish succession. He awoke realizing that he himself was the King of Spain. Mavra was frightened when her master revealed his identity, but she was only one of the stupid masses.

When the new king did not report to work for three weeks, someone was sent to inquire. The king then went to the office for a lark. When papers were put before him to copy, he sat blankly, waiting for everyone to realize who was sitting there. Finally he signed a paper Ferdinand VIII and went straight to the director's house. Entering her boudoir, he announced to Sof'ia that she would soon be happy with him in spite of their enemies' intrigues. The startled girl watched the intruder leave. She did not know that he alone had discovered that women were in love with the devil.

Since the Spanish delegates had failed to arrive, Poprishchin decided to make his own mantle out of his overcoat. He cut it into shreds and, to the horror of Mavra, adorned himself in it. Suddenly, however, he found himself in Spain. When put in a small room and told not to call himself Ferdinand VIII, he complained and was hit hard with a stick. He thought that the Grand Chancellor might really be the Grand Inquisitor and that he had fallen into the hands of the Inquisition. Sure enough, the Grand Inquisitor did appear. He beat Poprishchin and poured cold water on his head. The madman appealed to his mother for help before announcing that the Dey of Algiers had a wart under his nose. A speck on a pimple is the location of all humanity.

> Bobov, Dey of Algiers, Ferdinand VIII, Fidele, Fido, Filatka, Grand Chancellor, Grand Inquisitor, Griforii, King of Spain, Lidina, Madgie, Mahomet, Mavra, Philip II, de Polignac, Aksentii Ivanovich Poprishchin, Pushkin, Rose, Sofia, Sultan of Turkey, Wellington, Zverkov.

"The Portrait"

I

Passing an art gallery in the Shchukin Court of St. Petersburg, the artist Chertkov was attracted to the display in the gallery window. He was amazed at the poor quality of the paintings before him and wondered who would buy them. On the floor of the shop, he found a few dusty picutures which he began to examine. He was immediately struck by a face in one which showed that it had been painted by a master. It was a portrait of an old man with a malignant smile. The eyes were large, black, and lusterless. Chertkov was fascinated by the picture and sought to buy it. However, someone else joined in the bidding, and the artist had to pay all he had, fifty roubles. As he started to seize his treasure, he was taken aback by the living quality of the eyes. It was as if the eyes were still alive, not painted, but human. He left the picture and ran onto the street, trying to decide if some supernatural power were peering through those eyes against all the laws of nature. He went home to his room and looked at his own pictures. There was nothing masterful in them. His servant entered and mentioned that the landlord wanted the rent. Chertkov decided he would return to the gallery the next day and demand his money back. The servant lit a candle and left. Suddenly Chertkov shuddered. The picture he had bought was hanging on the wall. He called the servant, but the boy assured him that no one had entered the room. Chertkov's hair stood on end. He went over all the commonplace explanations to which one resorts when he wants to prove that something which has happened must have happened as he thinks. Yet he could find no explanation and tried not to look at the picture. However, his eyes were drawn there. He covered the art work with a sheet, but the eyes haunted him. He tried to sleep but could not. In a drowsy state, he saw the figure in the picture detach itself and come to his bedstead. The old man told him to paint portraits and he would help him become rich. Chertkov was stupefied but found the picture still covered with the sheets. Later he fell asleep.

The next morning a policeman came and demanded the rent for the landlord. When Chertkov said that he had no money, the policeman began looking for the artist's work. He uncovered the old man's portrait and took hold of the painting. A roll of gold coins fell from the back of the picture. Chertkov pretended that it was a legacy from his father and paid his debt. Then he rented a fashionable lodging and moved there. A woman soon arrived and asked that the artist paint her daughter Annette. He agreed and roughed out a sketch for her. The woman was not satisfied. The next morning Chertkov put an un-finished picture of Psyche on his easel. Annette and her mother arrived and were delighted with the picture he was painting, thinking that it was Annette. Chertkov finished the painting and sold it to them as if it really were Annette's portrait. When they left, his conscience bothered him. He had not been true to his art, but soon all of St. Petersburg flocked to him. He became wealthy. Genuine artists shrugged their shoulders when they saw how he wasted his talent, but the artist cared little for his craft. Gold became his passion.

One day Chertkov received an invitation to judge a picture by one of his former classmates, a young man who had sacrificed everything for his art. When Chertkov saw the purity and sincerity of the paintings, he was so struck emotionally that he ran from the gallery in tears. He realized how he had forsaken his talent. He began to buy fine paintings and destroy them. His wealth was used to demolish many a fine work of art. Soon he was mentally ill and died raving mad. His corpse was a thing of evil, dreadful to behold.

II

At an art gallery, a group of people stood before a loathsome portrait while a narrator revealed the history of the monstrous work of art. His father had been an artist of merit who went to money-lenders only in emergencies. In one such case, he thought of approaching Petromikhali, a miser with a frightful reputation, but learned the money-lender was dying. The artist assumed that the oncoming death was a sign that he should not go there. However, to his amazement, Petromikhali sent for him, asking him to bring his paints and brushes. When he arrived at the moneylender's, the withered head of the dying man raised up and flashed such eyes on the artist that he shuddered. The half-dead, wasted body demanded that the artist paint its portrait. With terror, the artist began his work. He worked quickly, fearing his subject's imminent death. When he had blocked in the wasted figure and began to create the details, the eyes suddenly became alive. The artist bound back in terror. Petromikhali begged him to continue, confessing that he had the power to live in the picture if it were completed. His eyes were already there. The artist could not lift a brush. Gold and promises could not force him to continue. He ran out as the moneylender died. Reaching his home, the artist found the unfinished portrait in his studio. He threw it into the fireplace and watched it burn, only to turn around and find the portrait on his wall. Soon his wife accidentally swallowed the pins she was holding in her mouth and died. Then his son fell from a window and was killed. The artist sent his other son, the narrator, to a military school while he entered a monastery. Ten years later, the narrator visited his father and the old man revealed a secret: The antichrist was returning to earth through souls of men like the moneylender. He would be destroyed in thirty years if someone told his story. The narrator mentioned that he saw his father thirty years ago and the startled audience watched the features of the portrait change completely. The eyes were no longer alive.

Annette, Princess B--, Chertkov, Erema, Eruslan Lazarevich, Foma, Khozrev-Mirza, Maecenas, Mars, Militrisa Kirbitevna, Petromikhali, Psyche, Sikher.

The Brothers Karamazov, F. M. Dostoevskii, 1880.
Part I.

Dmitrii, Ivan, and Alesha Karamazov were the sons of the notorious profligate and landowner Fedor Karamazov, whose debaucheries contributed to the early deaths of his two wives. The first, Adelaida, mothered his first son, Dmitrii, before the father's carousing drove her into the arms of a young student. At her death, the four-year-old Dmitrii was taken in by relatives and reared with the understanding that he was due a substantial inheritance from his father. Dmitrii grew up an emotional sensualist and became an officer in the military service. The duality of his character was evident in his noble and sadistic impulses. Fedor's second wife, Sofia, an heiress whose guardian objected to her marriage, gave birth to Ivan and Alesha before her husband's orgies caused her mental breakdown and death. Her guardian arranged for the upbringing of her sons. The intellectual Ivan grew into a writer and began making a name for himself in literary journals. The mystically inclined Alesha entered a monastery where he was the pupil of a famous Orthodox Church elder, Father Zosima. The three sons met at their father's large house when Dmitrii returned to collect his legacy and Ivan came to seek financial help. Alesha felt a strong friendship for Dmitrii but was disturbed by Ivan's atheism. Because of their disputes over money, the family agreed to meet in the monastery with Father Zosima, hoping the elder could help them settle their differences peacefully.

The Karamazovs were joined at the monastery by a former guardian of Dmitrii, Miusov, and his relative, Kalganov. Fedor conducted himself foolishly before Father Zosima, and the elder interrupted their talk for a visit with some pilgrims. One wealthy woman, Madame Khokhlakova, expressed doubts about her faith. Father Zosima stated that he would send Alesha to her and her crippled daughter, Lise. When the elder returned to the Karamazovs, Ivan revealed his theory that if immortality did not exist, then there can be no reason for virtue in the world. Fedor insulted Dmitrii by accusing him of having an interest in Grushenka, a local prostitute, while being betrothed to Katerina Ivanovna, the daughter of a former military commander. Dmitrii had saved the officer from scandal by giving Katerina 4,500 roubles to repay the funds her father had squandered.

In an emotional outburst, Dmitrii in turn accused Fedor of being interested in Grushenka. To the amazement of all, Father Zosima suddenly bowed to Dmitrii and left the room. Alesha accompanied the elder, who advised the novice to leave the monastery and go out into the world. Fedor, embarrassed by Zosima's departure, refused to dine with the others at the monastery and left. Rakitan, a liberal young seminarian, teased Alesha about Grushenka's designs on him and said that Zosima's bow to Dmitrii foretold of tragedy for the Karamazovs. Fedor abruptly returned, made a vulgar tirade against monks, and ordered Alesha to leave the monastery.

The Karamazov servants, Grigorii and Marfa, once had a six-fingered child which died in infancy. After the village idiot "Stinking Liza" was raped, supposedly by Fedor, and died in childbirth in the Karamazovs' bathhouse, the servants took her child Smerdiakov to rear. He was epileptic but became a servant in the Karamazov household when he grew up.

Dmitrii revealed to Alesha that he offered Katerina the money to save her father if she would come to his room, where he planned to seduce her. When she appeared, he felt sorry for the proud girl and gave her the money. Later, when a distant relative left Katerina a fortune, she repaid Dmitrii and offered to marry him. He accepted her proposal. When she gave him three thousand roubles to take to a relative, Dmitrii squandered the money on an orgy with Grushenka. Realizing that he did not want to marry Katerina, he begged Alesha to borrow three thousand roubles from their father, who kept that amount in a sack in the hope that Grushenka would come to him for a night.

Alesha found Ivan and Fedor arguing at the dinner table while his half-brother Smerdiakov served. Ivan insisted that there was no God while Alesha defended his faith in immortality. They were interrupted by Dmitrii, who entered looking for Grushenka. Not finding her, he seized his father, flung him on the floor, and kicked him in the head. Threatening him, Dmitrii ran out to search for Grushenka.

After a visit to Madame Khokhalakova's home, where he witnessed an argument between Katerina and Grushenka over Dmitrii, Alesha went to stay near the ailing Father Zosima. While there, Alesha received a love letter from the crippled Lise Khokhlakova.

Part II.

Alesha joined members of the holy community at the bedside of the dying Father Zosima. They all anticipated some sort of miracle after the elder's death. Father Zosima told Alesha to fulfill his responsibilities to his family. Alesha went to Fedor but was dismayed at his father's assertions that he would be a sensualist till death. Alesha left for Katerina's but met a group of boys who were stoning another small boy. When Alesha tried to help the attacked child, the boy bit Alesha's finger until it bled. Not understanding the boy's bitterness, Alesha went to the Khokhlakovs. Ivan and Katerina were there, and Alesha tried to convince them that they loved each other. Katerina stated that she could never abandon Dmitrii even if he married Grushenka. When Ivan left, Katerina told Alesha about a Captain Snegirev who had been brutally beaten by Dmitrii. She asked Alesha to take the destitute man and his family two hundred roubles. Alesha took the money to the home and saw the boy who had bitten him. The captain was too proud to accept the money although he was elated at first. Alesha returned to Madame Khokhlavkova's and reported his failure.

Having overheard a declaration of love between her crippled daughter Lise and Alesha, Madame Khokhlakova stated her disapproval; and Alesha asssured her that any plans for marriage would be in the future. Looking for Dmitrii, Alesha joined Ivan in a restaurant where the latter revealed his rejection of God's world, in which the innocent are allowed to suffer. Ivan related a prose poem he had written entitled "The Grand Inquisitor."

Based on St. Luke 4:1-13, the Grand Inquisitor attacked Christ for leaving man too weak to control his own freedom. If Christ had set up an earthly kingdom, man would have had security. If Christ had turned the stone offered by the devil into bread, man would have had spiritual and material sustenance. The Grand Inquisitor accused Christ of not understanding man's nature. To make up for Christ's error, a church was built in his name. The church is an earthly kingdom which makes up for man's weaknesses. Man willingly submits his freedom to the church in exchange for security. Christ did not respond to the Grand Inquisitor's accusations, but He did kiss his accuser.

When Ivan finished, he left, deeply depressed. Meeting Smerdiakov, Ivan learned three facts that made him aware that his half brother might be planning the murder of their father: (1) for no possible reason Smerdiakov had told Dmitrii the secret signals that Grushenka was to use if she decided to visit Fedor; (2) Smerdiakov feared that he was about to have an epileptic seizure which would give him an alibi if something happened to Fedor; and (3) Grigorii was ill and would not be in the house to protect Fedor from Dmitrii's wrath. However, Ivan decided to continue with his own plans and go to Moscow the next day.

When Fedor begged Ivan to sell a copse of wood for him in a neighboring town, Ivan relented and went. Smerdiakov fell down some steps and suffered the seizure he had predicted. Fedor was therefore left alone in the house to await Grushenka.

Alesha returned to the monastery in time to hear Father Zosima's last teachings. The elder confessed that Alesha resembled his dead brother Markel, both spiritually and physically, and that that was the reason for his strong love of the novice. Father Zosima's life was revealed. His followers heard the events which led the elder to his basic philosophy: through the voluntary acceptance of suffering, man finds redemption; everyone of us is responsible for all; and hell is spiritual, not material. He died calmly.

Part III.

When Father Zosima's remains began to putrify soon after they were placed in his coffin, the holy community and the townspeople were aghast. Many considered the premature decay as an evil omen. Rakitin ridiculed Alesha's grief and persuaded him to visit Grushenka. She had paid Rakitin to bring Alesha, but instead of seducing him, she developed a warm, compassionate friendship with him. Grushenka left for a tryst with a former lover, and Alesha went to Father Zosima's cell for prayer. He went to sleep, and the dead elder appeared to him in his dream, congratulating him for helping Grushenka. Alesha awoke with joy in his heart.

Dmitrii tried unsuccessfully to borrow money from acquaintances. He called on Grushenka, but she was not home. Outraged, he grabbed a brass pestle and ran to his father's where he gave Grushenka's secret signal. Fedor opened the window and stuck his head out the window. Dmitrii realized that Grushenka was not there and left. When Grigorii surprised him in the garden, Dmitrii hit him with the pestle. Fearful that he had killed the old servant, Dmitrii ran to Grushenka's and found out where his beloved had gone. Carrying a bundle of money and the pistols he had retrieved from a pawnbroker, Dmitrii went to the bar where Grushenka was visiting her friend. She greeted Dmitrii and soon realized that she loved him. During their celebration, police officers arrived and arrested Dmitrii for the murder of his father, who had been found dead and robbed. Perkhotin had reported Dmitrii's behavior. Dmitrii insisted that his money was an unused half of the money he had received from Katerina. Doubting his story, the officers took Dmitrii to prison while Grushenka promised him her undying love.

Part IV.

In jail, Dmitrii had a strange dream which caused him to feel that he was destined to suffer for the crimes of humanity. Meanwhile, Katerina and Ivan worked on a scheme in which Dmitrii would escape to America. Ivan went to Smerdiakov three times before the latter confessed to the murder of their father. Claiming to be an instrument of Ivan's beliefs, Smerdiakov blamed Ivan for planting the suggestion of murder in his mind. Taking the stolen money from his half brother, Ivan returned to his lodging, exhausted and ill. An apparition of the devil appeared and taunted him. That night Smerdiakov hanged himself.

At the trial, a strong case was presented against Dmitrii by the prosecutor, but the defense lawyer meticulously refuted the evidence as circumstantial. He asked for mercy so that Dmitrii could find regeneration in life rather than degeneration in prison. However, Katerina produced a letter from Dmitrii in which he declared that he could kill his father to obtain the money he owed her. Ivan told of Smerdiakov's confession; but Ivan suddenly began to see the devilish specter from his dream, and his instability greatly weakened the credibility of his testimony. Katerina took Ivan home to care for him. The jury found Dmitrii guilty. He was condemned to Siberia but agreed to an escape plan even though he knew he would hate America. He vowed to return to Russia as soon as possible. Katerina came and begged forgiveness from Dmitrii. Grushenka came but refused to forgive Katerina.

Little Il'iush died and Alesha went to the boy's funeral. Alesha talked with the boy's friends after the ceremony and told them to remember their immediate friendship forever. They appreciated Alesha's sincerity and shouted, "Hurrah for Karamazov."

Abraham, Aesop, Afanasii Pavlovich, Afimia, Agafia, Agafia Ivanovna, Pani Agrippina, Akim, Aleksander Aleksandrovich, Aleksei, Alexander of Macedon, Andrei, Anfim, Arina, Bakunin, Balaam's ass, Beliavskii, Belinskii, Bel'mesov, Benjamin, Bernard, Boileau—Despréaux, Bourbon, Caesar, Cain, Ceres, Chatskii, Chernomazov, Chichikov, Aleksei Ivanich Chizhov, Dante Alighieri, Dardanelov, Dardanus, Dashkova, Demidov, Diderot, Eisenschmidt, Ekaterina II, Elijah, Eliseev, Esther, Famusov, Fenardi, Mlle. Fenardi, Fenia, Ferapont, Fetiukovich, Foma, Gattsuk, Glafira, Gogol', Gorbunov, Gorstkin, Grand Inquisitor, Pope Gregory VII, Gridenko, Grigorii Vasil'evich, Grusha,

Grushenka, Hamlet, Heine, Herzenstube, Horatio, Hugo, Il'ia, Ilius, Il'iusha, Iosif, Ippolit Kirillovich, Isaac, Isaac the Syrian, Iul'ia, Jacob, Jenghiz Khan, Job, St. John, St. John the Merciful, Jonah, Joseph, Jupiter, Petr Fomich Kalganov, Kalmikov, Aleksei Fedorovich Karamozov, Dmitri Fedorovich Karamazov, Fedor Pavlovich Karamazov, Ivan Fedorovich Karamozov, Adelaida Ivanovna Karamazova, Sofia Ivanovna Karamazova, Karp, Kartashov, Katchalnikov, Katen'ka, Katerina Ivanovna, Katia, Khlestakov, Khokhlakova, Lise Khokhlakova, Kock, Kolbasnikov, Kolia, Kondrat'eva, Pavel Pavlovich Korneplodov, Korovkin, Kostia, Kramskoi, Kraotkin, Mikolai Ivanovich Krasotkin, Anna Fedorovna Krasotkina, Kravchenko, Kuvshinikov, Kuzmitchev, Lazarus, Lepelletier, Liaqavii, Librarian, Licharda, Lizaveta, Louis XI, St. Luke, Luther, Mahomet, Mikhail Makarovich Makarov, Maksimov, Maksimushka, Marfa Ignatievna, Mar'ia, Mar'ia, Mar'ia Kondratievna, Markel, Maslov, Matrena, Mastriuk, Mattei, Matvei, Mephistopheles, Mikhail, Mikhail, Mikhail Semenovich, Misha, Mitia, Mitrii, Petr Aleksandrovich Miusov, Miusova, Count von Moor, Franz Moor, Karl Moor, Morozov, Morozova, Mussialovich, Naaphonil, Napoleon I, Napoleon III, Nastas'ia, Nastas'ia Petrovna, Nast'ia, Natasha, Nazar Ivanovich, Nazarev, Nekrasov, Nikolai Parfenovich Neliudov, Nikita, Nosov, Nozdrev, Olga Mikhailovna, Olsufev, Onegin, Ophelia, Ostrovskii, Othello, Father Paisii, St. Paul, Pelletier, Petr Il'ich Perkhotin, Petr, Phaon, Phoebus, Pierrot, Piron, Trifon Borisovich Plastunov, Platon, Plotnikov, Podvystoski, Efim Petrovich Polenov, Polonius, Porfirii, Potemkin, Prodkhor, Prokhorich, Prokhorovna, Proserpine, Proudhon, Pushkin, Rachel, Mikhail Ospovich Rakitin, Rebecca, Richard, Sabaneev, Sade, Kuzma Kuzmich Samsonov, Sappho, Sarah, Schiller, Mavreikii Mavreikevich Schmertsov, von Schmidt, Schultz, Seraphicus, Shchedrin, Shkvornev, Silenus, Smaragdov, Pavel Fedorovich Smerdiakov, Lizaveta Smerdiashchaia, Smurov, Il'iusha Nikolaevich Snegirev, Nikolai Ilich Snegirev, Arina Petrovna Snegireva, Nina Snegireva, Varvara Snegireva, Sobakevich, Sofia, Von Sohn, Stepanida, Stepanida Il'inishna, Agrafena Aleksandrovna Svetlova, St. Sylvester, Tamerlane Tat'iana, Teucer, St. Thoma, Timofei, Tiutchev, Tolstoi, Trifon Borisovich, Trifon Nikitich, Trifonov, Tros, Turgenev, Tuzikov, Ulysses, Van'ka, Varsonofii, Varvara Aleksandrovna, Varvinskii, Vasen'ka, Vashti, Vas'ia, Varvara, Paisii Velichkovskii, Voltaire, Vrublegskii, Yorick, Zosima, Von Zon.

A Common Story, I. A. Goncharov, 1847.

Aleksandr Aduev, a spoiled young man, set out from his mother's country estate for St. Petersburg. He was leaving behind many luxuries as well as his unforgettable first love Sof'ia. Arriving in the city, the naïve Aleksandr sought the patronage of his uncle Petr Aduev, a stern, serious man, who had made his mark in the business world after leaving the country for the city. Petr could hardly tolerate his nephew's sentimental ideals or country manners. Life in the city was harsh for Aleksandr, and two events disillusioned him. He fell in love with the capricious Naden'ka Liubetskaia, who jilted him for a Count Novinskii. Then Aleksandr's childhood friend Pospelov came to St. Petersburg but did not let Aleksandr know. They met acccidentally on the street. When Pospelov invited Aleksandr to a party at his flat, the confused young man went but was bored with his friend's interest in cards. Aleksandr could not believe that Pospelov was the same friend who had ridden sixty miles to tell him goodbye when he left the country. Aleksandr felt deceived by love and friendship.

Feeling that he could never fall in love again, Aleksandr met Iulia Tafaeva, a pretty, educated, and wealthy young widow. She had been very unhappy in her marriage to an old man; and when she met Aleksandr, she fell madly in love with him, demanding that he be with her every moment. Aleksandr at first felt he had found a kindred soul; but the two stifled each other with their petty jealousies, and the marriage they had planned never took place.

After the affair with Iulia, Aleksandr neglected his work and his uncle chastised him for his indifference. The nephew did not care. He did not see any of his acquaintances and became chummy with Kostiakov, a man beneath Aleksandr's background and level of education. They went fishing together. Aleksandr sought only peace of mind. He began to dress sloppily. When an encounter with Liza, another young girl, proved disheartening, Aleksandr decided to return home. His mother was overjoyed at his return but could not understand the change in him. Boredom in the country soon overtook the disillusioned young man, and he returned to the city.

In an epilogue, a parallel between the lives of the nephew and uncle was disclosed. At thirty-two, a balding Aleksandr decided to marry a young woman because he was tired of living alone. Petr had done the same. Aleksandr, like Petr, had changed from a sentimental young idealist to a self-satisfied pragmatist. However, Petr had also undergone a change. In his rise to success, he had neglected his wife. She gradually became inert and withdrawn. The lovely soul that had once encouraged Aleksandr to write poetry was close to a mental breakdown. In desperation, Petr sold his factory, resigned from his position, and took Lizaveta Aleksandrovna to Italy for a cure. Petr had again set an example for Aleksandr, if he would follow it.

Aleksandr Fedorych (Sashen'ka) Aduev, Fedor Ivanych Aduev, Petr Ivanovich Aduev, Anna Pavlovna Adueva, Lizaveta Aleksandronva (Liza) Adueva, Aeschylus, Afansaii Savich, Agafia Nikitishna, Agashka, Agrafena Ivanovna, Aleksandr Stepanovich, Aleksandra Vasil'evna, Alexander of Macedon, Antigone, Anton Ivanych, Apollo, Arkhipych, Balzac, Barbier, Byron, Chateaubriand, Cooper, Dante Alighieri, Dashinka, Derzhaven, Drouineau, Drozhzhov, Timofei Nikonych Dubasov, Dumain, Evsei Ivanych, Fedorov, Fedos'ia Petrovna, Foma, Girin, Goethe, Mar'ia Gorbatova, Grunia, Gutenberg, Haller, Hesner, Hugo, Ignatii, Iulia, Ivan Andreevich, Ivan Ivanovich, Ivan Ivanych, Ivan Semenovich, Ivan Stepanych, Ivanchenko, Ivanov, Iziumov, Janin, Jupiter, Kaidanov, Kantemir, Karamzin, Katen'ka, Khozarov, Konev, Konigstein, Kostiakov, Krylov, Kuzma, Liza, Mar'ia Mikhailovna Liubetskaia, Nadezhda Aleksandrovna Liubetskaia, Lomonosov, Luk'ianov, Lunin, Marfa, Mar'oia, Mar'ia Ivanovna, Mar'ia Karpovna, Mar'ia Mikhailovna, Marlinskii, Mars, Masha, Matrena Mikhailovna, Matvei Matveich, Medvedev, Mercury, Mikhailo Mikhailych, Mikheev, Molière, Montaigne, Natasha, Newton, Nikitishna, Platon Novinskii, Oedipus, Evgenii Onegin, Orestes, Ozerov, Paganini, Pashin'ka, Pavel Savich, Petr Petrovich, Petr Sergeich, Petrarch, Phidias, Pospelov, Poulet, Praxiteles, Prokofii Astaf'ich, Proshka, Puzino, Pylades, Racine, René, Rubini, Sashen'ka, Schiller, Schmidt, Scott, Semele, Semen Arkhipych, Shakespeare, Sidorikha, Shachin, Smirnov, Sofia (Soniuchka), Sonin, Sophocles, Soulie, Stepan Ivanovich, Sue, Sumarokov, Surkov, Sylphs, Iulia Pavlovna (Julie) Tafaeva, Varen'ka, Vasilii, Venus, Verochka, Vesta, Volochkov, Voltaire, Vulcan, Watt, Weise, Vasil'ii Tikhonych Zaezzhalov, Zagoskin, Zagoretskii, Zaraiskii.

Crime and Punishment, F. M. Dostoevskii, 1866.
On a hot July evening in St. Petersburg, Raskol'nikov, a poverty-stricken young man, was walking the streets. He was preoccupied with thought and rather distraught. He had left his flat to avoid his landlady, to whom he owed money. His shabby clothes gave him a sinister appearance. When he went to an old woman pawnbroker,

Alena Ivanovna, he surprised her by the lateness of the hour and by his apparel. He pawned his watch for a measly sum and told her he would return in a few days to pawn a silver cigarette case. Watching her movements to find out where she kept her money, he caused her great suspicion by asking if she were always in the apartment alone. Upset by his question, she quickly escorted him from the flat. He began to have horrible thoughts which he decided were due to his hunger.

While sitting in a tavern, Raskol'nikov met an intoxicated man named Marmeladov. The latter revealed his problems: he was an alcoholic, and was unable to keep a job and support his wife and children. His second wife Katerina Ivanovna had been a widow who came from a respectable family and had married him out of desperation, being ill with tuberculosis. When he quit supporting her and the children, his daughter Sonia by his first marriage turned to prostitution as a means of giving the family financial aid. Their landlady forced Sonia to move to other quarters, but the girl continued to help the family. Suddenly Marveladov admitted that five days earlier he had broken open Katerina's strongbox and had remained drunk on the money ever since. He asked Raskol'nikov to accompany him home. He did but was chased out by Katerina, who thought Raskol'nikov was just another drinking partner. Raskol'nikov left but first placed some money on a table. Afterwards, he regretted his kindness, feeling that mankind does not deserve to be pitied.

The next day, Raskol'nikov was awakened by the house cook Nastasia, who informed him that the landlady Praskovia Pavlovna had asked the police to evict him for not paying his rent. She then gave him a letter from his mother. Raskol'nikov read it with interest. His mother informed him that there was little money left for his education. His sister Dunia had recently suffered much humiliation but was now in a fortunate position. She had accepted work as a governess with the Svidrigailov family, but the master of the household tried to seduce her. When his wife accidentally saw him during one of his efforts to take advantage of the hired help, she blamed Dunia and fired her. Then she spread rumors all over the town about the incident. Svidrigailov finally confessed the truth to his wife, and she made amends to Dunia by introducing her to a relative, a Mr. Luzhin. He was a prosperous forty-five-year-old man and soon offered to marry her. Dunia conceded. Raskol'nikov knew that she was marrying the man to help her family, and the thought disgusted him.

Aimlessly walking the streets, Raskol'nikov saw a man trying to pick up a young girl. Raskol'nikov became furious and called the man

Svidrigailov, associating him with the man who had tried to seduce his sister. He was about to fight with the man when a policeman intervened. The latter promised to accompany the girl home, and Raskol'nikov gave him money for his kindness. However, Raskol'nikov again regretted his compassion, realizing that indifference is the only practical way to accept this world.

Raskol'nikov started to his friend Razumikhin's but decided that he would go there after he had done "it!" He sat down for a rest and went to sleep. In a dream, he was seven years old, and with his father at the graves of his grandmother and brother. They witnessed the cruel beating of a horse. Raskol'nikov wanted to protect the animal, but his father took him away, saying that some men are brutal. Compassion and indifference were on his mind when Raskol'nikov awakened. He remembered the crime he was planning to commit and became disgusted with himself. Walking home, he saw Lizaveta Ivanovna, the pawnbroker's stepsister, and two merchants. He overheard part of their conversation and learned that Lizaveta would not be home the next evening at seven o'clock. He decided to carry out his plan. Taking an axe and a piece of wood wrapped up in paper as if it were something to be pawned, he went to the pawnbroker when he knew her stepsister would be gone. He forced himself into her flat when she opened the door and hacked her with the axe when she was trying to open the package he gave her. He took her keys and searched for her money. To his horror, Lizaveta returned and stood petrified by her dead stepsister. Raskol'nikov had not planned to kill her, but he quickly slashed her to death with the axe also. When he was about to leave, he noticed that the door was open. He closed it. Then he opened it and listened. There were voices. He closed it and waited. In a short time, two men came to the door. They rang and shouted. One went for the porter of the building; the other waited. Raskol'nikov was panic stricken. Fortunately, the other stranger went to find his friend and Raskol'nikov quickly went out of the apartment. He returned the axe to the porter's room and went to his own flat. After hiding the valuables he had stolen in a corner of his room, he fell asleep, exhausted. He was awakened by his landlady's maid, who brought him a police summons. He was fearful that he had been charged with murder. He went to the station and nervously asked his charge: it was for his back rent. Raskol'nikov's shabby dress drew the attention of the officials. When they talked of the murder of the pawnbroker, Raskol'nikov fainted and aroused the suspicions of the inspector Petrovich. He questioned Raskolnikov after he had revived but dismissed him without making an accusation.

Raskol'nikov left the station and hid his stolen goods under a large rock in an alleyway. Then he went to his friend Razumikhin. Raskol'nikov helped him with some translations, but became disinterested and returned home. For a few days Raskol'nikv lay ill with fever and talked irrationally. Razumikhin watched over his friend and had Doctor Zametov examine him. As the patient became better, he expressed radical views, maintaining that Napoleon had the right to commit crimes because he was above mankind, a superman. It was learned that the police believed that the murderers of the pawnbroker were the two men who had surprised Raskol'nikov in the old woman's apartment.

Dunia and Mrs. Raskol'nikov visited their ailing family member and asked his approval of Dunia's marriage to Luzhin. Raskol'nikov refused, believing that Luzhin was unworthy of his sister. The discussion ended in an argument, and Raskol'nikov went to a tavern where he met Zametov. They discussd the murder of the pawnbroker, and Raskol'nikov accused his acquaintance of thinking that he was the murderer. Leaving Zametov, Raskol'nikov went to the scene of the crime. When he asked if there was still blood on the floor, the painters in the apartment became suspicious. Raskol'niv left. He came upon a crowd in a street and found that the drunk Marmeladov had been run over by a coach. With help, Raskol'nikov managed to carry the dying man to his family. Leaving money for the destitute Katerina Ivanovna, Raskol'nikov joined Razumikhin and went to his own family. Luzhin had complained about Raskol'nikov's attitude toward him and insinuated that he gave his money to Sonia instead of to her family. Talking with his mother and sister, Raskol'nikov realized that his crime had made him alien to the world as well as to his family. Unexpectedly Sonia came and invited him to a funeral dinner for her father. Dunia and Mrs. Raskol'nikov did not accept the intruder at first but gradually warmed up to her.

Raskol'nikov and Razumikhin went to the inspector Petrovich's house to claim the watch and ring Raskolnikov had pawned with the murdered woman. Petrovich implied that he suspected Raskol'nikov of the murder. In an article the latter wrote about crime, he noted that the criminal becomes ill after committing an offense. There was also the theory that extraordinary men have the right to break the law because ordinary men are meaningless. Petrovich asked Raskol'nikov if he felt like an extraordinary type of man. The latter was sure that he was suspected of the murder. When he returned home, he retired and had a dream in which he tried to kill the pawnbroker but failed. It was motivated by a subconscious wish that he had not committed the crime. When he awoke, Svidrigailov was in his room. The newcomer confessed all his lustful, criminal acts to Raskol'nikov. Svidrigailov emerged as a person with a dual personality: he was considerate but also capable of the lewdest of acts.

Raskol'nikov went to his mother's and met Luzhin. A quarrel erupted between them, and Luzhin was exposed as a vain, petty, and mean character. When he left, everyone was happy and soon planned a publishing venture. Raskol'nikov went to Sonia, and they realized their mutual suffering had brought them together. He told her that he would tell her the next day who murdered the pawnbroker. Svidrigailov overheard the conversation through the wall, as his room was next to Sonia's. Raskol'nikov went to Petrovich's office. The latter was sure that Raskol'nikov was the murderer, but to his amazement, one of the painters confessed to the crime. Raskol'nikov went to the funeral dinner of Marmeladov. Luzhin came and accused Sonia of taking a hundred roubles from his room. Lebeziatnikov, a friend of Luzhin's, came and proved that Luzhin had planted the money on Sonia. He wanted to discredit her in the eyes of Dunia, hoping that she would marry him if she believed his stories about her brother and Sonia. Completely distracted by the confusion and arguing during the funeral dinner for her husband, Katerina Ivanovna went insane and died from a terrible attack of tuberculosis. Petrovich charged Raskol'nikov with the murder of the pawnbroker in spite of the painter's confession. Raskol'nikov was sure that Svidrigailov had told the police as well as his sister Dunia. He did tell Dunia and tried to seduce her, saying that he would tell no one about her brother if she submitted to him. She refused. Svidrigailov said that he was going to America but committed suicide.

Dunia went to her brother and told him that she knew about his crime. Raskol'nikov went to Sonia and informed her that he planned to confess to the police. When he was exiled to prison in Siberia for six years, Sonia went with him. His mother suffered a mental and physical breakdown and died, not really accepting the news about her son. Dunia married Razumikhin and kept in touch with her brother through Sonia. Raskol'nikov was disillusioned in the beginning but gradually saw that his theories led to anarchy. He and Sonia became closer and envisioned a new future together.

Abraham, Achilles, Afrasin'iushka, Alena Ivanovna, Aleshka, Amalia Ivanovna, Amalia Ludwigovna, Aniska, Dr. B——n, Babushkin, Bakaleev, Bartola, Berg, Princess Bezzemel'naia,

Bukh, Mr. Captain, Chebarov, Cyres, Daria Frantsovna, Nikolai
Dement'ev, Dmitrii, Duclida, Dushkin, Dussot, Fadeev, Fillipp,
Fil'ka, Gogol', Tsar Gorokh, Henriette, Il'ia Petrovich, Iushin,
Iusupov, Ivan Afanasevich, Ivan Mikhailovich, Izler, Johann,
St. John, Kapernaumov, Karl, Katia, Kepler, Kharlamov,
Kheruvimov, Ivan Ivanich Klopstock, Knopp, Kobelev, Kobilat-
nikova, Kokh, Kozel', Kriukov, Lazarus, Andrei Semenovich
Lebeziatnikov, Lewes, Amalia Frantsova Lippevekhzel', Lizaveta
Ivanovna, Luiza Ivanovna, Petr Petrovich Luzhin, Lycurgus,
Mack von Leiberich, Mahomet, Marlborough, Mangot, Marfa
Petrovna, Kolia Semenovich Marmeladov, Semen Zakharovich
Marmeladov, Katerina Ivanovna Marmeladov, Lida Semenovna
Marmeladova, Polenka Semenovna Marmeladova, Sofia Semen-
ovna (Sonia) Marmeladova, Martha, Massimo, Matvei, Mikolka,
Mit'ka, Napoleon I, Nastas'ia Petrovna, Natali'ia Egorovna, New-
ton, Nikodim Fomich, Nil Pavlich, Noah, Palmerston, Parasha,
Pashen'ka, Pestriakov, Piderit, Pokorev, Pole, Porfirii Petrovich,
Potanchikov, Potchinkov, Praskovia Pavlovna (Pashen'ka), Pri-
lukov, Pushkin, Radishchev, Raphael, Rodion Romanovich
(Rodia) Raskol'nikov, Avdot'ia Romanovna Raskol'nikova,
Pul'kheria Aleksandrovna Raskol'nikova, Rassudkin, Dmitrii Pro-
fovich Razumikhin, Resslich, Romeo, Rousseau, Rubenstein,
Schiller, Sharmer, Shchegol'skoi, Semen Semenovich Shelopaev,
Shil', Solon, Arkadii Ivanovich Svidrigailov, Marfa Petrovan
Svidrigailova, Prince Svirbei, Tereb'eva, Tit Vasil'ich, Afansai
Ivanovich Vakhurshkin, Varents, Viazemskii, Vrazumikhin,
Wagner, Aleksandr Grigorievich Zametov, Zeus, Zimmerman,
Zosimov.

Dead Souls, N. V. Gogol', 1842.
Part I.
A carriage of the type that bachelors ride in came into the town of
N——. Pavel Ivanovich Chichikov had arrived with his flunky Petrushka. The former rented a room with cockroaches peeking out of
every corner like so many black plums, and the latter settled into an
anteroom on a three-legged cot. In a word, everything was the same as
you could find anywhere else. The new arrival made calls on all the
high officials in the town and collected several invitations to teas,
dinners, and evenings at home. Having been well received, the hero
embarked on an enterprise that threw everyone into utter bewilder-
ment.

Leaving the town of N—— for an outing, Chichikov had his coach-man Selifan drive first to the estate of Manilov, a sugary, will-less sort of man who was bored in the country and eager for visitors. The landowner greeted his guest like a tomcat when you tickle him lightly behind the ears. It was soon evident that the host and hostess lived only to spoil each other while the rest of the estate went to rack and ruin. Chichikov learned that many of Manilov's souls, as the serfs were called, had died since the last census but that the landowner still had to pay tax on them until the next counting. Chichikov offered to buy the papers of the dead souls. Manilov did not understand the transfer and thought his guest was jesting. When Chichikov assured his host that the government would benefit from the legal stamp-duties, Manilov was happier, but still did not understand. However, as a well-meaning host, he signed over his dead serfs to his guest without payment, to the latter's delight.

Despite Manilov's entreaties, Chichikov drove off for other acquisi-tions. Selifan, however, was drunk and lost the way. A rain storm came, and the carriage turned over in the mud. Because of the storm, Chichikov had no time to flog his menial; there was time only to run to a nearby farmstead, the home of a Madame Korobochka. The old lady gave her guest a room with a hissing, croaking clock and a feather bed that sank to the floor. The next morning, the guest eased up to a purchase of dead souls and flabbergasted the hostess. While she could not comprehend the matter, she began to bargain with him for her deceased serfs. After considerable dickering, he bought the lot for fifteen roubles. Madame Korobochka then lost herself in the cares of her household, and God knows what strange notions strayed into her head. But then, isn't everything in the world arranged with wondrous whimsicality?

On the road again, Chichikov decided to stop at a tavern and fortify himself and his horses. Suddenly, there appeared the notorious gambler and liar Nozdrev, whom Chichikov had met in town. Nozdrev insisted that his new acquaintance accompany him to his estate. The host told one lie after another; and when Chichikov brought up a purchase of dead souls, the liar called his guest a liar. No persuasion worked on Nozdrev; he would not believe that Chichikov was telling him the truth. When the guest refused to play cards, the host was insulted. Forced into a game of checkers, Chichikov aroused Nozdrev's ire even further by an accusation of cheating. The host was about to beat up his guest when a captain of the police arrived to arrest Nozdrev for having accosted another landowner. In the confusion, Chichikov slipped out and made a hasty retreat.

The next landowner the dead-soul buyer visited was the sturdy and rough-hewn Sobakevich, who had a low opinion of everyone Chichikov tried to praise. The hostess had a face like a foreign speck on this earth and served enough food to keep her bear of a husband quite busy. Sobakevich did not register surprise when Chichikov brought up the purpose of his visit. The landowner merely asked a ridiculous price for his dead souls, and Chichikov became quite frustrated in making him lower the amount. Finally they agreed but only after the guest made a down payment. Sobakevich warned his guest not to visit a neighbor named Pliushkin, but Chichikov set off for that man's estate as soon as possible. The miser Pliushkin lived in sloth and filth. Chichikov quickly convinced the greedy creature to sign over his dead souls in order to avoid paying further taxes on them.

In the course of two and a half days, Chichikov was able to collect a goodly number of dead souls. Back in town, he legalized his purchases and celebrated his success with the chief of police. The townspeople, who thought the newcomer was buying live serfs for resettlement, held him in great regard. A ball was held, and every eligible woman was interested in meeting the rich landowner. The governor's daughter interested Chichikov because she would be a good catch, financially and socially. He was giving her great attention and parading about like a peacock when suddenly a voice that caused him to tremble resounded from the end of the ballroom. Nozdrev had arrived and quickly spread the story that the hero had been buying dead serfs. While people did not want to believe the noted liar, it was known that nothing is ever as it seems. The next morning, Madame Korobochka came to town, wanting to know the current price of dead souls. When she told two ladies about Chichikov's visit, they concluded that he was planning to abduct the governor's daughter. Soon everyone in the town was discussing the unusual purchases. A conference of the town officials concerning Chichikov was held. The postmaster told the story of a certain Captain Kopeikin, an armless, legless war veteran, who demanded compensation from the government for his misfortune. It was suggested that Chichikov and Kopeikin were one and the same. However, it was remembered that Chichikov possessed all four limbs and could not be the veteran. Nozdrev presented several theories, and the public prosecutor became so upset that he died. It was thought that Chichikov was a spy, a robber, and maybe even Napoleon in disguise. Meanwhile, the hero himself had been indisposed. When Nozdrev revealed to Chichikov his changed status in the town, the hero realized that he had no recourse but to leave. Hindsight is the Russian's strong point.

Chichikov began his career as a clerk, having received no legacy from his father. Progressing from customs officer to smuggler, Chichikov learned that souls could be mortgaged and set out to acquire a goodly sum, dead though they might be. Many delusions have overtaken this world! Where is the way out? Where is the path? Chichikov's troika took off like a bird.

And art not thou, Russia, soaring along like a spirited, never-to-be-out-distanced troika? All the nations and people must stand aside and give you the right of way.

Part II.

Chichikov arrived at the Tentetnikov estate and was charmed by the young bachelor host, who invited the traveler for a visit. Learning that Tentetnikov had a quarrel with a neighboring, retired general and that his host was in love with the general's daughter, Chichikov set off for the nearby estate. Not only did the traveler pacify the old general, but he also bought a cemetery full of dead souls. The jolly general was amused at Chichikov's account of his need for dead souls: he said that an aunt would leave him an estate if he obtained some serfs of his own; so he was buying serfs, dead ones.

On the way to the Koshkarev estate, Chichikov arrived by mistake at Petukh's property. The gluttonous host entertained the newcomer for several days. Chichikov met another guest, a very bored young man named Platonov, who invited the buyer of dead souls to his estate. Platonov agreed to travel with Chichikov and suggested that they stop off at his sister's place. Kostanzhoglo, the husband of Platonov's sister, ran his estate very well, Chichikov asked him many questions about land management. The guest suddenly had a desire to own his own property, and Kostanzhoglo informed him that a neighboring estate was for sale. Chichikov bought the land with the help of Platonov, who loaned him the money. Khlobuev, who sold the property, was a poor manager and squandered money on balls and dinners. He said that he had a rich aunt who would give to charities but would not help her relatives. Chichikov proceeded to the town where the old woman lived and managed to forge a will for her to his own advantage. However, he failed to insert a clause which cancelled all previous wills.

Chichikov was trying on a new suit when the police came to arrest him for tampering with the will of Khlobuev's relative. She had died, and two conflicting wills had appeared. In prison, Chichikov was visited by Murazov, a farmer who wanted to rehabilitate the prisoner, and by Samosvistov, a lawyer who agreed to fix things up for thirty thousand roubles. Chichikov agreed. The attorney went to his client's apartment, told the guards to watch it better, entered, and destroyed all compromising papers. Samosvistov soon created much confusion in the courts by starting suits and counter-suits. All the scandals in the county were tied in with Chichikov's case. The town officials agreed to free the prisoner if he would leave the area immediately. Chichikov complied most readily, stopping only to buy some wool for a new suit since the one he had on had been torn in a nervous fit in the prison.

Adelaida Sofronovna, Adel'geida Gavrilovna, Agrafena Ivanovna, Akul'ka, Aleksandr Petrovich, Aleksandra Gavrilovna, Aleksei Ivanovich, Andriusha, Anna Grigor'evna, Antinator Zakhar'evich, Antoshka, Bacchus, Bagration, Begushkin, Berebendovskii, Berezovskii, Aleksandr Dimitrievich Betrishchev, Ulin'ka Betrishchev, Sofron Ivanovich Bezpechnyi, Bikusov, Blokhin, Bobelina, Bobrov, Countess Boldyreva, Charlotte, Cheprakov, Pavel Ivanovich Chichikov, Chipkhaikhilidzev, Coucou, Dante, Denis Derebin, Derpenikov, Diogenes, Don Quixote, Drobiazhkin, Echartshausen, Elizavet-Vorobeii (Swallow), Emilia Fedorovna, Emel'ian, Fedor Ivanovich, Vasili Fedorov, Fedosei Fedoseevich, Fedot, Fenardi, Fetin'ia, Foma Bol'shoi (Big), Foma Malen'kii (Small), Franklin, Gremin, Grigorii, Grigorii Doezzhaine-doedesh' (Try-to-get-there-but-you-won't), Gambs, Gog, Homer, Ili'ia Il'ich, Il'ia Paramonych, Iuziakina, Ivan Antonovich, Ivan Grigor'evich, Ivan Petrovich, Ivan Potapych, Ivan Kolesso (Wheel), Judas, Kanapat'ev, Kanaris, Kanitolina, Karamzin, Kariakin Eremeii, Father Karp, Katerina Mikhailovna, Aleksandra Ivanovna Khanasareva, Kharpakin, Semen Semenovich Khlobuev, Khovanskii, Khrapovistkov, Khrulev, Khvostyrev, Kifa Mokievich, Kiril, Kiriusha, Kisloedov, Nastas'ia Petrovna Korobochka, Korovii Kirpich (Cow-dung Brick), Koskarev, Kos'ma, Konstantin Fedorovich Kostanzhoglo, Kotzebue, Krasnonosov, Krylov, Kutuzov, Kuvshinkin, Lancaster, La Vallière, Fedor Fedorovich Lenitskin, Lidin, Likhachev, Linskii, Macdonald Karlovich, Magog, Maklatura Aleksandrovna, Manilov, Alcides Manilov, Themistockius Manilov, Lizan'ka Manilova, Marfa, Mar'ia Gavrilovna, Mashka, Mavrocordo, Melan'ia, Miaoulis, Mikhail, Mikhailo, Mikheev, Uncle Mikhei, Mikheich, Milushkin, Uncle Miniai, Uncle Mitiai, Mizheuv, Mokii Kifovich, Afanasii Vasil'evich Murazov, Myl'noii, Napoleon I, Nozdrev, Onufrii Ivanovich, Ovid, Panteleimonov, Paramanov, Parasha, Pavel I (Petrovich), Pavlushka, Pelageia, Pelagia Igorovna, Fedor Fedorovich Perekroev, Perependev, Perkhunovski, Petr Varsonf'evich, Petrushka, Aleksasha Petukh, Nicolasha Petukh, Petr

Petrovich Petukh, Phyrov, Pimen the Bold, Pimenov, Pimenov, Platon Mikhailovich Platonov, Vasilii Mikhailovich Platonov, Pleshakov, Stepan Pliushkin, Aleksandra Stepanovna Pliushkina, Frol Vasil'evich Pobedonosnov, Petr Vasil'evich Pobedonosnov, Pochitaev, Polezhaev, Polikarp, Ponomarev, Poplevin, Popov, Porfirii, Praskov'ia Fedorovna, Praskushka, Predishchev, Antip Prokhorov, Prometheus, Proshka, Potseleuv, Rinaldi, Rosa Fedorovna, Petr Petrovich Samoilov, Samosvistov, Petr Savel'ev-Neuvazhai-Koryto (No-respect-for-the-pig-trough), Scheherazade, Selifan, Semen Ivanovich, Semiramis, Shakespeare, Shamsharov, Savelii Sibirikov, Sidor, Sidorovna, Solomon, Sopikov, Svin'in, Mikhail Semenovich Sobakevich, Feodul'ia Ivanovna Sobakevich, Sof'ia Aleksandrovna, Sof'ia Ivanovna, Sof'ia Rostislavna, Stepan Dmitrievich, Stepan Dmitrievich, Stepan the Cork, Suvorov, Sysoi Pafnut'evich, Themis, Maksim Teliatnikov, Andrei Ivanovich Tentetnikov, Trepakin, Trishka, Trukhachevskii, Vania, Vakhramei, Virgil, Varvar Nikolaich Vischnepokromov, Anton Volokita, Nikita Volokita, Werther, Young, Zavalishin, Zeus, Shukovskii, Ziablova, Zolotukha.

The Devils (The Possessed), F. M. Dostoevskii, 1867.

In a mid-nineteenth-century provincial Russian town, Stepan Verkhovenskii, a self-styled liberal and one-time university lecturer, became the tutor of Nikolai Stavrogin, the son of Mrs. Varvara Stavrogina, wealthy wife of a general and leading member of the local society. When the hostess became a widow, the tutor cherished thoughts of marriage with her. A love-hate relationship developed between them which lasted for twenty years. She dominated; he obeyed. She even chose his style of clothing. Hoping to create a stir in the literary world, they moved to St. Petersburg, where they associated with radical circles. Failing to start a literary journal, they returned to the provinces. Stepan journeyed to Berlin to prove his independence from Mrs. Stavrogina; however, he soon returned, realizing his emotional and financial dependence on her. A small group of liberals formed around Stepan to discuss progressive ideas: the idealist Shatov, the son of one of Mrs. Stavrogina's serfs; Liputin, a stingy, liberal busybody; Virginskii, a poor local official; Lebiatkin, the lover of Mrs. Virginskii; and Liamshin, a Jewish post-office clerk.

After his liberal education with Stepan, Nikolai Stavrogin finished his studies in St. Petersburg and then became an officer in the army. Resigning his commission, he lived a scandalous life in the slums of the capital city. In his confession (not printed in the original edition) he revealed sordid activities including child molestation. When his mother asked him to come home, he returned and caused several unusual incidents. He insulted the members of Stepan's liberal group; he pulled the nose of a man who had just said, "No one can lead me by the nose"; he kissed a hostess three times before her guests, causing her to faint; and he bit the ear of the provincial governor during a discussion. Considered ill with brain fever, Nikolai was confined to bed. After a few months, he seemed fully recovered. He then apologized for his behavior and left town. Mrs. Stavrogina received a letter from her childhood friend, Praskovia Drozdova, from Switzerland which revealed that Nikolai was courting her friend's daughter, Lisa Tushina. Mrs. Stavrogina traveled there with Dasha Shatova, whom she had reared along with the girl's brother Shatov. When Mrs. Stavrogina returned to Russia, she left Dasha abroad. Nikolai and Lisa broke their close relationship when he showed an interest in Dasha. He also became a friend of Petr Verkhovenskii, Stepan's son. The two young men found mutual agreement on political affairs. When Mrs. Drozdova returned to Russia and suggested to Mrs. Stavrogina that Dasha might be the cause of the split between Lisa and Nikolai, Mrs. Stavrogina decided to marry the twenty-year-old Dasha to the fifty-three-year-old Stepan. Knowing their dependency on their benefactress, Dasha and Stepan agreed to the repulsive plan. Yet when Stepan learned he was being used to cover up Nikolai's activities, the older man protested.

The narrator of the novel, Mr. G—v, knew the townspeople well. Heeding a request by Lisa Tushina to inquire about a certain crippled young woman, Mr. G—v went to see Shatov. He had two guests, Kirilov and Shigalev, with whom he had been in America. They had returned to Russia after working under the worst possible conditions. Shatov led Mr. G—v to Miss Lebiatkina, the deranged and talkative sister of Captain Lebiatkin. The next day, on the steps of the town cathedral, Miss Lebiatkina amazed a crowd when she kneeled before Mrs. Stavrogina. The latter, confused, decided to take the poor unfortunate home with her to discover why the girl had acted as she did. Lisa Tushina accompanied them, and a great scene took place after their arrival: Captain Lebiatkin came and tried to return some money Nikolai Stavrogin had given him. Mrs. Stavrogina was demanding to know the reason behind his action when Petr Verkhovenskii appeared. His father Stepan had seen little of him but welcomed him heartily. Mrs. Stavrogina was even more confused by Petr's chatter, especially when he suggested that Miss Lebiatkina was Nikolai's wife. Nikolai came, told Miss Lebiatkin she should not be there, and, denying she was his wife, escorted her away. Petr explained that Nikolai, out of his own generosity, had placed Miss Lebiatkina in a convent with an allowance. Her brother took her from the holy sisters and brought her here, using her allowance for his own means. Captain Lebiatkin did not deny Petr's comments but spoke of his family honor. When the captain left, he bumped into Nikolai in the hall. The latter made light of Petr's revelation, and Shatov struck Nikolai a hard blow in the face. The abused started to fight his attacker but withdrew to the confusion of all. Lisa fainted.

Petr Verkhovenskii became very busy: he ingratiated himself with Iulia Lembke, the governor's wife; he arranged for the Lebiatkins to move to an old wooden house across the river; and he tried to persuade Nikolai to remain true to the revolutionary cause which they had both believed in earlier. Nikolai was disillusioned and informed Shatov that the revolutionaries considered him a spy and might kill him. He also confessed to Shatov that he married Miss Lebiatkina as a whim but that the girl was a virgin. Gaganov, the son of the man whose nose Nikolai had pulled four years earlier, quarreled with Nikolai and demanded a duel. The latter asked Kirilov to be his second. He agreed and discussed his theory of the "man-god." Nikolai asked if he meant the "god-man." Kirilov corrected him, saying the "man-god" will come. Returning home in the dark, Nikolai met Fedka the convict, who intimated that Petr had sent him to inquire if a certain crime did not need to be committed against the Lebiatkins. Nikolai gave the destitute man some money and told him to leave him alone. Later Nikolai realized that Petr had entangled him in a plan to dispose of the Lebiatkins. The duel between Gaganov and Nikolai took place, and the latter was victorious without killing his opponent. The townspeople called Nikolai a hero. Petr was active all over the town: he disclosed that the governor had a collection of radical manifestoes; he caused strained relations between his father and Mrs. Stavrogina; and he created a disorder among the workers of the local factories.

Mrs. von Lembke led the town society in preprations for a literary fete in which the second-rate writer Karmazinov and Stepan Verkhovenskii would perform. Petr had gradually taken over his father's liberal discussion group and led them to radical measures. When Shatov denounced Petr as a spy and left, Petr forced four of the members to plan Shatov's murder. Petr confessed to Nikolai that he idolized him and wanted him to become the pretender when the revolution came, claiming that historically the Russian people always followed a pretender to the throne. Nikolai scoffed at Petr's suggestion, and the latter shouted, "I invented you."

Governor von Lembke agreed to a raid on Stepan Verkhovenskii's living quarters, and Hetzen's forbidden works were found there. Stepan went to the governor and complained. While there he witnessed the beating of dissident workers who had come quietly to express their grievances. Von Lembke wanted to call off the literary fete, but his wife forbade it. The fete was a complete failure. Petr had planted disrupters throughout the hall, and both speakers were embarrassed and mortified. An evening ball became a rout when a fire was discovered raging through some structures along the river. Captain Lebiatkin and his sister were found murdered in the wooden house to which Petr had taken them and which the fire had spared. When informed of the murders, Nikolai confessed that he knew of the possibility of the tragedy. Lisa was horrified and went to the scene of the crime. When she was recognized by the crowd, they stoned her and beat her to death because of her relationship with Nikolai. The latter quickly left town.

Petr revealed to his fellow conspirators that Fedka had murdered the Lebiatkins for robbery. He also informed them that the fanatic Krilov had agreed to cover up the group's proposed murder of Shatov. Kirilov was planning to commit suicide to prove he was the "man-god." He would leave a note saying that he had killed Shatov. Fedka denounced Petr as a scoundrel and viciously attacked him. Later Fedka was found dead outside the town. Unexpectedly, Shatov's wife Mar'ia returned after a three-year separation. She was ill and pregnant. Shatov procured Virginskii's wife for a midwife, and a boy was soon born. Shatov accepted the child, and a reconcilation took place between the couple. When he left his wife for a prearranged appointment, he went to his death. Shatov was attacked and shot by Petr, and then his body was weighted down with stones and cast into a pond. Petr then went to Kirilov for the note covering up the murder. Kirilov refused. Shatov had visited him and told him of his new happiness. Kirilov did not want to kill a man whose wife had just returned and was living nearby. Petr demanded that Kirilov carry out his part of the bargain. Claiming to be the "man-god" with the power to determine his own fate, Kirilov finally shot himself. Petr left the town by train. Mar'ia Shatova went to enquire about her husband and found Kirilov's body. She grabbed her baby and ran out into the dark, cold streets. When she was finally let into a home, she was so distracted that she became ill and died three days later. Her baby also perished from a cold. Liamshim confessed to the murder, and Shatov's body was found. One by one the murderers were captured. Only Petr remained free.

Stepan Verkhovenskii left the town in order to start a new life elsewhere. He traveled for some time before he became dangerously ill. An acquaintance he met in an inn notified Mrs. Stavrogina, and she came to her old friend. They were reconciled before he died. When Dasha received a letter from Nikolai asking her to go abroad with him, she showed the message to Mrs. Stavrogina. It was mailed from her large estate, and she immediately went there. Nikolai did not seem to be in the large mansion. An attic door on the top floor was found open, and Nikolai's body was hanging from a rafter.

Achilles, Aesthete, Agafia, Aleksei Egorovich, Alena Frolovna, Ancus Marcius, Andreev, Anton Lavrentevich, Augustin, Badinguet, Baron, Bazarov, Belinskii, Belshazzar, Berestov, Bismarck, Andrei Antonovich von Blum, Buechner, Byron, Cabet, Capefigue, Cassius, Chaadaev, Chernyshevskii, Madame Chevalier, Chopin, Cicero, Colonel, Columbus, Considérant, Copernicus, Countess, Criggs, Darwin, Dasha, Davydov, Derzhavin, Dickens, Dmitrii Mitrich, Ivan Drozdov, Mavrikii Nikolaievich Drozdov, Praskov'ia Drozdova, Dundasov, Erkel, Ernestine, Ermolaev, Esthete, Falstaff, Faust, Favre, Fedka, Fedor, Fedor Matveevich, Pavel Fedorov, Vassilii Ivanovich Filibusterov, Filippov, Foma, Fourier, Frenzel, Anton Lavrentevich G—v, Artemii Pavlovich Gagonov, Pavel Pavlovich Gaganov, Garin, General, Gluck, Goethe, Gogol', Granovskii, Grigorovich, Gulliver, Hamlet, Harry, Heckeren, Heine, Hertzen, Hoffmann, Horatio, Prince Igor, Iulia, Ivan, Ivan the Crown Prince, Ivan Filippovich, Ivan Osipovich, Anisim Ivanov, Julia, Jupiter, K—, Karmazinov, Kirilov, de Kock, Korobochka, Korovaev, Kraevskii, Kristofor Ivanovich, Krylov, Kubrikov, Kukol'nik, Kutuzov, L—n, Lame Teacher, Ignatius Lebiatkin, Mar'ia Timofeevna Lebiatkina, Le Febure, Andrei Antonovich von Lembke, Iulia Mikhailovna Lembke, Lermontov, Liamshin, Lilliputians, Liputin, Liputina, Littre, Lizaveta the Blessed, St. Luke, Lunin, Lynch, Maecenas, Mahomet, Major, Makar, Maksheeva, Prokhor Malov, Marfa Sergeevna, Maria the Unknown, Mar'ia, Mar'ia Timofeevna, Marie, Marshal's Wife, Martyn, Matresha, Maurice, Miasnichika, Millebois, Minerva, Minkhin, Minna, Moleschott, Molière, de Monbars, Nastas'ia, Natal'ia Pavlovna, Nikifor, Nikodimov, Nikolai I, Nina Savelevna, Nozdrev, Ophelia, Othello, Grigorii

Boganovich (Grishka) Otrepev, Pascal, Father Pavel, Perchorin, Petrov, Pierre, Plato, Pogozhev, Poins, Pompey, Mother Praskov'ia, Pripukhlov, Prokhorych, Proudhom, Pushkin, Quickly, Rachel, Radishchev, Raphael, Renan, Rousseau, Ryleev, Polin'ka Sachs, de Sade, Salzfisch, Sand, Semen Iakovlevich, Sevostianov, Shablykin, Shakespeare, Ivan Shatov, Dasha Shatova, Mar'ia Sharova, Shigalev, Sistine Madonna, Sloczewski, Slon'tsevskii, Sofia Antonovna, Solomon, Spigulin, Nikolai Vsevolodivich Stavrogin, Vsevolod Stavrogin, Varvara Petrovna Stavrogina, Stepanida Mikhailovna, Avdotia Tarapygina, Alesha Teliatnikov, Teniers, Tentenikov, Tikhon, Titov, Tocqueville, Tolachenko, Trojan, Turgenev, Tushin, Lisa Tushina, Tushina, Sof'ia Matveevna Ulitina, Verkhishin, Petr Stepanovich Verkhovenskii, Stepan Trofimovich Verkhovenskii, Miss Virginskaia, Mrs, Virginskaia, Virginskii, Vogt, Voltaire, Stepan Vysatskii, Fomka Zavialov, Zosima.

The Double, F. M. Dostoevskii, 1846.

Iakov Petrovich Goliadkin, a minor civil servant, arose from bed and looked into a mirror: a sleepy, weak-sighted, and rather bald image greeted him. He was pleased that no pimple had appeared during the night and that nothing untoward had happened. He counted his money: 750 roubles, a goodly sum. "A man could go a long way on this!" he thought and began looking for his servant Petrushka. Preparations had been made for Goliadkin's attendance at a party: a carriage was rented and proper clothes acquired. The civil servant dressed and dropped in on Dr. Rutenspitz for a consultation. The doctor advised him to have more social life. Goliadkin went to a restaurant where he accidentally met two young clerks from his office. He pretended to be a man-about-town but fooled only himself. When he arrived at his superior's house for the party, he was denied entrance. His embarrassment was heightened by the arrival of two "enemy clerks" from the office as he was leaving. Not to be denied, the offended clerk slipped into the ballroom through a back entrance. When a servant came to lead him away, Goliadkin avoided the menial and found himself in a position to extend his hand to Klara Olsuf'evna Berendeeva as if inviting her for the next dance. She gasped in horror, and Goliadkin was ushered from the room. Running home in a snowstorm, he suddenly met his own physical double and the personage terrified him. He followed his double to his own apartment but awoke the next morning unable to find a trace of him. He passed the episode off as a hallucination.

The next day at work, Goliadkin was surprised and deeply disturbed to find that his double was working in his own office. What was even stranger was that no one seemed to be bothered by the fact that his double was working there. His immediate superior Anton Antonovich Setochkin agreed that there was a strong resemblance between the two men, but was not disturbed by the fact that they looked alike and had the same name.

Meeting the problem head on, Goliadkin Senior invited Goliadkin Junior home with him for dinner. The double was shy and nervous in the beginning, and Goliadkin's hostility toward him quickly subsided. He even decided to take his double under his protection and use him for causing trouble with his "enemies." The plan, however, did not work. Goliadkin Junior quickly became one of the enemies instead of an ally. Goliadkin Junior received credit for work done by his Senior and he piled up bills which his Senior had to pay. Everyone seemed oblivious to what was happening; so Goliadkin Senior decided that there was a conspiracy against him. When he planned a confrontation with his double, the Junior punched the Senior in the stomach and pinched his cheeks to the amusement of the others in the office. Disgraced, Goliadkin Senior did not return to work but hid in an entranceway, bribing porters to find out what the office staff was saying about him. Discovered, he went to the office and was ignored by the staff. His servant left him, he lost his position, and his sanity was greatly affected. He went to another party at Berendeev's. It was as if everything that had happened since the last party was in his imagination. He hid in a stack of wood until the host asked him to enter the house. The guests were kind. Dr. Rutenspitz came and led Goliadkin away to an insane asylum. Goliadkin was shocked into reality, too late.

Alekseich, Andrei Filippovich, Bassavrikov, Bear, Olsufii Ivanovich Berendeev, Klara Olsuf'evna Berenedeeva, Brambeus, Briullov, Princess Chevchekhanova, Demosthenes, False Dmitrii, Eliseev, Evstafii, Fal'bala, Faublas, Fedoseich, Gerasimich, Iakov Petrovich Goliadkin (Junior), Iakov Petrovich Goliadkin (Senior), Homer, Iakov Petrovich, Ivan Semenovich, Judas, Karolina Ivanovna, Krylov, Mahomet, Maliutin, Martsimiris, Mikheev, Nedobarov, Ostaf'ev, Pelageia Semenovna, Pereborkin, Pet'ka, Petr, Petrushka, Pisarenko, Pushkin, Queen of Festivities, Rousseau, Krestian Ivanovich Rutenspitz, Semen Ivanich, Sergei Mikheevich, Anton Antonovich Setoshkin, Stolniakov, Suvorov, Prince Svinchatkin, Nestor Ignatievich Vakhrameev, Vasia, Villèle, Vladimir Semenovich.

The Eternal Husband, F. M. Dostoevskii, 1871.

Vel'chaninov, a tall, handsome man about thirty-eight years old, came to the conclusion that a man wearing a hat decorated with crepe was spying on him. He encountered the mysterious person a total of five times and began to create a mental romance about the strange figure. The look in the man's eyes haunted him. One night at two-thirty A.M., Vel'chaninov arose from his bed, unable to sleep. He looked out the window at the northern summer light. Suddenly he noticed a figure approaching his stairway. His heart began to beat rapidly. The stranger was coming toward him. He went to the door and soon heard breathing on the other side. When he opened the door quickly, the figure on the other side addressed him by his name. He recognized his old friend Trusotskii. They had not seen each other for nine years. Vel'chaninov was startled to learn that Trusotskii's wife Natal'ia was dead. She had carred out an adulterous affair with Vel'chaninov but dropped him when she tired of him. When the two old friends went to Trusotskii's apartment, Vel'chaninov met Liza, a nine-year-old girl whom he discovered to be his own daughter by Trusotskii's wife. Vel'chaninov observed the child's unhappiness and suggested that he be allowed to take the girl to a fine family where he knew she would be welcome. Trusotskii welcomed the opportunity and sent the girl in spite of her protestations. The Pogorel'tsev family was delighted to have Liza, but she was despondent and developed a fatal fever. When she died, Trusotskii did not attend the funeral. He did send money for her expenses.

Vel'chaninov did not see Trusotskii for some time. After they met once outside the cemetery gates where Liza was buried, they returned to Vel'chaninov's flat. Trustoskii informed his friend that he was planning to marry and invited him to visit his beloved in the country. Trusotskii took a diamond bracelet to his future bride, Nadezhda Zakhlebinina, but she was embarrassed and did not want to accept it. Her father, worried about the future of his numerous daughters, approved her acceptance of the gift as he had agreed to the wedding, with reluctance. Vel'chaninov noticed that the family did not care for Trusotskii. Nadezhda asked Vel'chaninov to return the bracelet to his friend because she was in love with another. During some outdoor games, Trusotskii was made to appear foolish and Vel'chaninov was glad to take his friend back to St. Petersburg. Aleksandr Lobov, the young man whom Nadezhda loved, came to Trusotskii and asked him to forsake his plans with the young girl. He revealed that he and Nadezhda had been sweethearts for years.

Trusotskii was very upset by the visit and the return of the bracelet. He spent the night with Vel'chaninov. In his despair, Trusotskii confessed his love for his friend and asked Vel'chaninov to kiss him. The latter hesitated but did kiss him. During the night, Trusotskii tried to murder his friend, but Vel'chaninov awoke in time to ward off the attack. He realized that his friend loved him from hatred, the strongest of all loves. Lobov later informed Vel'chaninov that he had put Trusotskii on a train and that the latter had relinquished his hold on Nadezhda. Trustoskii sent Vel'chaninov a letter from the deceased Natal'ia in which she confessed that Liza was Vel'chaninov's child. The latter understood why Trusotskii hated him.

Two years later at a train station, Vel'chaninov went to the aid of a lady who was having trouble leading a drunken young man along a platform. To Vel'chaninov's amazement, the lady's husband turned out to be Trusotskii. The drunken young man was a person whom the married couple were trying to help. The lady thanked Vel'chaninov for his help and asked him to visit them when she learned that her husband knew him. Trusotskii was embarrassed by the chance meeting and secretly asked his former friend not to visit them. The two parted on different trains in opposite directions forever.

Stepan Mikhailovich Bagautov, Glinka, Golubenko, Miten'ka Golubchikov, Jupiter, Katia, Kokh, Lipochka, Semen Petrovich Livtsov, Liza, Aleksandr (Sashenka) Lobov, Mar'ia Nikitichna, Mar'ia Sysoevna, Mavra, Nastia, Patroclus, Pelageia, Aleksandr Pavlovich Pogorel'tsev, Klavdia Petrovna Pogorel'tseva, Petr Kuz'mich Polosukhin, Predposylov, Mashka Prostakova, Quasimodo, Schiller, Stunend'ev, Thersites, Natal'ia Vasil'evna Trusotskaia, Slimpiada Semenovna (Lipochka) Trusotskaia, Pavel Pavlovich Trusotskii, Turgenev, Aleksei Ivanovich Vel'chaninov, Feodosii Petrovich Zakhlebinin, Zakhlebinina, Katerina Fedosevna Zakhebina, Nadezhda Fedosevna Zakhlebinina, Zavilevskii.

The Gambler, F. M. Dostoevskii, 1866.
Aleksei Ivanovich, the narrator of the novel, returned after a two-week absence to his post as tutor in the family of a general in the town of Roulettenburg, Germany. Aleksei was greeted rather coolly because the family was worried about their precarious financial position. They were hoping for news of the death of their wealthy relative Tarasevicheva, whom they called grandmother. After his return, Polina, the stepdaughter of the general, gave Aleksei some money and asked him to play roulette for her since she needed funds badly.

Because he loved her, he accepted the task, went to the casino and won an amazing sum: 1,600 gulden. He took the money to her and informed her that he would never play for her again. He gave as his reason that he was going to play for himself in the future, but he was actually afraid that he would lose her money. While the narrator was away, a Mademoiselle Blanche had come into the life of the general. He wanted to marry her, but his financial affairs would not allow it. There was also a new visitor to the family, an Englishman named Mr. Astley, who was also in love with Polina. When she insisted that Aleksei play roulette for her again, he succumbed but lost all her money. When Mademoiselle Blanche mentioned at dinner that she had seen him lose at the table that day, he said that the money was his own. Polina revealed to the narrator that the general had mortgaged his entire estate to a Frenchman, de Grieux. Their only hope now was the death of their grandmother. The narrator confessed his love to Polina, but she made fun of him. For a joke, she told him to insult a German aristocrat whom she knew at the spa, and the narrator immediately confronted Baroness von Wurmerhelm with an uncomplimentary remark. Baron von Wurmerhelm was an acquaintance of the general and informed him of what happened. Consequently the narrator was dismissed from his position as tutor of the general's two young children. The narrator decided to challenge the baron to a duel, but the general had Polina send him a note asking him to forget the matter. Aleksei told Astley about the incident and about his love for Polina. The Englishman revealed the past of Mademoiselle Blanche. She had first appeared in the town with an Italian nobleman, went from him to a Polish count, and ended up without money. When she asked Baron von Wurmerhelm to make a bet for her, the baroness had the police inform the young lady that her presence in the town was no longer desired. Blanche, however, was now courted by the general.

Instead of receiving news of the death of their grandmother, the general and his group were surprised to see the old woman herself appear at the hotel. Everyone was stunned. Grandmother Tarasevisheva informed the general that he would receive no money from her and set about giving orders to everyone. When she decided to visit the gambling tables, she had Aleksei escort her. She herself played and won twelve thousand playing on zero and rouge. While she was generous with her winnings with the servants, she still refused to give the general anything. That same afternoon, Grandmother Tarasevicheva demanded that Aleksei accompany her again to the tables; she lost fifteen thousand roubles. She was very upset by her losses and decided to return to Moscow, telling Polina that if she would return with her, she would take care of her. Polina refused, saying that she would come later. When the grandmother requested that Aleksei accompany her again to the tables, he refused. She went anyway and lost ten thousand roubles. The next day, to the consternation of the family and the excitement of everyone in the gambling hall, she played until she had lost over ninety thousand roubles. The family was ruined, and the old lady had to return to Moscow no longer wealthy. She even borrowed money from Astley for her trip. That night Polina came to Aleksei and showed him a letter from de Grieux. He had left, but Polina wished that she had enough money to pay off the general's debts to the Frenchman. Aleksei was suddenly inspired and asked Polina to wait an hour. He ran to the casino and in a series of spectacular wins amassed a fortune. When he went back to his room, he threw the money all over the table. Polina stayed the night with him, but the next morning she threw his money in his face and left. She had begged him to buy her but refused the payoff. She went away with Mr. Astley.

Mademoiselle Blanche invited Aleksei to Paris, where she set up a salon on his money. They lived a frivolous life while the money lasted. The general came, and Blanche became his wife. Aleksei returned to a spa in Germany and worked as a valet. He continued playing roulette, winning at times, losing at others. One day he met Astley and inquired about Polina. The Englishman confessed that Polina had loved Aleksei all the time and that she was presently in Switzerland. Astley gave his acquaintance some money, but it was only a small amount because he knew Aleksei would gamble with it. He did and lost it all at the tables, but he dreamed of winning a huge sum and going off to Polina. Gambling had become his obsession.

Albert, Aleksei Ivanovich, Amalchen, Empress Anna, Astley, Balakirev, Barberini, Blanchard, Cleopatre, Blanche de Cominges, Corneille, Fedor, Fedos'ia, Feeder, Grandmother, General, de Grieux, Hinze, Hoppe, Hortense, Katerina, de Kock, Lisette, Lovell, Marfa, Mar'ia Filippovna, Mezentsov, Misha, Nadia, Nil'skii, Perovskii, Blanche de Placet, Polina Aleksandrovna, Potapych, Praskov'ia (Polina) Aleksandrovna, Racine, Rothschild, Selma, Antonida Vasil'evna Tarasevicheva, Thérèse-philosophe, Timofei Petrovich, Baron von Wurmerhelm, Baroness von Wurmerhelm, Zagorianskii, Zagozianskii.

The Idiot, F. M. Dostoevskii, 1868.

On a wintry evening in a third-class coach of a train heading for St. Petersburg, two unusual young men chanced to meet. Prince Myshkin was returning to Russia after spending four years in Switzerland, where he had been treated for epilepsy at a sanitarium. His threadbare clothing and innocent facial expression attracted a fellow passenger, Parfen Rogozhin. Listening to the young men's conversation, the busybody functionary Lebedev joined in. He was amazed that Rogozhin would be in a third-class carriage when he had just inherited a huge fortune. Rogozhin explained that his brother had tried to beat him out of his inheritance but that by nightfall all would be his. Lebedev humiliated himself in trying to win the rich man's favor. When Rogozhin mentioned his love for the beautiful Nastas'ia Filippovna Barashkova, Lebedev identified her as the woman reared and kept by a Count Totskii. Rogozhin was amazed that Lebedev knew the truth about the beauty and accepted his services as a hanger-on. When the train reached St. Petersburg, Prince Myshkin was invited to his new acquaintance's home but declined in order to visit a distant relative, Mrs. Epanchina.

General Epanchin greeted their unexpected guest with concern. He was sure that Prince Myshkin had come for money, but his fears were soon allayed and he took a liking to the young man, who talked so naïvely he was almost idiotic. Prince Myshkin overheard the general's secretary, Gavrila Ivolgin, talk with his superior about a marriage being planned between the secretary and Nastas'ia Filippovna. Count Totskii wanted to be rid of the young woman whom he had reared and had offered the impoverished Gavrilla money to marry her. When Prince Myshkin saw a picture of Nastas'ia and exclaimed her name aloud, the general and his secretary were amazed. Prince Myshkin explained his meeting with Rogozhin to the listeners' concern. General Epanchin led Prince Myshkin to his wife and three daughters, Aleksandra, Adelaide, and Aglaia. The child-like Mrs. Epanchina soon took a liking to the young prince, and her daughters were fascinated and amused by his naïveté and interesting stories. When the visitor mentioned that Aglaia was almost as beautiful as Nastas'ia, a commotion started. Mrs. Epanchina demanded to see the picture which the prince had mentioned and sent him for it. Gavrila Ivolgin was furious when the prince came for the picture because the matter concerning his marriage was supposed to be a secret. He made the prince carry a note to Algaia, whom he wanted to marry. Prince Myshkin delivered the note, but Algaia would not answer. She was disgusted that Gavrila had even considered the marriage plan with Nastas'ia. That evening Gavrila escorted Prince Myshkin to his home, where his family let rooms. The head of the household was the drunken General Ivolgin, who was in debt to many and borrowed from anyone. Another lodger, the robust Ferdyshchenko, also knew Nastas'ia. To everyone's surprise, the beauty herself appeared at the Ivolgins'. Gavrila's sister Varva was rude to the "fallen" woman, but Nastas'ia pretended not to notice. Rogozhin came and offered Nastas'ia a hundred thousand roubles if she would marry him. Varvara Ivolgina was furious that such a scene could take place in her family's home and tried to slap her brother for bringing on such a disgrace. Her slap, however, fell on the poor Prince Myshkin, who had hastened to stop her. He forgave her in his simple, tolerant way. Nastas'ia told Gavrila and Rogozhin that she would give her answer to them that night. She quickly kissed Mrs. Ivolgina's hand and left.

At Nastas'ia's a curious group assembled. All the personages connected with her unhappy life were there. Prince Myshkin offered to marry her; but she laughed, asking what they would live on. To everyone's amazement, the prince produced a letter showing that he had inherited a fortune. Nastas'ia said that she could not take advantage of such a weakling. The hostess forced various people to tell the most disgusting thing that they had ever done. Ferdyshchenko admitted to a petty theft that caused an innocent maid to be fired. General Epanchin told a strange tale about his abuse of a woman who, unknown to him, was dead when he reviled her. Count Totskii told of deceiving a friend for a bouquet of camelias which a certain lady wanted. Nastas'ia suddenly asked Prince Myshkin if she should marry Gavrila, and the prince answered negatively. The hostess laughed and told Gavrila that she would follow the prince's advice. Suddenly Rogozhin came with a group of hangers-on. He presented Nastas'ia a hundred thousand roubles wrapped in a newspaper. She took the money and told Gavrila that she wanted to have one last look into his soul. She proposed that he could have the money if he would crawl to the fireplace and pull the money out of the fire with his bare hands after she threw it into the flames. An uproar took place from the guests; but Nastas'ia insisted that she would do with the money as she pleased, and Rogozhin agreed. She threw the packet of roubles into the fire amid the screams of her guests. Lebedev and others wanted to crawl in for it, but Nastas'ia held them all back, looking at Gavrila with blazing eyes. The horrified young man suddenly turned to leave and fainted. Nastas'ia took the burning packet out of the fire, smothered the flames, and threw it by Gavrila's side, declaring that the money was his when he awoke. Rogozhin and his gang of hangers-on led Nastas'ia to his carriage in a boisterous fashion as Prince Myshkin ran after him.

Rogozhin and Nastas'ia went to Moscow, followed by the prince.
The distraught beauty promised Rogozhin that she would marry him
but left him to return to St. Petersburg with the prince. Rogozhin
decided that he would surrender Nastas'ia to the prince; but his
jealously overwhelmed him, and he tried to kill his naïve friend. Just as
Rogozhin raised a knife to stab Prince Myshkin, the weakling had an
epileptic fit. Recovering, the prince went to Pavlovsk, where most of
his acquaintances had taken up residence. While there, he became a
victim of an extortion attempt. An ariticle written by Mr. Keller
accused the prince of depriving a Mr. Burdovskii of an inheritance
which was rightfully his. Burdovskii was supposed to be the son of
Pavlishchev, Prince Myshkin's benefactor who had left the prince a
fortune. Prince Myshkin, however, proved that Burdovskii was not
Pavlishchev's son, and the matter was dropped.

Gavrila returned the money to Nastas'ia, but Aglaia Epanchina
would not see him. Instead, she fell in love with Prince Myshkin, but
would not admit her feelings and treated the prince scornfully. When
Aglaia finally revealed her true feelings, Mrs. Epanchina was distressed, fearing that the prince was not capable of a successful
marriage. Reluctantly, the mother gave her consent and prepared an
evening party to introduce the prince to society. Mrs. Epanchina asked
the prince to remain quiet during the party lest he should commit
some social blunder and disgrace the family. To spite her mother,
Aglaia told the prince either to expound on his theory that "Beauty
will save the world," so that she could laugh, or to break an expensive
Chinese vase during the party. The prince refused her scheme; but
during a heated discussion, he did accidentally knock over the rare
vase, and stood staring at the pieces like an "idiot." Suddenly he was
seized by an epileptic fit and had to be carried home. The Epanchins
were cool toward him after the incident, but Mrs. Epanchina soon
forgave him and invited him again to their home.

A strange friendship developed between Nastas'ia and Aglaia
through a secret correspondence. When the latter asked Prince Myshkin to accompany her to her new friend's, he was amazed that they
had been communicating with each other. However, when they
arrived at Nastas'ia's, the two women's bitterness quickly came out,
and the hostess told Aglaia that she could take Prince Myshkin away
from her with just one word. When Nastas'ia fainted into the prince's
arms, Agalaia left, feeling that she had lost him. Nastas'ia and the
prince set their wedding day, and great preparations were made.
When she arrived at the church in her beautiful gown, she saw

Rogozhin in the crowd and suddenly called to him, asking him to save her. He immediately jumped into the carriage and escorted her away. Prince Myshkin accepted the news calmly, but many laughed at him for being an "idiot." He followed them to St. Petersburg but could not find them. When he discovered them at Rogozhin's house, he found that Rogozhin had killed Nastas'ia Filippovna by stabbing her under her left breast. In a weird scene, Rogozhin and Prince Myshkin spent the night together with the body of their beloved. Fearing that the body would smell by morning, they covered it and then lay down beside it. The next morning Prince Myshkin was found in an idiotic condition and sent back to the sanitorium in Switzerland. Rogozhin was sentenced to fifteen years at hard labor in Siberia and the loss of his fortune. Aglaia Epanchina married a Polish count who turned out to be a fraud. The Epanchins visited Prince Myshkin in Switzerland, but there was little hope that he would ever regain his mental powers or recover from his epilepsy.

Afanasii Ivanovich, Agashka, Aleksandr I, Aleksandra Mikhailovna, Anisia, Anna Fedorovna, Aramis, Armance, Athos, Dr. B——n, Bakhmutov, Petr Matveevich Bakhmutov, Filipp Barashkov, Nastas'ia Filippovna Barashkova, Bazancourt, Princess Belokonskaia, Bestuzhev, Sofia Bezpalova, Biskup, Bourdaloue, Madame Bovary, Antip Burdovskii, Burmistrov, Catherine, Princess de Chabot, Charras, Chebarov, Chernosvitov, Chopin, Columbus, Constant, Georges Dandin, Danilov, Daria, Daria Alekseevna, Davout, Vladimir Doktorenko, Don Juan, Don Quixote, Du Barry, Dumas, Ekaterina II, Emperor of Austira, Ivan Fedorovich Epanchin, Adelaida Ivanovna Epanchina, Agal'ia Ivanovna Epanchina, Aleksandra Ivanovna Epanchina, Lizaveta Prokof'evna Epanchina, Eropegov, Evgenii Pavlovich, Evlampia Nikolaevna, Famusov, Fedor, Fedoseev, Ferdyshchenko, Filisova, Gavrila Ardalionovich, Glebov, Gogol', Gorskii, Abbé Goureau, Hamlet, Hippolite, Holbein, Mar'ia Semenovna Ishchenko, Semen Ivanovich Ishchenko, Ivan Petrovich, Ardalion Aleksandrovich Ivolgin, Gavrila Ardalionovich Ivolgin, Nikolai Ardal'enovich Ivolgin, Nina Aleksandrovna Ivolgina, Varvara Ardal'enovna Ivolgina, Empress Josephine, Countess K——, Karamzin, Katia, Keller, Khludiakov, Kinder, King of Prussia, King of Rome, Kislorodov, Knif, Kolpakov, Vasilii Vasil'evich Konev, Koral'ia, Krylov, Kulakov, Kupfer, Kurmyshev, Lacenaire, Larionov, Lazarus, Kostia Lebedev, Lukian Timofeevich Lebedev, Elena Lebedeva, Liubov' Lebedeva, Vera Lukianovna Lebedeva,

Legros, Léon, Lermontov, Levitskaia, Aleksasha Likhachev, Lomonosov, Lubov', Mahomet, Malthus, Marfa Nikitishna, Mar'ia Aleksandrova, Mar'ia Alekseevna, Mar'ia Ivanovna, Marie, Marlinskii, Matrena, Mavra, Meierov, Millevoe, Molovtsov, More, Lev Nikolaievich Myshkin, Nikolai Lvovich Myshkin, Katerina Aleksandrovna Mytishcheva, Prince N——, Napoleon I, Napoleon II, Napoleon III, Nastas'ia Filippovna, Natal'ia Nikitishna, Nelaton, Nikifor, Nil Alekseevich, Nina Aleksandrovna, Nozdrev, Old Believer, Platon Ordynsev, Anfisa Alekseevna Ordynseva, Osterman, P——, Pafnut'evna, Abbot Pafnutii, Papushin, Pasha, Princess Patskaia, Nikolai Andreevich Pavlichev, Petr Zaharich, Petrov, Pirogov, Podkolesin, Podkumov, Pogodin, Porthos, Sergei Protushin, Proudhom, Ivan Petrovich Ptitsyn, Varvara Ardalianovna Ptitsyna, Pushkin, Evgenii Pavlovich Radomskii, Kapiton Alekseich Radomskii, Parfen Semenovich Rogoshin, Semen Parfenovich Rogozhin, Sen'ka Semenovich Ragozhin, Princess de Rohan, Rothschild, Rousseau, Rustan, Prince S——, Salazkin, Samson, Ivan Dmitrich Savelev, Schlosser, Schmidt, Schneider, Scopets, Sen'ka, Aleksei Ivanovich Shvabrin, Skopets, Sokolovich, Solovev, Sotskaia, Ivan Fomich Surikov, Mar'ia Petrovna Sutugova, Talleyrand, Tania, Terentev, Hippolite Terentev, Lena Terenteva, Marfa Borisovna Terenteva, Terentych, Jules Thibaut, Titan, Afanasii Ivanovich Totskii, Trepalov, Turgenev, Venus, Very, Timofei Fedorovich Viazovkin, Vilkin, Voltaire, Petia Vorkhovskii, Stepan Vorkhovskii, Prince Vygoretskii, Zalezhev, Zarnitzin, Zeidler, Zemtiuzhnikov, Zhdanov, Zhemarin, Mar'ia Petrovna Zubkova, Vera Aleksandrovna Zubova.

Mirgorod, N. V. Gogol', 1835.

"How Ivan Ivanovich Quarreled with Ivan Nikiforovich"

Ivan Ivanovich Perepenko was considered an excellent man. He had a fine farm with apple and pear trees. He ate melons and saved the seeds, marking the date he ate the melon and with whom. He was a widower with no children. His servant Gapka was a sturdy wench, and her children ran about the yard. Ivan was devout and attended church, but did not give to beggars. He was tall and thin.

Ivan Nikiforovich Dovgochkhum was a fine man. His garden was next to Ivan Ivanovich's, and they were friends such as the world had never seen. Ivan Nikiforovich never married and neither was he born with a tail, as a certain rumor stated. He was just a quiet, short, and squatty man.

One day Ivan Ivanovich saw a servant cleaning out Ivan Nikiforovich's house. She carried out so many things that Ivan Ivanovich expected the master himself to be carried out for airing. Suddenly she brought out a gun, and the observer was amazed. He knew his friend never used a gun, and Ivan Ivanovich was immediately possessed with the idea of owning that very weapon. He dressed and paid a visit to Ivan Nikiforovich, who was lying stark naked on the floor. Carefully, Ivan Ivanovich brought up the subject of the gun, even though Ivan Nikiforovich continued to bring the sinful word "devil" into the conversation. Any other time the mention of the word would have caused Ivan Ivanovich to cut the conversation short and leave. But he wanted the gun. When he offered a sow for the weapon, Ivan Nikiforovich refused. Two bags of oats were added to the offer, but it was again refused. The matter was dropped several times, but a sudden single word changed their lives forever. When Ivan Ivanovich persisted in his efforts, Ivan Nikiforovich called him a gander. The latter was so offended he left in a pique, which was to cancel all the fine relations that had ever existed between the two friends. The next day Ivan Nikiforovich built a goose pen next to his neighbor's fence. That night Ivan Ivanovich sawed the underpinnings of the building and it fell. He expected his neighbor to take vengeance for his destructive deed; so he decided to beat him to the punch by lodging a complaint against him.

The Mirgorod court house was busy when Ivan Ivanovich arrived. The court secretary was reading a case aloud, and the judge was not listening. The officials were surprised to see Ivan Ivanovich and read his complaint in astonishment. No sooner had he left than Ivan Nikiforovich came with a petition, but he got stuck in the door. The clerks pushed him through and read his complaint aloud. Both men accused each other of criminal actions. However, soon after the lodging of the complaints, Ivan Ivanovich's gray sow broke the city law and went into the public square. Not stopping there, she entered the court house and carried off Ivan Nikiforovich's petition. The police captain reported the incident to Ivan Ivanovich and asked him to dispose of the sow.

Ivan Nikiforovich heard of the incident and asked if the sow was the gray one. Learning that it was, he lodged another complaint, only this time against the sow as well as its accomplice, Ivan Ivanovich. He also threatened to take his complaint to a higher court, the one thing that moved the Mirgorod court into action. The judge wrote up a document which was registered and put on a shelf where it lay for three years. Meanwhile the police captain gave a large party. The guests tricked the two Ivans and brought them together for the occasion. When pressed into making up, the two old friends were about to fall into each other's arms when Ivan Nikiforovich made a fatal error: he accidentally repeated the insult and called his friend a gander. They parted as embittered enemies forever. The narrator visited Mirgorod twelve years later. He met both Ivans separately. Both were old and wasted; each claimed his lawsuit was to be settled soon in his favor. Depressed by the decimation of town and people, the narrator commented, "It is dreary on the earth, gentlemen."

Agafia Fedoseevna, Agrafena Trofimovna, Anton, Bokitko, Demian Demianovich, Dorofei Trofimovich, Ivan Nikiforovich Dovgochkhum, Nikifor Dovgochkhun, Elevfery Elevferievich, Eremeev, Evpl Akinfovich, Evtikhii Evtikhievich, Foma Grigorievich, Gapka, Garii, Anton Prokofievich Golopuz, Gorpina, Herod, Ivan Ivanovich, Ivan Nikiforovich, Liubii, Makar Nazarievich, St. Nikolai, Oryshko, Ivan Perepenko, Ivan Ivanovich Perepenko, Onisii Perepenko, Petr Fedorovich, Popov, Dorosh Tarasovich Pukhivochka, Savva Gavrilovich, Taras Tikhonovich, Zakhar Prokofievich.

"Old-World Landowners"

Afanasii and Pulkheria Tavstogub were as close and charming an old couple as one could ever meet in the Ukraine. They had no children and lived only for each other. Their little cottage was always warm and cozy. The doors sang in different keys, and the flies on the windows buzzed. Pulkheria ran the farm and looked after her husband. The abundance of their harvests allowed their serfs to steal a goodly amount without making any impression on the prosperity of the estate. The Tavstogubs lived and ate heartily. A snack or two before each meal was common, and food was used to cure a stomach ache. The couple rejoiced at the sight of visitors, and overfed and overtalked them. Life was ideal for the old couple until an unusual incident occurred.

Pulkheria had a cat that was always at her feet. She did not particularly like the animal; she was simply used to it. Once it disappeared for three days and returned acting like a wild forest cat. Pulkheria fed it, and it ate heartily; then it jumped out the window and ran. The mistress sank into thought. "It was death coming for me," she concluded; and nothing could change her mind. When Afanasii noticed that she was sad and was growing thinner, he asked with a tear what was wrong. She confessed that she knew she would die that summer and asked to be buried by the church fence in her gray dress. Afanasii wept like a child. Pulkheria arranged things for her husband so that his life would be easy after she left. Then she went to bed and died. Afanasii had a church funeral for his beloved and wept like a river.

Afanasii lived five more years. The house and farm became very run down. He cried and ate, more miserable with each day. Once in his garden he heard someone call his name. He turned and saw no one. It was Pulkheria calling him, he decided, and so he went home and died, leaving instructions to be buried in the church yard by his wife. The housekeeper and steward carried off many of the house's goods. A distant kinsman arrived and put the farm in the hands of trustees. The houses fell apart, the serfs ran off, and kinsman visited rarely.

Baucis, Iavdokha, de La Vallière, Napoleon I, Nichipor, Petr III, Philemon, Afanasii Ivanovich Tovstogub, Pulkheria Ivanovna Tovstoguba.

"'Taras Bul'ba"

Taras Bul'ba, a giant Cossack, was welcoming his sons after their return from a year's study in a seminary. Ostap, the older of the young men, took offense at his father's jibes at his seminary outfit and began exchanging blows with the old man to the latter's delight. The father soon embraced his son heartily, realizing that he had matured in spirit and strength. Taras turned to his younger son Andrei for a show of strength, but a woman's cries interrupted them. Taras did not want to heed his wife's entreaties for peace and quiet, but her embraces of the younger son stopped the men's skirmish. At a party for the local Cossacks in honor of his sons' arrival, Taras announced that he was taking his sons to the Sech the next day. The mother was saddened to see sons leave so quickly for the main camp of the Zaporozhian Cossacks, but she had to submit to her husband's will. She blessed her sons and gave them holy images to wear around their necks.

Taras Bul'ba was a true Cossack: he believed that the only good life was that of a soldier. He loved action in battle and adventure. Ostap shared his father's love for war and revelry, but he did not have his parent's leadership ability. Andrei was different from his father and brother. He had the potential to lead others but was also interested in scholarly subjects. His tragic flaw was his passion for women. They detracted him from his soldierly pursuits and invaded his dreams to torment him. He once saw a beautiful girl laughing from her window. Finding out that she was the daughter of a noted Polish nobleman, he brazenly stole into her boudoir one evening. He was inflamed with passion for her, but to his regret her father took her away soon afterward.

When Taras and his sons reached the Sech, they were greeted with noisy appellations and much camaraderie. Andrei and Ostap quickly adjusted to the wild, rebellious life of the Cossacks. When they needed money, they simply raided some merchant in a neighboring town. Their bravery and daring brought them recognition in the camp. Taras wanted his sons to know more than the drunken ways of the Cossacks; he wanted them to know fighting and adventure. When he suggested that the Cossacks attack some Turkish areas, he was informed that a treaty of peace existed between the Cossacks and the Turkish Sultan. Peace with the Turks did not appeal to the old Cossack; so he maneuvered to have a new camp leader elected. After much haranguing, Taras's friend Kirdiaga was selected; and he was quickly talked into setting up a raid on the coasts of Anatolia. Preparations were in progress when a group of Cossacks arrived and reported a Cossack defeat at the hands of the Poles. Jews were also accused, and a group of Jewish merchants were thrown into the Dnieper River to drown for vengeance. Only a merchant named Iankel escaped because he appealed to Taras for protection. The Cossacks decided to change their battle plans and invade Poland.

When the Zaporozhian troops arrived at the city of Dubno, they confronted high city walls giving security to a large Polish garrison. The Cossacks surrounded the city and cut off all food supplies. Waiting for the inhabitants to run out of food, the invaders gave themselves up to revelry and drunkenness. The inactivity of waiting bored Andrei and Ostap. One day, unbeknownst to Andrei, he was seen from the walls by the Polish beauty he had daringly visited some time before. That night she sent a Tartar servant to Andrei. The menial told him that her mistress was the beautiful blonde for whom he had once known passion and that she could lead him to the beauty if he chose. Andrei stole some bread and followed the servant through a secret entrance into the city. His traitorous act brought him face to face with his beloved. She was hungry, but he allowed her to eat little, fearing that she would become ill. They were soon in each other's arms. Andrei was given an honored place in the Polish society of the city and was soon observed by Iankel, who was trading there. The Jewish merchant returned to the Cossacks and reported to Taras what he had seen. The mighty warrior was furious and swore to avenge the family honor.

News from the Sech came. Tartars had invaded the Cossack territory. The Zaporozhian army at Dubno divided. Half returned to defend their lands while the rest stayed to pursue the battle for the beleaguered city.. Drunkenness prevailed during the lulls of battle, but one day there was great onslaught. Even Andrei appeared among the Polish troops. It was more than Taras could stand. He maneuvered his men so that they isolated his son from the enemy. Andrei showed no regret; and Taras shot him, leaving the body unburied. The Poles, however, were victorious and killed many Cossacks. Ostap was taken prisoner and Taras was seriously wounded. He awoke in a carriage returning to the Sech. The thought of his son in a Polish prison gave Taras no peace. He located the merchant Iankel and paid him to escort him to the city of Warsaw, where Ostap was imprisoned. Iankel placed Taras under a load of bricks and entered the hostile city. Bribes obtained an entrance into the jail for Taras, but a change of guards destroyed his chances of seeing his son. The next day on a city square, the old Cossack waited for the execution of the Cossack prisoners. When Ostap was brought forward and tortured, he cried out for his father. Taras bravely answered, "I hear you, my son." Miraculously, Taras was able to escape from the city, but he was pursued by the Poles. When he was safe in the Ukraine, he became the leader of a Cossack band. The Zaporozhian Cossacks finally made peace with their Polish enemy, but Taras would have nothing to do with the settlement. He led his band in further raids on Polish settlements. Five Polish regiments pursued him, and he was finally cornered but continued fighting so that his troops could escape. The Poles tied him to a tree and set him afire. As the flames rose, he called out cries of victory to his comrades escaping in boats in the distance.

Balaban, Borodatyi, Borodavka, Kasia Bovdug, Andrei Bul'ba, Ostap Bul'ba, Taras Bul'ba, Chervichenko, Cicero, Degtiarenko, Demetrovich, Doloto, Dorosh, Foma, Galiandovich, Maksim Golodukha, Mykita Golokopytenko, Gunia, Okhrim Guska, Haim, Horace, Ian, Iankel, Isaac, Judas, Juzysia, Khlib, Kirdiaga, Kobita, Koloper, Fedor Korzha, Kozolup, Kukubenko, Metelitsa, Mordecai, Okhrim Nash, Nevylychii, Nostugan, Ostranitsa, Pesherits, Pidisshok, Pisarenko, Pokrysha, Demid Popovich, Nikolai Potocki, Shilo, Shmul, Solomon, Thomas, Titan, Dmitro Tovkach, Vertykhvist, Vovtuzenko, Zadorozhny.

"Vii"
When the lilting seminary bell of the Bratskii Monastery rang out

every morning in Kiev, students of grammar, rhetoric, and theology trudged to their classes. They all looked forward to their June vacation when they could go off to their homes. One fine June, three students on their way home dropped off a main road to replenish their provisions at the first homestead they could find. They were the theologian Khaliava, the philosopher Khoma Brut, and the rhetorician Tiberii Gorobets. When darkness fell, the trio realized they had lost their way. Finally they saw a light and were let into an old woman's hut. When Khoma retured to a sheep's pen, he was suddenly joined by the old woman. He refused to sin with her, but she jumped on his back and made him run out over the farm. He realized she was a witch. When he was almost dead from running, he began chanting exorcisms against evil spirits. The chants slowed him down, and he was able to get out from under the fiendish creature and jump on her back. He grabbed a piece of wood and began beating her. She screamed and yelled, then began cooing. Khoma wondered if she were really an old woman. When she finally fell, he saw a beautiful girl before him. He had such strange emotions that he left her at full speed.

A short time later, Khoma was invited to the estate of one of the richest Cossack captains in the area. Before dying, the captain's beautiful daughter had expressed a wish that the seminarian Khoma Brut should read prayers over her for three days after her death. The philosopher felt that there was something ominous in the matter and did not want to do what had been asked of him. However, the rector and six strong Cossacks easily persuaded him. When the Cossacks stopped at a tavern and became drunk, Khoma thought of escaping; but he saw too many doors and could not leave. The next day he awoke in a busy village. He wandered to a hillside and again thought of escape: but a strong hand touched his shoulder, and he was advised against any plans of leaving. Then he was led to the Cossack captain. The old man wanted to know how his daughter could have heard of the pious philosopher. Khoma expressed ignorance and declared himself unworthy of the task. Still the old captain said that they would carry out his daughter's wishes. When the old man led Khoma to the coffin, the philosopher saw an indescribable beauty; but he realized that she was the witch he had killed.

Some of the Cossacks on the farm told Khoma that the dead girl had been known as a witch. They knew people ruined by her. Nikita the huntsman had withered into ashes after a romp with her, and Sheptun's wife and baby had been drained of blood by the witch. As evening fell, the villagers went to sleep, but Khoma was led to the church and locked in. He lit candles all over the building and sang prayers, but still the witch came out of her coffin and began groping for him. He drew a circle around himself and began pronouncing exorcisms. She drew near with opened dead eyes and gnashing teeth. At the circle she stopped; it was evident that her powers could not overcome it. When she returned to her coffin, the box sprang up with a hissing sound and flew all over the church, zigzagging around. Still she could not cross the circle, Finally dawn came, and the Cossacks released the harried seminarian. After a troubled sleep and a glass of vodka, Khoma felt better and talked with the villagers. Yet as evening approached, he was led back to the loathsome church. He quickly drew a circle around himself and began reading exorcisms, not looking at the coffin. He read for an hour and then peeked toward the black box. To his horror, the witch was standing at the edge of his circle. He heard her gnashing teeth and saw her waving arms. But she could not pass the line. Suddenly she screamed an incantation, whereupon evil creatures beat their wings on the window panes and scratched their claws on the railings. At dawn, the Cossacks found a half-dead philosopher. Much of his hair had turned white. Khoma begged the Cossack captain to release him from the last night of prayers, but to no avail. Even when he tried to run away, he was soon brought back. He had to face the last night.

Inside the church, Khoma again drew his circle and began recalling exorcisms. Suddenly the lid of the iron coffin broke open and the witch came out in horrible form. A whirlwind whistled and the church doors broke open, letting in a multitude of monstrous creatures. The corpse cried, "Bring Vii!" and suddenly a silence prevailed. In a sidelong glance, Khoma saw a squat, leg-rooted creature trudging heavily forward. Its eyelids hung to the ground. When it reached Khoma it said, "Lift my eyelids. I can't see." An inner voice told Khoma not to look; but he did, and the creature pointed a dirty finger at him. "There he is!" it cried. At once the multitude of creatures pounced on the philosopher, and his soul ran from his body in terror. In their ravaging, the creatures failed to hear the cock's crow. When it crowed a second time, it was too late. They all flew to the windows at once and were stuck there forever to rot all over the sacred building. The church was abandoned and soon overgrown with trees and thorns.

In Kiev, the bell ringer Khaliava and his friend Tiberii Gorodets had a drink in honor of their lost companion, who would still be alive if he had not been afraid. You have only to cross yourself and spit on a witch's tail to be safe from harm.

Khoma Brut, Dorosh, Tiberii Gorobets, Herodias, Iavtukh, Khaliava, Mikhita, Overko, Potiphar's wife, Sheptun, Spirid.

Notes from a Dead House, F. M. Dostoevskii, 1860.

After his prison term, Aleksandr Petrovich Gorianchikov was assigned by the government to live in a small village in Siberia. He taught small children for a living but lived to himself. The publisher of his memoirs met him while visiting a minor official in the town. After Gorianchikov's death, the publisher bought the deceased's notes from his landlady for twenty kopecks. The memoirs were published because of their interesting comments on criminology and Russian prisons.

After arriving at the Siberian prison in despair from the loss of his noble privileges, Gorianchikov was surprised at the freedom of the prisoners even though they were fettered and confined. In their leisure time, they indulged in singing, cursing, vice, pipe smoking, vodka drinking, and card playing. There were three classes of prisoners: the civilian convict-exiles, deprived of all their civil rights and status, "fragments broken off from society"; military criminals, not deprived of their rights, with short-term sentences followed by service in Siberian regiments; and the "Special Class," a fairly numerous group of the most terrible, predominantly military criminals. Every type of criminal and crime imaginable was represented in the prison. The Major in charge of the camp, nicknamed "Eight Eyes," was despised and hated by everyone for his petty cruelty and vindictiveness. He strove to "increase the bitterness of already embittered men."

Gorianchikov concluded that in the criminal himself, prison and hard labor only developed hatred, a thirst for forbidden pleasures, and terrible irresponsibility. "Prison does not reform the criminal but only secures society from his further attempts on its peace." There are insoluble problems concerning the equality of crime and criminal punishment. The same crime may have entirely different effects on two different men: one may not even consider himself wrong, while another may suffer from his stricken conscience, as well as from the outward punishment. Therefore, one man is punished more severely than another.

Prison was more difficult for a nobleman than the man from a lower class who was used to conditions of poverty. Work and money were forbidden in the prison fortress, but prisoners soon developed trades and had sources of income. There were tailors, money lenders, doctors, pawnbrokers and laundrymen among the convicts. They stole from one another shamelessly. They drank vodka and even arranged for women if they had enough money. Gorianchikov concluded that the guards had an exaggerated idea of the prisoners, expecting them to hurl themselves on their captors at any minute. The convicts were aware of this fear and became arrogant because of it. The best warden was the one who showed no fear.

Gorianchikov's notes revealed the personal histories of several convicts. Their tragedies were interwoven in descriptive scenes from prison life. The narrator's first trip to the bathhouse made a strong impression on him: the difficulty of taking off clothes over chains, the impact of walking through slime in a crowded, steamy room, and the conduct of the bathers. A pleasant remembrance was related to the Christmas celebrations allowed the captives. They ate on a grand scale—suckling pigs and geese—and presented a Christmas program which took considerable preparations, and included plays and songs. For one day of the year the prisoners were lifted out of their sordid lives and allowed to dream. The reactions of the convicts to the performances of their fellow prisoners were as notable as the acting itself. Gorianchikov had difficulty believing the reality of the psychological escape allowed by the Christmas party. His stay in the hospital gave him insights into other aspects of prison life. Some prisoners went merely for a rest, cleverly and deliberately fooling the doctors into believing that they were sick. Others that were ill showed the ravages of prison life and its ability to destroy convicts. Gorianchikov described in detail several prisoners who were recuperating from floggings and beatings with a rod. Their livid blue backs revealed the intensity of their punishment as well as their chance of survival. The latter depended greatly on the will of the prisoner, and his dream of life and freedom. Spirits were often kept high by pets of various kinds: dogs, geese, and a goat. Yet there was always the dream of escape. Two skillful and clever convicts, Kulikov and A—v, tried to leave the prison by bribing a discontented guard. After they had covered more than seventy miles of territory, they were captured and brought back to face even more severe punishments. The narrator concluded that prisoners exaggerate the idea of actual freedom. When Gorianchikov left the prison, he felt the greatest tragedy of the system was the loss of the talents and abilities of the men wasting their time in confinement.

A—chukovski, A—v, General Abrosimov, Akim Akimich, Akul'ka, Alei, Aleksandr. Almazov, Anchukovski, Ankudim Trofimich, Antonich, Vasilii Antonov, Aristov, Avdot'ia B—, B—kii,

B—m, Baklushin, Boguslawski, Brinvilliers, Briullov, Bulkin, Isaiah Fomich Bumstein, Dmitrii Bykov, Chekunda, Chekunov, Cherevin, Robinson Crusoe, Diatlov, Don Juan, Dranishnikov, Dumas, Dutov, Efim, Elkin, Fedka, Filatka, G—v, Gavril'ka, Gazin, Glinka, Gogol', Gorchakov, Aleksandr Petrovich Gorianchikov, Governor General, Grigorii Petrovich, Ivan Ivanovich Gvosdikov, Iankel', Ivan Matveich, K—ski, Kamenev, Karenev, Katerina, Kedril, Khavroshka, Khvasov, Kobylin, Koller, Korenev, Koshkin, Kulikov, Kvasov, Leporello, Lomov, Luka (Luchka) Kuzmich, de La Valliere, Luisa, M—, M—ski, Major, Mametka, Manilov, Maria Stepanovna, Mariashka, Martynov, Mikhailov, Mirecki, Miroshka, Mitrofan Stepanich, Fil'ka Morozov, Napoleon III, Narrator, Nastas'ia Ivanova, Netsvetaev, Nikita Gregorich, Nurra, Onufriev, Orlov, Osip, Ostrozhskii, Petrov, Petrovich, Potseikin, Roman, Quasimodo, de Sade, Shapkin, Shilkin, Ivan Semenich Shishkov, Shultz, Sirotkin, Skuratov, Smekalov, Sokolov, Stepan (Stepa) Dorofeich, Sushilov, T—vskii, Taras Bulba, Timoshka, Tokarzewski, Ustiantsev, Van'ka-Tan'ka, Varlamov, Vasia, Anton Vasil'ev, Zh—kii, Zherebiatnikov, Zibert, Zochowski, Zverkov.

Oblomov, by I. A. Goncharov, 1859.

In an apartment building with the population of an entire town, the nobleman Il'ia Ilich Oblomov was lying in bed one morning. The thirty-two-year-old nobleman with dark gray eyes had no definite expression of concentration on his face. His eyes were clouded with weariness and boredom. The handsome furnishings of the apartment were marred by dust-covered cobwebs, stains, and disorder. Oblomov was reticent to arise from bed because of four nagging problems he did not wish to confront: there was trouble on his estate, he was losing his apartment, there was an unpaid butcher bill, and his doctor had warned that his present state of idleness would mean certain death. Oblomov felt that it was more honorable to sit with folded hands than work and lost himself in daydreams. The latter were even applied to his problems in a threefold manner: he would imagine "how good it would be" if a problem were solved; then he would try to shift the responsibility to someone else; if there were no takers, he would decide that "perhaps it will get done somehow." He took no initiative except in his daydreams, during which he sometimes assumed the role of Napoleon.

Various acquaintances visited Oblomov as he lay in bed, Volkov, a dandy and gossip, related trivialities. Sudbinskii, a mealy-mouthed clerk, needed money. Penkin, a writer, read Oblomov his latest diatribe on almost almost all subjects known to man. Alekseev, a nondescript, used Oblomov as a listener. The last visitor, Tarantev, spoke cruelly of Germans, but came to borrow a waistcoat. Zakhar, Oblomov's servant, would not give him the coat because he had not returned the other clothes he had borrowed. After demeaning Stolz, Oblomov's friend from childhood, Tarantev left. Oblomov wished that his industrious and educated friend Stolz would come and solve the problems of the day. Zakhar pestered Oblomov, trying to force him into action, but the master preferred to dream.

Oblomov's dream world was a victory of the idealistic over the practical. Distorted memories of the idyllic life at Oblomovka, the family estate, when the hero was a boy, transposed the flabby nobleman into a reverie of tranquility. Zakhar had dressed Oblomov as a boy and had watched over him, fearful that he might fall and hurt himself. Overfed and over-attended, Oblomov daydreamed and listened to the adults spread superstitions and interpret dreams. Oblomov yearned for the security of his childhood.

Andrei Stolz was only half German, on his father's side. Russian was his native tongue, but he also knew German. His upbringing contrasted greatly with Oblomov's: Stolz rode horses, studied, and was all bone, muscle, and nerve. Oblomov could not understand his friend's zeal or why he had so many interests. To Zakhar's delight, Stolz persuaded Oblomov to dress and go out with him. During their outing, the ambitious friend tried to persuade the indolent one to accompany him abroad. When Oblomov referred to his problems, Stolz cried out, "Oblomovism," coining a phrase for Oblomov's indecisiveness.

Before leaving for the Continent, Stolz introduced Oblomov to Ol'ga Il'inskaia. Ol'ga sang beautifully, and Oblomov was overcome with new emotions. They felt close, and Ol'ga found a five-starred lilac, a symbol of love. Oblomov moved to the country to be near his new-found interest. Passion, however, frightened the hero and tempted him to withdraw. When Stolz wrote asking him to come to Europe, the weakling thought of using the trip to escape from his shame. Passion was an emotion he could not contend with. When Ol'ga put the hand which he had kissed up to his cheek, he was stunned. He wrote her a letter informing her that she was in error, that she could not love him. He found her crying in the garden; his weakness and inability to act had wounded her. The lilacs had withered. Yet his tenderness, solicitude, and concern for her happiness caused her to overlook his indolence and apathy. While she could not allow him to kiss her, she did put his hand on her heart to feel its beating. Both were enthralled: Oblomov went home to rest, and Ol'ga went to sing. The summer days passed in anxious delight, and Ol'ga finally kissed him on the cheek. He watched his cheek for days in the mirror to see if some trace of the kiss remained. He was in love.

When Tarant'ev notified Oblomov that he had rented an apartment for him at Agaf'ia Matveevna Pshenitsyna's, Oblomov was forced to move. The Il'linskii family moved to the city at the close of the summer, and Ol'ga and Oblomov met less regularly. Guests were always plentiful at the Il'inskiis', and Oblomov found it difficult to speak with his beloved. Gradually his visits became less frequent. Ol'ga made excuses for his absences, once even asking if a sty in his eye had kept him from coming. Feeble excuses could not stop the rift between them. Finally Ol'ga dared society's wrath and went to Oblomov's apartment alone. Her hero was horrified, and Ol'ga told him in parting that she doubted she was the aim of his life. At another meeting, she realized that all was over. Oblomovism had won.

Time passed, and Oblomov found the realization of his dreams: he was cared for like an infant by Agaf'ia Pshenitsyna, whom he married. His vegetative existence brought him the idle peace he had longed for. Stolz and Ol'ga married and led fruitful lives. At a final visit to Oblomov by Stolz, it was evident that Oblomovism had ruined his friend's life. While Oblomov had found security, he was financially and physically in the hands of Agaf'ia. He soon died of a stroke. Stolz took the son left from the liaison between Oblomov and Agaf'ia. At a chance meeting in a Moscow street, Stolz saw Zakhar, now reduced to begging. The successful businessman took the old man under his protection. He was the last victim of Oblomovism.

Achilles, Agaf'ia Matveevna, Aksin'ia, Akulina, Ivan Alekseivich Alekseev, Aleksei Naumych, Aleksei Sidorovich, Alesha Popovich, Matvei Andreich Al'ianov, Andriusha. Andriushka, Anis'ia, Anna Vasil'evna, Antip, Apollo Belvedere, Archimedes, Artemii, Averka, Bach, Balochov, Balthazar, Batiushkov, Beethoven, Belovodov, Bichurin, Brutus, Byron, Don Carlos, Chekmenev, Chloe, Cordelia, Correggio, Cottin, Dante, Dashen'ka Demka, Krivoi, Dmitriev, Dmitrii Arkadievich, Dobryna Nikitich, Dobrynin, Don Quixote, Duniasha, Emelia the Fool, Erard, Ernestine, Eruslan Lasarevich, Faust, Fedot, Foma Fomich, Galatea, Genlis, Goethe, Golikov, Misha Goriunov, Lidia Goriunova, Sof'ia Nikolaevna Goriunova, Herder, Hertz,

Herschel, Homer, Hugo, Ignashka, Il'ia Muromets, Ol'ga Ser-
geevna Il'inskaia, Irina Panteleevna, Ivan Gerasimych, Ivan Mat-
veich, Ivan Petrovich, Kalinnikov, Karamzin, Katia, Kheraskov,
Anna Andreevna Khlopova, Kolechichsha, Vasil'ii Sevast'ianych
Kolymiagin, Krylov, Marina Kul'kova, Kuz'ka, Kuz'minichna,
Kuznetsov, fon Langvagen, Laptev, Leonardo da Vinci, Liagaev,
Lizaveta Nikolvna, Login, Louis Philippe, Luka, Maevskii,
Makhmet-Ali, Makhov, Maklashin, Malan'ia Petrovna, Manfred,
Marfa, Mar'ia Mikhailovna, Mar'ia Nikolaevna, Mar'ia Onisimov-
na, Mar'ia Petrovna, Mar'ia Savishna, Mar'ia Semenovna, Matvei
Moseich, Metlinskii, Meyerbeer, Mexdrov, Prince Michel,
Michelangelo, Mikhilov, Militrisa Kibit'evna, Mina, Mot'ka, Moz-
art, Ivan Matveich Mukhoiarov, Irina Penteleevna Mukhoiarova,
Murashina, Mussinskii, Prince N—, Napoleon I, Nastas'ia Nas-
tas'ia Ivanovna, Natal'ia Faddeevna, Nemesis, Cornelius Nepos,
Nikita, Norma, Andrei Oblovov, Il'ia Oblomov, Il'ia Il'ich
Oblomov, Oblomova, Odontsov, Oleshkin, Ol'ga, Ovchinikov,
Prince P—, Pelageia Ignat'evna, Penkin, Peresvetov, Petr Pe-
trovich, Petrov, Petrushka, Prince Pierre, Kazimir Al'bertych
Pkhailo, Plato, Polkan, Prometheus, Vania Pshenitsyn, Agaf'ia
Matveevna Pshenitsyna, Masha Pshenitsyna, Pushkin, Pygmal-
ion, Raphael, Reinhold, "Robert le Diable," Rokotov, Rousseau,
Rubini, Samoila, Sand, Savinov, Say, Schiller, Schubert, Scott,
Semen, Semen Semenovych, Semenov, Shakespeare, Andrei
Ivanovich Shtol'ts, Ivan Bodganych Shtol'ts, Sonechka, Step-
anida, Stepanida Agapovna, Stepanov, Sud'binskii, Sue,
Sumarokov, Onisim Suslov, Svinkin, Sychuga, Mikhei An-
dreevich Tarant'ev, Taras, Tat'iana Ivanovna, Telemachus, Titan,
Titian, Prince Michel Tiumen'ev, Ulysses, Van'ka, Vasil'ev, Vasilii
Fomich, Vasilisa, Vas'ka, Vesta, Viasnikov, Volkov, Vytiagush-
kin, Werther, Wieland, Caleb Williams, Zakhar Trofimych, Isai
Fomich Zatertyi, Zavadskii, Zhukovskii, Zinaida Mikhailovna.

"The Overcoat," by N. V. Gogol', 1842.
    There was once a pockmarked, ninth-class clerk with a hemorrhoi-
dal complexion whose name was Akakii Akakievich Bashmachkin. He
was shown no respect in his office; he was like a fly in the room. The
clerks teased and played tricks on him. Only when the jokes were
unbearable did he say, "Let me be," which could have been "I am your
brother," from the tone of his voice. Akakii's clothes were always a
mess because he had the knack of passing under the windows just as

refuse was being discarded. He paid attention to nothing, except his copy work. Only when a horse breathed on his cheek would he realize he was not in the middle of a line but in the middle of the street.

Tortured by the St. Petersburg cold, which went through his worn, gauze-like overcoat, Akakii went to the tailor Petrovich. The latter was cursing his needle during a foul mood and immediately refused to mend Akakii's ragged coat. The poor clerk left bewildered. A bucket of lime fell all over him from a building under construction, but he did not notice. Deciding that the refusal had depended on the tailor's mood, Akakii waited until Sunday and returned to Petrovich. Again the tailor refused, even after a tip. Akakii realized that he had to have a new coat. He had forty roubles from years of saving, but he needed forty more. For a year he reduced his expenses: no evening tea, no candles at night, and no laundry except when absolutely necessary. However, his spirits brightened during his hardship. The new coat became an aim in life. Akakii discussed the material with the tailor for months. Finally the day came for the selection: the calico lining looked like silk, and the cat fur for the collar looked like marten.

The most solemn day in Akakii's life was when Petrovich escorted the new coat to its owner. Akakii welcomed it as he would a bride. Full of good spirits, he wore the coat to work. It was soon well known that he had a new possession, and his fellow clerks tried to persuade him to have a party in the coat's honor. The thought frightened him, and he tried to convince them that it was an old coat. One clerk took mercy and invited the group to his house. Akakii did not want to attend but agreed when told that it would be rude to refuse. That evening he did no copying but lay on his bed near his coat. When he donned it, he walked the long way through dimly lit streets to the clerk's house. Entering, he found a hall full of galoshes and overcoats. He left his prized possession and joined the guests. They yelled at him and went into the hall to see his new coat. Soon, however, he was abandoned for the card tables. When he became bored and tried to excuse himself, the guests forced him to drink two glasses of champagne. After midnight, he went into the hall, found his coat on the floor, and put it on as he went to the street. Walking into a dark, large square, Akakii was confronted by two men who took his coat and knocked him out. When he revived a few minutes later in the snow, he screamed. His coat was gone. A watchman on the square had seen two men and suggested that Akakii visit a police inspector the next day. The distressed clerk went home and spent a night such as can be imagined by those able to put themselves in another man's place.

For the first time in his life, Akakii missed a day of work. He was busy going from one office to another, all to no avail. The next day at work the office clerks did take up a trifling sum for him but soon began teasing him again. One clerk advised him to turn to an important personage for help. Akakii chose Stepan Varlamovich, a newly made important person who considered his own comments so important that he practiced them in front of a mirror. When Akakii came to Stepan's office, he was forced to wait a long time. When the poor clerk was finally shown in, the important personage was disgusted with the sight before him. Akakii explained his problem with great difficulty. only to be shamed by the important personage for having dared come to him about such a matter. Akakii was carried out almost unconscious. He arrived home ill and went to bed.

The next day a physician came. Even as he was prescribing a poultice, he told the landlady to order a coffin. Akakii had only another day to go. Apparitions visited him: he saw Petrovich and ordered a new coat; thieves crept under his bed; and he stood before the important personage. When Akakii gave up the ghost, he was quietly buried. Four days later the office inquired about him, learning only then that he was no more.

Rumors suddenly began circulating around St. Petersburg. A ghost which looked like a clerk was reported searching for a stolen overcoat and was pulling coats off everyone. When one of the department clerks saw the spirit, he recognized Akakii. The police were given orders to catch it at all costs. One officer did apprehend the ghost, but it sneezed so loudly that he had to wipe his face and it slipped away.

Unbeknownst to Akakii, he had not been forgotten by the important personage. Stepan Varlamovich could not forget the clerk who had stood before him so pathetically. Learning of the clerk's death, Stepan was depressed enough to attend a party as a way of escaping his thoughts. He was soon lost in frivolity. With the party over, he decided to visit a woman friend. On the way, he suddenly felt someone grab him from behind. He turned and looked with horror. It was Akakii as a ghost. Its face was white as snow, and it explained that it was taking the important man's coat since he had done nothing about the stolen one. Stepan almost died. He quickly ordered his coachman homeward, where he went and spent a wretched night.

After that incident, the ghost of Akakii was never seen again. Many, however, claimed that a ghost was still about. One watchman did see it and followed it into a dark area. He did not dare arrest it. It was a very tall ghost with a moustache. When it turned, it threatened with a huge

fist which seemed to symbolize the oppressive forces of the world. The
watchman cowered away, not looking for trouble. The ghost disappeared into the dark of night.

Anna, Akakii Akakievich, Akakii Akakievich Bashmachkin, Arina
Semenovna Belobriushkova, Dula, Eroshkin, Falconet, Ivan Ab-
ramovich, Ivan Ivanovich, Karolina Ivanovna, Khozdazat,
Mochius, Pavsikakhii, Petrovich, Sossius, Stepan Varlamovich,
Trifilii, Vakhtisii, Varadat, Varakhasii, Varukh.

Poor Folk, F. M. Dostoevskii, 1846.

This novel is in the form of letters between a middle-aged clerk,
Makar Alekseevich Devushkin, and a poor orphaned girl. Varvara
Alekseevna. While they were separated only by a courtyard, they
often communicated by letter. In the course of their acquaintance,
Devushkin began to help his friend financially, even though he was
practically impoverished himself. He sent her little gifts from time to
time and responded to her entreaties to stop his generosity by saying
that he was a lonely man and that helping her gave him pleasure.

Their letters were filled with humdrum details. He described the
dilapidated building in which he lived and complained of the air which
killed canaries brought into the abode. She mentioned her sewing or
reminiscenced about her past. She grew up in the country where her
father was a stewart on the estate of a Prince P—. She was happy
there; but after the Prince's death, the family moved to St. Petersburg,
where her father started a small business. When his endeavor failed
and he died, Varvara and her mother were forced to live with a
relative, an unpleasant woman named Anna Fedorovna. An orphaned
girl named Sasha also lived there, and Varvara studied with her under
the direction of Petr Pokrovskii, an impoverished student who
boarded with Anna Fedorovna. As children, Sasha and Varvara played
tricks on the tutor and exasperated him; but when they grew older,
Varvara wanted him to think of her as a young lady. Once she found
out that his birthday was coming; so she planned to buy him a set of
Pushkin's works. She found a set, but it was two roubles more
expensive than what she had. When she saw Pokrovskii's father also
buying books, she proposed that they pool their money and purchase
the Pushkin volumes. The old man agreed with pleasure. Varvara,
realizing that the father wanted to show his son that he had mended
his ways, allowed him to present the entire set of books to his son as if
they were only from him. A short time later, Pokrovskii's father died.
His demise was followed by the death of Varvara's mother, and the
poor girl was left without a friend in the world.

In Devushkin's building there was a writer named Rataziaev, whom Devushkin greatly admired. In his letters, he described several of the young author's romantic novels. Another lodger mentioned in Devushkin's letters was a man named Gorshkov, who lived in one room with his wife and three children. He had been dismissed from government service because of some sort of scandal, and the family lived in the direst poverty. He could not obtain another position because his case was pending before the courts. The matter was still unsettled after seven years. When Devushkin reported that Gorshkov had won his case, he also informed Varvara of a resulting tragedy. Evidently the news had been too much for the weakened man, and he died after receiving word of his acquittal.

During the course of their relationship, Devushkin's financial position worsened. Varvara was sick for a while, and her friend paid for help so that she would not have to enter a hospital. He became behind in his rent, and his landlady abused him. His clothes became worn with his elbows sticking out of his sweater. He was ashamed of his appearance, but he had no choice. When Varvara asked him for money so that she could move farther away from Anna Fedorovna, Devushkin tried unsuccessfully to borrow money. One day at work he left a line out of a document and was called before his superior. Devushkin was unable to defend himself; and while he was talking, a button fell off his coat. His superior noticed the shabby appearance of his worker and ordered that he be given an advance in wages since his work record was very good. However, Devushkin had already taken an advance in wages. When the rest of the clerks had left, the superior came to Devushkin and gave him a hundred roubles. The poor clerk was so overwhelmed that he kissed his benefactor's hand. The superior shook hands with him as if they were equal. While Devushkin's immediate financial problems were solved, he received painful news from Varvara. A wealthy man named Bykov had proposed marriage to her, and she had accepted because she saw no other means of saving herself. She confessed that she did not love him but had agreed to leave with him immediately for his estate in the country. Devushkin was distraught because he loved Varvara dearly; however, there was nothing he could do because he was just a poor clerk.

Aksentii Osipovich, Aksinia, Anna Fedorovna, Belkin, Bykov, Makar Alekseevich Devushkin, Duniasha, Efim Akimovich, Emel'ian Il'ich, Emel'ian Ivanovich, Ermak, Ermolaev, Evstafii Ivanovich, Fal'doni, Fedor Fedorovich, Fedora, Fedosii Ivanovich, Frolovna, Glasha, Gorshkov, Ivan the Terrible, Ivan Prokof'evich, de Kock, Kuchum, Lamonde, Lovelace, Markov, Masha, Natas'ia, Noah, Odoevskii, Prince P—, Pelageia Antonovna, Petinka, Petr Petrovich, Petr Zakharaovich (Petinka) Pokrovskii, Zakhar Petrovich Polrovskii, Prokofii Ivanovich, Pushkin, Rataziaev, Sasha, Shakespeare, Smel'skii, Snegirev, Stepan Karlovich, Teresa, Thedora, Theresa, Timofei Ivanovich, Ul'iana, V—, Varvara Alekseevna, Samson Vyrin, Zapol'skii, Ivan Prokof'evich Zheltopuz, Zinaida, Ziuleika.

The Possessed, F. M. Dostoevskii. See *The Devils*.

The Precipice, I. A. Goncharov, 1869.

Two gentlemen were seated in an untidy apartment discussing philosophy and social problems. The younger gentleman, the thirty-five-year old Raiskii, was youthful looking and sloppily dressed. He was a nervous, impressionable artist whose character was very changeable, turning quickly from a charming disposition to a cold, vindictive nature. The other gentlemen, the forty-five-year-old Aianov, was emaculately dressed and presented very proper manners. He lived in high society, where he was a welcome guest in many fine homes. He was a widower with a twelve-year-old daughter who was in a boarding school for girls. The two men decided to visit Raiskii's cousin, Sof'ia Belovodova, with whom he was infatuated.

Sof'ia was a young, beautiful widow who lived with two rich aunts. Raiskii tried desperately to broaden the horizons of his cold, aloof relative. He wanted to awaken passion in her and giver her a sense of the sufferings of her fellow man. Spending night after night with her in discussions, he could not transmit any of his own idealism to her. Raiskii finally realized the futility of his efforts to change Sof'ia's protected, narrow existence.

Raiskii went to the country to visit his great-aunt Berezhkova, whom he considered his grandmother. She lived on the Malinovka estate with two young female relatives. Berezhkova was an ideal woman and an accomplished proprietress. She was devoted to the family, was fair with the serfs, and managed her own estate. She also handled the affairs of the estates of Raiskii and her deceased brother's grandchildren. She could not understand Raiskii's disdain for practical matters; so she urged him to marry, settle down, and take over the control of his own estate.

At first Raiskii was quite taken by his relative, Marfen'ka, the youngest of Berezhkova's wards. The oldest, Vera, was away visiting a friend. Raiskii tried to direct Marfen'ka into intellectual pursuits, but she refused to read books unless they had a happy ending. She was pretty, joyful, and obedient to her grandmother. She spent her time with children, animals, and flowers. After a couple of weeks of admiring Marfen'ka's beauty and simplicity, Raiskii began to feel the boredom which always overtook him no matter what the endeavor. He never finished a painting or completed a novel. The idyllic country life became flat and tiresome.

When Vera returned, Raiskii's interests were again renewed. Vera was lovelier than her sister Marfen'ka and more mature: she was educated, determined, and quiet. She never laughed or cried, and always tried to conceal her expression if she was caused to smile. Although she loved her sister and grandmother, she never showed it. She could not confide her thoughts or feelings to anyone. There were two houses on the estate, one, a wooden rambling structure where Berezhkova and Marfen'ka lived, and another, a large old stone manor where Vera moved and lived by herself. Raiskii was intrigued by Vera's personality and wanted to earn her confidence. However, the more he tried to win her favor, the more distant she became, even evading him. She claimed that she loved freedom and hated being watched and followed. As usual with Raiskii, an image of physical beauty melted into passion. He loved Vera but felt she was in love with someone else. For a time he suspected Tushin, a landowner who was obviously in love with her. Yet she treated Tushin as a friend and nothing else. Vera's indifference soon plunged Raiskii into a depression filled with anger and disgust. He began to sketch peasants, nature, and the Volga; but nothing helped, and so he decided to leave.

Berezhkova gave a party for all the local gentry. One guest, Tychkov, was noted for his criticisms and recriminations, and people were afraid of him. When he was rude to a lady in a rather flashy dress, Raiskii reprimanded him. Tychkov turned his wrath on Raiskii, and the latter was about to throw him out of the house when Berezhkova interfered. Standing straight and erect, she denounced Tychkov for all his misdeeds. She accused him of taking bribes and of robbing his orphaned niece of all her money. Raiskii and Berezhkova became local heroes, Tychkov was ostracized from sociey and was soon doomed to lead a lonely life. Vera was much kinder to Raiskii after the incident, and he decided to stay in the country and try to win her love.

When Raiskii had inherited his father's estate, he had received a fine library which contained books he read as an adolescent. Having no

further interest in the books, he gave the library to a former schoolmate, Kozlov, who now taught Greek and Latin in a local school.
Kozlov loaned books to an acquaintance, Mark Volokhov, an intellectual known as a nihilist who had been sent to the province as a
punishment for some misdemeanor. After Raiskii met Volokhov at
Kozlov's, he learned that Volokhov was again in trouble for giving
politically dangerous books to young people in the school. Volokhov
asked Raiskii to take the blame for the students having possession of
the books because the material was from the library Raiskii had given
Kozlov. Raiskii was afraid that Kozlov would become involved and
lose his teaching position, his only source of income. Consequently,
Raiskii helped Volokhov and told the provincial governor that the
books were from the Raiskii library.

Behind the stone house where Vera lived was a precipice. The
garden of the estate used to run to its edge, and there was a ruined
arbor along it. Few people went to the precipice because there was a
suicide's grave nearby and most people were superstitious. In an
orchard near the precipice, Vera accidentally ran into Volkhov, who
was picking apples. An exchange about the ownership of the property
took place between them. Volokhov maintained that everything belonged to everyone. All was common property. It was evident that the
two young people were quite taken with each other. They began to
meet secretly near the precipice, arguing about everything. He was
impressed by her beauty and mind, and tried to persuade her to ignore
conventions and live with him so long as their passion lasted. At first
she was drawn to him by the novelty of his philosophy; but after she
had fallen in love with him, she tried to change his views. She was
willing to live with him if they could reconcile their ideals. But
Volokhov demanded that they catch a moment of happiness and not
hold each other down with conventions.

Vikan'tiev, a young landowner who lived with his mother across the
Volga, spent all of his free time from government service at Berezhkova's. He and Marfen'ka had been childhood friends, and so he
decided to marry her. No one was surprised at the young couple's
decision. Raiskii legalized a transfer of his Malinovka estate to Marfen'ka and Vera. The wooden house went to the former; the stone
manor, to the latter.

Raiskii became aware of Vera's meetings near the precipice, but he
did not know whom she met there. When he tried to follow her, she
became aware of his presence and begged him to leave her alone.
Raiskii left her after she had implored his trust. Volokhov, however,

persuaded Vera to deceive Raiskii by telling him that she loved Raiskii. Volokhov felt that the deception would detract attention from his meetings with Vera. Fearing that Berezhkova would find out about the meetings and become ill from worry, Vera decided that she would part from Volokhov. She asked Raiskii to prevent her from going to the precipice even if she tried forcefully to do so. Raiskii accepted the post of bodyguard. However, when Volokhov fired a shot in the distance to inform Vera that he was at the precipice, she fought with Raiskii in her efforts to leave. She insisted that it would be the last meeting and was going only to say goodbye. Yet she knew that if Volokhov had changed his attitudes, she would share her life with him. Raiskii waited all night for Vera's return. When she came in the morning, she quickly admitted that Volokhov had seduced her and then asked Raiskii to tell her grandmother everything.

Berezhkova was distraught at the news of Vera's affair and wandered about the estate for days. She was heard saying that an old sin had been punished. It was revealed that she too in her youth had succumbed to a young man whom she was not allowed to marry. As a result, she had never married. Hearing that Vera was ill, Berezhkova regained her strength and nursed her ward to health. Volokhov could not understand Vera's reaction to their affair, and wrote to her and waited for her near the precipice. She did not read his letters, and asked her friend Tushin to return them and tell Volkhov to leave her alone.

Town gossip began to associate Vera's name with Tushin, and there was talk of a second marriage in the family. Tushin wanted to marry Vera and hoped that he would be able to do so in time. He went to Volokhov and demanded that he leave town. Tushin told the townspeople that he had proposed to Vera but had been turned down.

After Marfen'ka's wedding, Raiskii went to Europe, hoping to become a sculptor and create a statue of Vera. His passion for her had ended, but he loved her as a sister. After two years abroad, he returned to what he realized he valued the most: Marfen'ka, Vera, Berezhkova, and Russia.

Afim'ia, Agaf'eia, Agashka, Ivan Ivanovich Aianov, Ol'en'ka Aianova, Akulina, Aleksei Petrovich, Andromache, Anna Borisovna, Anna Ivanovna, Anna Nikolaevna, Anna Petrovna, Anton, Antony, Apollo, Archimedes, Arina, Aristophanes, Aristotle, Armance, Armida, St. Augustine, Avdot'ia, I——B——, Bacchus, Bacon, Balakin, Barabbas, Basil, Basurman, Beethoven, Bellini, Paul Belovodov, Sof'ia Nikolaevna Belovodova, Tat'iana

Pestov, St. Peter, Petr, Petr I, Petr Petrovich, Phidias, Phoebus, Pichet, Pierre, Pontius Pilate, Plato, Plutarch, Popo Postumia, Praxiteles, Prokhor, Prometheus, Ptolemy, Pugachev, Pushkin, Pygmalion, de Querney, R—— K——, Rachel, Racine, Sof'ia (Sonechka) Raiskaia, Boris Pavlovich Ruskii, Michel Ramin, Raphael, Razin, Richard, Rinaldo, Rossini, Rubens, Sallust, Samson, Sandmann, Savelii, Savrasov, Scheherazade, Schmidt, Scott, Dashen'ka Semechkina, Semen, Serapinsbruder, Serge, Sergei Ivanovich, Sevast'ianov, Shakespeare, Sidor Sidorych, Silych, Sistine Madonna, Sof'ia Pavlovna, Sophocles, Spinoza, Stepan, Stepka, Sumarokov, Swift, Tacitus, Tamara, Taras, Tartuffe, Tasso, Telemachus, Teniers, Terentii, Thucydides, Titian, Anna Petrovna Todkeeva, Ivan Ivanovich Tushin, Anna Ivanovna Tushina, Nil Andreevich Tychkov, Ulita, Ustin'ia, I—— V——, Varvara Nikolaevna, Vasil'ev, Stepan Vasil'ev, Vasilii, Father Vasilii, Vasilii Nikitich, Vasilisa, Vas'ka, Vasiukov, Vas'ka, Vatrukhin, Tit Nikonych Vatutin, Velazquez, Venus De Milo, Verochka, Veronese, Nikolai Andreich Vikent'ev, Mar'ia Egorovna Vikent'eva, Viktor, Virginia, Vitali, Vlas, Mark Ivanych Volokhov, Voltaire, Wilhelm Meister, Werther, Xenophon, Zemfira, Zhukovskii.

A Raw Youth, F. M. Dostoevskii. See *The Adolescent*.

The Underground Man, F. M. Dostoevskii, 1864.
  Part I.
  "I am a sick man—I am a spiteful man. I am an unpleasant man. I think my liver is diseased—I refuse to treat it out of spite. I am well aware that I cannot get even with doctors by not consulting them. I know that I thereby injure myself and no one else—My liver is bad, well, let it get worse." Thus began the imaginary Underground Man who Dostoevskii said did exist in Russian Society because of the nature of the society itself.
  The forty-year-old Underground Man had lived for twenty years in his spiteful condition. He decided to write down his thoughts in order to criticize himself better. He had been in the civil service but did not accept bribes. He pretended to be spiteful and embittered to amuse himself. He cared not to succeed because only fools do. An intelligent man ought to be characterless; a man with character is limited.
  The Underground Man retired to his room when he received six thousand roubles in a will. He was suffering from hyper-consciousness. He knew the world too well and sought an escape whereby he

could be an insect or a complete scoundrel. He wanted to enjoy his
degradation to be conscious of his hopeless position. Normal man is
direct, seeks revenge, and cares only for himself. The Underground
Man envied normal men because they are not hyper-conscious. They
have not run up against the stone wall of apostasy. The Underground
Man knew the wall created by the laws of nature and natural science,
and he escaped his pathetic position by delighting in his despair. A
toothache brings delight because it humbles one. The result of the
Underground Man's consciousness was inertia, caused by his laziness.
He wished to develop the vice of gluttony in order to have a fat
stomach. A fat stomach could be something positive, something to
hold on to in a world where nothing is positive and there is nothing to
hold on to. Man's golden dreams are for something positive. There is
no such thing as choice for man. Any formulas for man's behavior
make him into an organ stop or a piano key. Man connot live in an
anthill or by the equation $2 + 2 = 4$. Man must preserve his indi-
viduality and therefore loves suffering, the origin of consciousness.
Such thinking might be considered irrational, but the irrational pre-
serves the individual.

Part II.

When the Underground Man was twenty-four, his life was lonely
and disorganized. He hated his own face and despised his fellow clerks.
He was a coward and a slave, by his own admission; but he felt that
cowardice and slavery were the fate of all decent men. He was
overwhelmed with depression and turned to vice in solitude at night.
Once while passing a tavern, he saw a gentleman thrown out the
window. He stood by a billiard table, and a tall officer took him by the
shoulders and moved him to another spot because he was blocking the
way of play. The Underground Man was terribly offended and left the
tavern. For several years he would stare at the officer with spite when
he saw him on the street. Once he followed the officer home. Finally
the Underground Man decided on revenge: he would run into the
officer on the street. Yet every time he tried his courage failed. Finally
he was able to bump into the officer, but the latter pretended that he
had not noticed. Still, The Underground Man felt avenged.

To escaspe his anguish, the Underground Man turned to daydreams
about being rich and serving mankind. Occasionally he would visit his
superior Anton Antonich Setochkin and sit for four hours listening
without saying a word. Another acquaintance whom he visited was
his former classmate Simonov. Once, after a year's absence, he went
to Simonov's and found two other former classmates there—Tru-
daliubov and Ferfichkin. The group was planning a party for another

classmate, Zverkov. To the consternation and disapproval of the others, the Underground Man invited himself to the party, promising to pay his share. When he arrived at the restaurant, he was an hour early; the others had failed to inform him that they had changed the time of meeting. When they arrived, Zverkov tried to be civil; but the Underground Man was hostile, and the others soon left him pouting alone. Later, after giving a tasteless toast, the Underground Man walked back and forth in the room for three hours. When the others decided to go to a house of dubious reputation, the Underground Man begged for money in order to accompany his classmates. Ferfichkin gave him some money, and they all left.

At the house, the Underground Man was confronted by a tall, strong-looking girl. He woke up at two o'clock with her by his side. He tried to make her feel ashamed. When Liza, the girl, finally cried, he asked her forgiveness and told her to come and see him. Borrowing money from Setochkin, The Underground Man was able to pay off his debts. However, he withheld his servant Grigorii's wages in order to exasperate the poor old man. When they quarreled, the Underground Man demanded that the servant go for the police. Apollon replied, "Whoever heard of a man sending for the police against himself." Liza came during their quarrel. The Underground Man tried to shame her, but she saw through his tirade. Although she was crushed by his unkind remarks, she saw that he was an unhappy man and felt genuine sentiment for him. She suddenly rushed to him and threw her arms around him, sobbing. The Underground Man fell on a sofa and cried. Then they rapturously embraced. Fifteen minutes later Liza realized that the outburst of passion had been one of revenge, not of love. So she left. The Underground Man cried out for her, but there was no answer. He found the five-rouble note he had given her the night they met. He started after her but stopped, believing that she would be happier in the future carrying her rage in her heart. The Underground Man never saw her again. He concluded that we never see "real life," since we prefer delusion. Even if we are granted some freedom, we immediately ask to be under control again.

The notes end, but the Underground Man did continue writing them.

Alexander of Macedon, Anaevskii, Apollon, Attila, Buckle, Churkin, Cleopatra, Countess, Prince D——, Princess D——, Ferfichkin, Ge, Gogol', Heine, King of Spain, Kolia, Kostan-zhoglo, Lermontov, Liza, Manfred, Napoleon I, Nekrasov, Officer, Olimpia, Petr Ivanich, Pirogrov, Podkharzhevskii, Pope,

Pushkin, Razin, Rousseau, Saltykov-Schedrin, Sand, Anton Antonich Setochkin, Shakespeare, Simonov, Trudoliubov, Underground Man, Vagengeim, Vaniukha, Zverkov.

The Village of Stepanchikogo, F. M. Dostoevskii, 1859.

Egor Rostanev, a forty-year-old widower, retired from the army and settled on an estate he had inherited, the village of Stepanchikogo. His mother, Madame Krakhotina, remarried a former general because she liked being called "Madame la Generale." Egor had to support two households, his own and that of his mother and stepfather, who was an invalid the last ten years of his life. Foma Fomich Opiskin came into the latter household as a reader for the cantankerous old general. Foma soon had the feminine half of the home under his spell. He read to them, interpreted their dreams, and preached on Christian virtues, convincing all that he was a sage. The general treated Foma badly, but his martyrdom only increased the ladies respect for him. When the general died, Foma rebuked Egor for mistreating his mother even though Egor had satisfied her every whim. The kindhearted son accepted the rebuke and moved his mother to Stepanchikogo, along with her entire retinue: a sourpuss old-maid companion, Miss Perepiltsin, numerous dogs, and the incredible Foma. It was at that time that Foma had begun to rule the household.

In St. Petersburg, Sergei Aleksandrovich, the narrator of the book and the nephew of Egor Rostanev, received a letter in which his uncle begged the nephew to marry a former ward, Nastia, who worked as a housekeeper in Egor's home. The letter was so vague on certain details that Sergei, who greatly revered his uncle, set out for Stepanchikogo. On the way he met Bakhcheev, a friend of his uncle, who informed him of the activities of Foma at Stepanchikogo. Foma dictated everything and once even declared two Wednesdays in one week when he mistook a Thursday for a Wednesday. Everyone in the household accepted his sage wisdom except for Egor's teenage daughter Sasha. Foma was trying to force Egor to marry a wealthy old maid, Tat'iana Ivanovna, and was persecuting the poor housekeeper Nastia, with whom Egor was in love.

Sergei arrived at Stepanchikogo quietly so as to talk with his uncle before meeting the others. The nephew soon realized his uncle's subservience to everyone in the household. When Sergei presented himself for tea, he slipped on a rug, and made a clumsy and embarrassing entrance. Except for the formidable Foma, the whole household was assembled, including some visitors: Pavel Obnoskin, a sarcastic young man, and his mother, a pretentious matron. Everyone was awaiting for Foma. Ezhivikin, the father of Nastia, came and tried to ingratiate himself with everyone. He was treated badly until he announced that Foma was not coming for tea. A general uproar took place. Egor finally confessed that Foma was offended because Egor had refused to call him "Your Excellency." Suddenly Sasha denounced Foma, calling him a liar, a cheat, and a bad influence. Madame la Generale fainted, and the audience was stunned. A servant boy, Falalei, entered crying. Foma had caught him dancing, and he was to be punished. Amidst the confusion, Foma himself suddenly appeared. Egor tried to introduce him to Sergei, but Foma paid no attention. He ridiculed the servant for dancing and delivered eloquent phrases on literature. Everyone listened to every word. When Gavrila, a servant, was summoned, Foma reduced the old man to tears with abuse. Gavrila finally burst out with a speech denouncing Foma. The company was aghast, and Madame la Generale demanded that Gavrila be put in fetters. However, at that moment, Sergei, who had controlled himself long enough, stepped into the middle of the assembly and announced that he shared Gavrila's sentiments about Foma. The latter was struck speechless, then screamed in indignation and stormed out of the room, followed by his toadies.

Sergei went into the garden and confronted Nastia. He told her that his uncle has asked him to marry her. Nastia was perturbed by his news and asked him to forget the matter. Sergei then asked her if his uncle loved her. She avoided the question and said that she was leaving the household. Sergei was called to his uncle, who announced that he was going to ask Foma to leave the household. The nephew was delighted and eavesdropped on his uncle's conversation with the petty tyrant. Foma turned down the money Egor offered him if he would leave; and Egor was so surprised he begged Foma to stay, even consenting to call him "Your Excellency." Sergei rebuked his uncle for giving in to the scoundrel, but Egor begged Sergei to wait for him in a small lodge on the estate until he could clear up a certain matter. Sergei complied and went to the lodge. Mizinchikov, a poor relative, came in and confessed that he wanted to marry the rich old maid Tat'iana, the very one Foma wanted Egor to marry. Mizinchikov planned an elopement but offered the old maid to Sergei if he would sign a note promising Mizinchikov money after the wedding. Sergei refused the ridiculous offer on moral grounds but did promise not to reveal the scheme, even though Mizinchikov had already told Obnoskin about it. When Egor came, he revealed that Foma had agreed that Nastia could stay in the household if Egor would marry Tat'iana. Sergei was disgusted and told his uncle about his conversation with Nastia. Later Sergei went walking and found his uncle in great distress. Foma had caught Egor kissing Nastia. Both nephew and uncle agreed that there would be bedlam the next day. Sergei was awakened by Bakhcheev, who informed him that Obnoskin had abducted the rich and befuddled Tat'iana. A great chase began. Egor, Sergei, and Mizinchikov caught up with the couple at a nearby estate. The rescue party took the crying old maid back back to Stepanchikogo in time for Foma's name-day party. During the festivities, Foma suddenly announced his departure. Again, bedlam! Foma said he could not stay in a house where the host took advantage of a housekeeper. Egor, enraged, threw Foma through a glass door; the victim went flying head over heels down the front entrance steps, landing in the yard among some broken glass. Again, pandemonium! Thunder clapped in the distance, and screams resounded in the room. Madame la Generale pleaded for Egor to bring Foma back. Nastia told Egor that she would leave because her presence was causing him nothing but trouble. However, Foma's carriage overturned in the storm and the tyrant was brought back, soaking wet. However, after rebuking Egor, Foma suddenly said that he would forgive him and allow his marriage to Nastia. The bewildered Nastia and Egor were asked to join hands and receive the blessing of Madame la Generale, which the equally surprised matron gave. Tat'iana came in and promised to give Nastia thirty thousand roubles for her wedding. Widespread rejoicing took place. Even Sasha and Nastia forgave Foma. Nastia and Egor married, and had children. With time, members of the household passed away, including Madame la Generale and Foma the sage. Nastia and Egor sometimes walked to his grave and remembered his sayings and what he ate. Sasha married and moved away. Mizinchikov became a successful landowner. Sergei planned a visit to Stepanchikogo in the near future.

Adelaida, Afanasii Matveich, Agrafena, Akulina Panfilovna, Alexander of Macedon, Andron, Arkhip, Stepan Alekseich Bakhcheev, Borozdin, Brambeus, Caesar, Clitus, Cook, Dasha, Egorushka, Elijah, Essbuketov, Evgrav Larionich Ezhevikin, Nastia Evgravovna Ezhevikina, Falalei, Fevron'ia, St. Foma, Gavrila, Pedro Gomez, Grishka, Hamlet, Iva Iakovlich, Judas Iscariot, Karamzin, Kholmskii, Koch, Komarinskii, Koreisha, Koronoukhov, Korovkin, Krakhotkin, Agafia Timofeevna Krakhotkina, Kuropatkina, Kuz'ma, Lermontov, Lomonosov,

Machiavelli, Malan'ia, Martyn, Matrena, Matvei Il'ich, Matvei Nikitich, Mercadante, Mitiushka, Ivan Ivanovich Mizinchikov, Nastenka, Noah, Pavel Semenich Obnoshkin, Afisa Petrovna Obnoskina, Oleadnrov, Foma Fomich Opiskin, Orpheus, Anna Nilovna Perepelitsyna, Polovitsin, Praskov'ia Il' inichna, Koz'ma Prutkov, Pugachev, Pushkin, Pykhtin, Pythagoras, Radcliffe, Egor Il'ich Rostanev, Il'ia Egorovich Rostanev, Aleksandra Egorvna Rostaneva, Katia Rostaneva, Rusapetov, Scribbler, Senkovskii, Serge, Sergei Aleksandrovich, Shakespeare, Frol Silin, Talleyrand, Tantsev, Tat'iana Ivanovna, Valentin Ignatevich Tikhontsev, Tiul'panov, Trishin, Ulanov, Vania, Vasil'ev, Vernyi, Gregorii Vidophliasov, Vlonskaia, Voltaire, Zuia, Zverkov.

CHARACTERS

Achukovskii. *Notes from a Dead House.* See Anchukovskii.

A——v. *Notes from a Dead House.* Once a nobleman, he was the most loathsome example of the depths to which a human being can sink. Completely degraded morally and ready to kill to indulge in his capricious pleasures, he was a moral Quasimodo.

Abraham. *The Brothers Karamazov* (2, 6, 1). The Biblical founder of the Hebrew nation (Gen. 12–23) who was mentioned in Father Zosima's biography when the elder discussed his acceptance of faith as a young man. *Crime and Punishment* (Epilogue 2). When Raskol'nikov was working in prison, he once gazed at the area where free men lived, and thought that time itself had stopped and that the age of Abraham had not passed.

Abrosimov, General. *Notes from a Dead House.* The officer for whom the prisoners presented their theatrical performance.

Achilles. *Crime and Punishment* (6, 6). Homer's hero in the *Iliad* who was invulnerable except in the heel. Just before Svidrigailov committed suicide, he approached a large house in front of which a man stood in an Achilles helmet. When the man saw Svidrigailov take out a gun, he said that it was not a fitting place for jokes. Svidrigailov told him to say that the victim said he was going to America and then he shot himself. *The Devils* (1, 5, 4). When Varvara Stavrogina ordered Stepan Verkhovenskii to ring the bell for a servant to show out Captain Lebiatkin, Stepan stated that Lebiatkin, too, had an Achilles heel. He meant Lebiatkin's problem with drink. *Oblomov* (1, 9). Oblomov's nurse told him about the Greek hero when Oblomov was a boy.

Acis. *The Adolescent* (3, 7, 2). A handsome Sicilian youth in Greek legend who was killed by his rival, the Cyclops Polyphemus. The blood flowing from Acis's body changed into water and formed the river Acis. See Lorrain, Claude.

Adelaida. *The Village of Stepanchikogo* (1, 3). A Russianized version of the name Adele. Vidopliasov said that the narrator's tie was the color Adelaida. In the 1840s and 50s, a dark blue color was mentioned in the Russian press as being Adelaida color.

Adelaida Sofronovna. *Dead Souls* A person whom Chichikov visited in
Simbirsk. The blonde girl at the ball began to yawn when he
told her about the visit.

Adel'geida Gavrilovna. *Dead Souls.* The sister-in-law of a certain
Bezprechnyi in Simbirsk. The blonde girl at the ball was bored
when Chichikov told her about visiting Bezprechnyi.

Aduev, Aleksandr Fedorych (Sashen'ka). *A Common Story.* The young
man who went to St. Petersburg when he was twenty to start
his career. His uncle Petr Ivanovich Aduev strove to make him
more sophisticated; and in ten years Aleksandr had acquired all
of the uncle's worst traits.

Aduev, Fedor Ivanych. *A Common Story.* Aleksandr Aduev's deceased
father and the brother of Petr Ivanovich Aduev.

Aduev, Petr Ivanovich. *A Common Story.* Aleksandr Aduev's uncle who
was a naïve idealist when he went to St. Petersburg. Petr
Ivanovich changed him into a practical but cunning person.

Adueva, Anna Pavlovna. *A Common Story.* The mother of Aleksandr
Aduev. She was a widowed landowner of limited means.

Adueva, Lizaveta Aleksandrovna. *A Common Story.* Petr Aduev's wife,
who consoled Aleksandr Aduev when he lost his beloved
Naden'ka. Lizaveta was unhappy with her husband.

Aeschylus (525–456 B.C.) *A Common Story* (1, 3). The father of Greek
drama. His bust was broken to pieces when Aleksandr Aduev
shook a table while erasing a letter that had ink spots.

Aesop. *The Brothers Karamazov* (1, 2, 8). The famous storyteller who was
mentioned by Miusov after he lost his temper in an argument
with Fedor Karamazov.

Aesthete, Mr. *The Devils.* See Esthete.

Afanasii Ivanovich. *The Idiot.* See Totskii, Afanasii Ivanovich.

Afanasii Matveich. *The Village of Stepanchikogo.* The uncle who left Egor
Rostanev three hundred serfs in a will.

Afanasii Pavlovich. *The Brothers Karamazov.* A former orderly whom
Father Zosima met after an eight-year separation. The elder
had beaten Afanasii up years ago and asked his forgiveness.

Afanasii Savich. *A Common Story.* An acquaintance of Aleksandr Aduev.
When Aduev was lonely in the big city of St. Petersburg, he
thought of his friend Afanasii in the country.

Aferdov. *The Adolescent.* A gambler who played at a roulette table across
from Arkadii Dolgorukii.

Afim'ia. *The Brothers Karamazov.* A serf who was sold by Father Zosima's
mother. *The Precipice.* A peasant woman who wanted to throw a
sick baby goose to a cat, but Marfen'ka protested.

Afrasin'iushka. *Crime and Punishment.* A woman who tried to drown herself in a canal. Raskol'nikov was a witness of the incident.

Agaf'ia. *The Adolescent.* A servant at the Touchards' when Arkadii Dolgorukii was in school. *The Brothers Karamazov.* The Krasotkins' servant. *The Devils.* Liputin's maid. *Precipice.* The servant who accompanied Marfen'ka to the cemetery.

Agaf'ia Fedoseevna. "Ivan Ivanovich and Ivan Nikiforovich, " in *Mirgorod.* The woman who bit off the tax assessor's ear. She used to visit Ivan Nikiforovich for weeks even though she had no connections with him. He wondered why she came but followed her every word.

Agaf'ia Ivanovna. *The Brothers Karamazov.* A half sister of Katerina Ivanovna. Dmitrii Karamazov said that Agaf'ia was not bad-looking in the Russian style: tall, stout, and with a full figure and beautiful eyes. She was a clever dressmaker and gave her services freely, but did not refuse payment if it was offered.

Agaf'ia Matveevna. *Oblomov.* See Pshenitsyna, Agaf'ia Matveevna.

Agaf'ia Nikitishna. *A Common Story.* The woman for whom Anton Ivanych saved some holy water.

Agashka. *A Common Story* A peasant girl who hit Aleksandr Aduev while playing and caused his nose to bleed. She was whipped by his father. *The Idiot.* The person whom Keller wanted to entertain when he took twenty-five roubles from Prince Myshkin. *The Precipice.* Before going for a visit to her future mother-in-law, Marfen'ka gave a jacket to the half-wit Agashka. Also, a blind laundress who liked to hang shirts on willow trees was named Agashka.

Agrafena. *The Adolescent.* Nikolai Semenovich's maid who found the baby Arina on the doorstep. *The Village of Stepanchikogo.* When Vidopliasov told the narrator his tie was the color Adelaida, the narrator asked if there was an Agrafena color. Vidopliasov repeated the wisdom which he had received from Foma Fomich Opiskin by saying that Agrafena was a common Russian name and could not be a color, whereas Adelaida was foreign and could be a color.

Agrafena Ivanovna. *A Common Story* A servant who ruled the Aduevs' household affairs. Evsei loved her. *Dead Souls.* The author spoke of the danger of using family names because someone was bound to show up with that very name and accuse the author of mentioning something untoward about him, for example, his visits to a certain Agrafena Ivanovna.

Agrafena Trofimovna. "Ivan Ivanovich and Ivan Nikiforovich," in
    Mirgorod. The police captain's wife who liked sausages made
    of blood and fat the way Gapka made them.
Agrippina, Pani. *The Brothers Karamazov*. The name which one of the
    Poles at Mokroe called Grushen'ka during Dmitrii Ka-
    ramazov's spree there.
Aianov, Ivan Ivanovich. *The Precipice*. A friend of Raiskii.
Aianova, Ol'enka. *The Precipice*. The daughter of Raiskii'a friend. He
    wrote Raiskii that the girl was doing well in school.
Akakii Akakievich. *"The Overcoat."* See Bashmachkin, Akakii
    Akakievich.
Akhmakov. *The Adolescent*. Katerina (née Sokolskaia) Akhmakova's
    husband, who was a general and who squandered her dowry
    on cards. He died after the premature death of his daughter,
    who swallowed phosphorous matches.
Akhmakova, Katerina. *The Adolescent*. The daughter of old Prince
    Sokolskii. She has a bashful and chaste face, and was intel-
    ligent. She captivated Aleksei Dolgorukii as she had fasci-
    nated his father, Versilov.
Akhmakova, Lidia. *The Adolescent*. Katerina Akhmakova's step-
    daughter, who died from sulfur poisoning.
Akim. *The Brothers Karamazov*. The peasant driver whose absence held
    up the transport of Dmitrii Karamazov from Mokroe after
    he had been arrested for the murder of his father.
Akim Akimich. *Notes from a Dead House*. An "extravagantly strange
    man," who was honest but quarrelsome, and was a man of
    all trades: carpenter, cobbler, shoemaker, painter, and lock-
    smith. He was serving twelve years for having a prince killed
    when he set fire to a fort. Akim had been a lieutenant in the
    Caucasus. His bunk was next to Aleksandr Petrovich
    Goriachikov's.
Aksentii Osipovich. *Poor Folk* The man who assaulted Petr Petrovich.
    Both were lodgers in the house where Devushkin lived.
    Devushkin witnessed the assault through a crack in the wall
    through which he was eavesdropping.
Aksin'ia. *Oblomov*. The wife of Antip, the serf who escaped being
    crushed under a falling balcony by moving away in time. *Poor
    Folk*. The sister-in-law of Fedor.
Akulina. *Oblomov*. Pshenitsyna's servant. *The Precipice*. Raiskii's serf
    who, according to Berezhkova, lived with Nikita.
Akulina Panfilovna. *The Village of Stepanchikogo*. Egor Rostanev's grand-
    mother who left Egor two hundred serfs.

Akul'ka. *Dead Souls.* Sobakevich's servant who ate all leftovers which Sobakevich said would go into the soup at the governor's house.
Notes from a Dead House. The poor girl who was beaten repeatedly by her parents because Morozov spread tales that he had slept with her. When she was sold in marriage to Shishkov, he discovered that she was innocent. However, he killed her when he found out that she loved her accuser.

Albert. *The Gambler.* The lover whom Mlle. Blanche took after setting up her salon in Paris on the narrator's money.

Alei. *Notes from a Dead House.* A likable young man who was one of the three brothers Goriachikov knew in Siberia. Alei was a Daghestanian Tartar and somewhat corrupted by prison life. Goriachikov taught him to read and write Russian in three months.

Aleksandr. *Notes from a Dead House.* The convict who was called by the feminine form Aleksandra and who had survived four thousand strokes of flogging because he was used to being beaten as a child.

Aleksandr I (1777–1825). *The Idiot* (4, 4). The tsar of Russia from 1801 to 1825. General Ivolgin claimed that when he served as a boy page to Napoleon I, he asked the Emperor to forgive Aleksandr I. Napoleon was supposed to have answered that he would kiss Aleksandr's feet.

Aleksandr Aleksandrovich. *The Brothers Karamazov.* A name mentioned by Mrs. Snegirev when she was relating the gossip which a deacon's wife had told her.

Aleksandr Petrovich. *Dead Souls.* Tentetnikov's teacher who demanded that his students study because he believed that a man did not have time in life for foolishness.

Aleksandr Stepanovich. *A Common Story.* The rich father of Aleksandr Aduev's fiancée.

Aleksandra Mikhailovna. *The Idiot.* A resident of Moscow. When General Ivolgin was conducting Prince Myshkin to the apartment of General Sokolovich, he led him by mistake to the apartment of Aleksandra Mikhailovna.

Aleksandra Gavrilvna. *Dead Souls.* The sister-in-law of a certain Bezprechnyi in Simbirsk. The blonde girl at the ball began to yawn when Chichikov told her that Aleksandra was visiting Bezprechnyi at the same time Chichikov was there.

Aleksandra Vasil'evna. *A Common Story.* The woman who sent regards to Adueva through Anton Ivanovich.

Alekseev, Ivan Alekseevich. *Oblomov*. The man who came to escort
Oblomov to Ovchinin's dinner. Alekseev was such a nondescript that people continually mixed up his name. Some
thought his patronymic was Ivanovich, others Vasil'ich, and
still others Mikhailovich. His family name was also confused.
Some called him Ivanov, others Vasil'ev, and still others Andreev.
Aleksei. *The Adolescent* (2, 9, 2). See Aleksei Mikhailovich. *The Brothers
Karamazov*. The name of the dead son of the peasant woman
Nastas'ia. Father Zosima told her that the child would be sad in
heaven because she had left her husband. The elder advised her
to return to him.
Aleksei Egorovich. *The Devils*. Mrs. Stavrogina's butler who spoke
decorously and edifyingly.
Aleksei Ivanovich. *Dead Souls*. The chief of police who was liked by
everyone but Sobakevich. *The Gambler*. The narrator, who had a
penchant for gambling and was a tutor in the general's household. He loved the general's stepdaughter Polina, but she played
with his affections. He was ruined by his obsession with gambling.
Aleksei Mikhailovich (1629–1676). *The Adolescent* (2, 9, 2). The Russian
tsar from 1645. The church near the school which Arkadii
Dolgorukii attended dated from the time of Tsar Aleksei.
Aleksei Naumych. *Oblomov*. The man who said he had been injured in a
sleigh ride, but Luka doubted his story.
Aleksei Petrovich. *The Precipice*. A man who was in dire circumstances
but was able to be on top again, according to Berezhkova.
Aleksei Sidorovich. *Oblomov*. When Oblomov asked for political news,
Alekseev told Oblomov that Aleksei Sidorovich's son had men-
tioned that there would be war but that he could not remember
with whom.
Alekseich. *The Double*. Olsufii Ivanovich Berendeev's servant who
refused admittance to Goliadkin after the latter had rented a
carriage to attend Berendeev's party.
Alena Frolovna. *The Devils*. Liza Tushin's nanny when Liza was a girl.
In Dostoevskii's home, a houseworker of the family for many
years was named Alena Frolovna.
Alena Ivanovna. *Crime and Punishment*. The old pawnbroker whom
Raskol'nikov murdered to "prove his theory of the amoral
superman." The old woman was cruel, and ugly and mistreated
her stepsister. Alena planned to leave her money to a monas-

tery so that perpetual prayers would be said for her. Raskol'nikov reasoned that her money would be better off helping others.

Alesha Popovich. *Oblomov* (1, 9). A Russian folk hero. Oblomov's nurse told him stories about Alesha and the ancient past.

Aleshka. *Crime and Punishment.* The younger workman in the apartment of the murdered Alena Ivanovna. Aleshka was amazed at Raskol'nikov's remarks when the murderer returned to the scene of the crime.

Alexander of Macedon (356–323 B.C.). *The Brothers Karamazov* (1, 2, 6). The Greek conqueror mentioned by Fedor Karamazov during his outbursts at the monastery. *A Common Story.* (3, 2). Tafaeva studied the Greek hero in her history lessons. *The Underground Man* (2, 8). The Underground Man felt that his servant Apollon had vanity befitting only Alexander the Great. *The Village of Stepanchikogo* (1, 7). Foma Fomich Opiskin felt that great poets could give peasants such virtues that Alexander the Great would envy them. (2, 6). Foma Fomich Opiskin felt that he himself was an unproven Alexander the Great.

Alexis. See Aleksei.

Al'ianov, Matvei Andreich. *Oblomov.* A guest at the Ovchinins' dinner when Alekseev tried in vain to escort Oblomov to the occasion.

Almazov. *Notes from a Dead House.* A convict who was difficult to get along with. He was youthful in appearance despite his advanced years.

Alphonsine. *The Adolescent.* The peculiar-looking creature who was at Lambert's after he had found Arkadii Dolgorukii in the street the night the boy was accused of stealing money in the casino. Alphonsine was tall, thin, and long waisted, and had sunken cheeks.

Amalchen. *The Gambler.* A name used for a German's girl friend. The narrator, in commenting on the German character, maintained that a German waits for years before marrying an Amalchen, or his girl, in order to save enough money. Meanwhile, the girl's breasts dry up.

Amalia Ivanovna. *Crime and Punishment.* The landlady of Katerina Ivanovna Marmeladovna. The latter always spoke condescendingly to her.

Amalia Ludwigovna. *Crime and Punishment.* The name Katerina Ivanovna Marmeladova called her landlady even though the woman insisted that her patronymic was Ivanovna.

Anaevskii, A. E. (1788–1866). *The Underground Man* (1, 8). The author of *Enhiridion the Curious* (1854), in which he stated that some feel that the Colossus of Rhodes was created by human hands, and others believe that it was created by nature. Anaevskii's comments became a popular source for jokes in the Russian press. The Underground Man mentioned the writer.

Ancheia. *The Adolescent.* Lambert's assistant.

Anchukovskii. *Notes from a Dead House.* A nobleman who was too simple and nondescript for Gorianchikov's liking. He was mentioned in the memoirs of Tokarzhevskii.

Ancus Marcius (640–616 B.C.) *The Devils* (3, 1, 3). In Karamazinov's long and ridiculous introduction at the literary fete, he described an absurd scene in which the legendary fourth ruler of Rome appeared.

Andreev. *The Adolescent.* A grubby, long-legged acquaintance of Lambert. He was continually trying to extort money from Lambert, who called Andreev "le grand dadais." Andreev squandered his sister's dowry and was a very unhappy person. Dostoevskii referred to him in much of the text as "the long-legged one." *The Devils.* A local wine merchant who talked with Stepan Verkhovenskii on erudite subjects and owed him four hundred doubles. Andreev informed Mrs. Stavrogina that the girl kneeling before her at the cathedral was Miss Lebiatkina.

Andrei. *The Brothers Karamazov.* The driver who took Dmitrii Karamazov to Mokroe to meet Grushen'ka.

Andrei Filippovich. *The Double.* Goliadkin's departmental head who gave Goliadkin murderous glances. He once met Andrei's carriage and pretended that he was someone else, making a complete fool of himself. Goliadkin referred to him as "the Bear."

Andriusha. *Dead Souls.* A peasant who helped untangle carriages when they collided. Also, Sof'ia Ivanovna's coachman who helped Sof'ia spread the alarming news of Chichikov's buying of dead souls. *Oblomov.* See Oblomov, Andrei. Also, a page whom Matvei boxed on the ear for not attending to his duties in St. Petersburg. Also, a servant at the Oblomov estate who was ordered to clear the debris after the balcony had fallen.

Andromache. *The Precipice* (1, 13). The wife of Hector during the Trojan wars. She was put to death with her son Astyanax when the Greeks captured Troy. Raiskii painted her picture.

Andron. *The Village of Stepanchikogo.* The cook at Stepanchikogo who was the uncle of Falalei and who was not able to teach his nephew to read Russian.

Andronikov, Nikolai Semenovich. *The Adolescent.* A man who looked after Versilov's interests. Before his death, Andronikov gave Kraft the letter that would help the Sokolskiis in their lawsuit with Versilov.

Anfim, Father. *The Brothers Karamazov.* An old man for whom Father Zosima had great affection.

Anikiia, St. *The Adolescent* (3, 1, 3). Dolgorukii mentioned St. Anikii, whose remains are located in the Zaonikiev Monastery of the Vladimir Virgin, founded about 1588. Anikii also is spelled Ioanikiia.

Anis'ia. *The Idiot.* Lebedev's sister whose son caused Lebedev much anxiety. *Oblomov.* Oblomov's cook who became Zakhar's wife.

Aniska. *Crime and Punishment.* The dressmaker of Svidrigalov's deceased wife. His spouse used to appear to Svidrigalov in ghostly form.

Ankudim Trofimich. *Notes from a Dead House.* A seventy-year-old man whose daughter Akul'ka became the center of a local controversy.

Anna, Empress. *The Gambler.* See Anna Ivanovna.

Anna. *The Adolescent.* See Versilova, Anna. *The Brothers Karamazov.* Anna was the name of an award created in 1735 by the Duke of Golstein. It was incorporated into Russian orders in 1797 during the reign of Pavel I (1754-1801). "The Overcoat." Anna was Akakii Akakievich Bashmachkin's former Finnish cook who worked for the police commissioner.

Anna Borisovna. *The Precipice.* The woman who was not supposed to have had a love in her lifetime, but Sof'ia was convinced that she did have.

Anna Fedorovna. *The Idiot.* The person whom General Ivolgin told Prince Myshkin he had not seen for some time because he no longer entertained. *Poor Folk.* A distant relative of Varvara. When Varvara's father died, she and her mother were forced by their poverty to live with Anna even though they did not like her character.

Anna Grigor'evna. *Dead Souls.* A most agreeable lady whom a lady just as agreeable came to visit.

Anna Ivanovna (1693-1740). *The Gambler.* The poorly educated, weak-minded, and lazy Russian Empress from 1730. The narrator Aleksei Ivanovich felt that his relationshilp to Polina Aleksandrovna might be similar to the jester Balakirev's relationship with the Empress Anna.

Anna Ivanovna. *The Precipice.* Tushin's sister who was a spinster and with whom Berezhkova compared herself. They both respected housekeeping and family traditions.

Anna Nikolaevna. *The Precipice.* An acquaintance of Berezhkova and Viken'tev. When Berezhkova prohibited Marfen'ka from studying horseback riding, Viken'tev mentioned that their acquaintance Anna Nikolaevna rode horseback.

Anna Petrovna. *The Precipice.* The actress who gave Raiskii an idea for a novel.

Anna Vasil'evna. *Oblomov.* An acquaintance of Sholtz. Ol'ga told Oblomov that Sholtz loved her more than he loved Anna Vasil'evna.

Annette. "The Portrait," in *Arabesques.* The eighteen-year-old girl whom Chertkov painted. She prefered to think that the picture of Psyche was she herself and bought the painting.

Antigone. *A Common Story* (2, 4). The daughter of Oedipus who accompanied her blind father in his wanderings. Meeting Liza, Aleksandr Aduev decided that she was like Antigone.

Antinator Zakhar'evich. *Dead Souls.* A popular figure in the town of N——. The townfolk began to love Chichikov as much as they cared for Antinator until they found about about Chichikov's buying of dead souls.

Antip (Antipka). *Oblomov.* A serf who carried water on the Oblomov estate. When Oblomov was a child, he would watch Antip's shadow and wonder about it.

Anton. *The Adolescent.* See Goremyka, Anton. "Ivan Ivanovich and Ivan Nikiforovich," in *Mirgorod.* A common character in the popular puppet theater of the nineteenth century. *The Precipice.* Vikent'eva's servant.

Anton Ivanych. *A Common Story.* Adueva's friend, who was a poor landowner and who was always dining at the table of others.

Anton Lavrentevich. *The Devils.* See G——v, Anton Lavrentevich.

Antonich. *Notes from a Dead House.* An older prisoner who was toothless and who would reply to a greeting, "Good morning, if you mean it."

Antonov, Vasilii. *Notes from a Dead House.* A tall, athletic man who was spiteful and bellicose. He was not a coward, but he surprised Gorianchikov once by surrendering some foot rags to Petrov without a fight.

Antony, Mark (83–31 B.C.). *The Precipice* (2, 10). The Roman who came into power after the assassination of Julius Caesar. Raiskii said that journalists were the present-day Antonys.

Antoshka. *Dead Souls*. Petukh's servant. Petukh called him a robber for not serving the hors d' oeuvres soon enough.

Apollo. *A Common Story* (2, 3). The Greek god of the sun. Tafaeva was enchanted by the story of the god's banishment to earth and his pranks there. *Oblomov* (2, 4). Shtolz reminded Oblomov that in his youth Oblomov had dreamed of seeing Apollo's statue in Italy. *The Precipice*. (4, 4) In the ecstasy of love, Raiskii felt that he was capable of creating a sculpture of Apollo.

Apollon. *The Underground Man*. The Underground Man's servant who made seven roubles a month and who aroused his master's hatred over every small and insignificant matter. The Underground Man could not release him because he felt the servant was chemically bound to his existence.

Aramis. *The Idiot* (1, 8). One of the *Three Musketeers* (1844) by Alexandre Dumas père (1802–1870). He was mentioned by General Ivolgin when thinking about his old friends General Epanchin and Prince Nikolai Myshkin. The latter was considered to be like Aramis.

Archimedes (287–212 B.C.) *Oblomov* (4, 5). The Greek inventor who developed a screw for moving water upward for irrigation. Shtolz felt that love moved the world the way Archimedes's screw moved water. *The Precipice* (2, 8). Raiskii said that men like Archimedes are the prime creators of progress in the world.

Arina. *The Adolescent*. A baby left on Nikolai Semenovich's doorstep. Nikolai ordered it to be taken to a foundling home, but Arkadii Dolgorukii offered to care for it. However, it died in a few days and Arkadii bought it a coffin. *The Brothers Karamazov*. One of the girls whom Dmitrii Karamazov asked for at Mokroe during his wild spree before his arrest. *The Precipice*. The village fool of whom Marfen'ka was afraid.

Aristophanes (450–380 B.C.). *The Precipice* (2, 7). The Greek comic dramatist noted for his satires of contemporary Greek life. Kozlov discussed the writer in class with the upper-level students.

Aristotle (384-322 B.C.). *The Precipice* (2, 7). The famous Greek philosopher whom Kozlov discussed in class with the upper-level students.

Aristov. *Notes from a Dead House*. The vile, base, despicable, and morally degraded convict loathed by the narrator. Aristov served the Major as a spy and informer, for which he was despised by Goriachikov but accepted, paradoxically by the other convicts.

Arkasha. *The Adolescent.* A diminutive for Arkadii. See Dolgorukii, Aleksei.

Arkhip. *The Village of Stepanchikogo.* The blacksmith who put the drunken Vasil'ev in the carriage till he sobered up. Arkhip told Vasil'ev's master Matvei Il'ich that his peasant was sick with colic.

Arkhipych. *A Common Story.* The yard keeper who talked with Evsenii when the latter was looking after the young Aleksandr Aduev.

Armance. *The Idiot.* A young woman of society whom Lebedev claimed he knew when he was running around with Likhachev. *The Precipice.* An actress to whom Belovodov gave a set of dishes which cost five thousand roubles. She then forgot to invite him for supper.

Armida. *The Precipice* (1, 6). A beautiful sorceress in Tasso's *Jerusalem Delivered.* Raiskii as a boy could not sleep after reading about Armida.

Artemii. *Oblomov.* A coachman friend of Zakhar.

Astley. *The Gambler.* An Englishman who was shy to the point of seeming stupid, but he was not. He blushed whenever Polina entered a room, and the narrator assumed that she loved him. Since Astley was wealthy, the narrator suggested to Polina that she marry him for his money.

Athos. *The Idiot* (1, 8). One of the *Three Musketeers* (1844) by Alexandre Dumas *père* (1802–1870). General Ivolgin considered himself to be like the most heroic musketeer, Athos.

Attila (d. 453). *The Underground Man* (1, 7). The Underground Man, in disputing Buckle's theory that civilization makes man less inclined to warfare, stated that most famous slaughterers have been the most civilized men. Even Attila the Hun could not match modern warmongers.

Augustine St. (354–430). *The Precipice* (1, 6). One author among many whose works Raiskii read in his father's library.

Augustin. *The Devils* (2, 5, 1). The name in the famous German song *Mein Lieber Augustin.* Liamshin created a musical piece which he played to Mrs. Lembke's delight and which won her favor. The music he wrote started with the French national anthem *The Marseillaise* and ended in *Mein Lieber Augustin.* It was reported that Lizmshin stole the music from a talented fellow who had passed through the town.

Avdot'ia. *Notes from a Dead House.* Cherevin's wife. Cherevin beat her after finding her with a lover. She agreed to wash his feet and drink the water. *The Precipice.* Kozlov's servant, who was stupid and sloppy. Volokhov called her an idiot.

Averianov. *The Adolescent.* The name on a promissory note which Stebelkov held, but the signature was a forgery. Arkadii Dolgorukii suggested that Stebelkov kept the note for no good reason.

Averka. *Oblomov.* The tailor who made a jacket for Il'iusha Oblomov with his mother's help.

Avistage. *The Adolescent* (3, 11, 1). One of the concubines of the aging Biblical King David (I Sam. 16, Kings 2). Arkadii Dolgorukii asked Lambert if he knew her story. When Lambert said he did not, Arkadii called him ignorant.

B——. *Notes from a Dead House.* See Boguslawski, J.

B——, Princess. "The Portrait," in *Arabesques.* The imagined friend of Annette. When Annette came to Chertkov to have her picture painted, Gogol' described her mentality as that of a young girl who was impatient to describe the flounces of some dress to her friend Princess B——.

B——, I——. *The Precipice.* The man who, according to Aianov, would be a minister's assistant.

B——kii. *Notes from a Dead House.* A nobleman who was consumptive, nervous, and irritable, but also kind and generous by nature. Gorianchikov could not bear B——kii's capriciousness and intolerance, and therefore refused to have relations with him.

B——m (Bem). *Notes from a Dead House.* An elderly man who impressed everyone most favorably. He was a coarse Philistine with the manners of a grocer grown rich through petty cheating. He did not know why he was billeted with the noblemen.

B——n, Dr. *Crime and Punishment.* The physician to whom Porfirii Petrovich went when he had a tickling feeling in his throat. The doctor told him that his lungs were affected from tobacco. Dostoevskii was probably referring to Dr. Sergei Petrovich Botkin (1832-1899), a well-known physician to Tsar Aleksandr II. *The Idiot.* The physician who warned Terentev that he had only two weeks to live.

Babushkin. *Crime and Punishment.* An acquaintance of Razumikhin. Raskol'nikov was once invited by Razumikhin to a housewarming at Babushkin's flat, but he refused.

Bacchus. *Dead Souls* (1, 11). The Roman god of wine. The clerks in the office where Chichikov worked when he was young offered frequent libations to Bacchus, thus demonstrating the paganism in the Slavic character. Chichikov did not drink and was singled out by his fellow workers. *The Precipice* (1, 10).The god whose figure riding on a barrel was on a clock in the old house where Raiskii was born.

Bach, Johann Sebastian (1685-1759). *Oblomov* (1, 2). The famous German composer. In the Mezdovs' home, the favorite topic of conversation was music, especially the work of Bach.

Bacon, Roger (1214-1292). *The Precipice* (1, 7). An English monk famous for his scientific experiments. He was regarded as a wizard in league with the devil. Kozlov showed Raiskii one of his books concerning the monk.

Badinguet. *Devils* (1, 2, 8). A stone worker. Louis Napoleon Bonaparte, the future Napoleon III, once ran from a fortress dressed as a stone worker. Afterwards his enemies referred to him as Badinguet. Stephan Verkhovenskii felt he was in the same position as Napoleon III when Vavara Stavrogina insisted that he marry Dasha Shatova.

Bagautov, Stepan Mikhailovich. *The Eternal Husband*. A young, elegant man belonging to the best society. He was mentioned as a true friend by Trusotskii when the latter came to Velchanikov.

Bagration, Petr Ivanovich, Prince (1765-1812). *Dead Souls* (1, 5). The Russian general of noble Georgian descent who participated in almost all engagements during the campaigns from 1805 to 1807. In 1812, he commanded the Second Western Army and died from wounds during the Battle of Borodino. His portrait hung among the pictures of Greek heroes in Sobakevich's living room.

Bakaleev. *Crime and Punishment*. The person in whose house Luzhin informed Raskol'nikov that he had found rooms for Mrs. Raskol'nikova and Dunia. Raskol'nikov was disgusted, calling the place cheap and filthy.

Bakhcheev, Stepan Alekseich. *The Village of Stepanchikogo*. Egor Rostanev's fat friend who informed the narrator about the goings-on at Stepanchikogo, especially about the activities of Foma Fomich Opiskin, whom Bakhcheev despised.

Bakhmutov. *The Idiot*. Ippolit Terentev's acquaintance who helped the medical man whom Terentev followed home in the dark.

Bakhmutov, Petr Matveevich. *The Idiot*. An active state counsellor who was an uncle of Bakhmutov, an acquaintance of Ippolit Terentev.

Baklushin. *Notes from a Dead House.* A convict in the special section who was known as "sapper." He was the gayest and most agreeable companion among the prisoners. He became involved in many disputes and never forgave a wrong. He was imprisoned for killing Schultz, a watchmaker who planned to marry Luisa, a girl whom Baklushin loved.

Bakunin, Mikhail A. (1814-1876). *The Brothers Karamazov* (1, 1, 2). The famed Russian anarchist whose revolutionary teachings led him around the world. He was in the United States in 1861. His major work was *God and the State* (1882). Petr Miusov knew Bakunin personally in Paris before returning to Russia, where he took Dmitrii Karamazov as a child from his father.

Balaam's ass. *The Brothers Karamazov* (1, 3, 6). In the Old Testament (Numb. 22-23), Balaam was a prophet who, persuaded to prophesy against the Israelites, rode an ass to his destination. But the animal stopped in a narrow pass and would not move. "And Jehovah opened the mouth of the ass, and she said unto Balaam, 'What have I done unto thee that thou hast smitten me these three times?' Then Jehovah opened the eyes of Balaam and he saw an angel before him." Fedor Karamazov used the name "Balaam's ass" for Smerdiakov.

Balaban. "Taras Bul'ba," in *Mirgorod.* A Cossack troop chief who chose to stay and fight the Poles when others went to fight Tartars.

Balakin. *The Precipice.* The man whom Berezhkova considered to be stupid though handsome. She felt that everyone had the possibility for success. She was sure that even Balakin would find a wealthy wife in spite of his stupidity.

Balakirev, Ivan Aleksandrovich (1699-1763). *The Gambler* (13). A court jester for Empress Anna Ivanovna (1693-1740). The anecdotes written by him were published in Moscow in 1839 and had wide circulation. The narrator felt that his relationship to Polina Aleksandrovna was similar to Balakirev's to the Empress Anna Ivanovna.

Balle. *The Adolescent* (1, 6, 2). The proprietor of the store in which Arkadii Dolgorukii bought some sweets for Prutkova.

Balochov. *Oblomov.* A serf who ran away from Oblomov's estate.

Balthazar. *Oblomov* (2, 5). A merchant in Shakespeare's *Comedy of Errors.* The word "Oblomshchina" was written in fire in Oblomov's dream, just as Balthazar saw a work written in fire during a feast.

Balzac, Honoré de (1799-1850). *A Common Story* (2, 3). The famous French writer whom Tafaeva read fervently.

Barabbas. *The Precipice* (3, 2). The robber who was released by popular
    demand in place of Jesus, according to a custom that one
    prisoner should be freed at an official feast. Tychkov called
    Mark Volokhov by this name.

Barashkov, Filipp. *The Idiot.* The deceased father of Nastas'ia Filippov-
    na. He had been a poor landowner.

Barashkova, Nastas'ia Filippovna. *The Idiot.* The daughter of a poor
    landowner. When he died, an aristocrat named Totskii took her
    under his care and seduced her. She was very beautiful and
    vacillated between marrying Rogozhin and Prince Myshkin.
    She was killed by the former on the day whe was supposed to
    marry the latter. The Prince insisted that she was insane. The
    two men spent the night with her corpse.

Barbara, Auntie. *The Adolescent.* A relative of the Andronikovs. Arkadii
    Dolgorukii stayed on her estate for a while.

Barberini. *The Gambler* (8). A famous Italian family noted since the
    thirteenth century. Astley explained to the narrator that Mlle.
    Blanche had come to the German spa with an Italian prince
    from the distinguished Barberini family.

Barbier. *A Common Story* A popular store in St. Petersburg. Surkov's
    expensive cane was purchased at Barbier's.

Baron. *The Devils.* A St. Petersburg aristocrat who visited Varvara
    Stavrogina. When he informed her and Stepan Verkhovenskii
    about the liberation of the serfs, the latter expressed his plea-
    sure too enthusiastically. Varvara later told Stephan that she
    would never forgive him for his conduct and did remind him of
    the incident thirteen years later.

Bartola. *Crime and Punishment* (2, 6). A man who was supposedly a
    descendant of the ancient Aztecs. He visited in St. Petersburg in
    1865. When Raskol'nikov was seeking news in the newspaper
    about the murder he had committed, he read the name Bartola.

Basencourt. *The Idiot.* See Bazancourt, Baron de.

Bashmachkin, Akakii Akakievich. "The Overcoat." The lowly ninth-
    level clerk whose family name meant "shoe" and whose first
    name sounds like the Russian work for baby-poo "kaki." Akakii
    is *Acacins* in Greek, meaning "without evil."

Bashutskii, Pavel Iakovlevich (1771-1836). *The Adolescent* (2, 1, 2). A
    general referred to by Versilov's landlord once and known for
    his stupidity when he was Commandant of St. Petersburg
    during the reign of Aleksandr I. Many anecdotes circulated
    about him.

Basil. *The Precipice..* Belovodova's friend, who Raiskii felt should be dropped from society.

Bassavriukov. *The Double.* The name of some arriving guests announced by a servant at Olsufii Berendeev's party when Goliadkin was going insane.

Basurman. *The Precipice* (2, 3). The hero of the historical novel of the same name by Ivanovich Lazhechinikov (1792-1869). Marfen'ka started reading the book, but when she discovered that the hero was executed, she stopped reading.

Batiushkov, Konstantin Nikolaevich (1787-1855). *Oblomov* (4, 9). Alekseev told Oblomov that Batiushkov was the best Russian author. Batiushkov was known for his sentimental elegies and lyrics.

Baucis. "Old World Landowners," in *Mirgorod.* See Philemon.

Bazancourt, Baron de (1767-1830). *The Idiot* (4, 4). Emperor Napoleon I's page, who died at the age of twelve, according to General Ivolgin. The general claimed that he then became the Emperor's new page. Bazancourt, however, had a much longer life than Ivolgin granted him.

Bazarov. *The Devils* (2, 1, 2). The famed fictional nihilist in I. S. Turgenev's book *Fathers and Sons* (1862). Petr Verkhovenskii claimed that he did not understand Turgenev's hero, and thought that he was a mixture of Gogol's Nozdrev and Lord Byron.

Bear. *The Double.* See Andrei Filippovich.

Beethoven, Ludwig van (1770-1827). *Oblomov* (1, 2). The famed German composer who added the emotional qualities of Romanticism to the formal precision of eighteenth-century music. In Mezdov's home, music was a favorite topic of conversation, especially the works of Beethoven. *The Precipice* (1, 14). For her birthday, Belovolova learned a Beethoven sonata which El'nin liked.

Begushkin. *Dead Souls.* A man whom Sobakevich suggested for a witness of the purchase deed when Chichikov wanted to buy dead souls.

Beliavskii. *The Brothers Karamazov.* A rich, handsome man who used to visit Fedor Karamazov and his wife; but he once slapped Fedor in front of his spouse, and she became furious that her husband did not challenge Beliavskii to a duel.

Belinskii, Vissarion Grigorievich (1811-1848). *The Adolescent* (2, 2, 3). A noted nineteenth-century Russian literary critic. Arkadii Dolgorukii picked up a book at Prince Sergei Sokolskii's and found it was from Belinskii's collected works. When Arkadii asked the prince if he were planning to enlighten himself, the prince became irritated. *The Brothers Karamazov* (4, 10, 6). Kolia Krasotkin spoke to the dying Il'iusha Snegirev about Belinskii. Kolia agreed with Belinskii, who wrote in a letter to N. V. Gogol' that Christ would have joined the revolutionaries if he had lived in the nineteenth century. *The Devils* (1, 1, 1). Stepan Verkhovenskii's name was mentioned for a short time by enthusiastic people along with the name of the famous critic. (1, 1, 9). The famous letter Belinskii sent to Gogol' was mentioned. Dostoevskii commented that it was comic for the Gogol' of that time to have received a letter chastising him for believing in a God "of some kind." (2, 7, 2). At the Virginskiis' group meeting, it was pointed out that Belinskii had debated with friends about the future organization of mankind.

Belkin. *Poor Folk* (June 27). The hero of *Tales of Belkin* (1831) by A. S. Pushkin (1799-1837), which were given to Varvara Alekseevna by Fedora.

Bellini, Vincenzo (1801-1835). *The Precipice* (4, 7). The composer of a duet which Sof'ia Belovodova sang with Milari. Gossip was started about her behavior during the song.

Bel'mesov. *The Brothers Karamazov*. A man whom Madame Khokhlakova had aided financially. She promised to help Dmitrii Karamazov also. Dmitrii thought that she had agreed to give him three thousand roubles which he needed to pay Katerina, but Madame Khokhlakova was not serious.

Belobriushkova, Arina Semenovna. "The Overcoat." The godmother of Akakii Akakievich Bashmachkin.

Belokonskaia, Princess. *The Idiot*. Mrs. Epanchina's acquaintance who was present at the party when Prince Myshkin broke the Chinese vase and had an epileptic fit.

Belovodov. *Oblomov*. A property owner whose estate was near Oblomov's.

Belovodov, Paul. *The Precipice*. Sof'ia's deceased husband.

Belovodova, Sof'ia Nikolaevna. *The Precipice*. Raiskii's twenty-five-year-old cousin who was a beautiful widow and who was from a family that had once been very wealthy.

Belshazzar. *The Devils* (3, 1, 2). The Biblical ruler known for his splendid feasts (Daniel 5, 2-4). For her literary fete, Mrs. von Lembke had the choice of a literary evening or an evening of reading with a Belshazzar feast. She choose the former to avoid expense.

Benjamin. *The Brothers Karamazov* (2, 6, 1). The Biblical son of Jacob (Gen. 35, 18) mentioned in Father Zosima's biography.

Berebendovskii. *Dead Souls*. A guest at the governor's ball.

Berendeev, Olsufii Ivanovich. *The Double*. A government counsellor who was head of a governmental department. He was referred to as His Excellency.

Berendeeva, Klara Olsuf'evna. *The Double*. The counsellor's daughter whom Goliadkin adored.

Berestov, Colonel. *The Devils*. The landowner who was playing cards in the train on which Petr Verkhovenskii made his escape.

Berezhkova, Tat'iana Markovna. *The Precipice*. Raiskii's great aunt who lived on his small estate with her two granddaughters. She also managed the estate.

Berezovskii. *Dead Souls*. The personal servant of Koshkarev.

Berg. *Crime and Punishment* (4, 1). A familiar name in St. Petersburg newspapers in the 1860's. He was noted for his management of theatrical attractions and his flight in a balloon. He also tried to develop a zoo in the Iusopov gardens.

Bernard, Claude (1813-1878). *The Brothers Karamazov* (4, 11, 4). The French physiologist and pathologist who was a follower of positivism. He was interested in the inner nervous system, and his theories are supposed to have influenced the French writer Émile Zola (1840-1902). Dmitrii Karamazov was familiar with Bernard's work.

Berry, Duc de (1778-1820). *The Adolescent* (1, 3, 2). The heir to the French throne who emigrated with his father in 1789 and returned to France after the Restoration of 1814. He was assassinated in Paris, February 13, 1820. Arkadii Dolgorukii claimed that James Rothschild knew the Duc was to be killed and sold the information for several millions. Arkadii, of course, was confused. Rothschild made millions by being the first to learn of Napoleon's defeat at Waterloo and then buying heavily on the London stock market.

Bestuzhev, Aleksandr Aleksandrovich (1797-1837). *A Common Story* (1, 2). The writer of historical adventure novels who published under the name Marlinskii. Gorbatova wanted Petr Aduev to read one of Marlinskii's books. *The Idiot* (1, 15). One of Rogozhin's followers at Nastas'ia Filippovna's party had been picked up on the street while he was stopping passersby and begging from them in the "florid style of Marlinskii."

Betrishchev, Aleksandr Dmitrievich. *Dead Souls*. The landowner who had bad relations with Tentetnikov. Chichkov called on Betrishchev to settle the quarrel between the two men.

Betrishchova, Ulin'ka. *Dead Souls*. The daughter of the landowner who had an estate near Tentetnikov's. The latter was in love with her for a while.

Bezpalova, Sof'ia. *The Idiot*. A woman who was in the tale which Totskii told at Nastas'ia Filippovna's party. Sof'ia was going to a ball with a bouquet of camelias, a flower prized at the time.

Bezpechnyi, Sofron Ivanovich. *Dead Souls*. The person whom Chichikov visited in Simbirsk. The blonde with whom Chichikov was talking at the ball began to yawn when he told of the visit.

Bezzemel'naia, Princess. *Crime and Punishment*. A society member whom Katerina Ivanovna Marmeladova knew in her youth. The princess had noticed Katerina at a ball and had blessed her when she married.

Bianco of Perugino (1445-1523). "Nevskii Prospect," in *Arabesques*. An Umbrian painter named Pietro de Cristoforo Vannuccio, who was a pupil of da Vinci. "Bianca" was his most famous work, and he was called by that name.

Bichurin. *Oblomov*. A friend who Shtolz thought was in love with Ol'ga.

Bikusov. *Dead Souls*. A wealthy landowner who had a niece. Nozdrev thought that Chichikov would have been smarter to court Bikusov's niece rather than the governor's daughter.

Biksup. *The Idiot*. An acquaintance of Parfen Ragozhin. When Ragozhin told Nastas'ia that he would give her forty thousand roubles, he mentioned that a certain Biskup would help him accumulate the money.

Bismarck, Prince Otto von (1815-1898). *The Adolescent* (1, 5, 4).The famous German statesman. Arkadii Dolgorukii felt that cheap things do not last long and that a quick understanding by the crowd is a sign of cheapness. Bismarck was accepted as a genius, but Arkadii felt ten years would change that opinion. *The Devils* (1, 2, 4). Stepan Verkhovenskii told Varvara Stavrogina that she was a Bismarck in her dealings with people. She denied it but claimed that she could see through hypocrisy. (2, 5, 1). When Liamshin played his musical piece for Mrs. Lembke (See Augustin), the narrator said that the change from one melody to another was like Jules Favre sobbing on Bismarck's bosom. In other words, it was like French sentimentalism giving in to German petty bourgeois or Philistinism. (See Favre, Jules.)

Bjoring. *The Adolescent.* The baron engaged to Katerina Akhmakova.

Blanchard, Marie (1778-1819). *The Gambler* (14). The wife of a noted balloonist. She perished when she let off firecrackers while traveling in a balloon. The balloon caught fire. While gambling, the narrator experienced a moment similar to what Madame Blanchard must have felt while falling from her balloon.

Blanche, Mlle. *The Gambler.* See Cominges, Blanche de.

Blokhin. *Dead Souls.* A landowner living in the vicinity of an inn where Chichikov once stopped to rest his horses and have a bite to eat.

Blum, Andrei Antonovich von. *The Devils.* A morose, awkward German clerk in the office of Governor Lembke. The governor had brought Blum with him from St. Petersburg in spite of his wife's opposition. Blum was a distant relative of Lembke, and had the same name and patronymic.

Bobelina. *Dead Souls* (1,5). The heroine of the Greek movement for independence in 1820 whose picture hung on the wall in Sobakevich's living room.

Bobov. "The Notes of a Madman," in *Arabesques.* A man who looked like a stork. In the letter of the dog Madgie to the dog Fedele, Madgie reported her mistress's conversation with Bobov and gave a description of him.

Bobrov. *Dead Souls.* Korobochka's neighbor who was a landowner.

Boccaccio, Giovanni (1313-1375). *The Precipice* (1, 6). The Italian poet and humanist, and author of the *Decameron*. Raiskii read his works.

Bochkov. *The Precipice.* A man who had three sons who drank, smoked, and played cards day and night. Marfen'ka considered them poor prospects for marriage.

Boguslawski, J. *Notes from a Dead House* (1, 7). A Polish revolutionary sentenced to hard labor in 1849. Dostoevskii had him work with Gorianchikov in the novel.

Boileau-Despréaux, Nicolas (1636-1711). *The Brothers Karamazov* (3, 8, 7). The French poet and critic known for his maxims. Maksimov claimed that he was once called Boileau at a masquerade because of the clever epigrams he quoted.

Bokitko. "Ivan Ivanovich and Ivan Nikiforovich," in *Migorod.* The man whose cow was stolen. His case was being considered at the court when Ivan Ivanovich came to lodge a complaint against Ivan Nikiforovich.

Boldyreva, Countess. *Dead Souls*. A person related to a certain general who was an acquaintance of Tentetnikov. The relationship between the two men was terminated by the countess.

Boris, Count. *The Precipice*. Pakhotin told a friend about a Count Boris who used to lose piles of gold at cards.

Borodatyi. "Taras Bul'ba," in *Mirgorod*. A name suggested for the election of the position of headman in the Cossack camp; but someone spoke against him, and the name was dropped. Later Borodatyi was killed when he stopped in battle to rob a dead nobleman.

Borodavka. "Taras Bul'ba," in *Mirgorod*. A Cossack about whom Taras inquired at the Zaporozhe Camp. He learned that Borodavka had been hanged in Tolopan.

Borovikov. *The Precipice*. A schoolmate of Raiskii.

Borozdin, I. P. (1803-1858). *The Village of Stepanchikogo* (1, 7). A second-rate poet whom Foma Fomich Opiskin put on the level of Pushkin and Lermontov, thus displaying his ignorance.

Bourbon. *The Brothers Karamazov* (1, 3, 4). Dmitrii Karamazov called himself a Bourbon which, after the French Revolution, meant a crude and impolite person.

Bourdaloue, Louis (1632-1704). *The Idiot* (2, 11). A Jesuit priest who was one of the most popular ministers during the reign of Louis XIV. The use of Bourdaloue in the chapter refers to the broad popularity of his sermons. His *Selected Words* was published in four volumes in Russian from 1821 to 1825.

Bovary, Madame. *The Idiot* (4, 11). The heroine of the French novel *Madame Bovary* by Gustave Flaubert (1832-1880). Prince Myshkin saw a copy of the novel at Nastas'ia Filippovna's when he was looking for Nastas'ia after she ruined their wedding plans. He put it in his pocket.

Bovdug, Kasia. "Taras Bul'ba," in *Mirgorod*. The oldest and most rejected man in the Cossack troop. He suggested that the Cossacks divide: half to liberate their fellow comrades from the Tartars and half to help liberate Cossacks captured by the Poles.

Brambeus. *The Double* and *The Village of Stepanchikogo*. See Senkovskii, Osip Ivanovich.

Brinvilliers, Maria Madellena, Marquise de (1651-1675). *Notes from a Dead House* (2, 3). The French aristocrat known for her cruelty to her subordinates. Gorianchikov wrote that some prison officials metted out punishments like a Madame de Brinvilliers. Dostoevskii mentioned her in an article in 1861 as a contrast to Pushkin's Cleopatra in his *Egyptian Nights*.

Briullov, Karl Pavlovich (1799-1852). *The Double* (7). The noted painter whose picture *The Last Day of Pompeii* was brought to St. Petersburg in 1834 and received much acclaim in the press. *Notes from a Dead House* (1, 5). The Major of the prison accepted A——v as a portrait painter compared to Briullov even though A——v had no talent.

Brut, Khoma. "Vii," in *Mirgorod*. The cheerful philosopher who liked to smoke, drink, and dance. A witch was his undoing, and he was devoured by dozens of demonic denizens.

Brutus Marcus (85-42 B.C.). *Oblomov* (1, 6). The Roman leader to whom Oblomov compared Shtolz for bringing him extra books to read. Oblomov considered Shtolz's effort as torturous as Brutus's effort against Caesar.

Buckle, Henry Thomas (1821-1862). *The Underground Man* (1, 7). The Underground Man disputed Buckle's argument that through civilization mankind becomes less bloodthirsty and less fitted for warfare. Dostoevskii was interested in Buckle's *History of Civilization in England* (1863) because Buckle also wrote about Russia and the Crimean War.

Buechner, Ludwig (1824-1899). *The Devils* (2, 6, 2). The German writer who was popular in the 1880's among liberal young people. He was noted for his work *Kraft und Stoff* (1855). In a district where Petr Verkhovenskii had been spending time, a lieutenant of the police went mad and bit his superior while receiving a reprimand. In the lieutenant's quarters, a candle was burning before Buechner's works.

Bukh. *Crime and Punishment*. The owner of the house in which Razumikhin lived. When Razumikhin tried to find Raskol'nikov, he searched for the house of Kharlomov. Both houses were actual places in St. Petersburg and are still standing today.

Bul'ba, Andrei. "Taras Bul'ba," in *Migorod*. Taras's younger son, who was more inventive than his brother Ostap and liked risky ventures. His love for a Polish girl led to his death as a traitor.

Bul'ba, Ostap. "Taras Bul'ba," in *Mirgorod*. Taras's younger son, who was more serious than his younger brother Andrei. Ostap was captured by the Poles and executed as his father looked on.

Bul'ba, Taras. "Taras Bul'ba," in *Mirgorod*. The Cossack chief who felt the Russians were the bravest of all men. He killed his traitorous son Andrei and watched his son Ostap's execution.

Bulgarin, Faddei Venediktovich (1789-1859). "Nevskii Prospect," in *Arabesques.* A Russian journalist and writer who published the journal *Northern Bee* (Severnaia pchela) from 1822 to 1828.

Bulkin. *Notes from a Dead House.* A queer little man who was silent and mistrustful. He attached himself to Varlamov.

Bumstein, Isaiah Fomich. *Notes from a Dead House.* A Jew about fifty years old. He was the most active man in the prison. He possessed undying self-confidence and perfect happiness. He was a jeweler by trade, and a source of distraction and entertainment for everyone. He was a comic mixture of simplicity, stupidity, and bashfulness.

Burdolakova, Seklettia. *The Precipice.* A deacon's wife. When Volokhov forged Vera's handwriting and sent Raiskii a letter asking that he give money to needy people, the person Raiskii was supposed to give the money was Burdolakova; but actually Volokhov was planning to intercept the letter and keep the money.

Burdovskii, Antip. *The Idiot.* The man who thought he was Pavlichev's son. In reality he was the son of the sister of a serf whom Pavlichev loved. His father was a surveyor named Burdovskii. He wanted money from Prince Myshkin because Pavlichev had not supported him but had helped rear the Prince. Therefore, Burdovskii reasoned that the Prince should give him at least as much as Pavlichev had spent on the Prince.

Burmistrov, Grigorii Semenovich. *The Idiot.* A man who General Epanchin claimed was an excellent interpreter of the Apocalypse. Epanchin ridiculed Lebedev when he tried to interpret the Apocalypse for a group at Pavlovsk.

Bykov. *Poor Folk.* The wealthy man who married Varvara and took her away. He also educated Pokrovskii because he had known and respected Pokrovskii's mother.

Bykov, Dmitrii. *Notes from a Dead House.* The man whom Shishkov sent to Morozov to tell him that he was going to shame him before the town for slandering innocent Akul'ka.

Byron, Lord George Gordon (1788-1824). *A Common Story* (1, 5). The poet whose elegant works Aleksandr Aduev spoke of. *The Devils* (2, 1, 2). Petr Verkhovenskii claimed that Turgenev's nihilist Bazarov was a mixture of Byron and Gogol''s Nozdrev. (3, 1, 3). In his ridiculous and long introduction at the literary fete, Karmazinov mentioned that the Russian genius in general has an occasional attack of Byronic spleen. *Oblomov* (2, 4). Oblomov once gave Byron as reading material to two sisters whom he was courting. *The Precipice* (1, 1). Aianov and Raiskii mentioned in conversation the subjects of beauty, women, boredom, and Byron.

Cabet, Étienne (1788-1856). *The Devils* (2, 7, 2). The French socialist noted for trying to set up a communal system on the Red River in Texas. After many difficulties he transferred the settlement to Nauvoo, Illinois, in 1849. The new settlement did not work, and Cabet died in St. Louis in 1856. After Shigalev presented his plan for a future organization of mankind, Petr Verkhovenskii called it rotten. However, it was defended by others who felt that socialists like Cabet had worked out worse systems.

Caesar, Caius Julius (100-44 B.C.). *The Brothers Karamazov* (2, 5, 5). The Roman Emperor mentioned by Ivan Karamazov in his noted philosophical poem. The Grand Inquisitor reprimanded Christ for not taking the sword of Caesar when it was offered so as to lighten the burden of mankind by setting up an earthly kingdom. (4, 11, 4). Dmitrii Karamazov told Alesha that it was no disgrace—even to Caesar—to be under the thumb of a woman. *The Precipice* (1, 8). Raiskii said that present-day journalists acted as if they were Caesar. *The Village of Stepanchikogo* (2,6). Foma Fomich Opiskin suggested that the household at Stepanchikogo appreciated only great men like Caesar, implying that he himself was on such a level.

Cain. *The Brothers Karamazov* (2, 5, 3). The Biblical murderer (Gen. 4, 9). When speaking with Alesha, Ivan asked if he were their brother Dmitrii's keeper and then added that Cain had said the same.

Calipso. *The Precipice* (3, 12). Atlas's nymph daughter who vainly sought to keep the shipwrecked Odysseus with her. Raiskii thought of Krilskaia as an aging Calipso in search of her love.

Canova, Antonio (1757-1822). *The Precipice* (5, 23). A notable Italian sculptor. Raiskii decided to be a sculptor like him.

Capefigue, Batiste-Honoré-Remond (1802-1872). *The Devils* (2, 5, 3). The French historian and author of *Histoire philosophique des Juifs* (1839). When Varvara Stavrogina criticized Stepan Verkhovenskii for the materials he gave her to read, she said he always gave her the works of Capefigue.

Captain, Mr. *Crime and Punishment*. The head clerk at the police station. While Raskol'nikov was at the station to answer a summons about his debts, he overheard the questioning of Luiza Ivanovna from a house of dubious reputation. She called the head clerk Mr. Captain.

Capulet. *The Precipice* (3, 15). A noble family in Verona in Shakespeare's *Romeo and Juliet*. The book Berezhkova wanted for her granddaughter concerned a family similar to the Capulets.

Carlos, Don (1788-1855). *Oblomov* (2, 4). The son of King Carlos IV. Don Carlos started a civil war which he lost and had to renounce his rights to the throne. He was mentioned in a dinner discussion.

Cassius (Gaius Cassius Longinus, d. 42 B.C.). *The Devils* (3, 1, 3). The instigator of the conspiracy against Julius Caesar in Shakespeare's play about the famous general. In Karamazinov's long and ridiculous introduction at the literary fete, he mentioned that a couple was sitting somewhere in Germany and beheld Pompey or Cassius on the eve of battle.

Catherine. See Katerina and Ekaterina.

Ceres. *The Brothers Karamazov* (1, 3, 3). The Roman protectress of the fruits of the earth. She was mentioned by Dmitrii Karamazov when he recited Schiller's poem "Hymn to Joy" ("*An de Freude*").

Chaadaev, Petr Iakovlevich (1793-1836). *The Devils* (1, 1, 1). An influential freethinker who was known as a foppish wit. Stepan Verkhovenskii was once mentioned for a short time by enthusiastic people as being on the level of Chaadaev.

Chabot. *The Idiot* (4, 10). A noted French family. Keller behaved toward Prince Myshkin as if he were marrying a member of the famous French family Chabot instead of Natas'ia Filippovna.

Charlemagne (742-814). *The Adolescent* (1, 5, 3). The King of the Franks and Emperor of the West. Arkadii Dolgorukii's favorite vision was of an average man without any particular talents who could face the world and feel superior to Charlemagne.

Charles. *The Precipice*. The Frenchman and friend with whom Kozlov spent much time reading.

Charlotte. *Dead Souls* (1, 7). The heroine of Goethe's novel *The Sorrows of Werther*. Chichikov, in a good mood, recited Werther's epistle to Charlotte while the buyer of dead souls was visiting Sobakevich. *The Precipice* (2, 22). Vera told Raiskii that sentimentality like Werther's was passé.

Charras, Jean Batiste Adolph (1810-1865). *The Idiot* (4, 4). The author of *Histoire de la Campagne de 1815, Waterloo* (1858). Charras criticized Napoleon. Dostoevskii read Charras's history at Baden Baden in 1867.

Chateaubriand, Vicomte François Réne de (1768-1848). *A Common Story* (2, 3). The French writer who was a forerunner of the Romantic movement. Tafaera confused the works of Chateaubriand with the writings of Voltaire. *The Precipice* (1, 10). Raiskii found Chateaubriand's works in his father's library and read them.

Chatskii. *The Adolescent* (1, 6, 3). The hero in Griboedov's famous play *Woe from Wit* (1824). Arkadii Dolgorukii remembered that his father Versilov quoted from the play. *The Brothers Karamazov* (2, 5, 1). Madame Khokhlokova thought that Alesha Karamazov was playing the role of Chatskii in his being magnanimous toward her daughter Lisa. *The Precipice* (1, 4). Sof'ia felt that Raiskii argued like Chatskii.

Chebarov. *Crime and Punishment.* The man who bought Raskol'nikov's IOU and had the police summon Raskol'nikov for payment. *The Idiot.* The agent who advised Antip Burdovskii to try and obtain money from Prince Myshkin.

Chechenin. *The Precipice* (2, 13). The man whose son returned from a vacation and announced that he needed three thousand roubles for a dowry.

Chekmenev. *Oblomov* (1, 9). A relative of Oblomov's mother. He owned seven serfs and visited the Oblomovs when Il'ia was a child.

Chekunda. *Notes from a Dead House.* A bread vender who also sold herself in the prison, to the narrator's surprise. He called her the dirtiest female in the world.

Chekunov. *Notes from a Dead House.* A prisoner in the hospital when Goriachikov was there. Chekunov had convinced the doctors for over a year that he had an aneurism, and thus escaped hard labor.

Cheprakov. *Dead Souls.* A landowner living in the vicinity of an inn where Chichikov stopped on the way to Sobakavich's.

Cherevin. *Notes from a Dead House.* A soldier in the penal battalion who was about fifty, and was sullen and pedantic. Cherevin was always moralizing and felt that all wives should be beaten.

Chernomazov. *The Brothers Karamazov.* The name Mrs. Snegireva called Alesha Karamazov when he came to give Snegireva some money. The name Chernomazov, while a slip of the tongue, actually throws light on the inner meaning of the name Karamazov. "Kara" means "black" in a Tartar language and "Chernyi" means black in Russian.

Chernosvitov, Raphael Aleksandrovich (b.1810). *The Idiot* (4, 4). A member of the Petrashchevskii Circle who was imprisoned in

1849. In 1854 he developed artificial legs for amputees. Lebedev claimed he had an artificial leg made by Chernosvitov, but General Ivolgin did not believe him.

Chernyshev Aleksandr Ivanovich (1785-1857). *The Adolescent.* A seventy-year-old minister who managed to make himself look thirty-five. Versilov's landlord referred to him. Even the tsar was amazed at Chernyshev's appearance.

Chernyshevskii, Nikolai Gavrilovich (1828-1889). *The Devils* (2, 4, 2). The leader of the radical intelligentsia in the 1860s who was known for his reactionary social theories. His book *'What Is to Be Done'* (1863) was on Stepan Verkhovenskii's table. The book bothered Stepan very much; he agreed with the socialistic ideals of the work in principle but feared them in practice.

Chertkov. "The Portrait," in *Arabesques.* The artist who sold his talent for gold and perished as a result.

Cherviakov. *The Adolescent.* An ill-mannered, pockmarked fool who was employed in a bank and lodged where Arkadii Dolgorukii lived.

Chervichenko. "Taras Bul'ba," in *Mirgorod.* A Cossack chief who was killed during the siege of the Polish fortress.

Chevalier, Madame. *The Devils.* The woman to whose home Lisa Tushin bought flowers for Stepan Verkhovenskii when Lisa returned to Russia.

Chevchekhanova, Princess. *The Double.* The person in whose chair Goliadkin started to sit when he forced his way into Klara Berendeeva's party. He was soon rebuked.

Chichikov, Pavel Ivanovich. *The Brothers Karamazov* (3, 8, 7). A literary figure from Gogol's *Dead Souls.* Kalganov mentioned the fictional hero at Mokroe. (4, 12, 6). Ippolit Kirillovich mentioned Chichikov as an example of a Russian not capable of setting an example for Europeans. Gogol' wanted Russia to be an example for the West. *Dead Souls.* The hero of the novel who felt that success in life was based on money; so he learned to take advantage of others. While he was successful in government service, he became involved in illegal activities which caused him to change his career several times. His most original escapade was his buying of dead souls in the hope of using their papers in various financial schemes.

Chipkhaikhilidzev. *Dead Souls.* A Georgian Prince who was present at the governor's ball.

Chizhov, Aleksei Ivanich. *The Brothers Karamazov.* A name mentioned by a market woman when Kolia Krassotkin was teasing a clerk.

Chloe. *Oblomov* (4, 8). The shepherdess beloved by Daphnis in *Daphnis and Chloe* by Longus (4th or 5th cent. A.D.). Stoltz thought of Chloe as a symbol of pastoral love.

Chopin, Frédéric François (1810-1849). *The Devils* (3, 1, 3). The renowned musical composer. In Karmazinov's long and ridiculous introduction at the literary fete, he described an absurd scene in which a water-nymph whistled a tune from Chopin. Dostoevskii was making fun of I.S. Turgenev, whose mistress Madame Viardot wrote a romance using A. S. Pushkin's poem "The Water-nymph" based on music by Chopin. *The Idiot* (1, 12). When General Ivolgin led Prince Myshkin to the wrong apartment, Ivolgin pretended that he knew the inhabitants who were not at home. He told the servant who answered the door to give a message to a certain Aleksandra Mikhailovna, with whom he pretended to have talked during a Chopin ballade at a party the last Thursday evening.

Chudin. *The Precipice.* The best pupil in Raiskii's class in school.

Churkin. *The Underground Man.* The owner of the store where the Underground Man bought a pair of black gloves and a decent hat in preparation for his confrontation with the officer.

Cicero, Marcus Tullius (106-43 B.C.). *The Devils* (2, 8, 1) The Roman philosopher, statesman, and orator. When Petr Verkhovenskii criticized Shigalev's plan for the reorganization of mankind, he stated that in such a system a Cicero would have his tongue cut out. "Taras Bul'ba," in *Mirgorod* (37). At the Zaporozhe camp were Cossacks who could not read, but some did know Cicero.

Cinderella. *The Precipice* (3,5). The heroine of the famous fairy tale. Raiskii thought of Cinderella when he was describing Belovodova's beauty to Vera.

Cleopatra (69-30 B.C.). *The Precipice* (2, 7). The Egyptian Queen of the Ptolemaic Dynasty. Kozlov called his wife a red-headed Cleopatra. *The Underground Man* (1, 7). The Underground Man stated that Cleopatra was fond of sticking gold pins into her slave-girls' breasts and derived enjoyment from their their screams and writhing.

Cléopâtre. *The Gambler.* A remarkable socialite. When Mlle. Blanche set up her Parisian salon on the narrator's money, women such as Cléopâtre visited.

Cléry. *The Precipice.* The French governess who did not stay long as Belovodova's teacher. She was fired.

Clitus (Cleitus). *The Village of Stepanchikogo* (2, 6). Alexander the Great's friend whom the conqueror killed in a rage. Foma Fomich Opiskin again showed his ignorance of history by saying that Caesar killed Clitus.

Colonel. *The Devils.* A former fellow officer of Governor Ivan Osipovich. He was in the room the day Nikolas Stavrogin bit the governor's ear.

Columbus, Christopher (1451-1506). The famous explorer. *The Devils* (1, 3, 7). Lisa Tushin remembered that Stepan Verkhovenskii taught her about Columbus's discovery of America. (2, 8, 1). Petr Verkhovenskii declared that he was so attached to Nikolai Stavrogin that without him he would be like Columbus without America. *The Idiot* (3, 5). In his article "My Essential Explanation," Hippolit Terentev mentioned that Columbus was more happy on the verge of discovering America than he was afterwards. *The Precipice* (3, 4). Thinking of Columbus, Raiskii concluded that all simple answers are difficult to conceive.

Cominges, Blanche de. *The Gambler.* A beautiful woman whom the general wanted to marry, but he waited in vain for an old relative to die and leave him a fortune. Mlle. Blanche was about twenty-five, with black eyes and yellowish whites. She dressed spectacularly and spoke in a husky contralto. Her real name was Blanche du Placet.

Considérant, Victor Prosper (1808-1893). *The Devils* (1, 2, 3). The French socialist who founded a communistic society in San Antonio, Texas. When Nikolas Stavrogin went to Liputin to apologize for kissing Mrs. Liputin in public, he noticed a volume by Considérant and asked Liputin if he were a Fourierist.

Constant. See Very, Constant.

Cook, James (1728-1779). *The Precipice* (1, 6). The famous English explorer whom Raiskii read about in his father's library. *The Village of Stepanchikogo* (1, 2). Foma Fomich Opiskin told some peasants that Cook discovered how many miles it is to the sun.

Cooper, James Fenimore (1789-1851). *A Common Story* (2, 4). The American writer. Aleksandr Aduev recommended that Lisa read Cooper instead of Byron.

Copernicus. Nicolaus (1473-1543). *The Adolescent* (1, 5, 3). The Polish astronomer famous as the proponent of the theory on the revolution of the planets around the sun. Arkadii Dolgorukii's favorite vision was of an average man without any particular talents who could face the world and feel superior to Copernicus. *The Devils* (2, 8, 1). When Petr Verkhovenskii criticized

Shigalev's plan for the reorganization of mankind, he stated
that in such a system a Copernicus would have his eyes gouged
out. *The Precipice* (2, 10). Raiskii said that it took mankind a long
time to accept Copernicus's theory on the rotation of the earth
on its axis, and he understood why. Rasikii had an aunt who still
believed in a brownie.

Cordelia. *Oblomov* (2, 9). The youngest daughter of King Lear in
Shakespeare's play *King Lear*. She was the only daughter who
loved him unselfishly. She was pure, devoted, and self-sacrific-
ing. Oblomov thought that Ol'ga's love for him was like Cor-
dilia's for her father.

Corneille, Pierre (1606-1684). *The Gambler* (15). The French playwright.
In a conversation with Mlle. Blanche, the narrator began to
paraphrase from Corneille's *Le Cid*. *The Precipice* (1, 10). Raiskii
found a work by Corneille in his father's library and read it.

Cornelia. *The Precipice* (2, 7). The mother of the Gracchi brothers of
ancient Rome. Kozlov called his wife Cornelia.

Correggio, Antonio Allegrida (1494-1534). The Italian painter.
Oblomov (2, 4). When Stoltz was trying to persuade Oblomov to
go abroad, he reminded him that he had wanted to see Correggio's paintings. *The Precipice* (5, 25). Raiskii paid respects to the
famous Italian painter's works in a museum in Dresden.

Cottin, Sophie (1773-1807). *Oblomov* (2, 4). The author of the book
Matilda (1805), which Oblomov once took away from his sister
when he gave her classics to read. *The Precipice* (5, 25). Raiskii
read *Matilda* instead of studying.

Coucou. *Dead Souls.* A Frenchman who was one of the guests at the
governor's ball.

Countess. *The Devils.* A person of whom Mar'ia Lebiatkina was suspicious. When Mar'ia became disturbed by Nikolai Stavrogin's
conversation with her, she accused him of being an imposter
and having been sent by this Countess. Mar'ia was not well
mentally. *The Underground Man.* A society figure listed as one of
the exotic members of the select group which walks along the
Nevskii Prospect in St. Petersburg where the Underground
Man decided to confront the officer.

Criggs. *The Devils* The governess of Dasha till the girl was sixteen.

Crusoe, Robinson. *Notes from a Dead House* (2, 5). The hero of the novel
by that name (1719) by Daniel Defoe (1659-1731), which was
translated into Russian in 1762. Gorianchikov said that a certain fugitive prisoner could have been a Robinson Crusoe of
sorts if conditions had been right for him.

Cunégonde. *The Precipice* (3, 16). The baron's daughter in Voltaire's *Candide, ou L'Optimisme* (1759). Vera and Marfen'ka were required to read Voltaire's work because of Berezhkova's insistance.

Cyrus of Persia (d. 529 B.C.). *Crime and Punishment* (1, 2). The founder of the Persian Empire. When Marmeladov was trying to teach Sonia, he had few books and finally had to stop her instruction. He noted that they stopped studying history after reaching Cyrus.

D——, Prince. *The Underground Man*. A society figure listed as one of the exotic members of the elite group that walked along the Nevskii Prospect in St. Petersburg.

D——, Princess. *The Underground Man*. During the party in the restaurant, the Underground Man's former classmates talked about the grace and beauty of a certain Princess D——.

Dandin, Georges. *The Idiot* (4, 1). The hero of the play (1668) by that name by Molière. Dostoevskii commented that not all husbands of low degree shout "Tu l'as voulu, Georges Dandin" (Act I, Scene 9), but millions do.

Danilov. *The Idiot* (2, 7). When Prince Myshkin stated that Danilovs are special cases among young people, he was referring to A. M. Danilov, a nineteen-year-old student who killed a money lender and his servant in 1866. Dostoevskii followed the trial very closely and Danilov was sentenced to nine years of hard labor in Siberia.

Dante, Alighieri (1265-1321). *A Common Story* (1, 2). The famous Italian writer. Aduev mentioned him as a known genius. *The Brothers Karamazov* (2, 5, 5). Ivan Karamazov named Dante in the philosophical poem about the Grand Inquisitor. Ivan stated that passages in the old Russian work *The Wonderings of Our Lady Through Hell* were as descriptive as Dante's writings. *Dead Souls* (1, 7). Gogol' wrote that Virgil served Dante as a collegiate registrar served his friends. *Oblomov* (4, 4). Shtolz commented that when Ol'ga answered his declaration of love with "foresaw and suffered," she might as well have pronounced Dante's remark, "Abandon all hope." *Oblomov* (1, 2). Penkov praised a poem about a bribe taker's love for a fallen women as if it had been written by Dante. *The Precipice* (1, 12). Reading Dante, Raiskii forgot everything around himself.

Dardanelov. *The Brothers Karamazov*. The teacher of the school boys. It was rumored that Kolia Krassotkin was smarter in mathematics and universal history than the teacher. Dardanelov loved Kolia and gave him private tutoring.

Dardanus. *The Brothers Karamazov* (4, 10, 5). A name mentioned by Kartashov as one of the founders of Troy.

Dar'ia. *The Adolescent.* The mother of Ol'ga, the girl who hanged herself. Dar'ia was a friend of Mrs. Stolbeeva. *The Idiot.* The maid who was fired when accused of taking a three-rouble note while working at Ishchenko's country house. Ferdyshchenko had taken the note and confessed at Nastas'ia Filippovna's party.

Dar'ia Alekseevna. *The Idiot.* A friend of Nastas'ia Barashkova. Dar'ia was present at Nastas'ia's birthday party.

Dar'ia Frantsovna. *Crime and Punishment.* A woman of evil character who led Sonia Marmaladova into prostitution.

Dar'ia Onisimovna. *The Adolescent.* A woman living across from Vassin.

Darwin, Charles Robert (1809-1882). *The Devils* (3, 1, 3). The English naturalist. In his long and ridiculous introduction at the literary fete, Karamazinov said that the Russian genius has accepted Darwinism and atheism.

Darzan, Aleksei. *The Adolescent.* An acquaintance of the forgerer Nashchokin. Arkadii Dolgorukii met both men at Prince Sergei Sokolskii's.

Dasha. *The Devils.* See Shatova, Dasha. *The Precipice.* A servant referred to by Raiskii. *The Village of Stepanchikogo.* A peasant girl of low reputation. Egor Rostanev suggested that the girl whom Sergei Aleksandrovich saw in the garden with Obnoskin was probably Dasha.

Dashen'ka. *A Common Story.* Petr Aduev's name for Naden'ka. *Oblomov.* A dancer with whom Misha Goriunov was in love. She was admired by the whole town.

Dashkova, Princess Ekaterina Romanovna (1743-1810). *The Brothers Karamazov* (1, 2, 2). The famous friend of Ekaterina II of Russia and Voltaire of France.

David. *The Adolescent* (2, 8, 2). The shepherd king of the Old Testament (1 Sam. 16-21, Kings 2). Old Prince Sokolskii remarked that there is art in the poetry of life; for instance, the Biblical David put a beautiful girl in bed with him in his old age to warm him up.

Davout, Louis Nicoles, Duke of Auerstast and Prince of Eckmukh (1770-1823). *The Idiot* (4, 4). A French general. According to General Ivolgin, when he was a page of Napoleon I in 1812, he knew General Davout and went riding with him.

Davydov, Denis Vasil'evich (1784-1839). *The Devils* (1, 5, 4). A poet. When Stepan Verkhovenskii referred to Captain Lebiatkin's drinking problem, he mentioned that Davydov had sung the praises of the bottle. He is known in Russian literature for his poems on battles and bottles.

Degtiarenko. "Taras Bul'ba," in *Mirgorod*. A brave Cossack who was knocked off his horse by a rich Pole in fine armor. The Cossack Shilo vanquished the Pole.

Dement'ev, Nikolai. *Crime and Punishment*. A painter who was suspected of murdering the old pawnbroker. He confessed to the murder even though he had not committed it.

Demetrovich. "Taras Bul'ba," in *Mirgorod*. A Cossack troop chief who chose to stay and fight the Poles when others went to fight the Tartars.

Demka Krivoi. *Oblomov*. The scribe for Oblomov's overseer at the estate Oblomovka.

Demian Demianovich. "Ivan Ivanovich and Ivan Nikoforovich," in *Mirgorod*. The judge at the town court who had all cases read aloud even though he did not listen.

Demidov. *The Brothers Karamazov*. A merchant mentioned by Fedor Karamazov.

Demosthenes (385-322 B.C.) *The Double* (4). The famous Greek orator. Dostoevskii wrote that to depict the wonders of Olsufii Berendeev's birthday party for his daughter Klara, one would need the eloquence of Demosthenes.

Denis. *Dead Souls*. A peasant. Petukh became caught in a fishing net while trying to give orders to Denis. *The Precipice*. An aristocrat who had squandered much money in his youth. He was a friend of Pakhotin.

Derebin. *Dead Souls* A man who, as Nozdrev remembered, was lucky enough to inherit his aunt's estate.

Dergachev. *The Adolescent*. The leader of the group composed of Vassin, Effin, and Kraft. The Dergachev group was the fictional equivalent of a secret society headed by A.V. Dolgushin. In July, 1874, the trial of the secret society's members was closely followed by Dostoevskii while he was writing *The Adolescent*.

Derpenikov. *Dead Souls*. A young man whom Murazov told the general-governor that he had unjustly treated.

Derzhavin, Gavrila Romanovich (1743-1816). *A Common Story* (2, 3). A famous Russian author whom Tafaeva had to study. *The Devils* (2, 2, 2). Captain Lebiatkin said he himself was a worm and not a god like Derzhavin, the famous classical writer of odes. *The Precipice* (1, 10). Raiskii read Derzhavin's works while visiting Berezhkova.

Desdemona. *The Adolescent* (2, 4, 2). The heroine in Shakespeare's play *Othello*. Versilov said that Othello killed Desdemona not out of jealousy but because he had been robbed of his ideal.

Devushkin, Makar Alekseevich. *Poor Folk*. The impoverished clerk who sacrificed his own means to help the young orphaned girl Varvara.

Dey of Algiers. "The Notes of a Madman," in *Arabesques*. The madman announced, after a moment of sanity, that the Dey of Algiers had a wart under his nose. The last Dey of Algiers lost the city to the French in 1830.

Diana. *The Precipice* (2, 2). The goddess of the hunt. Marfen'ka wanted a tablecloth that had Diana and her dogs embroidered on it.

Diatlov. *Notes from a Dead House*. A prison clerk who had influence over the head of the prison.

Dickens, Charles (1812-1870). *The Adolescent* (3, 5, 3). The famous English novelist. Trishatov asked Arkadii Dolgorukii if he had ever read Dickens's *Old Curiosity Shop*. *The Devils* (1, 1, 1). Stepan Verkhovenskii managed to publish an article on the moral nobility of knights in a journal that printed translations of Dickens's works.

Diderot, Denis (1713-1784). *The Brothers Karamazov* (1, 2, 2). The French philosopher and encylopedist mentioned by Fedor Karamazov in an anecdote which was not based on the truth. *The Precipice* (2, 7). Mark tore out some pages from Diderot's encyclopedia, and Kozlov lamented their loss.

Dido. *The Precipice* (5, 11). The Queen of Carthage and heroine of Virgil's *Aeneid*, written in the first century B.C. When Kozlov's wife was unfaithful, he felt that he had lost his Dido and went to visit Berezhkova.

Diogenes (412-323) B.C.). *Dead Souls* (1, 8). The Greek philosopher, whom Chichikov mentioned while talking with the governor's daughter. *The Precipice* (2, 13). Raiskii searched for an honest woman as Diogenes searched for an honest man.

Dmitriev, Ivan Ivanovich (1760-1837). *Oblomov* (4, 9). The Russian writer. Alekseev told Oblomov that he had heard that Dmitriev was one of the best such writers. *The Precipice* (2, 2). Raiskii remembered a poem about the Volga by Dmitriev and recited it to Marfen'ka.

Dmitrii. *Crime and Punishment.* One of the painters on the staircase in the building where Alena Ivanovna and her sister were killed by Raskol'nikov. Dmitrii was arrested for the crime.

Dmitrii the Pretender. (the False) (Lzhedmitrii) (d. 1610). *The Double* (8). The man who claimed to be the son of Ivan the Terrible. Goliadkin felt that Dmitrii was one of the few who ever gained from imposture.

Dmitrii Arkadievich. *Oblomov.* The person whom Alekseev quoted when he said that Dmitirev was one of the best Russian authors.

Dmitrii Donskoi (1350-1389). "Nevskii Prospect," in *Arabesques.* The medieval grand duke of Moscow who defeated the Tartars in the battle of Kulikovo (1380). He was the hero in a tragedy by V.A. Ozerov (1770-1816).

Dmitrii Mitrich. *The Devils.* Blum's helper during the raid on Stepan Verkhovenskii's living quarters. When they found copies of Hertzen's works in the apartment, Stepan begged Dmitrii Mitrich to keep the matter quiet.

Dobryrin. *Oblomov.* A neighbor near Oblomov's estate in the country. Taran'tev urged Oblomov to write to Dobrynin about the estate.

Dobryna Nikitich. *Oblomov.* Oblomov's childhood nurse who told him about travels and epic heroes.

Doktorenko, Vladimir. *The Idiot.* Lebedev's nephew who chastised his uncle for lying, and who wanted to attend the university but lacked funds. He came with Antip Burdovskii to protest against the prince for not giving Burdovskii money.

Dolgorukii, Arkadii Andreevich. *The Adolescent.* The twenty-two-year-old illegitimate son of Versilov. Dolgorukii was the narrator of the novel.

Dolgorukii, Makar Ivanovich. *The Adolescent.* Versilov's serf who was Arkadii's legal father. He was fifty when he married the eighteen-year-old Sof'ia, who became Versilov's mistress.

Dolgorukaia, Liza Makarovna. *The Adolescent.* Arkadii's sister, who was also fathered by Versilov. She was very blonde and almost towheaded. She had her mother's oval face, and Versilov's height and grace.

Dolgroukaia, Sof'ia Andreevna. *The Adolescent.* Makar's wife, who became Versilov's mistress and gave birth to his children. She married Makar because her dying father had commanded it.

Doloto. "Taras Bul'ba," in *Mirgorod.* A Cossack whom Taras greeted at the Zaporozhe camp.

Don Juan. *The Idiot* (4, 6). Don Juan Tenorio, the son of a leading family of Seville in the 14th century. His name has become a synonym for a rake, roué, and libertine. Prince N——, a conceited guest at the Epanchin's party, was considered a Don Juan. *Notes from a Dead House* (1, 11). In the play *Kedril the Gluttonous*, presented by the convicts, the hero was described as being something of a Don Juan. *The Precipice*. (1, 1, 1). Aianov called Raiskii a Don Juan.

Don Quixote de la Mancha. *Dead Souls* (2, 3). The famous character from Cervantes's novel by that name (1605). Konstanzhoglo was critical of foreign ideas among Russian landowners and felt there were new Don Quixotes among them. *The Idiot* (2, 1). Aglaia Epanchina hid the letter from Prince Myshkin in a book. When she noticed that it was *Don Quixote de la Mancha*, she laughed. *Oblomov* (4, 8). When Shultz thought of the question of truth, Don Quixote came to mind. *The Precipice* (1, 4). Pakhotin told Aianov that Don Quixotes are diversified in society.

Dorofei Trofimovich. "Ivan Ivanovich and Ivan Nikiforovich," in *Mirgorod*. The court assessor who said, "I say nothing," when he was asked to comment on Ivan Ivanovich's complaint.

Dorosh. "Taras Bul'ba," in *Mirgorod*. Taras's deceased brother, whom Iankel mentioned to Taras so that the Cossack would save his life. "Vii," in *Mirgorod*. One of the six strong Cossacks who came for Khoma Brut when he was supposed to read prayers over the beautiful dead witch.

Dovgochkhum, Ivan Nikiforovich. "Ivan Ivanovich and Ivan Nikiforovich," in *Mirgorod*. The lazy landowner who liked to lie around naked. He was shorter than his neighbor Ivan Ivanovich, and shocked the latter by his use of foul language, especially words such as "devil."

Dovgochkhum, Nikifor. "Ivan Ivanovich and Ivan Nikiforovich," in *Mirgorod*. Ivan Nikiforovich's father, a gentleman of the Mirgorod district.

Dranishnikov. *Notes from a Dead House*. One of the engineers in charge of convicts' work. He called the laborers "doctors."

Dredson. *The Precipice*. Sof'ia Belovodova's English governess who went back to England when the girl was sixteen.

Drobiazhkin. *Dead Souls*. A rural assessor who had the habit of bothering the wives and wenches of a certain village and who was killed by the villagers to keep him away. When the police inspected the slaying, they found out nothing; and since it did not matter to Drobiazhkin anymore, they dropped the matter.

Drouineau, Gustav (1880-1835). *A Common Story* (2, 3). A noted playwright who wrote *Rienzi, tribun de Rome* in 1826. Tafaeva considered Drouineau a hero.

Drozdov, Ivan. *The Devils*. A friend of the deceased General Stavrogin. In St. Petersburg, Drozdov was mentioned in a cartoon with Mrs. Starogina as "reactionary friends."

Drozdov, Mavrikii Nikolaievich. *The Devils*. A tall and handsome artillery captain who escorted Lisa Tushina to the Libiatkins' murder scene, where she was killed by a mob.

Drozdova, Praskov'ia. *The Devils*. A widow and childhood friend of Mrs. Stavrogina. Lisa Tushina was her daughter by a previous marriage.

Drozhzhov. *A Common Story*. A friend of Zaezzhalov. When Drozhzhov was facing dismissal from work, Zaezzhalov asked Petr Aduev to defend him.

Du Barry, Comtesse Marie Jeanne Bécu (1746-1793). *The Idiot* (2, 2). A mistress of Louis XV from 1768 to his death in 1774. She was guillotined in 1793. Lebedev's nephew claimed that his uncle prayed that the soul of the Comtesse Du Barry might rest in peace.

Dubasov. *The Adolescent*. A man referred to by Darzan as a person who always knew what was going on. To Arkadii Dolgorukii's surprise, Dubasov said that Katerina Akhmatova was going to marry Baron Bjoring.

Dubasov, Timofei Nikonych. *A Common Story*. The merchant to whom Aleksandr Aduev was forced to write a letter for his uncle Petr Aduev. In his agitation, Aleksandr wrote the wrong name and an incorrect notation of money due.

Duclida. *Crime and Punishment*. A woman in a saloon who begged Raskol'nikov for money.

Dula. "The Overcoat." A name on the page of names which Akakii Akakievich's mother examined when searching for a name for her son. She decided finally on his father's name Akakii.

Dumain. *A Common Story*. A friend of Aleksandr Aduev. Aleksandr spent a day with Dumain instead of carrying out a visit to Tafaeva.

Dumas, Alexandre, *fils* (1824-1895). *The Idiot* (1, 14). The noted French writer. When Totskii told his vilest experience at Nastas'ia Filippovna's party, he mentioned that Dumas's play *La Dame aux Camelias* (1852) was popular at the time his incident took place. *Notes from a Dead House* (1, 7). Petrov mentioned the French writer in a conversation with Gorianchikov.

Dundasov. *The Devils.* A cultured family which Stepan Verkhovenskii knew in Berlin. When he wrote Varvara Stavrogina that Mrs. Dundasova sent her regards, Varvara was repulsed.

Duniasha. *Oblomov.* A servant of Tat'iana Ivanovna. *Poor Folk.* The daughter of Samson Vyrin in the story "The Stationmaster" by A. S. Pushkin (1799-1837).

Dushkin. *Crime and Punishment.* A peasant who kept a dramshop facing the house where Alena Ivanovna lived. He once took some valuables to the police, saying that he bought them from Nikolai Dementev.

Dussot. *Crime and Punishment* (4, 1). The owner of a well-known restaurant in St. Petersburg.

Dutov. *Notes from a Dead House.* A prisoner condemned to two years at hard labor for attacking an officer who came to escort him to his flogging. According to Dostoevskii, a prisoner would do anything to postpone punishment.

Echartschausen, Karl (1752-1803). *Dead Souls* (1, 8). The German mystic and writer. The postmaster in the village where Chichikov went to buy dead souls liked to read the mystical writings of Echartschausen. *The Precipice* (1, 6). Raiskii read his works.

Edgeworth, Maria (1767-1849). *The Precipice* (2, 3). The English author of *Ellen,* a novel which Marfen'ka read and liked.

Efim. *Notes from a Dead House.* The prisoner who was on the road with Shapkin when the latter had his ears pulled by a police chief.

Efim Akimovich. *Poor Folk.* Makar Devushkin's colleague in the office who was known as the most touchy man on earth.

Egor Il'ich. *The Precipice.* The man whom Berezhkova mentioned as a person who was punished by fate because he was in love with rebellion.

Egor Prokhorych (Egorka). *The Precipice.* (1, 7). The Don Juan of Berezhkova's village. She called him by the long form of his name when she was displeased; otherwise he was Egorka.

Egorushka. A diminutive for Egor.

Eight Eyes. *Notes from a Dead House.* See the Major.

Eisenschmidt. *The Brothers Karamazov.* The German doctor who attended Father Zosima's brother. He assured the patient that he would live long but told the widowed mother that her son would soon die.

Ekaterina II (1729-1796). *The Brothers Karamazov* (1, 2, 2). The Empress mentioned by Fedor Karamazov in an anecdote not based on the

truth. *The Idiot* (4, 4). General Ivolgin claimed that when he was
a page of Napoleon I, the Emperor stopped before a portrait of
Ekaterina II and said, "That was a great woman." *The Precipice* (1,
14). The only Russian historical character whom Belovodova
remembered.

Elevferii Elevferievich. "Ivan Ivanovich and Ivan Nikiforovich," in
Mirgorod. A guest at the police captain's party, where a reconciliation of the two Ivans was attempted but failed.

Elijah. *The Brothers Karamazov* (2, 4, 1). The Jewish prophet whom Father
Ferapont mentioned when he told the little monk from Ob-
dorsk that the Holy Ghost had warned of a fool's visit that day.
The Village of Stepanchikogo (1, 2). The patron saint of Il'iusha
Rostanev.

Eliseev. *The Adolescent* (1, 6, 2). A popular store in St. Petersburg where
Arkadii Dolgorukii bought some sweets for Prutkova. *The
Brothers Karamazov* (3, 8, 5). The wine Dmitrii bought at Plot-
nikov's for his spree at Mokroe was bottled by the brothers
Eliseev, a noted firm in pre-revolutionary Russia. *The Double* (4).
Olsufii Berendeev purchased things for his daughter's birthday
party at Eliseev's.

Elizavet-Vorobeii. *Dead Souls*. A dead female serf whose name was
added to a list of male serfs by Sobakevich in his effort to cheat
Chichikov in a sale of dead souls.

Elkin. *Notes from a Dead House*. A shrewd man who was an old believer.
He took away Kulikov's business as a veterinarian.

El'nin. *The Precipice*. Belovodova's teacher of Russian. She had a crush
on him and learned all of her lessons well to impress him.

Elsevier. *The Precipice* (1, 16). The family name of the oldest printers in
Holland, dating from the sixteenth century. Kozlov said that
Volokhov had no respect for books and would even tear out a
page from a edition by Elsevier.

Emelia the Fool. *Oblomov*. A character from Russian folk literature.
Oblomov's nurse read him stories about Emelia.

Emel'ian. *Dead Souls*. Petukh's servant who was late in serving the hors
d' oeuvres and was severely reprimanded.

Emel'ian Il'ich. *Poor Folk*. A clerk who was fired in Devushkin's office.
He asked Devushkin to speak up for him.

Emel'ian Ivanovich. *Poor Folk*. An industrious and disinterested soul
who worked in Devushkin's office.

Emilia Fedorovna. *Dead Souls*. A second cousin of Pobedonosnov's
sister-in-law. The blonde with whom Chichikov was talking at

the ball began to yawn when he told of meeting Pobedonosnov in Penza. Emilia was also visiting Pobedonosnov at that time.

Emperor of Austria. *The Idiot* (4, 4). A reference to Joseph Karl Franz (1768-1835). According to General Ivolgin, who had been a page of Napoleon I, the Emperor claimed that his hatred for the Emperor of Austria was everlasting.

Epanchin, Ivan Fedorovich. *The Idiot.* The general who had three daughters. He was a man of no education who had risen from the ranks. He gave pearls to Nastas'ia Barashkova on her birthday.

Epanchina, Adelaida Ivanovna. *The Idiot.* The middle daughter of the Epanchin family. She was twenty-three years old and engaged to Prince S—.

Epanchina, Aglaia Ivanovna. *The Idiot.* The youngest daughter of the Epanchin family. She was twenty years old and fell in love with Prince Myshkin. Before she was to marry him, she visited Nastas'ia Barashkova, who informed her that she could take the Prince back and did. Aglaia later married an exiled Polish count.

Epanchina, Aleksandra Ivanovna. *The Idiot.* The oldest daughter of Lizaveta Prokof'evna and General Epanchin. She was twenty-five years old. If the arrangement between her father and Totskii had gone through, she would probably have married Totskii.

Epanchina, Lizaveta Profko'evna. *The Idiot.* The wife of General Epanchin. She had three daughters: Aleksandra, Adelaida, and Aglaia. She was distantly related to Prince Myshkin. Her character was changeable: she was childlike at times but flew into terrible rages once every three years, according to her husband.

Érard, Sébastien (1752-1831). *Oblomov* (4, 5). The famous French piano maker whose gold-inlaid piano stood in a prominent place at Sholtz's home.

Erema. "The Portrait," in *Arabesques*. A comic figure in seventeenth century carvings called *lubok*. Chertkov wondered about the taste of people who would buy a painting showing Erema.

Eremeev. "Ivan Ivanovich and Ivan Nikiforovich," in *Mirgorod*. The police captain's former light-cavalry commander.

Eremka. *The Precipice.* One of Berezhkova's peasants.

Erkel. *The Devils.* A second lieutenant at whose lodgings the five members of Petr Verkhovenskii's group met. Erkel belonged to the type of "small fools" who lack only the higher forms of reasoning powers. He had plenty of the lesser reasoning powers, especially cunning.

Ermak. *Poor Folk*. A hero in one of Rataziaev's novels. Ermak threw himself in the Irtish River when his beloved Ziuleika was accidentally killed by her blind father.

Ermolaev. *Poor Folk*. A writer in Devushkin's office whose eyes begged for a glass of vodka.

Ermolaev, General Aleksei Petrovich (1772-1861). *The Devils* (1, 5, 4). A noted Russian commander in the Caucasus. Captain Lebiatkin claimed that his grandfather was killed before the eyes of the general.

Ernestine. *Oblomov*. The governess at Oblomovka. She drank tea with Sholtz's mother.

Eropegov (Kapiton, Eroshka). *The Idiot*. A man whom General Ivolgin claimed to know. Ippolit Terentev did not believe that Eropegov existed. When confronted, General Ivolgin became confused about Eropegov's names and called him Kapiton and Eroshka.

Eroshkin, Ivan Ivanovich. "The Overcoat." The godfather of Akakii Akakievich Bashmachkin.

Eruslan Lasarevich. *Oblomov*. A comic hero from the Russian past whom Oblomov imagined himself to be in his dreams. "The Portrait," in *Arabesques*. A popular comic figure in seventeenth-century carvings called *lubok*. Chertkov wondered at the taste of people who would buy pictures showing Eruslan.

Esfiri. See Esther.

Essbuketov. *Village of Stepanchikogo*. A name Vidopliasov chose to exchange for his last name until Egor Rostanev pointed out that it was the name written on bottles of scent.

Esthete. *The Devils*. The name given to Stepan Verkhovenskii by a divinity student at the fete when he insulted Stepan by asking whether he had been justified in selling Fedka fifteen years ago to pay for a gambling debt.

Esther. *The Brothers Karamazov* (2, 6, 1). An Old Testament heroine (See Esther). The Persian King Ahasuerus chose her as his queen. She hid the fact that she was Jewish until she was able to use such information to save her own people. She was mentioned in Father Zosima's biography.

Eudoxie. *The Precipice*. The lady who married Prince Koko. Aianov reported the incident to Raiskii in a letter.

Evgenii Pavlovich. See Radomskii, Evgenii Pavlovich.

Evlampia Nikolaevna. *The Idiot*. The widow of a government clerk who visited the Epanchins. Her aim in life was to obtain things as cheaply as possible, and she was a cheat. Aglaia told Prince Myshkin that he had a similar philosophy.

Evsei Ivanych. *A Common Story*. Aleksandr Aduev's valet.

Evpl Akinfovich. "Ivan Ivanovich and Ivan Nikiforovich," in *Mirgorod*. A guest at the police captain's party, where a reconciliation between the two warring Ivans was attempted but failed.

Evstafii. *The Double*. Karolina Ivanovna's servant who was replaced by Petrushka when the latter abandoned Goliadkin.

Evstafii Ivanovich. *Poor Folk*. A clerk in Devushkin's office.

Evtikhii Evtikhievich. "Ivan Ivanovich and Ivan Nikoforovich" in *Mirgorod*. A guest at the police captain's party when a reconcilation was attempted between the two Ivans.

Eyre, Jane. *The Precipice* (2, 3). The heroine in the novel by that name (1847) by Charlotte Brontë (1816-1855). Marfen'ka read the book and could not sleep for two nights.

Ezhevikin, Evgrav Larionich. *The Village of Stepanchikogo*. The father of Egor Rostanev's ward. Ezhevikin was an embarrassingly ingratiating type, always bowing and wriggling.

Ezhevikina, Nastia Evgravovna. *The Village of Stepanchikogo*. Egor Rosanev's ward. Egor wanted his nephew to marry her.

Faddei Il'ich. *The Precipice*. The father of Egorka, a servant of Berezhkova. Egorka felt that her daughter Natal'ia had inherited the ugly mug of Faddei Il'ich.

Fadeev. *Crime and Punishment*. A store in St. Petersburg. Razumikhin mentioned that the store would give a customer a second suit for nothing if he wore out the one he had bought.

Falalei. *The Village of Stepanchikogo*. A peasant who had been made a house servant because he was pretty. Foma Fomich Opiskin punished him for dancing the Komarinskii. Falalei was pampered by Madame la Generale and stood by her chair during dinner, accepting lumps of sugar occasionally and smiling prettily.

Fal'bala. *The Double*. The landlady of a pension who was mentioned by Goliadkin. The name came from the poem "Count Nulin" by A. S. Pushkin (1799-1837).

Falconet, Étienne Maurice (1716-1791). "The Overcoat." The creator of a famous statue of Petr the Great in St. Petersburg. When clerks have no gossip to pass on, they retell the ancient joke about the commandant to whom it was reported that someone had hacked off the tail of the horse of the monument to Petr the First.

Fal'doni. *Poor Folk*. The servant of Makar Alekseevich's landlady. Fal'doni was a red-haired, swine-jowled, crooked lout. His name was taken from a popular French novel by N.G. Leonard (1744-1793) entitled *Teresa i Fal'doni* (1783), translated into Russian by M.T. Kachenovskii (1804).

Falstaff. *The Devils* (1, 2, 1). The great comic rogue in Shakespeare's play *Henry IV*. Stepan Verkhovenskii likened Nikolai Stavrogin's antics in St. Petersburg to the merrymaking of the Shakespearean characters in *Henry IV*. Varvara Stavrogina read the play but did not agree with Stepan. (1, 5, 6). When Petr Verkhovenskii related Nikolai Stavrogin's history to Mrs. Stavrogina, he mentioned that Captain Lebiatkin used to be Nikolai's Falstaff.

Famusov. *The Brothers Karamazov* (2, 5, 1). A character from A. S. Griboedov's *Woe from Wit* who was mentioned by Madame Khokhlakov after she eavesdropped on her daughter Lisa and Alesha Karamazov when they professed love for each other. *The Idiot.* (3, 1). Prince Myshkin referred to Famusov in conversation at the Epanchins' Swiss chalet at Pavlovsk. *The Precipice* (1, 4). The portraits of Sof'ia's grandmothers and great aunts looked like Famusovs in skirts to Raiskii.

Fanaritoova. *The Adolescent.* The upper-class family name of Versilov's deceased wife. Arkadii Dolgorukii was able to find out very little about her. She did give Versilov a son and daughter.

Faublas. *The Double* (10). The hero of the French novel *The Love Intrigues of Cavalier de Faublas* (1787) by J. B. Louvet de Couvray (1760-1747) which was translated into Russian in 1792. Goliadkin II referred to Goliadkin I as a Russian Faublas.

Faust. *The Adolescent* (3, 5, 3). The hero of Goethe's *Faust* (1790-1833), based on the scoundrelly magician and astrologer Dr. Johann Faust, who died about 1538. Trishatov stated that he would choose a theme like Faust if he were to compose an opera. *The Devils* (1, 1, 1). Stepan Verkhovenskii's unpublished play which was seized by Moscow authorities was in a lyrical dramatic form recalling the second act of Goethe's *Faust*. *Oblomov* (4, 8). Shtolz said that he and Ol'ga would not worry over philosophical questions as did Faust, but would silently live hard times. *The Precipice* (2, 5). Kozlov preferred elegies to Goethe's *Faust*.

Favre, Gabriel Claude Jules (1809-1880). *The Devils* (2, 5, 1). The noted French statesman. When Liamshin played his musical piece for Mrs. Lembke, the narrator said that the change of melody was as if Jules Favre were crying on Bismarck's shoulder. He referred to French sentimentalism and the German petty bourgeoise after the Franco-Prussian War of 1870.

Fedka. *The Devils.* The escaped convict from Siberia who was serving a life sentence for counterfeiting. He murdered the Lebiatkins and was himself later murdered after a quarrel with Petr Verkhovenskii. *Notes from a Dead House.* The governor's servant who had some control over his superior. Fedka, a diminutive of Fedor, almost went out of his mind when his dog Tresorka died.

Fedor. *The Devils.* The baptismal name of Fedka the convict. *The Gambler.* The footman whom Tarasevicheva sent home from Berlin on her way to Roulettenburg because she decided that she did not need him. *The Idiot.* A servant of the Epanchins.

Fedor Fedorovich. *Poor Folk.* A subordinate official about whom malicious gossip was being spread. Devushkin could not understand why Fedor did not do something about the rumors.

Fedor Ivanovich. *Dead Souls.* The new teacher of Tentetnikov who took over after Aleksandr Petrovich had died.

Fedor Matveevich. *The Devils.* The merchant to whom Stepan Verkhovenskii said he was going when he ran away at the end of the novel.

Fedora. *Poor Folk.* A friend and companion of Varvara.

Fedorov. *A Common Story.* A business partner of Petr Aduev.

Fedorov, Pavel. *The Devils.* The deceased valet of Mrs. Stavrogina, and the father of Shatov and Dasha.

Fedorov, Vasilii. *Dead Souls.* The name in an inscription on a store: "Vasilli Fedorov Foreigner." Chichikov read the sign while passing.

Fedoseev. *The Idiot.* The guest with General Epanchin when Prince Myshkin first came to visit.

Fedosei Fedoseevich. *Dead Souls.* A clerk in the administration office who was asked to hand over file N 368.

Fedoseich. *The Double.* The corpulent commissionaire who stood stiff as a ramrod at the office door to open it for His Excellency Osufii Berendeev.

Fedos'ia. *The Gambler.* A nurse in the general's household. *The Precipice.* When Raiskii returned to his estate, he was not sure whether a woman in the yard was Fedos'ia or Marina.

Fedos'ia Petrovna. *A Common Story.* The widow of Semen Arkhipych.

Fedosii Ivanovich. *Poor Folk.* A clerk in Devushkin's office.

Fedot. *Dead Souls.* Sobakevich's dead serf who had been of good character and born of a house wench. *Oblomov.* The carpenter who propped up the fallen balcony with logs to the satisfaction of head of the Oblomov family.

Feeder. *The Gambler.* Mr. Astley's relative who took Mlle. Selma from the casino the night the Baroness von Wurmerhelm had the police request that Selma leave.

Feklushka. *The Precipice.* A half-wit girl whom Raiskii listened to in his youth and drew a picture of in a cave.

Fenardi. *The Brothers Karamazov* (3, 8, 7). A character from Gogol's *Dead Souls.* During Dmitrii Karamazov's spree at Mokroe, Maksimov claimed to have known in real life certain characters from Gogol's book. Maksimov said that Mlle. Fenardi was a pretty girl who twirled around for four minutes, not four hours as Gogol' wrote. *Dead Souls* (1, 4). An acrobat from abroad who gave performances in the town of N—. She was admired by Nozdrev.

Fenia. *The Brothers Karamazov.* Grushen'ka's maid who lied to Dmitrii Karamazov when he tried to find out where Grushen'ka was on the night of Fedor Karamazov's murder.

Ferapont. *The Precipice.* A peasant whose name could not be made into a diminutive form by his owners.

Ferapont, Father. *The Brothers Karamazov.* A deranged monk who bitterly opposed Father Zosima. Ferapont claimed the Holy Ghost visited him daily in the form of a dove.

Ferdinand VIII. "The Notes of a Madman," from *Arabesques.* The name used by the madman to sign a document in his office after he thought that he had become the King of Spain.

Ferdyshchenko. *The Idiot.* An admirer of Nastas'ia Barashkova. He lodged at the Ivolgins' when Prince Myshkin went there to live. He was suspected of having stolen Lebedev's money, but General Ivolgin took it.

Ferfichkin. *The Underground Man.* A Russianized German who was a former classmate of the Underground Man. The latter considered him a blockhead.

Ferzing. *The Adolescent.* The commanding officer of an infantry regiment in Makar Dolgorukii's story of his life.

Ferzing, Mrs. *The Adolescent.* The wife of the infantry officer in Makar Dolgorukkii's story. She talked to the boy whom Makar wanted to rear just before the boy committed suicide by jumping into a river.

Fetin'ia. *Dead Souls.* Korobochka's servant who prepared a bed for Chichikov when he came in from the storm.

Fetiukovich. *The Brothers Karamazov.* A noted defense attorney who was brought from Moscow to defend Dmitrii Karamazov when he was accused of killing his father.

Feuerbach, Ludwig Andreas (1804-1872). *The Precipice* (4, 9). The German philosopher and author of *Philosophie und Christentum* (1834). Raiskii did not have the book in his library and asked Vera if she could obtain it.

Fevron'ia. *The Village of Stepanchikogo*. The name Mr. Bakhcheev used for Tat'iana Ivanova the morning he woke up the narrator to inform him of Tat'iana's abduction.

Fidele. "The Notes of a Madman," in *Arabesques*. The dog to whom the dog Madgie wrote the letters which were supposedly taken by Poprishchin.

Fido. "The Notes of a Madman," in *Arabesques*. The dog with whom the dog Madgie talked when Poprishchin overheard their conversation.

Filatka. "The Nevskii Prospect," in *Arabesques*. A popular name in Russian vaudevilles in the 1830's. *Filatka with Children* (1831) by P.I. Grigor'ev was often performed. "Notes of a Madman," in *Arabesques*. *Filatka and Miroshka* (1831) by P.G. Grigor'ev was popular in Russian vaudeville theater. It was criticized for lacking taste. *Notes from a Dead House*. The prisoners presented the play *Filatka and Miroshka* with great success.

Filibusterov, Vasilii Ivanovich. *The Devils*. A police inspector known for his zealous execution of his duties. He, ironically, informed von Lembke of the filibusters at the Spigulin factories.

Filipp. *The Adolescent*. The hairdresser who sold the tie to the tall guest at Lambert's the evening Arkadii Dolgorukii went there to learn why Dar'ia had given him Lambert's address. *Crime and Punishment*. Svidrigailov's serf who was supposed to have committed suicide to escape the cruelty of his master.

Filippov. *The Devils*. The owner of the house where the Lebiatkins lived. Shatov lived in the upstairs attic and Kirilov had a room in the Lebiatkins' flat. Filippov had a large red beard.

Filisova. *The Idiot*. The lady with whom Nastas'ia Filippovna lived after leaving her benefactor's. Prince Myshkin once tried to visit Nastas'ia, but Filisova said she was not at home.

Fil'ka. *Crime and Punishment*. Svidrigailov's serf who appeared to his master as a ghost. When informed about the specter, Raskol'nikov told Svidrigailov that he, Svidrigailov, was not well.

Fingal. *The Precipice*. (1, 6). The semi-mythological Gaelic hero who was the father of Ossian, the purported author of the long epic poem *Fingal* (1762). Raiskii drew the legendary Scottish hero instead of practicing his art lesson.

Foma (Thomas). *The Adolescent.* The peasant who was cheated by the merchant in Makar Dolgorukii's story about the child who had committed suicide. *The Brothers Karamazov.* A former soldier from whose room Dmitrii Karamazov spied on Grushen'ka. *A Common Story.* A peasant whom, according to Anton Ivanovich, the new doctor cured of stomach troubles. *The Devils.* A specialist in interior decorating who worked for Mrs. Stavrogina. She sent him to Stepan Verkhovenskii's place to clean it up in case Karamazinov called on him. *The Precipice.* A peasant whose daughter was baptized. "The Portrait," in *Arabesques.* A comic figure in seventeenth-century carvings called *lubok.* Chertkov wondered why people would buy paintings with Foma as the subject. He considered such art tasteless. "Taras Bul'ba," in *Mirgorod.* A Cossack with a blackened eye who poured vodka at the Zaporozhe camp.

Foma, St. See Thomas, St.

Foma Big (Bol'shoi). *Dead Souls.* The peasant to whom Petuckh was giving orders on how to pull fish into a net when Petukh himself became entangled.

Foma Fomich. *The Village of Stepanchikogo.* See Opiskin, Foma Fomich. *Oblomov.* The man with whom Sud'ibinskii had to work when he refused an invitation to dine with Oblomov.

Foma Grigorievich. "Ivan Ivanovich and Ivan Nikiforovich," in *Mirgorod.* A guest at the police captain's party where a reconciliation between the two warring Ivans was attempted but failed.

Foma Small (Malen'kii). *Dead Souls.* The peasant to whom Petukh was yelling and directing how to untangle the fish net Petukh was caught in.

Fourier, Charles (1772-1837). *The Devils* (1, 1, 1). The founder of a communistic social system. Stepan Verkhovenskii's unpublished play was seized by authorities in Moscow after the discovery of a group of subversives who were planning to translate Fourier's works. (1, 2, 3). When Nikolas Stavrogin went to Liputin to apologize for having kissed Mrs. Liputina in public, he asked if Liputin were a Fourierist. (2, 7, 2). When Shigalov spoke at the Virginskiis' group meeting, he mentioned the famous social philosopher Fourier as a naïve dreamer whose works are for sparrows, not humans. (3, 4, 2). Liputin denied he was a Fourierist when Petr Verkhovenskii questioned him about Fourier.

Franklin, Benjamin (1706-1790). *Dead Souls* (2, 3). The great American statesman and inventor. Koshkarev insisted that his peasants read about Franklin's lightning rods.

Frederick II, the Great (1712-1786). *The Precipice* (1, 14). The famous Prussian ruler. Belovodova remembered that Frederick played a role in history, but she was not sure when.

Frenzel. *The Devils*. A doctor friend of Shatov. When Shatov's wife returned sick, he wanted to call Frenzel. Shatov did not yet know that his wife had returned pregnant.

Frolovna. *Poor Folk*. A peasant weaver. When Varvara Alekseevna reminisced about her childhood, she remembered the sounds of Frolovna's spinning wheel.

Fyrov Abakum (Habakkuk Phyrov). *Dead Souls*. A runaway serf. Chichikov daydreamed about the life of the runaway.

G——v. *Notes from a Dead House*. The commandant who was at the prison only six months, but won the love and respect of the convicts.

G——v, Anton Lavrentevich. *The Devils*. The name of the narrator of the novel. He was a civil servant.

Gaganov, Artemii Pavlovich. *The Devils*. The man who hated Nikolai Stavrogin because of the insult he had given Artemii's father four years earlier. Through his spiteful remarks, he forced Nikolai into a duel. After Artemii missed his shot, Nikolai fired into the air. Insulted, he made Nikolai duel two more times, which was his right by law. Nikolai fired into the air both times after Gaganov failed to hit him.

Gaganov, Pavel Pavlovich. *The Devils*. A respected member of the town club who said, "They won't lead me by the nose," whereupon Nikolai Stavrogin pulled him by the nose for two or three steps and caused a scandal. The townspeople gave the insulted Gaganov an ovation everywhere he went, exchanging embraces with him and kissing him.

Galatea. *The Adolescent* (3, 7, 3). A sea nymph loved by the Cyclops Polyphemus, but she herself loved Acis. When her loved one was crushed under a huge rock by the jealous monster, she threw herself into the sea, joining her sister nymphs. See Lorrain, Claude. *Oblomov* (2, 9). Ol'ga saw herself in a situation as complicated as Galatea's.

Galiandovich, Pan. "Taras Bul'ba," in *Mirgorod*. The Polish gentleman who captured Iankel but spared him when he told his captor

that he could repay his debts only when he wanted to. Iankel
escaped and informed Taras about his son Andrei's treachery.
Galileo Galilei (1564-1642). The Italian astronomer and physicist who
advocated the Copernican system of earth rotation. *The Adolescent* (1, 5, 3). Arkadii Dolgorukii's favorite vision was of an
average man without any particular talents who could face the
world and feel superior to Galileo. *The Precipice* (2, 10). Berezhkova had no use for scientists such as Galileo. She preferred a religious explanation for everything.
Gambs. *Dead Souls* (2, 5). The owner of a famous furniture store in St.
Petersburg. *The Precipice* (1, 2). The couch in Pakhotin's apartment came from Gambs.
Gapka. "Ivan Ivanovich and Ivan Nikiforovich," in *Mirgorod*. Ivan
Ivanovich's servant who served him melons and brought an
inkstand so that Ivan could label the melon seeds. Gapka's
children ran about the yard, and she kept Ivan's keys.
Garas'ka. *The Precipice*. Berezhkova's peasant.
Garii. "Ivan Ivanovich and Ivan Nikiforovich," in *Mirgorod*. An early
nineteenth-century publisher of popular literature which was
cheap stuff for the semi-literate.
Garina. *The Devils*. The family name of the wife of Colonel Berestov.
Gattsuk, A.A. (1832-1891). *The Brothers Karamazov* (4, 11, 9). A journalist
who published the *Gazette of A. Gattsuk* and a religious calendar
from 1870 to 1880.
Gavrila. *The Village of Stepanchikogo*. Egor Rostanev's valet who once
looked after the narrator when he was a boy.
Gavrila Ardalionovich. *The Idiot*. See Ivolgin, Gavrila Ardalionych.
Gavril'ka. *Notes from a Dead House*. The prisoner whom Lomov attempted to murder when he learned that Gavril'ka had killed
the laborers on Lomov's father's farm. Lomov was punished for
his action.
Gazin. *Notes from a Dead House*. A peasant prisoner who was like a spider
and sold spirits. He was a frightful creature who produced a
hideous impression on everyone. When he was drunk, he was
dangerous and was sometimes beaten unconscious by other
prisoners. He was supposed to take pleasure in killing little
children.
Ge, Nikolai Nikolaivich (1831-1894). *The Underground Man* (1, 6). A well-
known Russian artist. In 1863, Ge exhibited his "Last Supper,"
and Dostoevskii thought the picture poorly conceived. The
Underground Man referred to Ge's picture.

General. *The Devils.* One of the most pompous members of the town club. He was a distant relation of the Gaganovs' and took great interest in Nikolai Stavrogin. *The Gambler.* A pompous personage who acted as if he were very wealthy, which he was not. He looked forward to the death of his Aunt Tarasevecheva in order to inherit her wealth. Her appearance at the German spa where he was staying greatly depressed him. He finally married Mlle. Blanche.

Genlis, Stephanie Felisita (1746-1830). *Oblomov* (1, 9). The French novelist whose works were translated into Russian. Oblomov's father read her novels aloud from three-year-old newspapers. *The Precipice* (2, 5). Marfen'ka read a novel by Madame Genlis.

Genzelt, Adolph L. (1814-1889). *The Precipice* (1, 14). A noted Russian pianist. Belovodova's mother wanted to hire Genzelt to teach her daughter; but when told that the girl had the talent to become a musician, the mother changed her mind.

Gérard, François (1770-1837). *The Precipice* (5, 25). The neoclassical French painter. Raiskii saw his grandmother in one of Gérard's painting.

Gerasimich. *The Double.* Olsufii's butler who explained to Goliadkin that Olsufii Berendeev had given orders not to receive him at the party.

Ghenghis-Khan. (1162-1227). *The Brothers Karamazov* (2, 5, 5). The famous Asian conqueror. The Grand Inquisitor stated that men such as Ghenghis-Khan represented the unconscious expression of the craving for universal unity.

Gibbon, Edward (1737-1794). *The Precipice* (2, 3). The historian who wrote *The Decline and Fall of the Roman Empire* (1776-1788). Marfen'ka found the work too heavy for her and did not finish it.

Girin. *A Common Story.* A merchant whose house was across from Tafaeva's dwelling.

Glafira. *The Brothers Karamazov.* Madame Khokhlavkova's maid.

Glasha. *Poor Folk.* An actress with whom Makar Devushkin fell in love in his youth.

Glebov, Stepan Bogdanovich (1672-1718). *The Idiot* (4, 5). The lover of Petr the Great's first wife Evdokia Lopukhina. Glebov was condemned to frightening torture and death.

Glinka, Mikhail Ivanovich (1803-1857). The composer of *A Life for the Tsar* (1836). *Eternal Husband* (12). When Vel'chanikov sang for the Zakhlebinins and their guests, he chose a song by Glinka. *Notes from a Dead House* (1, 11). When the prisoners performed the

Kamarinskii, the narrator noted that Glinka would have been satisfied with the music.

Gluck, Christoph Willibald (1774-1780). *The Devils* (3, 1, 3). The noted German composer. When Karmazinov gave his ridiculous introduction at the literary fete, he described an absurd scene in which Gluck was supposed to be playing in some rushes.

Goethe, Johann Wolfgang (1749-1838). *A Common Story* (1, 5). The famous German writer. Aleksandr Aduev referred to Goethe in a discussion on the grace of poetry. *Dead Souls* (1, 7). Chichikov discusses Charlotte, the heroine of Goethe's *Werther*. (1774). *The Devils* (1, 1, 9). Stepan Verkhovenskii said that he was rather an ancient pagan like "the great Goethe." *Oblomov* (2, 4). Oblomov wanted his girl friend to read Goethe. *The Precipice* (1, 1). Aianov and Raiskii mentioned the German writer in an argument about the value of life.(2, 22) Vera mentions Goethe's *Werther*.

Gog. *Dead Souls* (1, 5). A legendary evil king. In Sobakevich's opinion, the governor was like King Gog.

Gogol', Nikolai Vasil'evich (1809-1852). *The Adolescent* (1, 5, 1). The famous Russian eccentric and author of *Dead Souls*. Arkadii Dolgorukii called Gogol's hero Pliushkin a "simple type." *The Brothers Karamazov* (3, 8, 7). Kalganov said that Maksimov claimed to be the character Maksimov in Gogol's book *Dead Souls*. *Crime and Punishment* (4, 6). In talking with Raskol'nikov after Nikolai admitted being the murderer of the old pawnbroker, Porfirii Petrovich mentioned that Raskol'nikov always saw the comic side of things, which was a characteristic of the writer Gogol'. *The Devils* (1, 1, 9). Stepan Verkhovenskii mentioned a noted letter sent to Gogol' in 1847 by V. Belinskii in which the critic reviled the writer for his beliefs. (1, 3, 2). Dostoevskii stated that most Russian writers are forgotten after one generation, unlike Gogol', who had something original to say. (2, 1, 2). Petr Verkhovenskii claimed that Turgenev's nihilist Bazarov was a mixture of Gogol's Nozdrev and Lord Byron. (2, 2, 2). Captain Lebiatkin said that he had written his last story like the writer Gogol', who mentioned that his last story burst out of his heart. (3, 1, 1). The narrator said that suddenly people of station like Tentetnikov in Gogol's *Dead Souls* began to listen to the words of worthless individuals. *The Idiot* (3, 1). At the Epanchins' in Pavlovsk, Prince S— said that there is nothing Russian in Russian literature except for Lomonosov, Pushkin, and Gogol'. (4, 1). Dostoevskii mentioned Gogol's character Podkolesin from the play *The Marriage* (1842). (4, 1). Dostoevskii referred to Gogol's character Pirogov in "Nevskii Prospect."(4, 1). Dostoevskii cited the despicable character Nozdrev from Gogol's *Dead Souls. Notes from a Dead House* (1, 4). When the narrator saw Isaiah Fomich Bumstein, he was always reminded of the character Iankel in Gogol's "Taras Bul'ba." *The Underground Man* (2, 1). A reference was made to the character Konstanzhoglo from Gogol's *Dead Souls.*

Goliadkin, Iakov Petrovich (Junior). *The Double.* Goliadkin Senior's exact physical "double" with whom the Senior Goliadkin had discussions on his way to insanity.

Golaidkin, Iakov Petrovich (Senior). *The Double.* A middle-aged, extremely paranoid bureaucrat in a governmental department. Nervous and unstable, he began to converse with his own double, Iakov Petrovich Goliadkin (Junior).

Golikov, I. I. (1735-1801). *Oblomov* (1, 9). The Russian historian whose works Oblomov's father read at times.

Golodukha, Madsim. "Taras Bul'ba," in *Mirgorod.* The only Cossack who escaped when the Tartars raided the Cossack camp while the Zaporozhe Cossacks were fighting the Poles.

Golokopytenko, Mykita. "Taras Bul'ba," in *Mirgorod.* A brave Cossack who helped lead the final siege on the beleaguered Polish city. He brought Taras news of the death of several chieftains during the battle.

Golopuz, Anton Prokof'evich. "Ivan Ivanovich and Ivan Nikiforovich," in *Mirgorod.* A man who went about in a cinnamon-colored coat and who used to say that the devil himself tied the two Ivans together because they had such a fine friendship.

Golubenko. *The Eternal Husband.* The bridegroom who was stabbed in the stomach during his wedding ceremony by his best man Livtsov. Golubenko was marrying the woman whom Livtsov loved.

Golubchikov, Miten'ka. *The Eternal Husband.* A young man in the military service who continually caused trouble for his benefactors Pavel and Lipochka Trusotskaia. During a noisy scene which Golubchikov caused at a railway station, Lipochka accidentally met her husband's old friend Vel'chaninov.

Gomez, Don Petro. *The Village of Stepanchikogo* (2, 3). The hero of the humorous poem "Don Petro Gomez" by Kuz'ma Prutkov (A. K. Tolstoi) which Il'iusha Rostanev read for Foma Fomich Opiskin's name day.

Gorbatova, Mar'ia. *A Common Story*. Petr Aduev's sister-in-law who
    wrote Petr a letter about their youthful friendship, and asked
    him to send her yarn and books.
Gorbunov, I. F. (1831-1896). *The Brothers Karamazov* (4, 11, 9). An actor
    mentioned by the devil during Ivan's nightmare. Gorbunov was
    very successful, and Dostoevskii highly praised his ability.
Gorchakov, P.D. (1789-1868). *Notes from a Dead House* (2, 8). The gover-
    nor-general with three daughters who was referred to in the
    book. He actually had four daughters, three of whom visited
    him in Omsk.
Goremyka, Anton. *The Adolescent* (1, 1, 5). The hero of a short novel
    (1847) by that name by D. V. Grigorovich (1822-1879) about the
    severe conditions of the life of the peasants during serfdom.
Gorianchikov, Aleksandr Petrovich. *Notes from a Dead House*. The narra-
    tor of the notes who was a former gentry proprietor sent to
    prison after assassinating his wife.
Goriunov, Misha. *Oblomov*. The man with whom Volkov was going to
    Ekaterinburg when he invited Oblomov to accompany them.
Goriunova, Lidia (Liden'ka). *Oblomov*. The daughter of Sof'ia
    Goriunova. Volkov confessed to Oblomov that he was in love
    with Lidia.
Goriunova, Sof'ia Nikolaevna. *Oblomov*. The lady who was traveling
    with her family and who offered Oblomov a place in their
    carriage if he cared to ride with them.
Gorobets, Tiberii. "Vii," in *Mirgorod*. A peasant who was too young to
    drink or smoke. He wore a curl around his ear, and judging from
    the bumps on his head, he was a good fighter.
Gorokh, Tsar. *Crime and Punishment* (1, 1). A Russian fairy tale figure
    who represented a stupid oaf. Raskol'nikov lay in his room for
    days thinking foolish thoughts like Tsar Gorokh.
Goroshkin. *The Precipice*. An acquaintance of Openkin. They were not
    on good terms, and Openkin refused to drink at Goroshkin's.
Gorpina. "Ivan Ivanovich and Ivan Nikiforovich," in *Mirgorod*. Ivan
    Nikiforovich's cook.
Gorshkov. *Poor Folk*. A former officer who was discharged from
    government service for a crime he did not commit. He had lived
    in poverty with his family for seven years when his name was
    finally cleared. He died the day he received the pardon.
Gorskii. *The Idiot* (2, 7). A reference to A. Gorskii, the student who
    killed the merchant Zhemarin and his family in 1868. Dos-
    toevskii followed the trial closely. Gorskii declared himself a

non-believer, and Dostoevskii felt Gorskii represented the fruit of the nihilists of the 1860's. Prince Myshkin stated that Gorskiis are special cases among young men.

Gorstkin. *The Brothers Karamazov.* A merchant also known as Liagavii who wanted to buy some property belonging to Fedor Karamazov.

Goureau, Abbé. *The Idiot.* The Jesuit priest who converted Pavlishchev to Catholicism. When his convert died, the abbé tried to put a claim on the deceased's will.

Governor-General. *Notes from a Dead House.* See Gorchakov, P. D.

Grand Chancellor. "The Notes of a Madman," in *Arabesques.* The prison attendant who beat the madman. The latter ascribed the feat to the power of popular tradition in Spain.

Grand Inquisitor. *The Brothers Karamazov* (2, 5, 5). A literary figure created by Ivan Karamazov in his philosophical poem. The Grand Inquisitor belittled Christ for not understanding the true nature of man. In Christ's name, a church was built to make up for Christ's failings, according to the Grand Inquisitor. Christ's kissing the Grand Inquisitor at the end can be interpreted as acquiescence or triumph. "The Notes of a Madman," in *Arabesques.* When the Grand Chancellor beat the madman, he thought that he might have fallen into the hands of the Grand Inquisitor during the Spanish Inquisition.

Granovskii, Timofei Nikolaevich (1813-1855). *The Devils* (1, 1, 1). A professor of history at Moscow University. Stepan Verkhovenskii's name was mentioned for a short time by enthusiastic people along with Granovskii's. (2, 10, 3). Stepan Verkhovenskii reminded Karmazinov that they had met years earlier at a dinner for Professor Granovskii.

Granz. *The Adolescent.* The doctor who delivered Lidia Akhmatova's baby before Lidia died of sulfur poisoning.

Gregory VII, Pope (Hildebrand) (c. 1023-1085). *The Brothers Karamazov* (1, 2, 5). The Pope from 1073 to 1085. He was mentioned by Miusov.

Gremin. *Dead Souls.* A name used by Gogol' in a comparison. Chichikov was speechless before the governor's daughter "like some Gremin in a popular novel." The novels of A. A. Bestuzhev-Marlinskii (1797-1837) were very popular at that time.

Grech, Nikolai Ivanovich (1787-1867). "Nevskii Prospect," in *Arabesques.* A second-rate Russian writer. Gogol' mentioned that certain middle-class types make it into society and show their ignorance by putting Grech in the same sentence with Pushkin.

Gretchen. *The Adolescent* (3, 5, 3). A German diminutive of the name Margaret. Gretchen was the heroine of Goethe's *Faust*. When Trishatov mentioned that he would like to write an opera on the theme of *Faust*, he told the story of Gretchen in a musical setting similar to the plot of the opera *Faust* (1859) by C. F. Gounod (1818-1893).

Greuze, Jean Baptiste (1725-1805). *The Precipice* (1, 4). The noted French artist. Raiskii told Sof'ia that she was not so perfect or pretty as the women painted by Greuze. (5, 25) Raiskii saw the image of Marfen'ka in Greuze's sculptures in Europe.

Gridenko. *The Brothers Karamazov*. A copying clerk who sewed roubles into his hat.

Grieux, Monsieur de. *The Gambler*. The well-mannered and unscrupulous Frenchman who courted Polina and loaned the general money.

Grigorii, St. of Nyssa (c. 331-c. 396). *The Adolescent* (3, 1, 3). One of the four great fathers of the Eastern Church.

Grigorii. *Dead Souls*. A servant in Tentetnikov's household. "The Notes of a Madman," in *Arabesques*. In the dog's letter, he was the director's servant who said that Sof'ia's wedding was close at hand.

Grigorii Doezzhai-ne-doedesh. *Dead Souls*. The name of a dead serf whom Pliushkin sold to Chichikov. His name meant "Try to get there, but you won't."

Griogorr Petrovich. *Notes from a Dead House*. The guard whom Sirotkin killed in a fit of depression.

Grigorii Vasil'evich. *The Brothers Karamazov*. An old servant in the Karamazov household who cared for Dmitrii Karamazov before the Miusovs took him from his father. Grigorii was gloomy, stupid, obstinate, and argumentive.

Grigorovich, Dmitrii Vasil'evich (1822-1899). *The Devils* (1, 1, 9). The Russian author of *Anton the Wretched* (1847) (Anton Goremkya). Liputin pointed out at a meeting of Stepan Verkhovenskii's society that even high-society ladies had been moved by the book and wrote their managers from Paris instructing them to be kinder to the peasants.

Grishka. *The Village of Stepanchikogo*. Bakhcheev's servant whom the master often scolded.

Grunia. *A Common Story*. Petr Aduev's name for Naden'ka.

Grusha. *The Brothers Karamazov*. A diminutive of Grushen'ka.

Grushenka. *The Brothers Karamazov*. See Svetlova, Agrafena Aleksandrovna.

Gubonin Petr Ionovich (1825-1894). *The Adolescent* (1, 5, 2). A wealthy
  Russian financier. Arkadii Dolgorukii was sure that he could be
  as wealthy as Gubonin.
Guizot, François Pierre Guillaume (1787-1874). *The Precipice* (2, 22).
  The French historian whom Raiskii recommended to Vera. She
  tried reading his works but found them boring.
Gulliver, Lemuel. *The Devils* (1, 1, 1). The hero of Jonathan Swift's novel
  Gulliver's Travels (1726). Dostoevskii mentioned the hero as a
  typical man who could not break his habits. He shouted at
  carriages in London as if he were still among the small Lillipu-
  tians. *The Precipice* (2, 3). Marfen'ka told Raiskii that she had read
  Gulliver's Travels.
Gunia. "Taras Bul'ba," in *Mirgorod*. The experienced friend and advisor
  of Ostranitsa, the headman of the new Cossack force.
Guska, Okhrim. "Taras Bul'ba," in *Mirgorod*. A Cossack whose man-
  gled body fell to the ground during the fighting for the besieged
  Polish city.
Gutenberg, Johann (c. 1398-c. 1468). *A Common Story* (1, 2). The inventor of printing whom Petr Aduev considered a genius.
Gvozdikov, Ivan Ivanovich. *Notes from a Dead House*. A man whose five
  daughters studied under the tutelage of Gorianchikov. The
  narrator first met Gorianchikov at Gvozdikov's.

Haim (Khaivalokh). "Taras Bul'ba," in *Mirgorod*. A Jewish contractor in
  the city besieged by the Cossacks. Seeking news of the Cossacks, Taras asked Iankel' whom he had seen in the city,. Iankel'
  answered that he had seen only Haim.
Haller, Karl Ludwin von (1768-1854). *A Common Story* (2, 3). The author
  of a popular German reader. When Tafaeva wanted to study
  German literature, she could find only Haller's reader.
Hamlet. *The Brothers Karamazov* (3, 8, 5). Shakespeare's famous hero.
  Dmitrii mentioned Hamlet when he went to buy things at
  Plotnikov's store for the spree at Mokroe. (4, 12, 9). A comment
  in the crowd during a trial recess was, "We have only Karamazovs, and they [Europeans] have Hamlets." *The Devils* (1, 3,
  7). Lisa Tushina remembered that Stepan Verkhovenskii told
  her the story of Shakespeare's *Hamlet* when she was his pupil.
  The Idiot (3, 4). Lebev called Hamlet's famous "To be or not to be"
  a very contemporary theme. *The Precipice* (3, 13). Raiskii compared himself to Hamlet and Kozlova to Ophelia after her
  impassioned attack on him. *The Village of Stepanchikogo* (2, 5). Foma

Fomich Opiskin advised Egor Rostanev to read *Hamlet* in order to understand the sufferings of Opiskin's soul.

Harpagon. *The Adolescent* (1, 5, 1). A miser from Molière's play *L'Avare* (1668). See Molière.

Harry, Prince. *The Devils* (1, 2, 1). The nickname of Prince Henry in Shakespeare's *Henry IV*, Part II. Stepan Verkhovenskii called Nikolai Stavrogin after Prince Harry.

Heckeren, Baron Jacob Theodore. *The Devils* (2, 1, 5). The Dutch ambassador to the Russian court and a noted decadent. His sole beneficiary was Georges d'Anthes, who killed A. S. Pushkin in a duel over the latter's wife. When Stavrogin went to Kirilov and asked him to be his second in a duel with Artemii Gaganov, Kirilov reminded him that Pushkin had acted hastily in writing to Heckeren about Georges d'Anthes.

Hector. *The Precipice* (1, 13). The son of Priam, King of Troy. Raiskii drew a head of Hector instead of a torso as required by the Academy of Art.

Hecuba. *The Adolescent* (1, 8, 3). The second wife of Priam in Homer's *Iliad*. After the fall of Troy, Hecuba fell to the Greeks. She was metamorphosed into a dog and threw herself into the sea. "On to Hecuba" has come to mean "to the main point." Arkadii Dolgorukii stated that Kraft shot himself to prove his main point and go "on to Hebuca."

Heine, Heinrich (1797-1856). *The Brothers Karamazov* (4, 11, 9). The German poet known for his lyrical poems and witticisms. He was mentioned by the devil in Ivan's nightmare. *The Devils* (3, 1, 3). In Karamazinov's long and ridiculous introduction at the literary fete, he mentioned that the Russian genius had a grimace from Heine. *The Underground Man* (1, 11). In the second volume of his book *About Germany*, in *Admittances* (1853-1854). Heine said that no man can write truthfully about himself. He accused Rousseau of telling lies about himself in his *Confessions* (1781-1788).

Helen. *The Precipice.* See Edgeworth, Maria.

Henriette. *Crime and Punishment.* The girl who was hit in eye by a drunkard in Luisa Ivanovna's house. Because of the scandal, Luisa was summoned to the police station.

Hercules. *The Precipice* (1, 6). The hero of Greek myth who was possessed with superhuman strength. When Raiskii heard music, he sometimes felt he was strong enough to replace Hercules.

Herder, Johann Gottfried (1744-1803). *Oblomov* (2, 1). The German
  writer whose works Sholtz read aloud to his father at the age of
  eight.

Hermann. *The Adolescent* (1, 8, 1). The hero of A. S. Pushkin's "The
  Queen of Spades." The imaginative hero had considerable
  influence on Russian literature.

Herod, King (73?-4 B.C.) "Ivan Ivanovich and Ivan Nikiforovich," in
  Mirgorod. The ruler of Judea who was known for his wickedness.
  He was mentioned as a character in the puppet theaters which
  were popular in nineteenth-century Russia.

Herodias. "Vii," in *Mirgorod*. The wife of Herod (Gen. 39), the ruler of
  Judea at the time of Christ's birth. One of the most popular
  plays at the Kievan monastery was about Herodius.

Herschel, Sir William (1738-1822). *Oblomov* (2, 9). The English astronomer whom Oblomov once mentioned to Ol'ga Il'inskaia. She
  became interested in astronomy.

Hertz, Henry (1806-1888). *Oblomov* (2, 1). A German composer.
  Sholtz's mother cried when her son had a bloody nose and
  consoled herself by playing the music of Hertz.

Hertzen, Aleksandr Ivanovich (1812-1870). *The Adolescent* (3, 7, 2). The
  noted Russian socialist, writer, and critic. Arkadii Dolgorukii
  asked Versilov if he intended to join Hertzen when Versilov
  went abroad with the intention of becoming an emigré.
  Hertzen as an emigré in London wrote the noted journal *The
  Bell. The Devils* (1, 1, 1). Stepan Verkhovenskii's name was for a
  short time mentioned along with Hertzen by enthusiastic people. (2, 6, 2). When the lieutenant of the police went mad in the
  district where Petr Verkhovenskii had spent some time, the
  narrator commented that the lieutenant was the type that
  would have gone to the Marquesas Island like Hertzen's cadet if
  he had had the money. Hertzen's cadet was P. A. Bakhmetiv,
  who was described in Hertzen's *Past and Thoughts* (2, 6). (2, 6, 4).
  When Blum talked of raiding Stepan Verkhovenskii's home for
  forbidden books, he mentioned that Hertzen's works were
  probably there. (2, 7, 1). Virginskii's stupid relative, called the
  Major, had passed on thousands of copies of Hertzen's periodi-
  cal *The Bell* which was published in London and smuggled into
  Russia. The major never read it but felt duty bound to deliver it
  since it was given to him to do so. (2, 9, 1). Hertzen's works were
  seized when the authorities raided Stepan Verkhovenskii's
  living quarters. (3, 4, 2). Liputin asked Petr Verkhovenskii if he

wrote the poem read at the literary fete. Liputin was sure that Hertzen had not written it. (3, 8, 1). In Stravrogin's letter to Dasha Shatova before his suicide, he mentioned that he, like Hertzen, had taken up residence in Switzerland and asked her to go there with him. Hertzen, losing his citizenship in Russia in 1851, took up residence in Switzerland.

Hesner, Solomon (1730-1788). *A Common Story* (2, 3). The Swiss poet whose sentimental works were popular in Russia in the early nineteenth century. Tafaeva read one of his books.

Herzen. See Hertzen.

Herzenstube. *The Brothers Karamazov*. An old doctor in the town who gave testimony in Dmitrii Karamazov's favor at the trial.

Hinze. *The Gambler*. A young man of frivolous nature for whom the narrator served as a valet while living in Baden.

Hippolit. *The Idiot*. See Terentev, Ippolit.

Hoffman. "Nevskii Prospect," in *Arabesques*. A high-class bootmaker who was a friend of the ironmonger Schiller. When Pirogov followed the blonde to the strange house, he came upon the drunken Hoffman.

Hoffman, August Heinrich (1798-1874). *The Devils* (3, 1, 3). The German writer of romantic stories. In Karmazinov's long and ridiculous introduction at the literary fete, he described an absurd scene in which Hoffman appeared. Dostoevskii was making fun of I. S. Turgenev's work *Enough* (1865), which has the line "Hoffmanism is not terrible, no matter in what form it appears." Dostoevskii had Hoffman appear in a scene where a water nymph whistled a tune from Chopin.

Holbein, Hans (1497-1543). *The Idiot* (1, 6). The famous painter known as "the Younger." Prince Myshkin told Aleksandra Epanchina that she had a shadow of sorrow in her face like the Dresden Madonna painted by Holbein. Dostoevskii saw the picture in 1867, but in 1870 the Dresden picture was verified as a copy of the original hanging in the Darmstart museum. (2, 3). Prince Myshkin identified a painting at the Rogozhins' apartment as a copy of a work by Holbein.

Homer. *Dead Souls* (1, 7). The name of the poet to whom is assigned the authorship of the *Iliad* and the *Odyssey*. Chichikov came to the conclusion that the chairman of the town of N— could prolong meetings the way Homer's Zeus prolonged days and shortened nights. *The Double* (4). Dostoevskii wrote that only a talent such as Homer's could attempt to describe the wonders of Olsufii

Berendeev's birthday party for his daughter Klara. *Oblomov* (4, 9). The pen of Homer was needed to describe all the provisions in the house of Pshenitsyna. (1, 9). The stories of Oblomov's nurse were as vivid as Homer's. *The Precipice* (1, 6). Raiskii read Homer's *Iliad* and *Odyssey* in his youth.

Hoppe. *The Gambler* (4). The name of a banking firm in Amsterdam and London.

Horace (short English for Quintus Horatius Flaccus (65-8 B. C.). "Taras Bul'ba," in *Mirgorod*. The famous Roman lyricist and satirist. Tovkach was not considered a scholar like Horace.

Horatio. *The Brothers Karamazov* (3, 8, 5). The friend of Hamlet in Shakespeare's play *Hamlet*. Dmitrii Karamazov mentioned Horatio while drinking at Plotnikov's store before setting out for Mokroe. *The Devils* (1, 5, 6). Varvara Stavrogina regretted that her son Nikolai did not have a friend like "some gentle Horatio" to look after him in his youth.

Horatius. *The Adolescent* (2, 1, 4). A legendary hero of ancient Rome who was supposed to have sent his sons to die for the empire. Arkadii Dolgorukii wanted Versilov to be a dominating father like Horatius. *The Precipice* (3, 9). Volokhov was disgusted that Kozlov used Horatius as reading material for his students, as for instance, in the play *Horace* (1640) by Pierre Corneille (1606-1684).

Hortense. *The Gambler*. A woman of society in Paris who attended Mlle. Blanche's salon.

Hugo, Victor Marie (1802-1885). *The Adolescents* (3, 8, 1) The famous French poet, novelist, and dramatist. Versilov stated that painful memories are like great scenes in literature which are painful to think about, for instance, the scene where the escaped convict meets the little girl in Hugo's *Les Misérables* (1862). *The Brothers Karamazov* (2, 5, 5). Ivan Karamazov mentioned Hugo in his philosophical poem "The Grand Inquisitor." In Hugo's *Notre-Dame de Paris* (1831), the Virgin Mary appeared during the reign of Louis XI. *A Common Story* (2, 3). Tafaeva talked about Hugo and Montaigne as if they were from the same period. *Oblomov* (3, 5). Ol'ga Il'inskaia thought about Hugo's poems during a meeting with Oblomov in the Summer Garden. *The Precipice* (2, 8). Kozlov suggested that Raiskii read Hugo's *Napoleon le petit* (1853).

Humboldt, Baron Alexander Friedrich (1769-1856). *The Precipice* (3, 14). The famous German naturalist mentioned by Raiskii.

Hymen. *The Precipice* (1, 3). The Greek god of marriage. People were
wondering when Hymen would put chains on Sof'ia.

I—— V——. *The Precipice*. An acquaintance of Aianov. In a letter to
Raiskii, Aianov wrote that he had to finish writing because he
had a serious game of cards upcoming at I—— V——'s.

Iago. *The Adolescent* (2, 5, 3). The famous traitor of Shakespeare's play
Othello who was mentioned in a conversation between Versilov
and Arkadii Dolgorukii.

Iakov. *The Precipice*. Berezhkova's old servant who served at her table.

Iakov Petrovich. *The Double*. See Goliadkin, Iakov Petrovich.

Ian. "Taras Bul'ba," in *Mirgorod*. A guard who was replaced in the
Polish prison, upsetting Iankel's plan for taking Taras to the
captured Cossacks.

Iankel. *Notes from a Dead House* (1, 4). A character from Gogol's "Taras
Bul'ba." The narrator always thought of the fictional character
when he saw Isaiah Fomich Bumstein. "Taras Bul'ba," in
Mirgorod. The Jew who begged Taras for his life when the
Cossacks were throwing Jews into the Dnieper and laughing as
they drowned. Taras spared Iankel because he knew Taras's
deceased brother Dorosh. Later, Iankel informed Taras about
his traitorous son Andrei.

Iavdokha. "Old-World Landowners," in *Mirgorod*. The housekeeper
whom Pulkheria Tavstoguba told to look after her master after
her mistress's death.

Iavtukh. "Vii," in *Mirgorod*. One of the six Cossacks who came for
Khoma Brut at the monastery. His nickname was Kovtun, and
he believed that the dead captain's daughter was a witch.

Ignashka. *Oblomov*. A peasant at Oblomovka. Oblomov's father asked
each of his peasants where he was going. Ignashka was planning to sharpen knives.

Ignatii. *A Common Story*. Liubetskaia's servant.

Igor', Prince (—945). *The Devils* (1, 1, 9). The Prince of Kiev from 912.
Dostoevskii wrote that nationalism had never existed in Russia,
but he did not include the times of Prince Igor'. (1, 2, 7). Stepan
Verkhovenskii was planning to teach Dasha Shatova about the
medieval poem *The Lay of Igor's Army* when Varvara Stavrogina
cancelled Daha's lessons.

Il'ia. *The Brothers Karamazov*. The father of the deformed girl Lizaveta
who was called "Stinking Liza." Il'ia had lost everything and
lived many years as a poor workman. *The Precipice*. Pakhotin

mentioned Il'ia as a man who received a bonus when others did not.

Il'ia Il'ich. *Dead Souls.* A popular figure in the town of N— whom the townspeople like as much as they did Chichikov when he first came to town.

Il'ia Kuz'mich. *The Precipice.* Berezhkova's uncle, who brought the woman a shawl from the East which she wore on holidays.

Il'ia Paramonych. *Dead Souls.* A merchant whom the chief of police invited to see a trotter.

Il'ia Petrovich. *Crime and Punishment.* The assistant police superintendent who was known for his explosive temperament.

Il'ia Muromets. *Oblomov.* An epic hero from the Russian *byliny.* As a child, Oblomov's nurse read him about the hero.

Iliia. See Elijah.

Il'inskaia, Ol'ga Sergeevna. *Oblomov.* The girl who was introduced to Oblomov by his friend Sholtz. Ol'ga fell in love with Oblomov; but his ways destroyed their chances, and she married Sholtz. She had a marvelous singing voice.

Ilius. *The Brothers Karamazov.* A name mentioned as one of the founders of Troy by Kartashov in a discussion of history.

Il'iusha. *The Brothers Karamazov.* See Snegirov, Il'iusha. *The Precipice.* Berezhkova's peasant.

Ioan Milostivyi (6th-7th cent.). *The Brothers Karamazov* (2, 5, 4). John the Merciful, who helped a poor sick man from his own false self-laceration. Ivan Karamazov mentioned the religious figure while explaining his rebellion against God to his brother Alesha. Dostoevskii read I. S. Turgenev's translation (1877) of Gustave Flaubert's *La Légende de Saint-Julian-l'Hospitalier* (1876).

Ioann Vasil'evich III (1440-1505). *The Precipice* (1, 6). A famous Russian tsar. Raiskii was interested only in Ioann III and Ioann IV when he studied history.

Ioann Vasil'evich IV (1530-1584) (Ivan the Terrible). *Poor Folk* (June 2). Devushkin felt that Rataziaev's play *Ermak and Ziuleika* was right out of the times of Ivan IV. *The Precipice* (1, 6). Raiskii was interested in Ivan the Terrible when he studied history.

Iosif, Father. *The Brothers Karamazov.* A librarian at the monastery who read the Bible by Father Zosima's coffin before the body began to give off an unpleasant odor. Iosif gave little significance to the early decomposition of the body, but others felt that it showed the judgment of God.

Iov (—1607). *The Precipice* (1, 6). A protégé of Boris Godunov. He was persecuted after the death of Boris. When Raiskii was threatened with punishment, a priest told about the sufferings during the time of Tsar Boris.

Ippolit Kirillovich. *The Brothers Karamazov*. The public prosecutor who conducted the trial against Dmitrii Karamazov.

Irina. *The Precipice*. A name used by Berezhkova to describe the sort of peasant she would help in childbirth.

Irina Panteleevna. See Mukhoiarova, Irina Panteleevna.

Isaac. *The Brothers Karamazov*. The Biblical son of Abraham (Gen. 24-28), mentioned in Father Zosima's biography. "Taras Bul'ba," in *Mirgorod*. A Jew who denied that the pillagers of churches in the Ukraine were Jews. The Cossacks refused to believe him, and threw him and his friends into the Dnieper to drown. The Cossacks laughed at the misery of the dying men.

Isaac the Syrian. *The Brothers Karamazov* (1, 3, 1). A religious figure whose sermons were highly valued. Grigorii had a copy of the sayings and sermons of the noted religious mystic. (4, 11, 8). Ivan read mechanically from the sermons of Isaac when he went to Smerdiakov for the final interview about his father's murder.

Ishchenko, Mar'ia Semenovna. *The Idiot*. The daughter of the host at the country house where Ferdyshchenko stole the three-rouble note. She played the piano for the guests.

Ishchenko, Semen Ivanovich. *The Idiot*. An acquaintance of Ferdyshchenko. When Ferdyschchenko told the story of his theft at Nastas'ia Filippovna's party, he mentioned that his base action took place at Ischenko's country house.

Isis *The Precipice* (4, 4). The chief female deity of Egyptian mythology. Vera seemed to Raiskii to be like Isis, full of mystery.

Iulia. *The Brothers Karamazov*. Madame Khokhlakova's maid. *A Common Story*. Petr Aduev used this name when talking about Naden'ka. *The Devils*. Mrs. Lembke's first name. When she was an old maid, she was called Iulia.

Iushin. *Crime and Punishment*. A man who rented rooms in Bakaleev's house. When Luzhin said that he had found rooms for Mrs. Raskol'nikova and Dunia at Bakaleev's, Raskol'nikov was disgusted because Iushin lived there, and the place was filthy and cheap.

Iusupov. *Crime and Punishment*. One of the wealthiest families in tsarist Russia. The park named for the family was a common meeting place for middle-class people in the nineteenth century. When Raskol'nikov was on his way to murder Alena Ivanovna, he passed through the Iusupov gardens.

Iuziakina. *Dead Souls.* The general's relative who broke up the friendly relationship between the general and Tentetnikov.

Ivan. *The Devils.* The name which Mar'ia Shatova chose for her newborn son. She knew that the child was not Shatov's. *The Precipice.* Vikent'eva's servant.

Ivan the Crown-Prince (Tsarevich). *The Devils* (2, 8, 1). A name created for Nikolai Stavrogin by Petr Verkhovenskii. When Petr discussed with Nikolai the possibilities of an overthrow of the government in Russia, he proclaimed that the people would follow a leader who appealed to them and he would create Stavrogin into that leader—Ivan the Crown Prince. Petr based his theory on the Russian peasant followings of former pretenders to the Russian throne. See Ostrepev, Grisha.

Ivan the Terrible. See Ioann Vasil'evich IV.

Ivan Abramovich. "The Overcoat." The visitor in the office of the important person when Akakii Akakievich sought help in finding his stolen coat.

Ivan Afanasevich. *Crime and Punishment.* The former boss of Marmeladov and a man of modern political ideas.

Ivan Andreevich. *A Common Story.* A new doctor whom Aleksandr Aduev's mother wanted to call when Aleksandr was sick.

Ivan Antonovich. *Dead Souls.* A clerk in charge of the purchase deeds for serfs in the town of N——.

Ivan Bogdanovich. *The Precipice.* A country doctor whom Marfen'ka talked into making calls on poor, sick peasants.

Ivan Egorovich. *The Precipice.* The deceased husband of Kritskaia.

Ivan Filippovich. *The Devils* (2, 8, 1). A name created for Nikolai Stavrogin when he wanted to become the pretender to the throne of Russia. Dostoevskii derived the name from two historical pretenders of a noted sect of eunuchs: Daniel Filippovich and Ivan Timofeevich. The sect, founded in the eighteenth century, had a legend that an ancestor would come from the Urals and spread the sect of eunuchs into the West.

Ivan Gerasimych. *Oblomov.* A former colleague of Oblomov whom he preferred to visit rather than see friends of Sholtz.

Ivan Grigor'evich. *Dead Souls.* The chairman of the office where, according to Sobakevich, the officials talked about Chichikov.

Ivan Iakovlich. *The Village of Stepanchikogo.* See Koreisha, Ivan Iakovlich.

Ivan Ivanovich. *A Common Story*. A friend of Aleksandr Aduev. When Aleksandr was homesick in Paris, he thought of his friend Ivan back home. Also, a teacher hired for Tafaeva was named Ivan Ivanovich. "Ivan Ivanovich and Ivan Nikiforovich," in *Mirgorod*. See Perpenko, Ivan Ivanovich. Also, the man who winked was the second Ivan Ivanovich in the story. *The Precipice* (1, 13). The painter who told Raiskii that he had talent but needed to study. (2, 1). The second Ivan Ivanovich in the novel was Raiskii's friend to whom Raiskii gave papers from his great aunt to read. (3, 2). A third Ivan Ivanovich in the work was the young clerk whom Tychkov reproved for courting Kritskaia. (3, 20). The fourth Ivan Ivanovich was the husband of Natal'ia Ivanovna.

Ivan Ivanych. *A Common Story*. The clerk who brought tobacco to the head of the department. *The Precipice*. A professor whom students called a prophet.

Ivan Kolesso (Ivan the Wheel). *Dead Souls*. One of Korobochka's dead serfs.

Ivan Matveich. *Notes from a Dead House*. A volunteer foreman at the work camp. *Oblomov*. See Mukhoiarov, Ivan Matveich. *The Precipice*. Vikent'ev fished with Ivan Matveich only fifteen minutes before he caught a large carp which he took to Berezhkova.

Ivan Mikhailovich. *Crime and Punishment*. The father of Katerina Ivanovna. He had been a civil colonel in line to be a governor. His family lived very well, and Katerina Ivanovna told her children of her luxurious life at home.

Ivan Nikiforovich. See Dovgochkhum, Ivan Nikiforovich.

Ivan Osipovich. *The Devils*. The former governor of the provincial town and a relative of the Stavrogins. He was a "bit of an old woman."

Ivan Petrovich. *Dead Souls*. A man who was described as a person full of authority with his subordinates, but small and stupid in the presence of his superiors. *The Idiot*. See Ptitsyn, Ivan Petrovich. *Oblomov*. The man who received the order of St. Vladimir. *The Precipice* (1, 1). A worker at the Aianovs' who told pleasantries and gave candy to pretty women. (3, 2). The second Ivan Petrovich in the novel was Berezhkova's landowner neighbor who was interested in politics.

Ivan Potapych. *Dead Souls*. A merchant who lost a fortune. Murazov told Khlubaev that Ivan Potapych was happier working as a clerk than he had been when he was rich.

Ivan Profof'evich. *Poor Fold*. A clerk who Devushkin maintained was the only person in his office staff who wrote as well as he did.

Ivan Semenovich. *A Common Story.* A favorite teacher of Aleksandr
   Aduev. Ivan's lectures delighted his students. *The Double.* The
   clerk who sat in Goliadkin's place at the office when the latter
   was absent.

Ivan Stepanych. *A Common Story.* A man described as the type who
   readied his house for social events when the summer passed.

Ivanchenko. *A Common Story.* The man who received a promotion
   instead of Aleksandr Aduev.

Ivanov. *A Common Story.* Aleksandr Aduev's co-worker who retired; his
   place was then given to Ivanchenko instead of to Aleksandr. *The
   Devils.* Gaganov's former servant who recognized Stepan Verkhovenskii in the country.

Ivlev. *The Precipice.* A friend of Aianov. They played cards together.

Ivolgin, General Ardalion Aleksandrovich. *The Idiot.* A former officer
   who was ruined by drink. He was a notorious liar. He claimed to
   have been Napoleon's servant when he was captured by the
   French as a boy. Ivolgin kept a mistress and stole four hundred
   roubles from Lebedev, but later returned them. He died at the
   end of the novel.

Ivolgin, Gavrila (Gania) Ardal'enovich. *The Idiot.* General Epanchin's
   secretary who was supposed to marry Nastas'ia Barashkova in
   the plot worked out by Totskii. He was marrying her for
   money, to the great shame of his proud but poor family. When
   Nastas'ia ran away with Rogozhin, Gania quit his job. Later he
   helped Prince Myshkin in the Burdovskii matter. Gania found
   out that Pavlichev was not Burdovskii's father.

Ivolgin, Nikolai Ardal'enovich (Kolia). *The Idiot.* General Ivolgin's
   youngest son, who became Prince Myshkin's friend. He went to
   school, looked after his father, and helped his sister Varia with
   errands.

Ivolgina, Nina Aleksandrovna. *The Idiot.* The proud but improverished
   wife of the drunken general. She did not want her son Gania to
   marry for money.

Ivolgina, Varvara Ardal'enovna. *The Idiot.* The proud daughter of the
   impoverished Ivolgin gamily. She married Ptitsyn. She was
   against Gania's marriage to Nastas'ia Barashkova and visited
   the Epanchin family on behalf of her brother's interest in
   Aglaia.

Iziumov. *A Common Story.* The merchant who liked to chase doves from
   his roof every morning.

Izler, Ivan Ivanovich. *Crime and Punishment* (2, 6). The owner of a
popular St. Petersburg summer garden where mineral water
was sold. He often advertised in the papers in the 1860's.

Jacob. *The Brothers Karamazov* (2, 6, 1). The Biblical patriarch of the book
of Genesis (28-32) who was mentioned in Father Zosima's
biography. *The Precipice* (2, 19). After Berezhkova ordered
Openkin out of the house, he told Iakov about Jacob's arguments with God (Gen. 28-32).

Janin Jules (1804-1874). *A Common Story* (2, 3). The author of *Histoire de la
littérature dramatique* (1858). Tafaeva thought of Janin as an exceptional person.

Jenghiz-Khan. *The Brothers Karamazov.* See Ghenghis-Khan.

Job. *The Brothers Karamazov* (1, 3, 1). The Biblical figure who underwent
many tribulations. Grigorii was fond of the story of Job. (2, 6, 1).
The story of Job had a great influence on Father Zosima before
he became a monk.

Job. *The Brothers Karamazov.* An old revered monk who died at the age of
105. He had been a celebrated ascetic, fasting in silence.

Johann. *Crime and Punishment.* The father of Amal'ia Ivanovna. During
the funeral dinner for Marmeladov, Katerina Ivanovna and
Amal'ia Ivanovna argued over their respective backgrounds.
Amal'ia claimed that her father was a burgomeister named
Johann. Katerina laughed, and the two women had a fight.

John, St. *The Brothers Karamazov* (2, 6, 2). Father Zosima read a Biblical
verse from St. John (12, 24) to a man who later confessed his
sins. *Crime and Punishment* (4, 4). When Raskol'nikov and Sonia
discussed the Bible, Sonia read aloud from St. John (11, 19-31)
where Lazarus was raised from the dead.

John the Merciful. *The Brothers Karamazov.* See Ioann Milostivyi.

Jonah. *The Brothers Karamazov* (2, 6, 1). The Biblical figure of the Book of
Jonah who was mentioned in Father Zosima's biography.

Joseph. *The Brothers Karamazov* (2, 6, 1). A Biblical hero in the book of
Genesis (37, 39-50). He was sold into slavery by his jealous
brothers. Father Zosima mentioned him in his biography.

Josephine, Empress (1763-1814). *The Idiot* (4, 4). The first wife of
Napoleon I. General Ivolgin said that when he served as a page
to the French Emperor, he inspired Napoleon to write to the
Empress Josephine. The general failed to remember that
Napoleon divorced Josephine in 1809.

Juan, Don. See Don Juan.

Judas. *Dead Souls* (1, 5). The disciple who betrayed Jesus to his enemies (Matt. 26,49). Sobakevich felt that the people in the town of N-- were Judases and swindlers. *The Double* (8). Goliadkin referred to Petrushka as a Judas when he failed to deliver the note which Goliadkin had written to his double. "Taras Bul'ba," in *Mirgorod*. Taras thought of his son Andrei as a Biblical Judas after Andrei went over to the Poles. *The Village of Stepanchikogo* (1, 8). When Egor Rostanev tried to persuade Foma Fomich Opiskin to leave by giving him money, Opiskin accused him of being a Judas, the deceiver of Christ (Matt. 26, 49).

Judith. *The Precipice* (4, 8). The legendary Jewish heroine who tricked and killed Holofernes. Her story is told in the Apocryphal book of Judith. Raiskii thought that Vera was as cruel as Judith.

Julia. See Iulia.

Jupiter. *The Brothers Karamazov* (4, 12, 14). The Roman god mentioned by Fetiukovich at Dmitrii Karamazov's trial. *A Common Story* (1, 2). Aleksandr Aduev thought that the head of his department could pose as a Jupiter. (2, 3). Tafaeva liked the story of Jupiter's love of an earthly girl. *The Devils* (1, 2, 4). The supreme deity of Roman mythology. Stepan Verkhovenskii, in describing the new governor, von Lembke, stated that a railway clerk will act like Jupiter if given an order to carry out. *The Eternal Husband* (7). Trusotskii said that Vel'chanikov was from the race of Jupiters—god-like, ruling, and judgeful of man by his own petty nature.

Juzyaia. "Taras Bul'ba," in *Mirgorod*. A Polish girl who went to the square in Warsaw with her boy friend to see the Cossacks tortured.

K——, Count. *The Devils*. An aristocrat from St. Petersburg who lived in Paris and accepted Nikolai Stavrogin as his son.

K——, Countess. *The Idiot*. A Russian lady who entered a Catholic convent abroad. Ptitsyn commented that Russians sometimes cannot stand up against those foreign rogues who seek to convert them.

K——ski. *Notes from a Dead House*. A Polish nobleman, quiet and kind, who paced the yard in his leisure time. He wanted to preserve his health by fresh air and exercise.

Kaidanov, I. K. (1782-1843). *A Common Story* (2, 3). The Russian historian who played down the influence of Alexander the Great on later history. Raiskii read his historical studies.

Kalmikov. *The Brothers Karamazov*. Captain Snegirev's landlady.

Kalganov, Petr Fomich. *The Brothers Karamazov*. A distant relative of Miusov and an acquaintance of Dmitrii's who attended the party at Mokroe. Kalganov was thoughtful but absentminded. Miusov tried to persuade the good-looking relative to go abroad to a university.

Kalinnikov. *Oblomov*. A financier in St. Petersburg. When Sholtz's father sent him to the capital, he told his son to stop at Kalinnikov's for three hundred roubles to start his new life.

Kamenev. *Notes from a Dead House*. A notoriously cruel highway bandit. The narrator once saw Kamenev but felt that the convict Gazin looked more cruel.

Kapanat'ev. *Dead Souls*. Korobochka's neighboring landowner.

Kanaris, Constantine (1790-1877). *Dead Souls* (1, 5). A hero of the Greek War for Independence. He defeated the Turkish fleet. His portrait hung in Sobakevish's living room.

Kanitolina. *Dead Souls*. Fedot's mother, who was a house wench.

Kantemir, Prince Antioch (1764-1723). *A Common Story* (2, 3). The noted classical writer. Tafaeva's Russian teacher brought her Kantemir's works to read.

Kapernaumov. *Crime and Punishment*. The family with whom Sonia Marmeladova roomed after she became a prostitute. All the members had cleft palates.

Karamazov, Aleksei Fedorovich (Alesha). *The Brothers Karamazov*. Fedor's youngest son, who was deeply religious. He was an early lover of humanity and adopted the monastic life.

Karamazov, Dmitrii Fedorovidh (Mitia). *The Brothers Karamazov*. Fedor's oldest son, who hated his father and was convicted of murdering him.

Karamazov, Fedor Pavlovich. *The Brothers Karamazov*. The head of the Karamazov household, who was noted for his depravity and cynicism. His murder by one of his sons caused a sensational trial in which Dmitrii was convicted.

Karamazov, Ivan Fedorovich. *The Brothers Karamazov*. The second son of the family, who was tormented by philosophical questions on the value and meaning of life. He early showed an unusual aptitude for learning and attended a university when he grew up. He published brilliant reviews of books on various subjects.

Karamazova, Adelaida Ivanovna (née Miusova). *The Brothers Karamazov*. Fedor Karamazov's first wife and the mother of Dmitrii. She was a beautiful girl of noble background, and the author did not explain why she married the puny weakling Fedor Karamazov. It was said that she beat up Fedor in their marriage squabbles and finally ran off with a divinity student. She died of either typhus or starvation in a garret in St. Petersburg.

Karamazova, Sof'ia Ivanovna. *The Brothers Karamazov*. Fedor Karamazov's second wife, and the mother of Ivan and Alesha. She was a deacon's daughter who had been reared by an old woman who was an insufferable tyrant. Sof'ia eloped with Fedor and was treated miserably. She died when Alesha was born.

Karamzin, Nikolai Mikhailovich (1766-1826). *A Common Story* (2, 3). The author of the twelve-volume *History of the Russian State* (1816-1824). After reading French novels, Tafaeva did not like to read the works of Karamzin. *Dead Souls* (1, 7). Some of the town folk in N—— even read Karamzin's history. *The Idiot* (1, 1). Lebedev mentioned Karamzin's history when referring to Prince Myshkin's historical name. *Oblomov* (4, 9). A friend of Alekseev's thought that Karamzin was the best Russian author. *The Precipice* (1, 10). While spending the summer at Berezhkova's estate, Raiskii read Karamzin. *The Village of Stepanchikogo* (1, 3). The author of *Frol Silin* (1791), in which Foma Fomich Opiskin saw epic qualities when it was actually a sentimental tale.

Karenev. *Notes from a Dead House*. A dangerous man with very little or no intelligence. The convicts left him alone.

Kariakin Eremei. *Dead Souls*. A runaway serf whom Chichikov bought from Pliushkin.

Karl. *Crime and Punishment*. The bouncer in Luiza Ivanovna's house of dubious reputation. When he received a hit in the eye by a boisterous man, Luiza summoned the police.

Karmazinov. *The Devils* A supercilious, pretentious novelist who was a relative of Mrs. von Lembke. Dostoevskii patterned the literary figure after I. S. Turgenev (1818-1873).

Karolina Ivanovna. *The Double*. A German woman who had been Mr. Goliadkin's landlady before the novel began. Goliadkin called her a vile, beastly, brazen German. "The Overcoat." A woman of German extraction whom Stepan Varlamovich decided to visit after attending a party.

Karp. *The Brothers Karamazov*. A dangerous culprit who Grigorii said fathered Smerdiakov. *Dead Souls*. A village priest who would someday find the money of Pliushkin tucked away in a bureau drawer. *The Precipice*. A name used by Raiskii when speaking of general literary types.

Kartashov. *The Brothers Karamazov.* An eight-year-old boy who read
Kolia Krassotkin's book on Troy.

Katchalnikov. *The Brothers Karamazov.* The justice of the peace who said
that Dmitrii was unstable.

Katen'ka. *The Brothers Karamazov.* A diminutive for Katerina Ivanovna.
A Common Story. Petr Aduev kept inventing names for Naden'ka,
for instance, Katen'ka.

Katerina. *The Gambler.* Polina Aleksandrovna's deceased mother whom
Tarasevicheva had highly respected. Because of her feelings,
the old lady offered to take Polina back to Russia and care for
her. *Notes from a Dead House.* When the narrator went to
Gorianchikov's lodging after his death, he learned that his
former acquaintance had taken a fancy to his landlady's granddaughter and had had a mass sung for her in church. *The
Precipice.* Sof'ia's friend with whom she planned to go to the
Summer Garden.

Katerina Ivanovna. *The Brothers Karamazov.* A colonel's beautiful daughter who offered Dmitrii Karamazov her body to save her
father's honor in a scandal. Dmitrii loaned her the money she
needed but did not take advantage of her. When she returned
the money, she offered to be his wife. He accused her of loving
her own virtue, not him, and deserted her for Grushen'ka.
Crime and Punishment. See Marmeladova, Katerina Ivanovna.

Katerina Mikhailovna. *Dead Souls.* The sister-in-law of Pobedonosnov.
The blonde with whom Chichikov was talking at the ball began
to yawn when he told of visiting in Penza and meeting Katerina
Mikhailovna.

Katia. *The Brothers Karamazov.* A diminutive for Katerina Ivanovna.
Crime and Punishment. A girl in a low haunt who sang gutter
songs. Svidrigailov heard her before committing suicide. *The
Eternal Husband.* When Vel'chanikov was looking for Trustoskii
after Liza's death, he went to a house where a certain Katia
remembered Trustoskii. She said that she would help find him
but did not. *The Idiot.* Nastas'ia Filippovna's maid, who was
frightened at Rogozhin's entrance at the party with a band of
drunken followers. *Oblomov.* Ol'ga Il'inskaia's maid who said
that Ol'ga talked in her sleep during her infatuation with
Oblomov.

Kedril. *Notes from a Dead House* (1, 11). A character from the play *Kedril the
Gluttonous,* which was presented by the prisoners. The work was
based on a comedy entitled *Don Pedro,* which was printed in a

collection called *Russian Dramatic Works 1672-1725* by N. S. Tikhonravov in 1874. Don Pedro was changed to Pedrilo and then to Kedril.

Keller. *The Idiot.* The man who wrote the article denouncing Prince Myshkin. In a satirical way the article said that the prince should give money to "Pavlichev's son" Burdovskii. It also insulted Burdovskii's mother.

Kepler, Johann (1571-1630). *Crime and Punishment* (3, 5). The noted German astronomer. Raskol'nikov maintained that if one or more persons would have to be sacrificed to bring the theories of Kepler to light, the sacrifice would be justified.

Kh--. *The Precipice.* Aianov and Raiskii's mutual friend.

Khaliava. "Vii," in *Mirgorod.* A tall, broad-shouldered theologian who had a habit of stealing anything in his reach. He had a gloomy temper and liked to hide in tall grass when he was drunk.

Khanasareva, Aleksandra Ivanovna. *Dead Souls.* Khlobuev's rich aunt who did not help her relatives.

Kharlamov. *Crime and Punishment.* A property owner. Trying to find Raskol'nikov, Razumikhin remembered that his friend once lived in a house owned by a certain Kharlamov, but he was mistaken. Raskol'nikov lived in Bukh's house. Both houses are extant.

Kharpakin. *Dead Souls.* Korobochka's neighboring landowner.

Khat'kov. *The Precipice.* The man who spread the gossip about Sof'ia's faux pas.

Khavroshka. *Notes from a Dead House.* A bread vender who sold her wares in the prison.

Kheraskov, Mikhail Mikhailovich (1773-1807). *Oblomov* (1, 9). The classical writer whose work *Rossiiada* (1779) was read to Oblomov by his father.

Kheruvimov. *Crime and Punishment.* A bookseller and publisher of natural-science manuals whom Razumikhin described to Raskol'nikov.

Khlestakov, Ivan Aleksandrovich. *The Brothers Karamazov* (4, 11, 9). The famous literary figure from Gogol's play *Revizor* (1836). The devil mentioned the noted trickster in Ivan Karamazov's nightmare.

Khlib. "Taras Bul'ba," in *Mirgorod.* The leader of the Pereiaslav troops who were killed while having a drinking bout. Khlib was taken prisoner by the Poles and displayed naked to the Cossacks from the city walls.

Khlobuev, Semen Semenovich. *Dead Souls*. A ruined landowner whose estate was inspected by Chichikov with the intention of purchase.

Khlopova, Anna Andreevna. *Oblomov*. A woman with six children.

Khludiakov. *The Idiot*. The tenants in the Rogozhins' house. The Khludiakovs were members of the sect called *Skoptsy*. See *Skopets*.

Khokhlakova. *The Brothers Karamazov*. The mother of the crippled Lise. Madame Khokhlakova had severe religious convictions and took her daughter to holy men in the hope of obtaining a miraculous cure.

Khobhalakova, Lise. *The Brothers Karamazov*. The daughter of Madame Khokhlakova. Lise was engaged to Alesha Karamazov but broke off the engagement. She was a cripple who was spoiled and demanded her own way in all matters. She believed that men declare that they hate evil, but secretly they love it. She read nasty books and loved the murder of Fedor Karamazov.

Kholmskii. *The Village of Stepanchikogo*. The family in the novel *The Kholmskii Family* (1832) by D. N. Begichev (1786-1855). Ezhevikin compared his own family to the Kholmskiis.

Khovanskii, Prince Aleksandr Nikolaevich (1771-1857). *Dead Souls* (1, 11). A Minister of Finance who signed paper money. Bribes became known as "Khovanskii's letter of recommendation."

Khozarov. *A Common Story*. A family that Aleskandr Aduev considered on the level of animals.

Khozdazat. "The Overcoat." A name suggested to Akakii Akakievich's mother for her son, but she settled on Akakii.

Khozrev-Mirza. "The Portrait." A Persian prince who was the head of the embassy in St. Petersburg in August, 1829, when the famed Russian writer A. S. Griboevdov (1795-1829) was killed in Persia.

Khrapovistkov. *Dead Souls*. A name derived from the Russian verb to snore (Khrapet'). Gogol' mentioned the phrase "to drop in on Khrapovistkov," which meant to sleep and snore.

Khrulve. *Dead Souls*. The man who was in charge of accepting reports on the Koshkakev estate before it was closed.

Khvasov. *Notes from a Dead House*. A convict who was a master of deception. Nobody believed him.

Khvostyrev. *Dead Souls*. The man from whom Nozdrev stole a pup.

Kifa Mokievich. *Dead Souls*. A man inclined to intellectual speculation who did not correct his son in fear that the town of N— would think his son was a bad boy.

Kilian. *The Adolescent.* A clerk in a downstairs office in the building where old Prince Sokolskii lived.

Kinder. *The Idiot.* An acquaintance of Rogozhin. At Nastas'ia Filippovna's party, Ptitsyn said that Rogozhin was collecting 100,000 roubles for the hostess and Kinder was helping him.

King of Prussia. *The Idiot* (4,4). A reference to Frederick William III (1797-1840). According to General Ivolgin, when he was a page of Napoleon I, the Emperor claimed that his hatred of the King of Prussia was everlasting. Ivolgin was noted for his prevarications.

King of Rome. *The Idiot* (4,4). See Napoleon II.

King of Spain. "The Notes of a Madman," in *Arabesques.* The madman who came to the conclusion that he was the King of Spain. *The Underground Man* (2,1). Dostoevskii referred to the madman in Gogol's story.

King of Sweden. *The Adolescent* (2,1,2). A reference to Charles X (1622-1660), who saw a visionary assembly of Swedish parliamentarians in the royal palace. Versilov's landlord mentioned the king's vision.

Kirdiaga. "Taras Bul'ba," in *Mirgorod.* The Cossack whom Taras helped select as headman of the Zaporozhe camp. A fist fight settled the election.

Kiril. *Dead Souls.* The dean of the church in the town of N—.

Kiril Kirilovich. *The Precipice.* A man who was happy and then became grief stricken when his wife left him. Berezhkova used him as an example in a discussion of fate. She felt that fortune acts negatively on people who are always happy.

Kirilov. *The Devils.* An idealist who wanted to prove his self-will by killing himself. Before his suicide, Petr Verkhovenskii forced him to sign a letter accepting the guilt for Shatov's murder.

Kirilov, Semen Semenovich. *The Precipice.* Raiskii's teacher at the Art Institute who did not approve of the portraits of Belovodova painted by Raiskii.

Kiriusha. *Dead Souls.* Khlobuev's servant who was ordered to bring champagne to celebrate the purchase of an estate by Chichikov. *The Precipice.* Berezhkova's servant who was very attentive.

Kisha. *The Precipice.* The piano tuner who had a calendar with a picture of a Spanish prince.

Kislorodov. *The Idiot* (3,5). A student whose name means "oxygen" in Russian. He was mentioned by Ipollit Terentev. Dostoevskii was indicating that the possessor of the name had oxygen but not a soul. He was making fun of the nihilistic students of the period.

Kisloedov. *Dead Souls.* A town official in N——.

Klopstock, Friedrich Gottlieb (1724-1803). *The Precipice* (2,5). A German writer. Kozlov tried to read Klopstock's works but could not finish them because of their lack of appeal.

Klopstock, Ivan Ivanich. *Crime and Punishment.* A chief counselor who did not pay for the half-dozen linen shirts which Katerina Ivanovna Marmeladova made for him. He drove her away, saying that the shirt collars were not made like the pattern.

Knif. *The Idiot.* The man who cheated Parfen Ragozhin in cards when he was squandering the money which his father had entrusted to him.

Knopp. *Crime and Punishment* (5,1). The owner of a noted store in St. Petersburg where foreign items, especially English, were sold. Lozhin realized that if he had showered Dunia with gifts from stores like Knopp's, she would not have turned him down so easily.

Kobelev, General. *Crime and Punishment.* A person being sought by someone in the address bureau. When Razumikhin searched for Raskol'nikov, he found his address at the bureau and overheard someone discussing General Kobelev.

Kobilatnikova. *Crime and Punishment.* An acquaintance of Lebeziatnikov. At the Marmeladov funeral dinner, Lebeziatnikov explained that he was late because he was visiting Kobilatnikova. After his arrival, Lebeziatnikov exposed Luzhin's accusation of theft against Sonia Marveladova as a false claim.

Kobita. "Taras Bul'ba," in *Mirgorod.* A young Cossack who killed a fine-looking Pole before he himself was shot in the temple.

Kobylin. *Notes from a Dead House.* A narrow-minded and stupid convict who was generally good-natured.

Kock, Paul de (1794-1871). *The Adolescent* (2,8,2). The French novelist noted for his portraiture of cheap dissipation in low and middle-class life in Paris. Old Prince Nikolai Sokolskii said that Kock had neither a sense of measure nor good taste, but did have some talent. *The Brothers Karamazov* (1,3,4). Dmitrii Karamazov mentioned the writer of dissipation in Paris. *The Devils* (1,1,5). Stepan Verkhovenskii read Kock secretly in the garden. (1,2,4). Varvara Stavrogina accused Stepan Verkhovenskii of reading only Kock and nothing else. *The Gambler* (13). The narrator read Kock's books because there was nothing else to do in the evening. *Poor Folk* (June 26). Makar Devushkin saw a novel by Kock at Rataziaev's and was shocked. He informed Varvara that the book was not for her eyes to see. *The Village of Stepanchikogo* (2,3). Foma Fomich Opiskin secretly read the novels of Kock.

Kokh. *The Eternal Husband.* An old friend of the Trusotskiis who was a doctor. Natal'ia looked forward to his aid, but she died before he came. *Crime and Punishment.* Kokh was the name of the young man who came to the door of Alena Ivanovna after Raskol'nakov had killed her.

Koko, Prince. *The Precipice.* The friend of Aianov and Raiskii who married Eudoxie. Aianov informed Raiskii of the marriage.

Kokorev, Vasilii Aleksandrovich (1817-1889). *The Adolescent* (1, 5, 2). A wealthy financier in Russia. Arkadii Dolgorukii was sure that he could become as wealthy as Kokorev.

Kolbasnikov. *The Brothers Karamazov.* The master of classical studies in the boys' school. Kolia Krasotkin told Il'iiusha Snegirev on his sickbed the latest epigram the boys had written about the teacher of classics.

Kolechichsha. *Oblomov.* The nurse who wove stories about epic heroes for Oblomov when he was a child.

Kolia. *The Brothers Karamazov.* A diminutive for Nikolai Krasotkin. *The Underground Man.* Zverkov's friend who had three thousand serfs and who helped Zverkov in an intimate affair.

Koller. *Notes from a Dead House.* The Polish guard whom Kulikov and A——v were able to talk into participating in their escape plan.

Koloper. "Taras Bul'ba," in *Mirgorod.* A Cossack about whom Taras inquired at the Zaporozhe camp. He learned that Koloper's hide had been torn off at Kizkir.

Kolpakov. *The Idiot.* A man who General Ivolgin claimed had been buried for six months and then turned up alive. The general told the story to the great consternation of his wife.

Kolymiagin, Vasilii Sevast'ianych. *Oblomov.* A guest at Ovchinin's dinner.

Kondrat'eva. *The Brothers Karamazov.* The well-to-do widow who nursed Lisaveta while she was pregnant with Fedor Karamazov's illegitimate son. Lizaveta escaped from her house and gave birth to Smerdiakov in the Karamazovs' bathhouse.

Konev. *A Common Story.* A business partner of Petr Aduev. *The Idiot.* The acquaintance who informed Parfei Ragozhin about his father's demise.

Konigstein. *A Common Story.* The tailor who made the clothes for Aleksandr Aduev which his uncle did not approve of.

Koral'ia (Coralie). *The Idiot.* A woman of society whom Lebedev claimed he knew very well when he was running around with Likhachev.

Koreisha, Ivan Iakovlich (1780-1861). *The Village of Stepanchikogo* (1,1). A lame-brained prophet who had a following in Moscow. Foma Fomich Opiskin had an influence on the ladies in the Rostanev household similar to the influence which Koreisha had on the citizens of Moscow who believed the sick man's prophesies.

Korenev. *Notes from a Dead House.* A former brigand chieftain who was a ferocious brute. He represented a complete triumph of flesh over the spirit. But the narrator felt that he was a coward compared to Orlov. He taught Gorianchikov how to take clothes off over his chains in the shower room.

Korneplodov, Pavel Pavlovich. *The Brothers Karamazov.* The lawyer whom Dmitrii Karamazov consulted about his inheritance.

Kornoukhov. *The Village of Stepanchikogo.* Egor Rastanev's acquaintance whose wife, sister, and cousin were insulted by Egor during a theater performance. Egor asked his friend who the ugly scarecrow was in the box next to him, and he answered that it was his cousin. Egor changed the victim to the next lady, and she was Kornoukhov's sister. The final attempt to change the blunder fell on Kornoukhov's wife.

Korobochka, Nastas'ia Petrovna. *Dead Souls.* The greedy old landowner who gave Chichikov refuge during a terrible storm. She went to town to find out the going price for dead serfs. *The Devils* (1, 3, 8). Stepan Verkhovenskii maintained that Praskovi'ia Drozhdova was as spiteful and provocative as Gogol's literary figure Korobochka.

Korovaev. *The Devils.* The man to whom Captain Lebiatkin passed off counterfeit French notes.

Korovii Kirpich (Cow-dung-brick). *Dead Souls.* A dead serf whom Chichikov agreed to buy.

Korovkin. *The Adolescent.* The name which Arkadii Dolgorukii thought he was called by a guest at Lambert's when Arkadii went there to satisfy his curiosity as to why Dar'ia had given him Lambert's address. *The Brothers Karamazov.* A former schoolmate mentioned by Ivan Karamazov during his nightmare. *The Village of Stepanchikogo.* Egor Rostanev mentioned him as a man he had met while traveling. Sergei Aleksandrovich could not understand why his uncle had interrupted their conversation to mention Korovkin.

Korzha, Fedor. "Taras Bul'ba," in *Mirgorod*. A Cossack killed by a Pole from a princely family. The Pole was then killed by a Cossack.

Koshkarev. *Dead Souls.* A landowner who was called crazy by his neighbors. He wanted his peasants to read science and art books, and preferred that the women dress as ladies.

Koshkin. *Notes from a Dead House.* The convict who played the role of the Brahmin in the play *Kedril the Gluttonous*, presented by the convicts.

Kos'ma. *Dead Souls.* The peasant to whom Petukh gave orders on how to pull the fish net that Petukh was entangled in.

Kostanzhoglo, Konstantin Fedorovich. *Dead Souls.* Platonov's brother-in-law, who was an excellent agriculturist.. *The Underground Man* (2, 1). A fictitious landowner from Gogol's *Dead Souls* (1852).

Kostia. *The Brothers Karamazov.* The seven-year-old son of the doctor's wife who rented rooms in the Krasotkin home.

Kostiakov. *A Common Story.* Zaezzhalov's old friend who lived in St. Petersburg. Zaezzhalov asked Petr Aduev to drop in on Kostiakov when Petr was in the northern capital.

Kotzebue, August Friedrich Ferdinand von (1761-1819). *Dead Souls* (1, 1). The German dramatist who spent much time in Russia. His play was given in the town of N—— when Chichikov stopped there.

Kovrigin. *The Precipice.* An excellent student whose name was given as an example to Raiskii.

Kozel'. *Crime and Punishment.* A German cabinetmaker in whose house the Marmeladovs lived.

Kozlov, Leontii. *The Precipice.* A deacon's son who knew Greek and Latin. He became a friend of Raiskii at the university.

Kozlova, Ul'iana Andreevna (Ulia, Ulin'ka). *The Precipice.* The wife of Leontii Kozlov. She continually spoke badly of others.

Kozolup. "Taras Bul'ba," in *Mirgorod*. A Cossack whom Taras greeted at the Zaporozhe camp.

Kraevskii, A. A. (1810-1889). *The Devils* (1, 1, 6). The publisher of the journal *Notes of the Fatherland* who was hated by Dostoevskii for exploiting his workers. Kraevskii kept the editorial offices of his journal in his home, which still stands in Moscow.

Kraft. *The Adolescent.* Efin Averev's friend whose face was free of the slightest suspicion of wickedness, but he was not innocent. He was blonde and twenty-six years old.

Krakhotkin. *The Village of Stepanchikogo*. The former officer who was forced to resign from the service through "an unpleasant incident." He was broke and married Egor Rostanev's mother as a means of livelihood. He soon became an invalid and spent the last years of his life making everyone miserable. Foma Fomich Opiskin came into the household as his reader.

Krakhotkina, Agaf'ia Tiofeevna. *The Village of Stepanchikogo*. Egor Rostanev's mother, who married a general at forty-two in order to be secure in her old age. She blamed her son for her marriage because he did not want to stay a bachelor and support her. Rostanev had to support his mother and her new husband.

Kramskoi, Ivan Nikolaevich (1837-1887). *The Brothers Karamazov* (1, 3, 6). An artist who was an enemy of the democratic artist movement of the 1860's. Dostoevskii knew the painter personally, and both artists respected each other's work.

Krasnonsov. *Dead Souls*. An official in the town of N——.

Krasotkin. *The Brothers Karamazov*. An official whose son became Alesha Karamazov's disciple.

Krasotkin, Nikolai Ivanovich. *The Brothers Karamazov*. The young boy who was spoiled by his mother but had the respect of his classmates. He was stabbed with a penknife by Il'iusha Snegirov. Later he became Alesha Karamazov's disciple.

Krasotkina, Anna Fedorovna. *The Brothers Karamazov*. The mother of Kolia who lived in a small house near Plotnikov's shop.

Kravchenko. *The Brothers Karamazov*. The physician who declared that Katerina Ivanovna's father was ill and thereby helped him escape governmental inspectors when he was involved in a scandal.

Kristofor Ivanovich. *The Devils*. An acquaintance of Lisa Tushina in Switzerland. When Nikolai Stavrogin and Lisa met the next day after the fire that disrupted the town ball, she said that she did not wish to stay as long as Kristofor Ivanovich once did. Nikolai did not recall the incident she referred to.

Kritskaia, Polina Karpovna. *The Precipice*. A local lioness of society who attracted Raiskii with her free speech and daring glances. She loved admirers and spread untrue rumors about the size of her following.

Kriukov. *Crime and Punishment*. The man who had just left a cab with a lady on his arm when he witnessed Nikolai Dement'ev and Dmitriri fighting on the ground after the murder of Alena Ivanovna.

Krylov, Ivan Andreevich (1768-1844). *The Adolescent* (1, 6, 3). The noted
Russian fabulist whose poems were loved by Arkadii Dolgorukii. *A Common Story* (2, 1). When Aleksandr Aduev was
disappointed, he read Krylov's fables. *Dead Souls* (1, 11).
Chichikov's school teacher did not like Krylov's fables. *Dead
Souls* (1, 11). Chichikov's school teacher did not like Krylov
because he wrote, "Drink, but know what you're doing." *The
Devils* (1, 1, 9). Shatov stated that the critic V. Belinskii was like
the inquisitive man in Krylov's fable who did not notice an
elephant in a museum of curiosities. Shatov felt that Belinskii
overlooked the Russian people in his famous letter to Gogol'. (1,
5, 4). When Captain Lebiatkin asked if he could read his poem
"The Cockroach," Varvara Stavrogina thought that he wanted to
read a fable by Krylov, who used insects in his poems. *The Double*
(4). When Goliadkin thought of the line "To open it you simply
raised the lid," he was thinking of Krylov's fable "The Small
Chest" ("Larchik") (1808), which described several clever attempts to open a chest except in the obvious way. The theme of
the fable is that difficulties should not be seen where they do
not exist. *The Idiot* (1, 13). At Nastas'ia Filippovna's party, Ferdyshchenko cited Krylov's fable "The Aged Lion" ("Lev
sostarevshiisia," 1825) and said that he and General Epanchin
represented the figures in the fable: the General was the lion,
and Ferdyshchenko was the ass. The General agreed with the
latter. *Oblomov* (2, 1). In childhood, Sholtz studied Krylov's
fables.

Kubrikov. *The Devils*. A sixty-two-year-old man who claimed that
during the trouble in the town he was under the influence of
the "Internationale." The first International was named by Karl
Marx in 1864.

Kuchum. *Poor Folk*. A character from a story by Rataziaev. Kuchum
supposedly killed his daughter by accident. He was blind and
entered her tent to kill her lover Ermak, but killed her instead.

Kudriumov. *The Adolescent*. The redheaded youth at Dergachev's who
was rather rude with Arkadii Dolgorukii when he refused to
agree with certain political arguments.

Kukol'nik, Nestor Vasil'evich (1809-1868). *The Devils* (1, 1, 5). A second-
rate Russian poet. Varvara Stavrogina fell in love with a portrait of the writer when she was a girl. The portrait was painted
by K. P. Briullov in 1836. Varvara modeled Stepan Verkhovenskii's clothes after the apparel in the writer's picture. (2,

9, 1). When Stepan Verkhovenskii burst out crying after the raid on his living quarters, the narrator was amazed that the man who had borne himself as high as Kukol'nik could have fallen so low.

Kukubenko. "Taras Bul'ba," in *Mirgorod*. A Cossack suggested as a new headman; but someone shouted that his mother's milk was still dribbling from his mouth, and he was dropped from consideration. Kukubenko was chief of the Nezamaikovskii troops. He was later killed in battle.

Kulakov. *The Idiot*. The occupant of the apartment to which General Ivolgin led Prince Myshkin by mistake while they were looking for General Sokolovich. The name Kulakov was on the door of the apartment, but the occupant was not at home.

Kulikov. *Notes from a Dead House*. The veterinarian who was replaced by Elkin. Kulikov was energetic and tried to escape with the help of a guard. He was unsuccessful in his attempt.

Kul'kova, Marina. *Oblomov*. The serf who gave birth to quadruplets. The news gave the estate Oblomovka some notoriety.

Kunigunde. *The Precipice* (5, 10). A legendary lady in Kynast Castle, which was built over an abyss. She vowed not to marry anyone who could not ride around the rim of the canyon. Many perished, but one succeeded and then spurned her. Vera thought of her despair after she had parted with Mark.

Kuntz. "Nevskii Prospect," in *Arabesques*. A carpenter who was a drinking companion of Schiller the ironmonger.

Kupfer. *The Idiot*. A man who had signed some IOUs. When an unknown carriage drove up to a group at Pvalovsk, a strange voice called to Evgenii Rodomskii that he was not to worry because Rogozhin had bought up Kupfer's IOUs. Rodomskii maintained that he knew nothing about any IOUs. Prince S—— later identified the voice as that of Nastas'ia Filippovna.

Kurmyshev. *The Idiot*. The man who tried to hit Nastas'a Filippovna after she had hit him with a whip. Prince Myshkin restrained him from hitting her, and Kurmyshev challenged him to a duel. Their difficulties were settled by Rodomskii.

Kuropatkina. *The Village of Stepanchikogo*. An actress who ran away with an officer during a performance without waiting until the end of the play. Egor Rostanev told the actress's tale to the great displeasure of Foma Fomich Opiskin.

Kutuzov. *The Devils*. A man who attended Stepan Verkhovenskii's circle but died soon after its formation.

Kutuzov, Mikhail Illarionovich, Prince of Smokensk (1745-1813). *Dead Souls* (1, 3). The famous Russian general whose portrait was hanging in Korobochka's living room.

Kuvshinikov. *The Brothers Karamazov* (3, 8, 7). A literary character from Gogol's *Dead Souls* who Maksimov maintained was actually a person from real life. Maksimov also claimed to be the Maksimov in Gogol's masterpiece. *Dead Souls.* Kuvshinikov was one of the officers at the fair with Nazarov.

Kuz'ka. *Oblomov.* A peasant at the Oblomov estate. In that corner of the earth where Oblomovka was located, nothing much ever happened. At the most, the village boys might declare that a horrible snake was after Kuz'ka.

Kuz'ma. *A Common Story.* The husband of Agashka, Aleksandr Aduev's childhood playmate. *The Precipice.* A servant at Raiskii's estate Malinovka. Also, the second Kuz'ma in the novel was Vikent'eva's servant. *The Village of Stepanchikogo.* The barber at Stepanchikogo whose duty it was to curl Falalei's hair on holidays.

Kuz'ma Fedotych. *The Precipice.* A merchant who had great respect for Berezhkova.

Kuz'minichna. *Oblomov.* The nurse of Ol'ga Il'inskaia. Ol'ga thought that Oblomov looked at her the way her nurse used to.

Kuzmitchev. *The Brothers Karamazov.* A name mentioned by a market woman when Kol'ia Krasotkin was teasing a clerk.

Kuznetsov. *Oblomov.* A former colleague of Oblomov. Sud'binskii informed Oblomov that Kuznetsov had married.

Kvasov. *Notes from a Dead House.* The convict known as an idle chatterer. He brought the news that the Major was leaving.

L——n. *The Devils.* See Lunin, M.S.

Lacenaire, Pierre François (1800-1836). *The Idiot* (3, 8). The famous French murderer who killed others as a protest against society. After Ippolit Terentev tried to kill himslef, Radomskii called him a Lacenaire. Dostoevskii included an article about Lacenaire in his journal *Vremia (Time)* (1861, #2, 1-50).

Lambert, Maurice. *The Adolescent.* Arkadii Dolgorukii's schoolmate who became a crook and cringed before everyone.

Lame Teacher. *The Devils.* A guest at the Virginskii's group meeting who defended Shigalev's theory on the organization of mankind. He also confronted Petr Verkhovenskii by asking him to answer his own question on whether he would inform the police if he knew of a planned political murder. Petr had forced several to compromise themselves with their answer and was embarrassed when the lame teacher put him in the same situation.

Lamonde. *Poor Folk* (June 1). The writer of a French grammar book published in Moscow in 1831.

Lancaster, Joseph (1778-1838). *Dead Souls* (1, 8). The educator who established the system whereby the teacher worked with the best students and they in turn worked with the weaker students.

Langvagen, Baron von. *Oblomov*. Ol'ga Il'inskaia's guardian and the only friend of Ol'ga's aunt.

Laptev. *Oblomov*. A runaway serf from Oblomov's estate.

Larionov. *The Idiot*. The staff captain who died and was replaced by Prince Nikolai Myshkin.

La Vallière, Duchesse de. Françoise Louise de la Baume le Blanc (1644-1710). *Dead Souls* (1, 10). A favorite of Louis XIV. She was mentioned in the novel *Viconte de Bragelonne* by Alexandre Dumas père. Chichikov read about her when he was sick with a cold, not knowing that the town was discussing his purchase of dead souls from various landowners. *Notes from a Dead House* (1, 7). The novel *Countess de Vallière* (1804) by S. F. Genlis (1746-1830) was translated into Russian in 1805. "Old-World Landowners," in *Mirgorod*. A picture of Louis XIV's mistress hung on the walls of the Tovstogubs' cottage.

Lavinia. *The Precipice* (2, 7). In mythology, Lavinia was the daughter of the King of Italy. Kozlov called his wife Lavinia at times.

Lavrovskii. *The Adolescent*. Arkadii Dolgorukii's school friend with whom Arkadii often discussed the joys of being married.

Law, John (1671-1729). *The Adolescent* (1, 5, 2). The Scottish financier who escaped to the Continent after being condemned to death for killing Eward Wilson in a duel. When his financial dealings in France collapsed, he declined Tsar Petr I's invitation to take charge of Russia's finances. Law died poor and forgotten in Venice.

Lazarus. *The Brothers Karamazov* (2, 6, 3). The Biblical figure (Luke 16) who was mentioned by Father Zosima in his biography. *Crime and Punishment* (3, 5). Razumikhin asked Raskol'nikov if he believed that Lazarus had risen from the dead. Raskol'nikov answered that he did believe it literally. (4, 4). When Sonia and Raskol'nikov were discussing the New Testament, Sonia asked about Lazarus. (Epilogue 2). Raskol'nikov thought of Lazarus at the end of the book, the indication being that he too will become a new man. *The Idiot* (3, 5). In Ippolit Terentev's article "My Essential Explanation," the Biblical figure Lazarus is mentioned.

Lefebure. *The Devils.* The person who exposed Praskov'ia Drozdova's lie about a Hussar officer's marriage proposal when Praskov'ia was in a boarding school.

Lebedev, Kostia. *The Idiot.* A school friend of Kolia Ivolgin. They bought a hedgehog from a peasant and were persuaded by Aglaia Epanchina to sell the animal to her.

Lebedev, Lukian Timofeevich. *The Idiot.* The clerk who met Prince Myshkin and Parfen Rogozhin on the train to St. Petersburg. He became a hanger-on in Parfen's band and helped him collect 100,000 roubles with which to buy Nastas'ia Barashkova. Lebedev helped Keller write an article denouncing the prince.

Lebedeva, Elena. *The Idiot.* Lebedev's wife, who died in childbirth five weeks before Prince Myshkin came to St. Petersburg.

Lebedeva, Liubov'. *The Idiot.* Lebedev's infant daughter, whose mother died in childbirth.

Lebedeva, Vera Lubianovna. *The Idiot.* Lebedev's daughter, who was so filled with grief after Prince Myshkin lapsed into idiocy that she fell ill. She later began a correspondence with Evgenii Radomskii.

Lebeziatnikov, Andrei Semenovich. *Crime and Punishment.* A young man with progressive ideas. He shared a room with Luzhin and revealed the latter's dishonesty when Sonia Marmeladova was accused of theft. Lebeziatnikov believed in free love, equality for women, and communal societies.

Lebiatkin, Captain Ignatius. *The Devils.* The lover of Mrs. Virginskii. He claimed to be an army captain. He was killed with his sister by Fedka the convict.

Lebiatkina, Mar'ia Timofeevna. *The Devils.* The cripple whom Nikolai Stavrogin married as a joke. Mentally unbalanced, she spent her days telling her own fortune with cards. She was murdered by Fedka.

Lebrecht. *The Adolescent.* The deceased owner of the apartment where Arkadii Dolgorukii went to an auction and bought an album in red morocco.

Legros. *The Idiot.* The criminal whom Prince Myshkin, while living abroad, saw guillotined.

Lembke, Andrei Antonovich von. *The Devils*. The governor who replaced Ivan Osipovich. With Lembke's arrival, a noticeable
change took place in the town society's attitude toward Varvara
Stavrogina and Stepan Verkhovenskii. Lembke was from the
elite class of old Russia, well-educated and proud.

Lembke, Iulia Mikhailovna von. *The Devils*. The wife of the governor.
She created a large fete that turned into a scandal. She was
always for both sides of a matter: for the aristocratic element
and for the free-and-easy manners of young people. Peter
Verkhovenskii gained her favor by the grossest flattery.

Lenitsin, Fedor Fedorovich. *Dead Souls*. Tentetnikov's former department head who informed Tentetnikov that if he were not
satisfied he could retire. He did.

Léon. *The Idiot*. The name Swiss children called Prince Myshkin when
he lived in Switzerland. The Prince's name "Lev" means "lion"
in Russian.

Leonardo da Vinci (1452-1519). *Oblomov* (1, 2). In Mezdov's house,
people spoke about Venetian art and of Leonardo da Vinci..

Lepelletier. *The Brothers Karamazov*. See Pelletier.

Leporello. *Notes from a Dead House* (1, 11). The notorious valet to Don
Giovanni in Mozart's opera (1787) by that name. A servant was
described as a Leporello in the play *Kedril the Gluttonous*.

Lermontov, Mikhail Iur'evich (1814-1841). *The Devils* (1, 5, 8). The
famous Russian poet and novelist. When Mr. G——v, the
narrator, described Nikolai Stavrogin's character after Shatov
had hit him, he mentioned that Nikolai had more malice in him
than Lermontov had. The famous Russian writer was known
for his quick temper and died in a duel he caused through his
own malice. *The Idiot* (1, 11). When Kolia Ivolgin mentioned
Lermontov's play *The Masquerade* (1834) to Prince Myshkin, he
referred to the rebuke of Prince Zvedzdich by Arbenin. *The
Underground Man* (2, 5). The Underground Man knew he was
acting in a romantic vein like a Lermontov hero. *The Village of
Stepanchikogo* (1, 7). Foma Fomich Opiskin could not understand
why Lermontov did not write moral poems for the peasants.

Lev Petrovich. *The Precipice*. A man who Sof'ia claimed could love
without showing it. She mentioned Lev in an argument with
Raiskii.

Levitskaia, Countess. *The Idiot*. The aristocrat who was a favorite of a
guest at the Epanchins'. When he stated that he had left Vienna

to escape from Catholics who wished to convert him, Belokonskaia reminded the guest that he had left to join the countess in Paris.

Lewes, George Henry (1817-1878). *Crime and Punishment* (1, 2). The author of *The Physiology of Common Life* (1859) which was popular among nihilist students in the 1860's. Marmeladov said that Sonia had read Lewes's work on physiology.

Liagaev. *Oblomov*. A man whose possessions consisted of two shirts and a ruler. Oblomov mentioned him while telling Zakhar about the perils of moving to another flat.

Liagavii. *The Brothers Karamazov*. The real name of Gorstkin. "Liagavii" means "setter dog" in Russian.

Liamshin. *The Devils*. A Jewish post-office clerk who attended Stepan's circle and played the piano. While helping to murder Shatov, he became hysterical and had to be subdued.

Librarian, Father. *The Brothers Karamazov*. A monk at the monastery when the Karamazovs met there.

Licharda. *The Brothers Karamazov* (2, 5, 6). A servant of the king in the famous medieval tale *Bova-Korolevich*, which appeared in Russia not later than the middle of the seventeenth century. Smerdiakov called himself Licharda when Dmitrii Karamazov demanded that he keep a lookout for Grushen'ka.

Lichten. *The Adolescent*. The doctor who prescribed an ointment for Makar Dolgorukii's problem with his legs.

Lidiia. *The Precipice*. A cousin of Sof'ia whom she visited in boarding school.

Lidin. *Dead Souls*. A name used by Gogol' in a comparison. Chichikov was speechless before the governor's daughter like some character with the name Lidin in a popular novel.

Lidina. "The Notes of a Madman," in *Arabesques*. A woman who thought she had blue eyes, but they were green. She was mentioned in Madgie the dog's letters to the dog Filene. Madgie reported her mistress's conversations about Lidina.

Likhachev. *Dead Souls*. A merchant with a pleasant disposition who played cards with Nozdrev.

Likhachev, Aleksasha. *The Idiot*. The man Lebedev followed around like a stooge, meeting various courtesans and young ladies, including Nastas'ia Barashkova.

Lilliputians, *The Devils* (1, 11). The small people whom Lemuel Gulliver encountered in Jonathan Swift's satirical novel *Gulliver's Travels* (1726).

Linskii. *Dead Souls*. A name used by Gogol' in a comparison. Chichikov
was speechless before the governor's daughter like some character with the name Linskii in a popular novel.

Lipochka. *The Eternal Husband*. See Trusotskaia, Olimpiada Semenovna.

Lippevekhzel', Amalia Frantsova. *Crime and Punishment*. The Marmeladovs' landlady, who would not allow Sonia to live with the
family after she was forced to take a yellow ticket upon regis-
tering as a prostitute.

Liputin. *The Devils*. The liberal scandalmonger who was the oldest
member of Stepan Verkhovenskii's group. Liputin confessed to
the police about the activities of Petr Verkhovenskii. Liputin
was known as an atheist.

Liputina. *The Devils*. The young and pretty hostess whom Nikolai
Stavrogin suddenly kissed three times at a party and caused a
scandal.

Lisa. See Liza.

Lise. See Liza.

Lisette. *The Gambler*. A woman of society who frequented the salon set
up by Mlle. Blanche in Paris. The salon was supported by the
narrator's money.

Littré, Maximilien Paul Émile (1801-1881). *The Devils* (2, 8, 1). The
French philosopher of positivism. When Petr Verkhovenskii
discussed the overthrow of the Russian government with
Nikolai Stavrogin, he pointed out that crime is insanity according to Littre. However, Dostoevskii made an error. The theory
that crime is insanity was the idea of the Belgium mathematician A. Ouetelet (1796-1874). The theory was made popular in
Russia in the writings of V. A. Zaitsev (1842-1882), a critic on
the *Russkoe slovo* (*Russian Word*) in the 1860's.

Litvinov. *The Adolescent*. A woman who roomed next to Vasin in a
boardinghouse. She once yelled through the wall some information which proved that she had been eavesdropping.

Liubetskaia, Mar'ia Mikhailovna. *A Common Story*. Naden'ka's mother,
who, according to Petr Aduev, had a wart on her nose.

Liubetskaia, Nadezhda Aleksandrovna (Naden'ka). *A Common Story*. A
woman with whom Aleksandr Aduev fell in love, to the neglect
of his studies.

Liubii. "Ivan Ivanovich and Ivan Nikiforovich," in *Mirgorod*. An early
nineteenth-century publisher of popular literature for the
semi-literate.

Livius, Titus. *The Precipice*. See Livy.

Livtsov, Semen Petrovich. *The Eternal Husband.* An acquaintance of the
  Trusotskiis when they lived in T——. Vel'chanikov met him
  when he, Vel'chanikov, was having an affair with Natal'ia.
  Livtsov served as best man at the wedding of his true love.
  During the ceremony he stabbed the bridegroom in the stomach, but the victim lived.
Livy. (Titus Livius) (59 B.C. - A.D. 17). *The Precipice* (1, 12). The Roman
  historian noted for his *History of Rome* in 142 volumes. Raiskii
  read some of his works after reading Plutarch.
Liza. *The Brothers Karamazov.* See Khokhlakova, Lise. *A Common Story.*
  The girl who fell in love with Aleksandr Aduev, whereupon he
  pretended to be cool to her affection. He attempted seduction,
  but her father sent him away. *The Eternal Husband.* The daughter
  of Vel'chanikov and Natal'ia Trusotskaia. The child was tall,
  slim, and pretty. She did not know that Vel'chanikov was her
  father. *The Precipice.* Kozlova used to gossip with sentences like:
  "Liza was talking with a man by the fence at daybreak!" *The
  Underground Man.* The prostitute whom the Underground Man
  invited to his apartment. When she came, he was too proud to
  accept the love she offered.
Lizaveta. *The Brothers Karamazov.* A poor child whom Father Zosima
  blessed when he met a group of peasants who had come to see
  him. Later Father Zosima sent her the money a wealthy woman
  had donated for the poor.
Lizaveta the Blessed. *The Devils.* A saintly nun who lived in a cage at the
  nunnery where Miss Lebiatkina stayed.
Lizaveta Livanovna. *Crime and Punishment.* The kind, good-natured, and
  simple half-sister of the old pawnbroker Alena Ivanovna. Lizaveta was uncouth in appearance, remarkably tall with long
  feet that looked as if they were bent backwards. She was
  continually with child. Raskol'nikov murdered her when she
  returned home unexpectedly after he had killed the old pawnbroker.
Lizaveta Nikolaevna. *Oblomov.* A girl who, according to Pshenitsyna,
  was an excellent seamstress.
Lobov, Aleksandr (Sashen'ka). *The Eternal Husband.* The childhood
  sweetheart of Nadezhda Zakhlebinia. He wanted to marry her,
  but the older Trusotskii had a claim on her hand. When Lobov
  asked his rival to forget Nadezhda, he refused. Finally,
  Nadezhda demanded her freedom because she loved Lobov.
Login. *Oblomov.* The landowner who received twelve thousand roubles
  for his estate instead of the seventeen thousand he expected.

Lomonosov, Mikhailo Vasil'evich (1711-1765). *A Common Story* (2, 3). The famous Russian scientist and author whom Tafaeva had to study. *The Idiot* (3, 1). At the Epanchins' Swiss chalet at Pavlovsk, Prince S—— said that in Russian literature there was nothing except for Lomonosov, Pushkin, and Gogol'. *The Village of Stepanchikogo* (2, 3). Egor Rostanev hoped that his son Il'iusha would read something from Lomonosov's poetry for Foma Fomich Opiskin's name day. However, the boy read a humorous poem by Kuz'ma Prutkov.

Lomov. *Notes from a Dead House.* A wealthy peasant's son who was accused of killing some laborers to whom he owed money. When he learned that the real murderer Gavril'ka was in prison with him, Lomov tried to kill him. He failed and was severely punished.

Lorrain, Claude (1600-1682). *The Adolescent* (3, 7, 2). The French landscape painter whose original name was Claude Gellée. Versilov told Arkadii Dolgorukii about seeing Lorrain's painting "Acis and Galetea" in the Dresden museum and somehow always called it "The Golden Age."

Louis XI. (1423-1483). *The Brothers Karamazov* (2, 5, 5). The King of France from 1461 to 1483. Ivan Karamazov told of heavenly powers that were brought down to earth in plays during the reign of Louis XI.

Louis Philippe (1773-1850). Oblomov (2, 1). The ruler of France from 1830 to 1848. A gentleman at a dinner spoke so familiarly about Louis Philippe that Oblomov was disgusted.

Lovelace. *Poor Folk* (August 11). The flatterer of women in the novel *Clarissa Harlowe* (1749) by Samuel Richardson (1689-1761). When the office force found out about the relationship between Varvara and Devushkin, they called him Mr. Lovelace.

Lovell. *The Gambler.* The name of a well-known sugar refinery. Mr. Astley informed the narrator in their final conversation that he was a partner in the firm of Lovell.

Lozgin. *The Precipice.* A boy who did not want to go to church on Sunday. He was flogged and confessed that his older brother said that there was no God.

Lubov' (Lubochka). *The Idiot.* Lebedev's infant daughter.

Luchka. See Lushka.

Lucia. *The Adolescent* (2, 4, 3). The heroine in the opera *Lucia di Lammermoor* (1835) by G. Donizetti (1797-1848). Versilov and Arkadii Dolgorukii heard strains from the opera in a restaurant.

Lucretia. *The Precipice* (2, 7). The legendary Roman woman who stabbed herself after being dishonored by Sextus. Kozlov said that his wife looked like Lucretia but was unlike her in that she would accept favors.

Luisa. *Notes from a Dead House.* A German girl with whom Bakhlushin was in love. She was affectionate, smiling, and wonderfully neat. He killed Schultz when the older man took Luisa away from him.

Luiza Ivanovna. *Crime and Punishment.* The owner of a brothel. When Raskol'nikov went to answer a summons at the police station after murdering the pawnbroker, the head clerk told a gaily dressed, pimple-faced lady to sit down and conduct herself properly.

Luka. *Oblomov.* A carpenter whom Oblomov's father had admired even though he built steps that shook like a cradle.

Luka (Luchka) Kuz'mich. *Notes from a Dead House.* A small, feeble convict with a pointed nose. He was easily offended and very conceited. Even though he was supposed to have killed six men, very few of the immates were intimidated by him.

Luke, St. *The Adolescent* (3, 10, 2). The author of the Gospel of St. Luke in the New Testament. After Makar Dolgorukii's funeral, Sof'ia Dolgorukaia asked her son Arkadii to read from the Bible; he chose a chapter from St. Luke. *The Brothers Karamazov* (2, 6, 11). The patron saint of physicians mentioned in Father Zosima's biography. *The Devils.* The epigram to Chapter One of the book is a quotation from St. Luke (8, 32-36).

Lukeria. *The Adolescent.* The old cook at Versilov's. She loved listening to Arkadii Dolgorukii's stories.

Luk'ianov. *A Common Story.* An acquaintance of Petr Aduev. In an effort to stop her husband from berating his nephew Aleksandr, Petr's wife mentioned a letter from Luk'ianov.

Lunin. *A Common Story.* The man whom Aleksandr Aduev considered to be a perfect ass.

Lunin, M. S. (1787-1845). *The Devils* (1, 5, 8). An exiled Decembrist who was known for his enjoyment of excitement and danger. The narrator, speaking of Stavrogin's bravery, mentioned that he was more fearless than Lunin.

Lushka. A diminutive for Luka. See Luka.

Luther, Martin (1483-1546). *The Brothers Karamazov* (4, 11, 9). The leader of the Reformation in Germany. Luther's ink refers to a legend that the devil appeared to tempt Luther when he was translating the Bible. Luther supposedly threw his inkwell at him. An ink blotch on the wall of Luther's prison cell was considered a result of the incident.

Luzhin, Petr Petrovich. *Crime and Punishment.* A successful lawyer and businessman who wanted to marry Dunia Raskol'nikova. He was a cousin of the Svidrigalovs and was forty-five years old. He had the impression that he could buy anything he wanted, but Dunia broke off her engagement with him when his dishonesty was exposed. He tried to accuse Sonia Marmeladova of stealing money from him.

Lycurgus. *Crime and Punishment* (3, 5). The legendary Spartan lawgiver. Raskol'nikov maintained that men like Lycurgus were criminals because in making new laws they broke old laws; yet their crimes were justified.

Lynch. *The Devils* (1, 4, 4). A name based on the act of lynching in the lawless West in America in the nineteenth century. When Shatov talked of his experiences in America with Mr. G——v, he mentioned that Lynch's law was terrible.

M——. *Notes from a Dead House.* A convict who became a friend of A——v only to be deceived by him. Later when they met, A—— would laugh at M—— for trusting him.

M——. *The Precipice.* The man who tried to make Ainov drunk so that he would shed light on the gossip about Sof'ia Belovodova.

M——ski. See Mirecki, Aleksandr.

Macaulay, Thomas Babington (1800-1859). *The Precipice* (2, 22). The English statesman and author. Raiskii received one of Macaulay's books for Vera.

Macbeth, Lady. *The Precipice* (4, 8). The heroine of Shakespeare's play *Macbeth*. Raiskii though that Vera was capable of a crime like Lady Macbeth, who instigated her husband to murder.

Machiavelli, Niccolò (1469-1527). *The Adolescent* (3, 12, 4). The famed Florentine statesman whose name stands as an epithet for an unscrupulous politician. Arkadii Dolgorukii wrote that at certain moments madmen are capable of Machiavellian cunning. *The Precipice* (1, 10). Raiskii read Machiavelli's writings while visiting his great aunt Berezhkova. *The Village of Stepanchikogo* (1, 8). Foma Fomich Opiskin implied that Sergei Aleksandrovich probably told Egor Rostanev that Opiskin was some sort of Machiavelli.

Macdonald Karlovich. *Dead Souls*. A man who showed up in the town of N—— during the upheaval about Chichikov's buying of dead souls.

Mack von Leiberich, Baron Karl (1725-1828). *Crime and Punishment* (4, 5). The Austrian general who surrendered his army to Napoleon I in 1805 while surrounded at Ulm. Porfirii Petrovich mentioned the general in a conversation with Raskol'nikov.

Madgie. "The Notes of a Madman," in *Arabesques*. The dog that talked to another dog outside the store where the madman was standing. He heard Madgie tell the dog Fidele that the dog Fido was supposed to have delivered a letter to her.

Maecenas, Gaius Cilnius (d. 8 B.C.). *The Devils* (1, 1, 2). A Roman patron of men of letters such as Horace and Virgil. Varvara Stavrogina was described as a female Maecenas. "The Portrait," in *Arabesques*. Gogol' stated that inheritors of wealth often spend fortunes trying to be Russian Maecenases.

Maevskii. *Oblomov*. The Il'inskiis' friends who were invited to their box during a theatre performance.

Magog. *Dead Souls*. The vice governor who, in Sobakevich's opinion, was as evil as the people of the legendary King Gog.

Mahomet (570?-632). *The Adolescent* (2, 1, 4). The titular name of the founder of Islam. Arkadii Dolgorukii referred to a passage in the Koran where Allah bid the Prophet to look upon troublesome creatures as He would on mice. *The Brothers Karamazov* (4, 10, 5). Mahomet was in the title of the book which Kolia Krasotkin traded for another book for the sick Il'iusha Snegirev. The book *A Relative of Mahomet; or, Complete Foolishness* was a translation from the French and was printed in 1785. *Crime and Punishment* (3, 5). Raskol'nikov maintained that men like Mahomet were criminals because in making new laws they broke old laws; yet their crimes were justified. *The Devils* (3, 5, 5). When Kirilov warned Shatov that the five seconds of eternal harmony he felt could be the beginning of an epileptic fit, Kirilov mentioned that the time element was like the legend about Mahomet's pitcher. Mahomet was awakened by the angel Gabriel and flown to Paradise. In leaving, he bumped into a pitcher but returned fast enough to catch the vessel before it hit the floor. *The Double* (4). During Klara Berendeeva's party, Goliadkin looked at a man wearing a wig and thought of Arab emirs who wore green turbans to symbolize their kinship with the Prophet Mahomet. *The Idiot* (2, 5). After leaving Rogozhin and heading for Pavlovsk, Prince Myshkin remembered the marvelous moment in which the Prophet Mahomet saw all the dwellings of Allah. "The Notes of a Madman," in *Arabesques*. The madman noted that the Mohammedan faith was spreading in Europe.

Major. *The Devils*. A stupid relative of Virginskii. The major liked liberals and in his youth distributed copies of Hertzen's *The Bell*. See Hertzen. *Notes from a Dead House*. The prison commandant who gambled and was partly under the control of his servant Fedka. The Major was called "Eight Eyes" by the prisoners.

Makar. *The Devils* (1, 1, 7). A name used in a popular phrase in the later nineteenth century. "Where Makar never drove his sheep" was used as a reference to police persecution. Stepan Verkhovenskii translated the phrase into French.

Makar Nazarievich. "Ivan Ivanovich and Ivan Nikiforovich," in *Mirgorod*. A guest at the police captain's party where a reconciliation between the two warring Ivans was attempted but failed.

Makarov, Mikhail Makarovich. *The Brothers Karamazov*. The district police inspector who questioned Dmitrii Karamazov about the murder of his father Fedor Karamazov.

Makarov, Savin. *The Adolescent*. The peasant remembered by Makar Dolgorukii because the ignorant fellow refused to look through his master's microscope.

Makhmet-Ali (1769-1840). *Oblomov* (2, 4). An Egyptian King who wanted to dig the Suez canal and establish irrigation. Oblomov heard about him at a dinner.

Makhov. *Oblomov*. The man who took the position vacated by Sud'binskii in the department where Oblomov used to work.

Maklashin. *Oblomov*. The man who held a dinner every Friday for his friends.

Maklatura Aleksandrovna. *Dead Souls*. A cousin of the daughter-in-law of Petr Varsonf'evich. The blonde with whom Chichikov was talking at the ball began to yawn when he told of meeting Maklatura.

Maksheeva. *The Devils*. A woman to whom Shatov was referred for a midwife. However, Mrs. Virginskaia went to help Marie Shatova.

Maksimov. *The Brothers Karamazov*. A sixty-year-old landowner of Tula who was poor and lived off the generosity of others such as Grushen'ka. At the monastery, Fedor Karamazov accused

Maksimov of being von Sohn, a man killed in a famous murder case. Fedor's ridiculous accusations were the beginning of the scandalous scene which he caused at the holy place. (3, 8, 7). Maksimov claimed to be the character Maksimov in Gogol's *Dead Souls*. *Dead Souls*. The landowner whom Nozdrev thrashed. Later Nozdrev was charged "for inflicting bodily injury with rods in a drunken condition."

Maksimushka. *The Brothers Karamazov*. A diminutive for Maksimov which was used by Grushen'ka.

Malan'ia. *The Village of Stepanchikogo*. A housekeeper at Stepanchikogo who sprinkled Falalei with magic water so that he would not dream of the white bull.

Malan'ia Petrovna. *Oblomov*. A woman who was always in good spirits. Oblomov wanted her to visit at Christmas.

Malek-Adel'. *The Precipice* (1, 6). The Moslem general who was a character in the novel *Matilda* (1802) by Sophie Cottin (1773-1807). Raiskii read the book and was agitated by it.

Malgasov. *The Adolescent*. Makar Dolgorukii's old master who had a microscope through which Makar first saw the properties of water. He was disturbed by what he saw.

Maliuev. *The Precipice*. One of the best students when Raiskii was in school.

Maliutin. *The Double* (4). The owner of a fashionable St. Petersburg store where Olsufii Berendeev bought things for his daughter Klara's birthday party.

Malov, Prokhor. *The Devils*. The man who served as a witness at Nikolai Stavrogin's marriage to Miss Lebiatkina.

Malthus, Thomas Robert (1766-1834). *The Idiot* (3, 4). The author of *An Essay on the Principle of Population* (1789). Malthus warned that hunger and poverty would be the result of an unchecked population growth. Lebedev referred to Malthus as a friend of humanity.

Mametka. *Notes from a Dead House*. A little figure with high cheekbones who was a comical figure in the prison.

Mamykin. *The Precipice*. A farmer who moved from Moscow to the country near Berezhkova's estate.

Mamykina, Nasten'ka. *The Precipice*. A young neighbor whom Berezhkova wanted Raiskii to marry, but he did not even want to meet her.

Manfred. *Oblomov* (4, 8). The hero of Byron's poem (1817) by that name. Shtolz said to Ol'ga that they were not like Manfred, who fought monumental questions with fervor. Shtolz felt it best to weather hard times with bowed heads. *The Underground Man* (2, 2). Manfred's disgust with a world fraught with injustice was mentioned.

Mangot. *Crime and Punishment.* A teacher of French. When Katerina Ivanovna Marmeladova described her plans for her family, she said that she would take them away to where she once lived so that the Frenchman Mangot could teach her children.

Manilov. *Dead Souls.* A landowner who lacked the strengths of a successful proprietor. His surroundings, interests, and speech showed his undeveloped character. The furniture in his house was only partially upholstered, and his books were never completely read. His steward managed the estate. The name Manilov was derived from the Russian verb *manit'* ("to entice"). However badly though the lonely and bored Manilov wanted to entice Chichikov to prolong his visit, the buyer of dead souls departed after achieving his goal. *Notes from a Dead House* (2, 2). When the prisoners talked about the former prison officer Smekalov, Gorianchikov was reminded of the sugary fictional character Manilov in Gogol's *Dead Souls*.

Manilov, Alcides. *Dead Souls.* Manilov's younger son, whose name is one of the names of Hercules, son of Alcaeus.

Manilov, Themistocles. *Dead Souls.* The eight-year-old son of Manilov who was named after the Greek general who commanded the fleet of Athens at Salamis (480 B.C.).

Manilova, Lizan'ka. *Dead Souls.* Manilov's charming wife.

Marfa. *A Common Story.* The porter's wife who heard Aleksandr Aduev's sobs after Aleksandr had learned that Naden'ka did not love him. *Dead Souls.* Pliushkin's servant who was ordered to bring the dried-out Easter cake for tea. *The Gambler.* Grandmother Tarasevichev's ward who accompanied the old lady on travels. *Oblomov.* A servant in the Oblomov household who would have been considered a witch if anyone had even accused her. Also, a second Marfa was a servant in the Il'inskii household.

Marfa Ignat'evna. *The Brothers Karamazov.* A servant in the Karamazov household and the wife of Grigorii Vasil'evich. She wanted to leave the Karamazovs after the liberation of the serfs and open a small shop in Moscow. Grigorii told her she was "talking nonsense since every woman is dishonest." Her one child by Gregorii had six fingers on one hand, and her husband called it a dragon and hated it. It died after a fortnight.

Marfa Nikitishna. *The Idiot.* A cousin of the late Nikolai Andrievich Pavlishchev. Prince Myshkin remembered her as a severe person.

Marfa Petrovna. *Crime and Punishment.* See Svidrigailova, Marfa Petrovna.

Marfa Posadnitsa (15th cent.). *The Precipice* (5, 7). A legendary defender of freedom in the city of Novgorod. Raiskii compared Berezhkova to her because they both helped others.

Marfa Sergeevna. *The Devils.* The late Mrs. Gagonov's sister who broke her leg getting out of her carriage at the fete.

Marfa Vasil'evna (Marfen'ka). *The Precipice.* Berezhkova's young relative who called her grandmother. Marfa spent her time with children, animals, and flowers, refusing to read books that did not have happy endings. She was pretty and obedient.

Marfen'ka. *The Precipice.* See Marfa Vasil'evna.

Margarita. *The Precipice.* A German who was Sof'ia Belovodova's nurse as a child.

Mar'ia. *The Adolescent.* Nikolai Semenovich's wife, who was greatly concerned with Arkadii Dolgorukii's welfare when Arkadii lived in her home as a student. Also, a second Mar'ia was Prutkova's Finnish maid, who had a grating voice. *The Brothers Karamazov.* One of the girls Dmitrii Karamazov asked to sing during his spree at Mokroe. Also, a second Mar'ia was a peasant market woman whom Kolia Krasotkin spoke to. *A Common Story.* Petr Aduev called Naden'ka by the name Mar'ia, which displeased Aleksandr Aduev. *The Devils.* A maid whom Varvara Stavrogina sent to clean up Stepan Verkhovenskii's place in case Karmazinov called on him.

Mar'ia the Unknown. *The Devils.* A name given Miss Lebiatkina by her brother when he talked about his sister with Varvara Stavrogina.

Mar'ia Aleksandrovna. *The Idiot.* A resident of an apartment. When General Ivolgin led Prince Myshkin to what he thought was the apartment of General Sokolovich, the name on the door was Kulakov. The general pretended that it did not matter. When informed by a servant that Mar'ia Aleksandrovna was not at home, Ivolgin paid his respects and left.

Mar'ia Alekseevna. *The Idiot.* A character from the play *Woe from Wit* (1825) by A. S. Griboedov (1795-1829). The line "What will Princess Mar'ia Alekseevna say?" became a popular saying. Ippolit Terentev mentioned the princess when saying goodbye to the assembled gathering at Pavlovsk.

Mar'ia Filippovna. *The Gambler*. The sister of the general who was expecting a large inheritance from Tarasevicheva.

Mar'ia Gavrilovna. *Dead Souls*. The sister-in-law of Bezpechnyi in Simbirsk. The blonde with whom Chichikov was talking at the ball began to yawn when he told of his visits to other cities and his meeting with Mar'ia Gavrilovna.

Mar'ia Ivanovna. *A Common Story*. Liubetskaia's friend. Liubitskaia went to visit him and then returned home with Count Novinskii. *The Idiot*. Ferdyshchenko stole a three-rouble note from Mar'ia Ivanovna's work table. He told about his theft at Nastasi'a Filippovna's party. When his tale caused the others to feel disgust toward him, he was irritated and asked why they expected a pleasant story when they had asked to hear about the vilest thing he had ever done.

Mar'ia Karpovna. *A Common Story*. Soniushka's mother who was a neighbor of the Aduevs.

Mar'ia Kondrat'evna. *The Brothers Karamazov*. Dmitrii Karamazov's landlady's daughter, who loved Smerdiakov. She was a romantic type who thought duels must be lovely, a perfect picture of gallantry. Dmitrii learned from her of Smerdiakov's illness the night of Fedor Karamazov's murder.

Mar'ia Mikhailovna. *A Common Story*. Liubetskaia's friend who visited Liubetskaia one afternoon. *Oblomov*. Ol'ga Il'inskaia's aunt, who supervised Ol'ga very lightly.

Mar'ia Nikitichna. *The Eternal Husband*. Nadezhda Fedosevna Zakhlebinina's girl friend who was a brunette with a comical face. Trusotskii dreaded her.

Mar'ia Nikolaevna. *Oblomov*. A girl who was an excellent seamstress, according to Pshenitsyna.

Mar'ia Onisimovna. *Oblomov*. A friend of the Oblomovs who loved mushroom pies.

Mar'ia Petrovna. *Oblomov*. A name which Oblomov thought of when he daydreamed about the bliss of marriage or about the pleasure of having company. *The Precipice*. A man who Raiskii thought should be hated by the villagers. Yet if some Mar'ia Petrovna saw him, she would fall at his feet once he called to her.

Mar'ia Savishna. *Oblomov*. A woman who visited the Oblomov estate. Oblomov was brought from school to see her.

Mar'ia Semenovna. *Oblomov*. Ol'ga Il'inskaia's dear friend whom Oblomov wanted as a companion for Ol'ga on a trip to the Summer Garden.

Mar'ia Stepanovna. *Notes from a Dead House.* Akul'ka's mother, who beat the girl after Fil'ka Morozov had spread stories about her.

Mar'ia Sysoevna. *The Eternal Husband.* The owner of the furnished rooms, which Trusotskii rented.

Mar'ia Timofeevna. *The Devils.* See Lebiatkina, Mar'ia Timofeevna.

Mar'ia Vasil'evna. *The Precipice.* A woman who rode horseback. After Berezhkova forbade Marfen'ka to accept the saddle from Viken'tev, he mentioned their acquaintance Mar'ia Vasil'evna and her equestrian activities.

Mariashka. *Notes from a Dead House.* A bread vendor who sold more than bread in the prison, to the narrator's surprise.

Marie. *The Devils.* The wife of Shatov. He called her by the French form of the name Mar'ia. *The Idiot.* A young woman in the village in Switzerland where Prince Myshkin was being cured. She was a consumptive and had been deceived by a man. She returned to her village in disgrace. Everyone turned her out. When her mother died, she worked as an assistant cowherd. Only the children whom Prince Myshkin encouraged would help her. Finally she died.

Marina Antipovna (Marishka). *The Precipice.* The beautiful and unfaithful wife of Savel'ich. When Raiskii returned to his estate, he was surprised at what an attractive woman Marina had become.

Mark Antony. See Antony, Mark.

Markel. *The Brothers Karmazov.* Father Zosima's older brother, who had a hasty and irritable temper, but was kind-hearted and never ironical. He died very young.

Markov. *Poor Folk.* The man from whom Makar tried to borrow money, but he was turned down.

Marlborough, Jouhn Churchill, First Duke of (1650-1722). *Crime and Punishment* (5, 5). The famous English general. Katerina Marmeladova became hysterical after the funeral of her husband, and proposed that she and her children should sing on the streets. One of the songs she chose was a French folk song based on the famous Duke of Marlborough.

Marlinskii. See Bestuzhev, Aleksandr Aleksandrovich.

Marmeladov, Kolia Semenovich. *Crime and Punishment.* Sonia Marmeladov's little half-brother.

Marmeladov, Semen Zakharovich. *Crime and Punishment.* The head of the Marmeladov family who was an alcoholic and whose drinking kept his family in poverty. He met Raskol'nikov in a tavern.

Marmeladov held firm to his faith in Christ through all of his troubles. He was killed when he stumbled under a horse-drawn carriage.

Marmeladova, Katerina Ivanovna. *Crime and Punishment*. The tall, slender, and pretty second wife of the drunkard Marmeladov. She had been happily married to an infantry officer who was killed. She was educated and hard-working. Though she was chronically ill with tuberculosis, she strove to keep her family together. She was Sonia's stepmother, and the mother of Polenka, Lida, and Kolia.

Marmeladova, Lida Semenovna. *Crime and Punishment*. Sonia Marmeladova's youngest half-sister.

Marmeladova, Polenka Semenovna. *Crime and Punishment*. Sonia Marmeladova's half-sister, whom Sonia helped support by her street walking.

Marmeladova, Sof'ia Semenovna (Sonia). *Crime and Punishment*. A fair, thin girl who was eighteen years old, kind, and religious. She turned to prostitution to provide for her family. She did not become bitter but felt personal degradation. Her faith became the foundation for Raskol'nikov's redemption and regeneration.

Marmontel, Jean François (1723-1799). *The Precipice* (1, 10). The French writer who was known for his tragedies and the philosophical novel *Belisaire* (1767). Raiskii read the writer's works during the summer he spent on the estate of his Aunt Berezhkova.

Mars. *The Adolescent* (2, 4, 3). The Roman god of war. While having tea with Arkadii Dolgorukii, Versilov referred to a policeman as a son of Mars. *A Common Story* (2, 3). Tafaeva liked the comedies written about ancient gods like Mars. "The Portrait," in *Arabesques*. Gogol' referred to people living in the district of Kolomna as sons of Mars.

Marshal's wife. *The Devils*. The town hostess who provided a place in her mansion for the literary fete which was such a catastrophe.

Martha. *Crime and Punishment* (4, 4). The sister of Lazarus, whom Christ brought forth from the dead (St. John 11, 19-31). Sonia read the passage aloud to Raskol'nikov.

Martsimiris, Vizier. *The Double* (4). A name in a book title which Goliadkin thought of. Dostoevskii was referring to a book printed in 1782 and entitled *A Tale About the Adventures of the English Lord George and about the Brandenburg Margrave Frederick Louise with an Aggregation of the History of the Past Turkish Vizier Martsimiris and the Sardinian Queen Thérèse.*

Martyn. *The Devils* (2, 2, 1). A name which Dostoevskii added to an old expression. In the author's Siberian notes he wrote, "He grabbed up the pie, as Martyn did soap." *The Village of Stepanchikogo.* The servant who ate soap, according to Falalei.

Martynov. *Notes from a Dead House.* A convict who had seven years left on his sentence when Gorianchikov was freed.

Masha. *A Common Story.* A young peasant woman whom Aleksandr Aduev liked. His mother made her a maid. *Poor Folk.* The granddaughter of Makar Devushkin's former landlady.

Mashka. *Dead Souls.* Sof'ia Ivanovna's maid who noticed how pale her mistress became after hearing about Chichikov's buying of dead souls. *The Precipice.* A peasant woman who lived in a barn with Prokhar, according to Berezhkova.

Mashutka. *The Precipice.* Berezhkova's house servant who was always dirty.

Maslinikov. *The Precipice.* A sensitive schoolmate of Raiskii.

Maslov. *The Brothers Karamazov.* The name of the father and son who wanted to buy land from Fedor Karamazov.

Massimo. *Crime and Punishment* (2, 6). A man who was supposedly a descendant of the ancient Aztecs. He visited St. Petersburg in 1865. When Raskol'nikov read the newspapers for information about the murders he had committed, he saw an article about Massimo.

Mastriuk. *The Brothers Karamazov* (3, 8, 5). A figure from "Mastriuk Temriukovich," a folk song about a young lad who had everything and nothing. Dmitrii Karamazov mentioned him while talking with Petr Il'ich Perkhotin.

Matrena. *The Brothers Karamazov.* Grushen'ka's cook who had been with Grushen'ka since childhood. Matrena told her the story of the sinner burning in hell who was pulled out by an onion until she kicked away other sinners who tried to hold on to her. She then fell back into the flames. *The Idiot.* The Ivolgins' cook. Also, a second Matrena was the servant for Ippolit Terentev. *The Precipice.* Berezhkova would help peasant girls such as some Matrena, who was having an illegitimate child. *The Village of Stepanchikogo.* The girl whom Vidopliasov was supposed to marry until Foma Fomich Opiskin objected.

Matrena Fadeevna. *The Precipice.* The woman who was embracing Kiriusha when Berezhkova approached. Matrena broke the embrace and ran away.

Matrena Mihkailovna. *A Common Story.* The woman who sent regards to Adueva via Anton Mikhailych.

Matrena Semenovna. *The Precipice*. The maid whom Egor Prokhorych invited to look through the crack in the wall of Raiskii's room.

Matresha. *The Devils*. The child whom Nikolai Stavrogin molested.

Mattei, Count. *The Brothers Karamazov*. The person to whom Ivan Karamazov wrote in Milan for a cure from his hallucinations.

Matthew, St. *The Adolescent* (3, 3, 4). One of the twelve disciples of Jesus. In Makar Dolgorukii's story, the merchant who had caused a child to commit suicide read St. Matthew 18, 6 and felt condemned.

Matvei. *The Adolescent*. Arkadii Dolgorukii's coachman. *The Brothers Karamazov*. The peasant with whom Kolia Krasotkin spoke while walking with Smurov. *Crime and Punishment*. In Raskol'nikov's dream, before Mikalka began beating the mare, he complained that his bay horse had run off with a certain Matvei.

Matvei Il'ich. *The Village of Stepanchikogo*. The master of Vasil'ev, the peasant who sobered up in a broken-down coach and could not get out of the vehicle.

Matvei Matveich. *A Common Story*. Aleksandr Aduev's acquaintance who always went for a walk in the evening.

Matvei Moseich. *Oblomov*. A general's valet who came out in the yard and boxed the ears of a young page for not being in the house.

Matvei Nikitich. *The Village of Stepanchikogo*. The master of Gavrila's grandfather who, Gavrila claimed, helped hang the rebel Pugachev to an aspen tree.

Mavra. *The Eternal Husband*. A serving girl who brought Vel'chanikov coffee to his room. *The Idiot*. A servant of the Epanchins. "The Notes of a Madman," in *Arabesques*. The madman's Finnish servant, who demanded tidiness and reminded him that he was absentminded. *The Precipice*. Vikan'teva's robust housekeeper.

Mavrocordato, Alessandro (1791-1865). *Dead Souls* (1, 5). The hero of the Greek war for independence whose picture hung in Sobakevich's living room.

Maurice. *The Devils*. See Drozdov, Mavrikii Nikolaievich.

Medvedev. *A Common Story*. The man who had a court order against Zaezzhalov.

Meierov. *The Idiot*. The owner of the house across from Ippolit Terentev's window. The sick boy liked looking at the red brick walls of the house.

Meister, Wilhelm. *The Precipice*. See *Wilhelm Meister*.

Melakholikha. *The Precipice*. Berezhkova's peasant woman who treated sick peasants with folk remedies.

Melan'ia. *Dead Souls.* Sof'ia Ivanovna's seamstress who started making dressed in the latest styles for her mistress.

Mephistopheles. *The Brothers Karamazov* (1, 3, 8). The leering tempter in the Faust legend mentioned by Fedor Karamazov. (4, 11, 9). In Ivan Karamazov's nightmare, the devil mentioned that Mephistopheles declared to Faust that he desired evil but did only good. In his notebooks for 1876-1877, Dostoevskii wrote that man could say that he aches for the good but does evil.

Mercandante, Saverio (1795-1870). *The Village of Stepanchikogo* (1, 8). The Italian composer whose works were popular in Russian theaters during the 1830's and 1840's. Foma Fomich Opiskin, in his questionable erudition, mentioned the composer in the same context with Macchiavelli, probably because the names began with "M" or because he confused Mercandante's name with Dante.

Mercury. *A Common Story* (1, 2). The son of Zeus. A clerk in a department store reminded Aleksandr Aduev of Mercury.

Metelitsa. "Taras Bul'ba," in *Mirgorod*. A Cossack whose body was raised on a spear during the fighting for the besieged Polish city. His name means "little snowstorm" in Russian.

Metlinskii, Count. *Oblomov.* An aristocrat who used the services of two seamstresses. Pshenitsyna told Oblomov that he should also take advantage of the seamstresses' fine work.

Meyer, Madame. *The Precipice.* A schoolmistress. Marfen'ka and Verochka studied for five years under her tutelage.

Meyerbeer, Jacob (Jakob Liebmann Beer) (1791-1864). *Oblomov* (2, 5). The noted opera composer. Oblomov told Ol'ga Il'inskaia that Meyerbeer's music sometimes moved him.

Mezdrov. *Oblomov.* The family that was always discussing music and art.

Mezenskii. *The Precipice.* The gentleman who spread the rumor in society about Sof'ia Belovodova's faux pas.

Mezentsov. *The Gambler.* An acquaintance of the general at Roulettenbrug.

Miaoulis, Andreas Bokos (1768-1835). *Dead Souls* (1, 5). A Greek admiral during the war of independence whose picture hung in Sobakevich's living room.

Miasnichika. *The Devils.* An acquaintance of Kirilov. Petr Verkhovenskii asked Kirilov to locate someone for him at her house.

Michel, Prince. *Oblomov.* A guest at the manor house Sholtz's father managed. The prince taught Andrei Sholtz how to box.

Michelangelo (Michelangelo Buonarrotti) (1475-1564). *Oblomov* (2, 4). The great Italian artist. In trying to persuade Oblomov to travel abroad, Sholtz reminded Oblomov that he once wanted to see all of Michelangelo's works.

Michelet, Jules (1798-1874). *The Precipice* (2, 3). The French historian whose works were considered too difficult by Marfen'ka.

Mikhail. *The Brothers Karamazov.* The warden of the hermitage. Also, a second Mikhail was the man who confessed a murder to Father Zosima. *Dead Souls.* The flour dealer about whom Nozdrev told a big lie. Nozdrev maintained that Mikhail and his wife were the godmother and godfather to the same child, but it was not allowed in the Russian church that a godmother and godfather could be a married couple.

Mikhail Andreevich. *The Precipice.* The man whom Vikent'ev's mother wanted him to visit. She was continually giving her son suggestions which he resented.

Mikhail Semenovich. *The Brothers Karamazov.* A member of the audience at the trial of Dmitrii Karamazov.

Mikhailo. *Dead Souls.* Tentetnikov's valet who held a towel for his master until he finally quit rubbing his eyes.

Mikhailo Mikhailych. *A Common Story.* Adueva's friend who did not observe Lent, to the horror of Adueva.

Mikhailov. *Notes from a Dead House.* The man who talked Sushilov into changing places with him on the way to Siberia. Also, a second Mikhailov was a man Goriachikov knew in the prison hospital. He was a young, pleasant-looking person.

Mikheev. *A Common Story.* A store owner from whom Adueva bought material for her son's traveling clothes. *Dead Souls.* Sobakevich's dead serf who had been an excellent coach maker. *The Double.* A caretaker at the office where Goliadkin worked.

Mikhei. *Dead Souls.* A peasant who was supposed to have witnessed the execution of the criminal Stepan the Cork, according to Chichikov's imagination.

Mikheich. *Dead Souls.* The man whom the kind chief of police asked when they were going to play *gorki* again.

Mikhilov. *Oblomov.* A man whom Oblomov gave as an example of a person very much like himself. *The Precipice.* The person who accused Belovodova's mother of neglecting her daughter and inviting unworthy people to her house.

Mikhita. "Vii," in *Mirgorod.* A brave, fine huntsman who, according to Spirid, was bewitched by the mistress of the estate. She once rode on his back all over the farm, and soon afterwards he withered away into just a heap of ashes.

Mikolka. *Crime and Punishment.* The cruel cart driver who beat his horse unmercifully in Raskol'nikov's dream.

Milari, Count. *The Precipice.* A young man who was a fine musician. Belovodova's father brought the charming count to meet her.

Militrisa Kibit'evna. *The Adolescent* (3, 12, 1). A Russian folktale princess. Prutkova asked Arkadii Dolgorukii if he remembered Militrisa. When he asked who she was, he was told that she was the earthly queen of his ideal. *Oblomov* (1, 9). When Oblomov was a child, his nurse told him that he would some day marry Militrisa. "The Portrait," in *Arabesques.* One of the shops in the Shchukin Court had a picture of the folktale princess from "Bova-Koralevich" of the seventeenth century.

Milushkin. *Dead Souls.* A dead serf sold to Chichikov by Sobakevich, who told a town official that the serf was still alive.

Millebois. *The Devils.* A high-spirited civil servant whom Governor von Lembke once knew. Under the stress of his position, the governor liked to recall how he once caught a sparrow in a park with his friend Millebois.

Millevoye, Charles (1782-1816). *The Idiot* (3, 7). A French writer. The stanza quoted by Ippolit Terentev in his article "My Essential Explanation" was not by Millevoye but by Nicolas Joseph Florent Gilbert (1751-1780). They are the last lines of the poet's work *Ode Imitée de Plusierus Psaumes,* written eight days before his death after a fall from a horse.

Milton, John (1608-1674). *The Precipice* (2, 5). The great English poet. Kozlov preferred Milton to all other other writers.

Mina. *Oblomov.* The woman whom Oblomov helped to support, pretending that he had loved her in his youth.

Minerva. *The Adolescent* (2, 8, 1). The Roman goddess of wisdom and patroness of the arts. Stebelkov called Anna Versilova a Greek statue of Minerva except that she wore fashionable clothes. *The Devils* (3, 1, 1). The narrator mentioned that Mrs. Stavrogina, like other other Minervas, helped the most worthless people. *The Precipice* (3, 2, 1). Marfen'ka had a terrifying dream in which Minerva and other statues attacked her.

Miniai. *Dead Souls.* A peasant who mounted a horse attached to a carriage.

Minkhin. *The Devils.* A name used to designate an average girl. The narrator stated that von Lembke could have been a clerk and married to some Minkhin. It was his marriage to the forty-year-old Iulia that raised him to the ranks because she was a former princess.

Minna. *The Devils.* A name used to designate an average girl. The narrator felt that von Lemke would have married some Minna if Iulia had not come along.

Misha (diminutive for Mikhail). *The Brothers Karamazov.* Perkhotin's boy, whom Dmitrii Karamazov sent to Plotnikov's store for provisions for the spree at Mokroe. *The Gambler.* The general's son, whom the narrator took for walks. The child's inheritance was squandered by the general.

Mirecki, Aleksandr. *Notes from a Dead House.* A prisoner who took part in a revolutionary conspiracy against the tsar and was sentenced to ten years at hard labor.

Miroshka. *Notes from a Dead House.* A character in the play *Filatka and Miroshka* (1831) by P.G. Grigor'ev. The prisoners presented the play most successfully.

Mitia (diminutive for Dmitrii). *The Brothers Karamazov.* See Dmitrii Karamazov.

Mitiai. *Dead Souls.* A peasant who helped untangle Chichikov's carriage when it was caught on another vehicle.

Mitiushka. *The Village of Stepanchikogo.* A postillion who played the tambourine in the orchestra at Stepanchikogo.

Mitka. *Crime and Punishment.* A name that was called up the staircase when Raskol'nikov was waiting on the landing after killing Alena Ivanovna.

Mitrii. *The Brothers Karamazov.* The person whom Ivan Karamazov hired to inform his father that he had not gone to Chermashnia.

Mitrofan Stepanich. *Notes from a Dead House.* The uncle of Akul'ka who believed the stories about her and said that her marriage to Shishkov was not honest.

Mitrofania, Abbess (Baroness Praskov'ia Rosen). *The Adolescent* (Epilogue, 3). An abbess who was tried and found guilty of forging checks and falsifying a will. Arkadii Dolgorukii wrote that Anna Versilova had a personality on a level with the abbess.

Miusov, Petr Aleksandrovich. *The Brothers Karamazov.* The cousin of Fedor Karamazov's first wife who managed to have Dmitrii taken away from Fedor in childhood.

Miusova. *The Brothers Karamazov.* The family name of Fedor Karamazov's first wife Adelaida.

Mizinchikov, Ivan Ivanovich. *The Village of Stepanchikogo.* The narrator's second cousin, who had squandered his money and was living at

Egor Rostanev's. He seemed crushed by life and agreed with everything. He plotted to elope with Tat'iana Ivanovna for her money, but his plan failed. Later, with Egor's help, he became a successful landowner.

Mizhuev. *Dead Souls*. Nozdrev's brother-in-law, who stopped with him at the inn where they met Chichikov. Mizhuev was amazed at the lies Nozdrev told and sometimes disputed his statements.

Mochius. "The Overcoat." A name which Akakii Akakievich's mother considered for her son before she settled on Akakii.

Mokii Kifovich. *Dead Souls*. Kifa Mokievich's son, who was very strong and pestered people continually.

Molchalin. *The Precipice* (1, 5). A noted character in the play *Woe from Wit* (1824) by A. S. Griboedov (1795-1829). Anna Petrovna used the character Molchalin in a play which she was writing.

Moleschott, Jacobus (1822-1893). *The Devils* (2, 6, 2). A popular writer in the 1860's among liberal young people. In a district where Petr Verkhovenskii had been spending time, a lieutenant of the police went mad and bit his superior while receiving a reprimand. In the lieutenant's quarters, a candle was burning before Moleschott's works.

Molière. *The Adolescent* (1, 5, 1). The pseudonym of the noted French dramatist Jean Baptiste Poquelin (1622-1673). Arkadii Dolgorukii wrote that Molière's character Harpagon was a simple type. See Harpagon. *A Common Type* (2, 3). Tafaeva commented that Molière wrote only for the theater. *The Devils* (1, 3, 2). Dostoevskii stated that most Russian writers are forgotten and neglected after one generation because they were unlike Molière, who had something original to say. *The Precipice* (1, 5). Anna Petrovna borrowed a character from Molière for a play she was writing.

Molochnikov. *The Pricipice*. A very happy family who were friends of Berezhkova.

Molovtsov. *The Idiot*. The man at the Vauxhall who said that Nastas'ia Barashkova should be whipped. She heard him, and picked up a cane from a young man near her and hit Molovtsov across the face. He raised his arm to strike her but was prevented from doing so by Prince Myshkin.

Monbars, Prince de. *The Devils* (1, 5, 4). The name which Captain Lebiatkin said he wished was his own. It is possible that Dostoevskii used the name of the famous sea pirate Monbars, who became a hero of romances and dramas, for instance, J. B. Picquenard's *Monbars l'Exterminateur* (1807).

Mongeot, Madier de (1814-1892). *The Adolescent* (3, 5, 3). A French parliamentarian. When two Polish gentlemen were discussing French politics in a restaurant, Andreev overheard one of them mispronounce Mongeot's name. Andreev stood up and made a rather ugly scene for no real purpose.

Montague. *The Precipice* (3, 15). The rival family of the Capulets in Shakespeare's *Romeo and Juliet*. Berezhkova made Marfen'ka and Vera read a book that had a family similar to the Montagues.

Montaigne, Michel Eyquem de (1533-1592). *A Common Story* (2, 3). The noted French writer. Tafaeva mixed up his name with that of Montaigne.

Montesquieu, Baron de la Brède et de. Charles de Secondat (1689-1755). *The Precipice* (1, 10). The French writer whose works Raiskii read while visiting Verezhkova.

Montferant, Auguste-Richard de (1789-1858). *The Adolescent* (2, 1, 2). The architect of St. Isaac's Cathedral in St. Petersburg. He advised breaking up the rock by the Pavlovskii Barracks. This event took place in a tale told to Versilov by his landlord.

Moor, Count von. *The Brothers Karamazov* (1, 2, 6). A name which Fedor Karamazov gave to himself. It was based on the fictional family by that name in I. F. Schiller's *The Robbers* (1781).

Moor, Franz. *The Brothers Karamazov* (1, 2, 6). The name which Fedor Karamazov called his son Ivan. See Moor, Count von. *The Precipice* (2, 15). Raiskii called Volokov a Russian Karl Moor.

Mordecai. "Taras Bul'ba," in *Mirgorod*. A Jew in Warsaw to whom Iankel went when he wanted to help Taras.

More, Thomas (1478-1535). *The Idiot* (4, 5). The English humanist and one of the founders of utopian socialism. Lebedev stated that More made the remark, "Pierce my heart, but not my head."

Morozov. *The Brothers Karamazov*. The former owner of a book that Kolia Krasotkin swapped for the book which he gave to Ii'iusha Snegirev on his sickbed.

Morozov, Fil'ka. *Notes from a Dead House*. The young man who spread rumors that he had slept with Akul'ka. He actually loved her himself and did not want her to marry another. The rumors led to her murder.

Morozova. *The Brothers Karamazov*. Grushen'ka's landlady, who was a widow and led a secluded life with her two unmarried nieces.

Moses. *The Precipice* (4, 9). The Biblical figure under whose leadership the Israelites left Egypt (Exod. 1). Raiskii felt that while Berezhkova knew all the vices written in Moses's tablet, she could not help Vera morally or physically.

Mostotil'aikov. *The Precipice* (1, 6). The man who translated into Russian *Jerusalem Delivered* by Torquato Tasso (1544-1595).

Mot'ka. *Oblomov.* The serf who reported that the remaining part of the balcony was ready to fall. *The Precipice.* The peasant to whom Vas'ka reported his forthcoming death.

Mozart, Wolfgang Amadeus (1756-1791). *Oblomov* (2, 5). The great Austrian composer. Oblomov told Ol'ga Il'inskaia that he liked music, but at times he could not stand to hear even Mozart.

Mukhoiarov, Ivan Matveich. *Oblomov.* The brother of Agaf'ia Pshenitsyna. He was a dishonest government clerk, who, with the aid of Tarant'ev, tried to cheat Oblomov out of some money.

Mukhoiarova, Irina Panteleevna. *Oblomov.* The wife of Ivan Matveich Mukhoiarov.

Murashina. *Oblomov.* The woman whom Sub'binskii planned to marry.

Murazov, Afanasii Vasil'evich. *Dead Souls.* The wealthy business manager whom Chichikov envied.

Murillo, Bartolomé Esteban (1617-1682). *The Precipice* (5, 25). The great Spanish painter. When traveling in Europe, Raiskii saw Vera in all of Murillo's works of art.

Mussialovich. *The Brothers Karamazov.* A former lover of Grushen'ka. At Mokroe, Dmitrii Karamazov offered him three thousand roubles if he would leave and take his friend Vrublevskii with him. The Pole refused to leave Grushen'ka, and Dmitrii accused him of wanting to marry her for the money she had saved. At the murder trial, Mussialovich spoke so proudly that Dmitrii yelled out "Scoundrel!", causing an uproar.

Mussinskii. *Oblomov.* An acquaintance of Goriuev. After the ballet, Goriuev could not have tea with Oblomov because he had to visit Mussinskii.

Myl'noi. *Dead Souls.* A landowner who lived in the vicinity of the inn where Chichikov stopped after leave Korobochka's.

Myshinskii. *The Precipice.* A man who gossiped about Sof'ia Belovodova's faux pas.

Myshkin, Prince Lev Nikolaievich. *The Idiot.* An epileptic who was sent to Switzerland for a cure when he was child. Professor Schneider sent him back almost cured. The Prince inherited a fortune and offered to marry Nastas'ia Filippovna Barashkova. She refused and left with Rogozhin. Myshkin followed but decided to let her marry him. Myshkin then fell in love with Aglaia Epanchina and proposed. Nastas'ia told Aglaia that she could take back the prince if she chose and did take him from

Aglaia. Nastas'ia, however, returned to Rogozhin, who killed her. Myshkin spent the night with her dead body.

Myshkin, Nikolai Lvovich. *The Idiot.* The idiot's father, who died in Elissavetgrad when Lev was a child.

Mytishcheva, Katerina Aleksandrovna. *The Idiot.* A woman in the tale which Totskii told at Nastas'ia Filippovna Barashkova's party. Katerina bought up all the camellias in the area before a ball.

N——, Prince. *The Idiot.* A charming, witty, and forthright man who was convinced that he was the sun which had risen to shine down on the Epanchins' drawing room. Prince Myshkin found N—— delightful and considered him a Don Juan. *Oblomov.* Oblomov thought that being invited to Prince N——'s was to reach the apex of society.

Naafonil. *The Brothers Karamazov* (1, 2, 8). A neologism based on the word Afor or Athos, the famous monastery on a peninsula in Greece.

Nadia. *The Gambler.* The general's daughter whom the narrator took for walks. Her father squandered her inheritance.

Nadexhda Nikitishna. *The Precipice.* A woman whom Marfen'ka envied because Nadezhda had seven children.

Napoleon I (1769-1821). *The Adolescent* (1, 5, 3). The famous French ruler. Arkadii Dolgorukii's favorite vision was of a man without talents who could face the world and feel superior to the French Emperor Napoleon. (3, 7, 1). Versilov said that a photograph catches a person at a random moment so that even a Napoleon may look stupid. *The Brothers Karamazov* (4, 10, 6). Kolia Krasotkin quoted Napoleon's remark, "Les femmes tricottent," while Kolia was talking with Il'iusha Snegirev on his sickbed. *Crime and Punishment* (3, 5). Raskol'nikov maintained that men like Napoleon were criminals because in making new laws they broke old laws; yet he felt their crimes were justified. (3, 6). Raskol'nikov called Napoleon a real master because he got away with the monstrous things he did in the name of progress. (4, 5). Porfirii Petrovich mentioned to Raskol'nikov that if Porfirii had been in the army, he would not have been a Napoleon, but maybe a major. (5, 5). During his confession of murder, Raskol'nikov mentioned Napoleon. (6, 5). In explaining his letter to Dunia before trying to seduce her, Svidrigailov mentioned that Raskol'nikov considered himself a Napoleon. *Dead Souls.* (1, 10). The city officials of the town of N—— thought that

Chichikov might be Napoleon in disguise. *The Idiot* (3, 8). Aglaia
Epanchina asked Prince Myshkin if he daydreamed that he was
a field marshal who defeated Napoleon. (4, 4). General Ivolgin
maintained he had been a page of Napoleon in 1812. *Oblomov* (1,
6). Oblomov saw himself as Napoleon in his dreams. "Old-
World Landowners," in *Mirgorod*. Afanasii Tovstogub liked to
talk with visitors about politics. He was sure the French had a
secret agreement with England to free Napoleon. *The Underground Man* (1, 7). The Underground Man referred to Napoleon
to dispute H. T. Buckle's theory that civilization makes man less
fitted for warfare. Blood flowed in streams during Napoleon's
time. (2, 9). When the Underground Man asked Apollon to
bring tea for Liza, he stood before his servant with arms crossed
à la Napoleon.

Napoleon II, Joseph François Charles (1811-1832). *The Idiot* (4, 4). The
son of Napoleon I and Marie Louise of Austria. Napoleon gave
his son the title King of Rome and abdicated his throne in his
son's favor in 1814.

Napoleon III (1808-1873). *The Brothers Karamozov* (2, 5, 2). The French
ruler known as "the Little Napoleon." Smerdiakov showed his
ignorance when he said that Napoleon I was the father of the
present Emperor of France. Napoleon III was the son of
Napoleon I's brother Louis Napoleon, King of Holland. *The Idiot*
(1, 2). When Prince Myshkin came to St. Petersburg, he wore a
small beard in a style named after Napoleon III, the Emperor of
France from 1852. *Notes from a Dead House* (1, 7). Petrov asked
Gorianchikov to explain how a president became an emperor.
He referred to Napoleon III, who was President of the Second
Republic of France after 1848. In 1852, he proclaimed himself
Emperor. *The Precipice* (1, 8). Kozlov, in an argument with Raiskii
about journalism, hinted that even Emperor Napoleon III would
use deception to achieve a goal.

Narrator. *The Idiot*. See G——v. *Notes from a Dead House*. The gentleman
who met Gorianchikov and published the notes received from
him under the title of the book. *The Village of Stepanchikogo*. See
Sergei Aleksandrovich.

Nash, Okhrim. "Taras Bul'ba," in *Mirogorod*. A brave Cossack who
helped lead the final siege on the Polish city.

Nashchokin, Ippolit. *The Adolescent*. A professional forger who led a
forgery ring in which Prince Sergei Sokolskii was involved.

Nastas'ia. *The Adolescent*. A servant of Vasin's landlady. *The Brothers*

Karamozov. A woman peasant who came to Father Zosima on a pilgrimage, asking him to pray for her dead son Aleksei. *The Devils.* Stepan Verkhovenskii's maid, whose simple acceptance of faith was alien to her master's beliefs. *Oblomov.* The guests at a dinner table surmised that the next guest would be Nastas'ia if a candle went out. *Poor Folk.* A laundress.

Nastas'ia Filippovna. *The Idiot.* See Barashkova, Nastas'ia Filippovna.

Nastas'ia Ivanovna. *Notes from a Dead House.* A widow who continually offered assistance to those in exile. *Oblomov.* A hanger-on in the Oblomov household.

Nastas'ia Petrovna. *Crime and Punishment.* The servant girl of Praskov'ia Pavlovna, Raskol'nikov's landlady. *The Brothers Karamazov.* A name mentioned by Mrs. Snegirev when she told about a gossipy deacon's wife. *The Precipice.* The guest at Berezhkova's party whom Tychkov teased.

Nasten'ka (diminutive for Nastia). *The Village of Stepanchikogo.* See Ezhevikina, Nastia.

Nastia. *The Brothers Karamazov.* The eight-year-old daughter of the doctor's wife, who rented rooms in the Krasotkins' house. *The Eternal Husband.* A red-haired girl who was a friend of the Zakhlebinin daughter when Vel'chanikov visited with Trusotskii.

Natal'ia Egorovna. *Crime and Punishment.* The crippled daughter of Praskov'ia Pavlovna. Raskol'nikov once planned to marry Natal'ia, but the unfortunate girl died before their plan could be carried out.

Natal'ia Faddevna. *Oblomov.* A woman who came as an unexpected guest at the Oblomovs' estate. If a candle went out in a room, the family considered it a sign that someone like Natal'ia was coming for a visit. *The Precipice.* The girl who wanted to look through a hole in the wall of Raiskii's room.

Natal'ia Ivanovna. *The Precipice.* The guest at Berezhkova's party who translated into French a remark by Tychkov about the young people in attendance. He said that they looked fresh and healthy. Also, a second Natal'ia Ivanovna was the priest's wife, who was a friend of Vera.

Natal'ia Nikitishna. *The Idiot.* A cousin of the late Nikolai Andreevich Pavlishchev. Prince Myshkin remembered her as a saintly person.

Natal'ia Pavlovna. *The Devils.* A woman in society. When the authorities raided Stepan Verkhovenskii's living quarters, Stepan claimed that the public prosecutor was condescending toward him. Yet the prosecutor was the man who had been thrashed for hiding in the boudoir of the charming Natal'ia Pavlovna.

Natasha. *The Brothers Karamazov*. The name Kolia Krasotkin called the peasant named Mar'ia. *A Common Story*. Another name for Naden'ka invented by Peter Aduev. *The Precipice*. Raiskii's lost love. She was a lovely young girl whom he loved, but he neglected her and became bored with her. When she became sick and died, he realized his mistake. Also, a second Natasha in the novel was a servant of Vera. Together they cut out blouses for peasants.

Nazar Ivanovich. *The Brothers Karamazov*. A chief porter.

Nazarev. *The Brothers Karamazov*. A merchant who was a member of the jury at Dmitrii Karamazov's trial for murder.

Nedobarov. *The Double*. A former master of Goliadkin's servant Petrushka.

Nekrasov, Nikolai Alekseevich (1821-1878). *The Adolescent* (1, 7, 1). A Russian poet known for his peasant and bourgeois themes. Makar Dolgorukii was still handsome and reminded Arkadii Dolgorukii of a line from a poem by Nekrasov: "dark-visaged, tall and spare." *The Brothers Karamazov* (2, 5, 4). When Ivan Karamazov described the beating of a horse while speaking about the cruelty of man, Dostoevskii had in mind the poem "About the Weather: Street Impressions" (1859) by Nekrasov. *The Underground Man* (2, 1). Part II of the novel begins with a quotation from the poetry of Nekrasov.

Nelaton. *The Idiot*. A physician in the French court in Paris who, General Ivolgin claimed, came to doctor him when he was wounded at Sevastopol.

Neliubova. *The Precipice*. Belovodova's cousin who told Mikhilov that Sof'ia Belovodova paid special attention to her teacher El'nin.

Neliudov, Nikolai Parfenovich. *The Brothers Karamazov*. A young investigating lawyer at Dmitrii Karamazov's trial.

Nemesis. *Oblomov* (4, 4). The goddess of retribution, especially retributions on presumptuous or wicked mortals. When Sholtz declared his love to Ol'ga Il'inskaia, she felt that she was a victim of Nemesis. Ol'ga appreciated Sholtz's intentions, but she had a sense of guilt about her feelings toward Oblomov.

Nepos, Cornelius (99-32 B.C.). *Oblomov* (1, 3). A Roman historian. Oblomov was studying Nepos's works when his father decided that he had had enough education and stopped his studies.

Neptune. *The Precipice* (1, 2). The god of the sea. The doorman of
  Pakhonin's sisters reminded one of Neptune.

Netsvetaev. *Notes from a Dead House.* The convict-actor who brandished
  a cane as if he were remembering a childhood memory in which
  he saw a dandy carry on a cane.

Nevylychii. "Taras Bul'ba," in *Mirgorod.* A Cossack chief who chose to
  go fight the Tartars instead of fighting the Poles. He was killed
  in action.

Newton, Sir Isaac (1642-1727). *A Common Story* (1, 2). The famed
  English scientist. Petr Aduev told Aleksandr Aduev that Newton was an example of a talented man. *Crime and Punishment* (3, 5).
  Raskol'nikov maintained that if one or several people would
  have had to be sacrificed to bring the theories of the English
  scientist Newton to light, then the sacrifice would have been
  justified.

Nichipor. "Old-World Landowners," in *Mirgorod.* The carriage driver
  who told Pulkheria Ivanovna Tovstagubova that the oak trees
  in her forest had simply fallen down. She accepted his answer
  but doubled the watch on her pear trees.

Nikifor. *The Devils.* A word that represented nature in the poem "The
  Cockroach" by Captain Lebiatkin. He read the work to Varvara
  Stavrogina, causing her to become very angry. *The Idiot.* The
  orderly for General Epanchin when he was a second lieutenant.
  Nikifor reported the missing bowl which caused Epanchin to go
  and berate an old landlady. Unbeknownst to him, she was dying
  while he berated her.

Nikita. *The Brothers Karamazov.* The peasant woman Nastas'ia's husband. *Oblomov.* The Il'inskiis' servant who heard that Oblomov
  was planning to marry Ol'ga Il'inskaia. *The Precipice.* One of
  Marina Antipovna's lovers.

Nikita Gregorich. *Notes from a Dead House.* The man who refused to
  marry Akul'ka after Morozov had spread tales about her.

Nikita Sergeevich. *The Precipice.* A teacher who told some children that
  there was no God, causing a great commotion in the neighbor-
  hood.

Nikitishna. *A Common Story.* A peasant healer whom Aleksandr Aduev's
  mother called in to cure him once when he was ill.

Nikodim Fomich. *Crime and Punishment.* A district police superintendent.

Nikodimov. *The Devils* (2, 10, 3) A literary figure in a work by Karmazinov, who said that he showed all the faults of the Westerners in Nikodimov's character. Dostoevskii was actually

making fun of the remark by I. S. Turgenev that he showed the
faults of the Westerners in the character of Panshin in the book
A Gentry Nest (1859).

Nikola, St. *The Precipice* (2, 18). A Russian saint. Openkin called on St.
Nikola to witness that he never lied or did evil to people.

Nikolai, St. (Nicholas). "Ivan Ivanovich and Ivan Nikiforovich," in
Mirgorod. The wonder-working saint mentioned by the narrator
when wishing he had a coat like Ivan Ivanovich's.

Nikolai I, Emperor. (1795-1855). *The Devils* (1, 3, 8). The Russian ruler
known for his despotism. A picture of Nikolai I was hanging in
Kirilov's room.

Nikolai Andreevich. *The Precipice*. Berezhkova's friend who used God's
name in vain.

Nikolai Ivanovich. *The Precipice*. The husband of Natasha, Vera's servant. Nikolai read and explained *The Lives of the Holy Fathers* to
both of them.

Nikolai Ivanych. *The Adolescent*. A relative of Prince Sergei Sokolskii.

Nikolai Semenovich. *The Adolescent*. The landlord with whom Arkadii
Dolgorukii lived while in high school.

Nil Alekseevich. *The Idiot*. The department head who asked Lebedev to
expound on the antichrist. Later Nil fell out of his carriage and
died immediately. Lebedev claimed that he had predicted Nil's
demise.

Nil Pavlich. *Crime and Punishment*. A clerk. When Raskol'nikov went to
the police station to confess to the murder of the pawnbroker,
Il'ia Petrovich asked the clerk Nil Pavlich who it was that had
committed suicide that morning. Raskol'nikov learned that it
was Svidrigailov.

Nil'skii, Prince. *The Gambler*. An acquaintance of the general who was
visiting when Tarasevicheva arrived and spoke so offensively
to the general. She asked who the mousy little man was,
referring to Prince Nil'skii, but not knowing that he understood
Russian.

Nimrod. *The Precipice* (3, 24). In the Bible (Gen. 10, 9) Nimrod was the
"mighty hunter before the Lord." Raiskii called Tushin a hunter
like Nimrod.

Nina Aleksandrovna. *The Idiot*. See Ivolgina, Nina Aleksandrovna.

Nina Savelevna. *The Devils*. A maid who came to Stavrogin's lodgings in
St. Petersburg.

Nini. *The Precipice*. Pakhotin's girl friend who ordered dinner at a farm
in the country.

Noah. *Crime and Punishment* (2, 1). The Biblical figure who built the famous ark (Gen. 6, 9). When the head clerk at the police station described the building where Alena Ivanovna had been murdered, he said that it was a regular Noah's ark. *Poor People* (April 8). Makar Devushkin described his lodgings as a Noah's ark of sounds and confusion. *The Village of Stepanchikogo* (1, 1). The Rostanev household became a Noah's ark soon after it had moved to Stepanchikogo.

Norma. *Oblomov* (2, 7). Ol'ga Il'inskaia sang the *Casta Diva* from the opera *Norma* (1831) by Vincenzio Bellini (1802-1835).

Nosov. *The Brothers Karamazov* (3, 8, 7). During Dmitrii Karamazov's wild spree at Mokroe, Maksimov maintained that the character Nozdrev in Gogol's *Dead Souls* was really called Nosov.

Nostugan. "Taras Bul'ba," in *Mirgorod*. A Cossack chief who chose to go fight the Tartars instead of fighting the Poles.

Novinskii, Count Platon. *A Common Story*. The man who called on the Liubetskiis every day and taught Naden'ka how to ride horses. His activities made Aleksandr Aduev very jealous.

Nozdrev. *The Brothers Karamazov* (3, 8, 7). The literary figure from Gogol's *Dead Souls* who was mentioned during Dmitrii Karamazov's spree at Mokroe. See Nosov. (4, 12, 6). Ippolit Kirillovich mentioned Nozdrev at Dmitrii Karamazov's trial, saying that Nozdrev was not a good example of a Russian. *Dead Souls*. The notorious liar who was a contemptible character. An incessant gambler and cheat, he delighted in showing off his possessions, lying continually about their value or how he had obtained them. He was one of the landowners who exposed Chichikov's scheme of buying dead souls. *The Devils* (2, 1, 2). The obnoxious, vile-tempered character in Gogol's masterpiece. Petr Verkhovenskii claimed that I. S. Turgenev's hero Bazarov was a mixture of Nozdrev and Lord Byron. (2, 1, 7). Shatov reminded Slavrogin that Nozdrev in *Dead Souls* tried to catch a hare by its hind legs.

Nurra. *Notes from a Dead House*. A Lezghian who was built like Hercules with light blue eyes and features of an Ugro-Finnish cast. He was always jolly and well-liked by all. He was pious and fasted before Moslem holidays. A kind, sympathetic soul, he longed to return to the Caucasus.

Oblomov, Andrei (Andriusha). *Oblomov*. The son of Oblomov and Agaf'ia Matveevna.

Oblomov, Il'ia. *Oblomov.* The landowner whose son became the personification of the superflous man in nineteenth-century Russia.

Oblomov, Il'ia Il'ich. *Oblomov.* A thirty-two-year-old, nice-looking man with out a trace of intelligence in his face. He was not stupid, just incredibly lazy. He was waited on so much as a child that he never learned to make decisions. He preferred to daydream about a happy existence. In a sense, he achieved his dream. He ended as a child, fully protected from the outside world by Agaf'ia Matveevna.

Oblomova. *Oblomov.* Oblomov's deceased mother.

Obnoskin, Pavel Semenich. *The Village of Stepanchikogo.* A young man about twenty-five who, in spite of his chic dress, was shabby and common. He was a guest for tea when the narrator arrived at his uncle Egor Rostanev's. Obnoskin carried out Mizichinkov's plan and eloped with Tat'iana Ivanovna only to lose her when Egor Rostanev came to her rescue.

Obnoskina, Anfisa Petrovna. *The Village of Stepanchikogo.* A fat lady about fifty years old who dressed tastelessly and who was a guest at Egor Rostanev's when Sergei Aleksandrovich arrived at his uncle's.

Odoevskii, Vladimir (1804-1869). *Poor Folk.* A noted Russian writer. The epigraph to the story was taken from Odoevskii's story "The Live Corpse" ("Zhivoi mertvets") (1839).

Odontsov. *Oblomov.* The neighbor near the Oblomovs' estate who built a road with another neighbor when Oblomov failed to act on his proposal to build a road near Oblomovka.

Oedipus. *A Common Story* (2, 4). The famed Greek hero who blinded himself for having killed his own father and having married his own mother. Liza's father reminded Aleksandr Aduev of Oedipus.

Officer. *The Underground Man.* The gentleman who picked up the Underground Man and set him out of his way by the billiard table. The Underground Man plotted revenge on the officer for years, finally bumping into him on the street. The officer paid no notice to the event, but the Underground Man felt avenged.

Old Believer. *The Idiot.* A member of a schismatic religious movement in the mid-seventeenth century. The member refused to accept the liturgical reforms of the Patriarch Nikon. Parfen Rogozhin's father was an old believer.

Oleandrov. *The Village of Stepanchikogo*. A name which Vidiplasov chose to exchange for his own last name, but he later changed his mind.

Oleshkin. *Oblomov*. Il'ia Oblomov's former colleague who became a general.

Ol'ga. *Oblomov*. See Il'inskaia, Ol'ga.

Ol'ga Mikhailovna. *The Brothers Karamazov*. Makarov's eldest granddaughter.

Ol'ga Onisimovna (Ol'ia). *The Adolescent*. The daughter of a poor woman in the building where Vasin lived. Ol'ga hanged herself because of her poverty and her shame for having gone to a brothel. She was tricked into the latter.

Olimpia. *The Underground Man*. The girl whom Zverkov claimed for himself when the classmates left their reunion party for a brothel.

Olimpiada. *The Adolescent*. A stepdaughter of a cousin of old Prince Sokolskii for whom he had set aside a dowry.

Olimpiada Izmailovna, Princess. *The Precipice*. A woman who made the sins of others her own business. She visited Sof'ia's aunts and upset them to the point that they quit receiving guests.

Olsufev. *The Brothers Karamazov*. The man who murdered a merchant.

Omar (7th Cent.). *The Precipice* (1, 16). The Arab warrior who conquered Egypt and ordered the burning of the library in Alexandria. Kozlov compared him with Mark Volkkhov.

Onegin, Eugene. *The Brothers Karamazov* (4, 10, 6). The titular hero of the famous novel in verse (1820-1830) by A. S. Pushkin (1799-1837). While talking with Alesha Karamazov, Kolia Krasotkin mentioned his admiration of the work. *A Common Story* (2, 3). Tafaeva was given Pushkin's famous work and liked it so well that she memorized verses from it.

Onufriev. *Notes from a Dead House*. A convict whose girl friend was pockmarked but was not a beggar.

Onufrii Ivanovich. *Dead Souls*. Tentetnikov's uncle who told his nephew to prepare for government service by copying documents.

Openkin, Akim Akimovich. *The Precipice*. Berezhkova's guest who visited friends to escape his wife.

Ophelia. *The Brothers Karamazov* (1, 1, 1). The famous heroine in Shakespeare's *Hamlet*. The narrator mentioned a young romantic girl who threw herself from a precipice into a raging river to drown as Ophelia did in the play. *The Devils* (1, 5, 6). When Varvara

Stavrogina lamented her son Nikolai's past, she commented that he never had an Ophelia in his life. *The Precipice* (3, 13). Ophelia was remembered by Raiskii after Kozlova seduced him.

Opsikin, Foma Fomich. *The Village of Stepanchikogo.* The notoriously petty eccentric. First hired as a reader for General Krakhotkin, Foma Fomich gradually acquired a marvelous influence over the feminine half of the household. He was a cowardly creature and an outcast from society, but incredibly vain. Dostoevskii wrote, "A base soul escaping from oppression becomes an oppressor."

Ordynsev, Platon. *The Idiot.* A landowner. When Totskii told about his vilest deed at Nastasi'ia Filippovna's party, he told an incident that occurred when he was a guest at the estate of the Ordynsevs.

Ordynseva, Anfisa Alekseevna. *The Idiot.* The wife of Ordynsev. At Nastas'ia Filippovna's party, Totskii told a tale about an ailing woman named Ordynseva who loved camellias. Totskii foiled her would-be lover's plans by obtaining the only camellias in the district for her.

Orestes. *A Common Story.* (2, 1). The son of Agamemnon and Clytemnestra in classical mythology. Orestes was ready for any sacrifice in the name of friendship. Aleksandr Aduev mentioned Orestes when speaking about friendship.

Orlov. *Notes from a Dead House.* A haughty, superficial man who was condemned to be flogged. The narrator was curious to see him after the punishment because Orlov had enormous will power. He returned in dreadful shape, his back swollen a livid blue, but the next day he was up and about. The most terrible thing was his spiritual numbness, a complete triumph of the flesh over the spirit.

Orlov. A. A. (1791-1840). "Nevskii Prospect," in *Arabesques.* The author of moralistic tracts for the illiterate masses.

Orpheus. *The Village of Stepanchikogo (7).* The Thracian poet of Greek legend who could change hearts with his song. Foma Fomich Opiskin claimed that he, like Orpheus, could change the crude manners of the servants with song.

Oryshko. "Ivan Ivanovich and Ivan Nikiforovich," in *Mirgorod.* The girl whom the court judge ordered to bring some tea instead of winking at the clerks.

Osip. *Notes from a Dead House.* A cook who was teased affectionately by the other inmates.

Ossian (Oisin) (3rd Cent.). *The Precipice* (1, 6). The legendary Gaelic bard. Raiskii read poems supposedly by him published in 1760 by James Macpherson (1736-1796).

Ostaf'ev. *The Double.* A clerk who would buy anything for ten kopecks. Goliadkin tried to receive information about his fellow workers from Ostaf'ev.

Osterman, Count Andrei Ivanovich (1686-1747). *The Idiot* (4, 5). A German-born Russian diplomat during the reign of Petr I and Empress Anna. When Elizabeth I came to the throne, Osterman was sentenced to death on the wheel, but later his sentence was commuted to exile in Siberia.

Ostranitsa. "Taras Bul'ba," in *Mirgorod.* The headman of the new Cossack force that rose to avenge the forces that had ravaged the Cossack lands.

Ostrovskii, Aleksandr Nikolaevich (1823-1886). *The Brothers Karamazov* (4, 12, 13). The Russian playwright mentioned by Fetiukovich at Dmitrii Karamazov's trial.

Othello. *The Adolescent* (2, 4, 2). The titular hero of Shakespeare's play. Versilov said that Othello killed Desdemona not out of jealousy, but because he had been robbed of his ideal. *The Brothers Karamazov* (3, 8, 3). When Dmitrii pursued Grushen'ka to Mokroe, he reflected on Pushkin's comment that Othello was not jealous but trustful. His soul was shattered when his ideal was destroyed. *The Devils* (1, 4, 1). Lisa Tushina read the first act of *Othello* to her mother Praskov'ia Drozhdova. *The Precipice* (4, 4). Raiskii was like Othello in that he did not have a suspicious nature but did have bursts of passion.

Otrepev, Gregorii Boganovich (Grishka). *The Devils* (2, 2, 3). The man who was known as the False Dmitrii. He pretended to be the son of Tsar Ioann IV. When captured he was shot and burned, and his ashes were then shot from a cannon. He was mentioned by Mar'ia Lebiatkina as a pretender.

Ovchinikov. *Oblomov.* A man who invited Oblomov to dinner.

Overko. "Vii," in *Mirgorod.* One of the six strong Cossacks who came to fetch Khoma Brut to the beautiful dead witch.

Ovid (Publius Ovidius Naso) (43 B.C.-17 A.D.). *Dead Souls* (1, 3). The author of *Metamorphoses,* to which Gogol' referred.

Owen, Robert (1775-1858). *The Precipice* (5, 18). The English utopian socialist whom Raiskii thought of when he considered Tushin's successful business enterprises.

Ozerov, Vladislav Aleksandrovich (1769-1816). *A Common Story* (2, 3). A Russian author whose works were read by Tafaeva.

P——. *The Idiot.* The name given to Pavlishev in a story from a weekly humorous newspaper which Kolia Ivolgin read to a gathering at Pavlovsk. The story made fun of Prince Myshkin. *Poor Folk.* Varvara's father worked on the estate of Prince P——. When new owners took over the estate, Varvara's family moved to St. Petersburg. *Oblomov.* Oblomov did not see any reason to shake Prince P——'s hand. He did not care to show that he knew an important person.

P——, B——. *The Precipice.* A member of society. Princess Olimpiada found out from B—— P—— that Milari had a fiancée in Italy and did not have any serious intentions toward Sof'ia Belvodova.

P——, P——. *The Precipice.* A member of society. In a newsy letter, Aianov wrote that P—— P—— lost seventy thousand roubles at cards.

Pafnut'ev. *The Precipice.* The previous governor, who was much stricter than the present one, according to Tychkov.

Pafnut'evna. *The Idiot.* A servant of Rogozhin.

Pafnutii, Abbot. *The Idiot* (1, 3). The founder of a monastery on the River Volga in the fourteenth century.

Paganini, Nicolò (1782-1840). *A Common Story* (2, 5). The legendary violinist and composer. Aleksandr Aduev was at a concert when a stranger looked at his face and remarked, "All that man's feelings are in his face, while I heard Paganini and didn't raise an eyebrow."

Paisii, Father. *The Brothers Karamazov.* A wise theologian and close friend of Father Zosima. He tried to give comfort to Alesha after Zosima's death.

Pakhotin, Nikolai Vasil'evich. *The Precipice.* Sof'ia Belovodova's father, who spent all of his money after his wife's death, leaving very little for Sof'ia.

Pakhotina, Anna Vasil'evna. *The Precipice.* Sof'ia Belovodova's old rich aunt, the sister of Nadezhda.

Pakhotina, Nadezhda Vasil'evna. *The Precipice.* Sof'ia Belovodova's old rich aunt, the sister of Anna.

Palmerston, 3rd Viscount, Henry John Temple (1784-1865). *Crime and Punishment* (2, 3). The English Prime Minister of the Tory Party (1855-1865). By calling Raskol'nikov's hat by the name Palmerston, Razumikhin referred to its age and condition. *The Precipice* (1, 2). Pakhotin was described as handsome and joyful as Palmerston.

Panteleimon. *The Precipice.* A peasant. Berezhkova called all peasants by the diminutive forms of their names, but she could not find a suitable diminutive for Panteleimon.

Panteleimonov. *Dead Souls.* A dead serf whom Pliushkin sold to Chichikov.

Papushin, *The Idiot.* The Moscow merchant who left his fortune to Prince Myshkin's aunt. The prince received the estate from the aunt.

Paramanov. *Dead Souls.* A dead serf whom Pliushkin sold to Chichikov.

Paramanskaia, Galendukha. *The Precipice.* A name thought up by Raiskii. He regarded it as wicked to marry some Galendukha Paramanskaia just for her money and diamonds. His grandmother wanted him to marry the Mamykins' daughter.

Parasha. *Crime and Punishment.* A servant girl. In a conversation with Raskol'nikov, Svidrigailov assured him that his sister Dunia was chaste. Svidrigailov did admit to taking advantage of a black-eyed wench named Parasha who also worked in his home as did Dunia. *Dead Souls.* Anna Grigor'evna's maid.

Parny, Evariste Désiré Desforges, Chevalier de (1753-1814). *The Precipice* (1, 6). The French poet known for his love poems. In his youth, Raiskii read Parny.

Pascal, Blaise (1623-1662). *The Devils* (1, 2, 4). The French religious thinker and author of *Pensées.* Stepan Verkhovenskii stated that he was not a Pascal when Varvara Stavrogina accused him of never saying something short and to the point. Stepan maintained that Russians do not know how to say anything in their native tongue and so far have said nothing.

Pasha. *The Idiot.* A servant of Nastas'ia Filippovna Barashkova. *The Precipice.* A servant referred to by Raiskii.

Pashen'ka. *Crime and Punishment.* See Praskov'ia Pavlovna. *A Common Story.* Petr Aduev reminded Aleksandr Aduev of his love for Naden'ka, referring to her as Pashen'ka.

Pashutka. *The Precipice.* A young girl who waited on Berezhkova. Standing in the corner knitting, she was ready to serve her mistress at any moment.

Patroclus. *The Eternal Husband* (7). The friend of Achilles who was killed while wearing his friend's armor. Achilles was greatly saddened by the loss. The poem quoted in the book was "Das Siegesfest" (1803) by Schiller. It was translated into Russian ("Torzhestvo pobeditelei") in 1828.

Pataskaia, Princess. *The Idiot*. A member of society. Lebedev claimed that when he ran around with Likhachev, he met a certain Princess Patskaia.

Paul. *The Precipice* (2, 5). The hero of *Paul and Virginia* (1788), a popular romance by Bernardin de St. Pierre. The book was in Raiskii's library, and Marfen'ka read it.

Paul, St. *The Brothers Karamazov* (2, 6, 1). The Biblical apostle mentioned in Father Zosima's biography.

Paul. See Pavel.

Pauline. *The Precipice*. One of Pakhotin's girl friends.

Pavel, Father. *The Devils*. The chief priest at the cathedral in the provincial town. He delivered solemn sermons which people wanted him to publish, but he could not make up his mind.

Pavel I (1754-1802). *Dead Souls* (1, 3). The Russian ruler known for his madness. Kutuzov's uniform in the picture hanging in Korobochka's living room looked like one worn in the time of Tsar Pavel I.

Pavel Savich. *A Common Story*. A landowner. Anton Ivanych apologized for being late by saying that his horse stepped on a nail on Pavel Savich's bridge.

Pavlichev, Nikolai Andreevich. *The Idiot*. The benefactor of Prince Myshkin. When Pavlichev met Professor Schneider in Berlin, he sent Myshkin to Switzerland for a cure of his epilepsy in Schneider's clinic there. Pavlichev died three years later. He was also involved in the life of Antip Burdovskii. The latter's mother was a sister of a serf-girl whom Pavlichev loved. She died. Pavlichev took her sister under his care and gave an education. She married a land surveyor named Burdovskii, who gave up his job because of his wife's dowry, took to drink, and died. Pavlichev helped Antip's mother and that generosity led to the false rumor that Antip was his son.

Pavlushka. *Dead Souls*. Nozdrev's servant whom Nozdrev called to beat up Chichikov.

Pavsikakhii. "The Overcoat." A name which Akakii Akakievich's mother considered for her son, but she later settled on Akakii.

Perchorin. *The Devils*. (3, 1, 3). The individualistic and romantic hero of M. Iu. Lermontov's novel *The Hero of Our Time* (1842). In Karmazinov's long and ridiculous introduction at the literary fete, he mentioned that the Russian genius in general had something of Pechorin in it.

Pelageia. *Dead Souls*. The servant girl whom Korobochka sent with

Chichikov to guide him to the main road after he had left her estate. *The Eternal Husband.* Velchanikov's servant from Novgorod. Having a young girl servant bothered Velchanikov since he was a bachelor, but she was so efficient that he was satisfied.

Pelageia Antonovna. *Poor Folk.* A literary character in a work by Rataziaev which Makar Devushkin praised as humorous.

Pelageia Ignat'evna. *Oblomov.* One of the hangers-on in the Oblomov household.

Pelageia Igorovna. *Dead Souls.* The sister of Petr Varsonof'evich's daughter-in-law. The blonde with whom Chichikov was talking at the ball began to yawn when he told of meeting the relatives of Petr Varsonof'evich.

Pelageia Petrovna. *The Precipice.* A servant. Egor Prokhorych drilled a hole into Raiskii's room and invited Pelageia to peek.

Pelageia Semenovna. *The Double.* Goliadkin Junior's aged aunt whom he discussed with Goliadkin Senior.

Pelageia Sergeevna. *The Precipice.* A peasant woman. Egor Prokhorych was such a Don Juan that he only had to call to Pelageia and she submitted.

Pelletier, Pierre Joseph (1788-1832). *The Brothers Karamazov* (4, 10, 7). The French chemist who isolated quinine. He was recommended to Mrs. Snegirova by the town doctor.

Penkin. *Oblomov.* Oblomov's liberal friend who wrote two articles a week for a newspaper.

Pereborkin, Colonel. *The Double.* The former master of Goliadkin's servant Petrushka.

Perekroev, Fedor Fedorovich. *Dead Souls.* An acquaintance of Chichikov. The blonde with whom Chichikov was talking at the ball began to yawn when he told of visiting a certain Perekroev in the province of Riazan.

Perepelitsyna, Mlle. Anna Nilovna. *The Village of Stepanchikogo.* Madame Krakhotin's favorite toady companion who had spite against the whole universe. She had no eyebrows, and her lips were as thin as a thread.

Perependev. *Dead Souls.* The man who played cards with Nozdrev at Likhachev's. Nozdrev told Chichikov that Perependev had stated how sorry he was that Chichikov had not been there, but Chichikov did not know Perependev or Likhachev. It was just another lie from the lips of Nozdrev.

Perepenko, Ivan. "Ivan Ivanovich and Ivan Nikiforovich," in *Mirgorod*. Ivan Ivanovich's father, who was a clerk but was referred to by his son as "Ivan of Blessed Memory." Ivan Nikiforovich called him a notorious drunkard.

Perepenko, Ivan Ivanovich. "Ivan Ivanovich and Ivan Nikiforovich," in *Mirgorod*. The good landowner whose head was like a radish, tail downwards. He was thin and tall, and spoke so well that listening to him "gave one the sensation one has when someone is searching one's hair for lice."

Perepenko, Onisii. "Ivan Ivanovich and Ivan Nikiforovich," in *Mirgorod*. Ivan Ivanovich's grandfather whose lineage was not related to a gander, according to the narrator.

Peresvetov. *Oblomov*. Sud'binskii's colleague who received a better salary than Sud'binskii but did not work so well.

Perkhotin, Petr Il'ich. *The Brothers Karamazov*. A young civil servant who loaned Dmitrii Karamazov money on the night of the murder. He planned to marry Madame Khokhlakova, but she finally spurned him. Perkhotin wrote a humorous poem for her entitled "On the Convalescence of the Swollen Foot on the Object of My Affections." After Madame Khokhlakova turned him down, he wrote a paragraph about her in a gazette called *Gossip*.

Perkhunovskii. *Dead Souls*. A guest at the governor's ball.

Perovskii, General V. A. (1795-1857). *The Gambler* (1). A Russian military figure. When the narrator told the general and his family about his experiences in Paris, a Frenchman objected to a story about a French officer who shot a child in 1812. The general advised him to read General Perovskii, whose memoirs were published in the *Russkii Arkhiv* in 1865 and were probably read by Dostoevskii.

Perugino, Il (Pietro Vannucci) (1446-1523). *The Precipice* (1, 14). An Umbrian painter of the early Renaissance who was a teacher of Raphael. Raiskii's girl friend Natasha was like a figure in a Perugino painting: clean, trusting, and loving.

Persherits. "Taras Bul'ba," in *Mirgorod*. A Cossack whom Taras greeted when he escorted his sons to the Zaporozhe camp.

Pestov. *The Precipice*. An acquaintance of Openkin, who spent three days at Pestov's to escape his wife's nagging.

Pestriakov. *Crime and Punishment*. The man who was with Kokh when they found the murdered pawnbroker and her sister. They were both accused of murdering them.

Peter. See Petr.

Petinka (diminutive for Petr). *Poor Folk.* Gorshkov's son who died.
Pet'ka.*The Double.* A name used by Dostoevskii to refer to a typically
fine young dancer at the birthday party of Klara Olsuf'evna
Berendeeva.
Petr. *The Adolescent.* Prince Sergei Sokolskii's servant. *The Brothers
Karamazov.* A serf of a murdered woman who was mentioned in
Father Zosima's biography. *The Double.* See Petrushka, a dimin-
utive for Petr. *The Precipice.* Petr (Petrushka) Berezhkova's valet.
Petr, St. *The Precipice* (4, 4). One of the twelve disciples of Jesus. In an
ecstasy of love, Raiskii was ready to rebuild St. Petr's cathedral
in Rome.
Petr I, Velikii (the Great). (1672-1725). *The Precipice* (1, 6). The Russian
tsar from 1689 to 1725. Raiskii was not captivated by Russian
history, but he did have some interest in Petr I.
Petr III (1728-1762). "Old-World Landowners," in *Mirgorod.* The Russian Emperor from 1761 to 1762 who was killed by followers of
his wife Ekaterina II. She then ascended the throne.
Petr Fedorovich. "Ivan Ivanovich and Ivan Nikiforovich," in *Mirgorod.*
The police captain who lost a button from his coat two years
previously, and the police were still looking for it. He moved
slowly because as he limped, he threw his wounded leg so far to
the side that it cancelled out the work done by the other leg.
Petr Il'ich. See Perkhotin, Petr Il'ich.
Petr Ivanich. *The Underground Man* (2, 1). A literary figure from I. A.
Goncharov's novel *A Common Story* (1847). Dostoevskii referred
to Petr Ivanich Aduev, who was adroit in business.
Petr Petrovich. *A Common Story.* A common name. While Petrs were all
over the town, Aleksandr Aduev became lonely in St. Petersburg when he moved there. *Poor Folk.* The man assaulted by
Aksentii Osipovich. Devushkin witnessed their encounter
while eavesdropping through a crack in the wall. *Oblomov.*
Lecturing Zakhar, Oblomov used the name Petr Petrovich as a
model for a better type of servant. *The Precipice.* An old doctor
who was sent for when Berezhkova was once sick. Also, a
second Petr Petrovich was a professor highly respected by his
students.
Petr Sergeich. *A Common Story.* An acquaintance of Adueva, from
whom Anton Ivanych brought Adueva a greeting.
Petr Stepanovich. *The Adolescent.* The teacher in Makar Dolgorukii's
story about the merchant who did not know how to rear a boy
whom he took into his home.

Petr Valerianovich. *The Adolescent*. Makar Dolgorukii's acquaintance who lived ten years in a desert to escape the bonds of matrimony. He refused to take holy vows and believed that science would someday answer all questions.

Petr Varsonf'evich. *Dead Souls*. An acquaintance of Chichikov. The blonde with whom Chichikov was talking at the ball began to yawn when he told of meeting Petr Varsonf'evich in Viatka.

Petr Zakharich. *The Idiot*. A clerk who told Lebedev that the department head Nil Alekseevich had died as Lebedev predicted.

Petrarch, Francesco (1304-1374). *A Common Story* (2, 1). The Italian poet. Aleksandr Aduev quoted Petrarch while describing his love for Naden'ka to his aunt.

Petromikhali. "The Portrait," in *Arabesques*. An extremely rich money lender who kept every penny he made. There were rumors that he sometimes gave away money but made such demands that people ran in horror.

Petrov. *The Idiot*. A friend of Kolia Ivolgin and Kostia Lebedev. Petrov gave them money to buy Schlosser's history book, but instead they bought a hedgehog. Aglaia Epanchina later bought the animal from them and sent it to Prince Myshkin. *Notes from a Dead House*. An unpredictable drifter with no real aims in life. He was considered the most desperate man in the prison. He was actually an informer. *Oblomov*. The man who Oblomov insisted was an disenchanted with life as he was.

Petrov, Anton (d.1861). *The Devils* (1, 1, 9). A peasant in the province of Kazan who stirred up a mutiny among his fellow peasants. In suppressing the uprising, tsarist troops killed many. Later Petrov was shot after being condemned by a court. When a similar incident happened near Skvoreshniki, the Stavrogin estate, Stepan Verkhovenskii went to the governor and declared that he had had nothing to do with the affair.

Petrovich. "The Overcoat." The tailor who advised Akakii Akakievich to have a new coat made. *Notes from a Dead House*. An invalid prisoner who grumbled and stayed to himself.

Petrushka. *Dead Souls*. Chichikov's flunky, who watched his master take three hours to dress. Petrushka means parsley in Russian. *The Double*. Goliadkin's servant. *Oblomov*. Oblomov's servant at the estate Oblomovka.

Petukh, Aleksasha. *Dead Souls*. Petr Petukh's son, who was home on vacation.

Petukh, Nikolasha. *Dead Souls*. Petr Petukh's son, who was home on vacation.

Petukh, Petr Petrovich. *Dead Souls*. The landowner who was pulling
    fish out of a net when Chichikov came to call on him. Chichikov
    thought he was calling on Koskarev.
Phaon. *The Brothers Karamazov* (3, 8, 7). The Greek youth who rejected
    Sappho's advances, causing her to throw herself into the sea.
    Maksimov mentioned him in a poem which he quoted during
    Dmitrii Karamazov's spree at Mokroe.
Phidias (5th Cent. B.C.). *A Common Story* (2, 6). A Greek sculptor of the
    Periclean age whom Petr Aduev mentioned while discussing
    art. *The Precipice* (5, 23). Raiskii decided to go to Rome and try to
    be a sculptor like Phidias.
Philemon. "Old-World Landowners," in *Mirgorod*. In Greek legend, the
    husband of Baucis. This devoted couple gave food and shelter to
    Zeus and Hermes after others had refused them. As a result of
    their generosity, Zeus spared their lives in the flood which he
    unleashed on their neighbors. The Tavstogubs were a devoted
    couple like Philemon and Baucis.
Philip. See Filipp.
Philip II (1527-1598). "The Notes of a Madman," in *Arabesques*. The
    Spanish king who came to the throne in 1556, heading a
    Catholic reaction in Europe. During his reign, the Spanish
    Inquisition reached its zenith. In his notes, the madman men-
    tioned that his servant Mavra was surprised to hear that he was
    the King of Spain because she associated the title with Philip.
Phoebus. *The Brothers Karamazov* (3, 8, 5). An epithet of Apollo men-
    tioned by Dmitrii Karamazov when he discoursed on his love of
    life with Perkhotin. The latter was alarmed at Dmitrii's be-
    havior when he bought back the pistols he had pawned. *The
    Precipice* (3, 14). Raiskii told Vera that Tushin was like Phoebus:
    healthy, strong, fearless, and handsome.
Phyrov, Abakum (Habakkuk Phyrov.) *Dead Souls*. A runaway serf who
    appealed to Chichikov's imagination. Chichikov daydreamed
    about him.
Pichet. *The Precipice*. The owners of a local millinery store. Kritskaia
    admired a hat which she assumed had come from Pichet's.
Piderit, M. *Crime and Punishment* (5, 3). A journalist. At Marmeladov's
    funeral dinner, Lebeziatnikov explained to those assembled
    that he had come late because he dropped off an article by
    Piderit at Madam Kobilatnikova's.
Pidisshok. "Taras Bul'ba," in *Mirgorod*. A Cossack about whom Taras
    inquired at the Zaporozhe camp. He learned that Pidisshok's
    head had been sent to Constantinople in a barrel of brine.

Pierre. The French for Petr (Peter). *The Devils*. The name by which Stepan Verkhovenskii addressed his son Pierre when they met for the first time in ten years. *Oblomov*. A guest on the estate managed by Sholtz's father. Prince Pierre taught Sholtz about military uniforms. *The Precipice*. Sof'ia Belovodova was sure that Prince Pierre loved someone but was not showing it.

Pierrot (French for "little Peter"). *The Brothers Karamazov* (4, 12, 2). A favorite character of pantomime, a sort of clown-lover. Dmitrii Karamazov referred to his father Fedor at the trial as a Pierrot.

Pilate, Pontius (26 B.C.-36 A.D.). *The Adolescent* (2, 4, 3). The Roman Governor of Judea. Versilov told Arkadii Dolgorukii that his landlord had tried to convince a lodger that the British parliament once appointed a committee of jurists to review the trial of Jesus and Pilate. *The Precipice* (4, 9). Raiskii thought that the question "Where is the truth?" was Pilate's major concern.

Pimen the Bold. *Dead Souls*. The owner of the pub where Petrushka spent most of his time in the town of N--.

Pimenov. *Dead Souls*. A dead serf sold to Chichikov by Pliushkin.

Pirogov, Lieutenant. "Nevskii Prospect," in *Arabesques*. One of the officers who formed a sort of middle class in Petersburg and who passed for well-bred, highly educated young men. *The Underground Man* (2, 1). A reference was made to Gogol's hero in the story "Nevskii Prospect."

Pirogov, Nikolai Ivanovich (1810-1881). *The Idiot* (1, 12). A famous Russian surgeon who General Ivolgin claimed came to him when he was wounded at Sevastopol. Actually, Dr. Pirogov did administer to the wounded at Sevastopl, even journeying to St. Petersburg to plead for an improvement of medical facilities in the war zone.

Piron, Alexis (1689-1773). *The Adolescent* (1, 5, 3). A French satirical poet. Arkadii Dolgorukii felt that if he were as rich as a Rothschild, such a writer as Piron would not outshine him. *The Brothers Karamazov* (3, 8, 7). Maksimov mentioned Piron, who was noted for his epigrams. He was called a "machine à saillies."

Pisarenko. *The Double*. The clerk who came to Goliadkin when he was hiding behind the stove. To Golaidkin's surprise, Pisarenko delivered the information that Ostaf'ev was sent for. "Taras Bul'ba," in *Mirgorod*. A Cossack whose cut-off head spun in the air with its eyelids beating, during the fighting for the besieged Polish city.

Piskarev. "Nevskii Prospect," in *Arabesques*. A timid, modest, simple-hearted artist whose passion ruined him and brought on his suicide.

Pkhailo, Kazimir Al'bertych. *Oblomov*. A guest at Ovchinin's dinner.

Placet, Blanche du. See Cominges, Blanche de.

Plastunov, Trifon Borisovich. *The Brothers Karamazov*. The innkeeper at Mokroe when Dmitrii Karamazov went on a spree.

Plato (427?-347 B.C.). *The Devils* (2, 7). The famous Greek philosopher. When Shigalev spoke at the Virginskiis' group meeting, he mentioned Plato as a naïve dreamer whose works are for sparrows, not humans. *Oblomov* (4, 9). The Platonic aspects of Oblomov's personal philosophy were indicated by the author. *The Precipice* (1, 16). Leontii Kozlov wrote Raiskii a letter and mentioned that he wanted Raiskii to see his library, including the works of Plato. (2, 14). Kozlov was referred to as Plato.

Platon, Metropolitan (Levshin, Petr Egorovich) (1737-1812). *The Brothers Karamazov* (1, 2, 2). The religious figure mentioned by Fedor Karamazov when he made up an anecdote about Diderot. Miusov accused Fedor of lying, and Fedor did not rebuke him. Fedor was referring to a historical anecdote: when the philosopher Diderot wanted to show his contempt for religion to the Metropolitan Platon, he said, "There is no God." The Holy man answered, "The madman says in his heart that there is no God, but you say it aloud." Diderot was so taken aback, he did not answer.

Platonov, Platon Mikhailovich. *Dead Souls*. Petukh's neighbor, who was a handsome young man but was perpetually bored.

Platonov, Vasilii Mikhailovich. *Dead Souls*. Platon's brother, who managed their estate very well.

Pleshakov. *Dead Souls*. A landowner who was a neighbor of Korobochka.

Pliushkin, Stepan. *The Adolescent* (1, 5). The obnoxious character in Gogol's *Dead Souls* to whom reference was made. *Dead Souls*. A greedy, grotesque, dirty old man whose estate had deteriorated into a vile mess. His serfs were dying off like flies because of poor treatment. Chichikov thought that a shepherd had a better diet than Pliushkin.

Pliushkina, Aleksandra Stepanovna. *Dead Souls*. Pliushkin's oldest daughter, who ran off with an officer.

Plotnikov, Pavel Ivanovich. *The Brothers Karamazov*. The shopowner from whom Dmitrii Karamazov bought goods for his trip to Mokroe. Dostoevskii himself liked to buy tidbits in this shop.

Plutarch (46-120 A.D.). *The Precipice* (1, 6). The Greek writer who wrote many biographies of famous Greeks and Romans. Raiskii read Plutarch in a vain attempt to escape from life.

Pobedonosnov, Frol Vasil'evich. *Dead Souls.* An acquaintance of Chichikov. The blonde with whom Chichikov was talking at the ball began to yawn when he told of visiting Pobedonosnov in the province of Penza.

Pobedonosnov, Petr Vasil'evich. *Dead Souls.* The family that Chichikov visited in the province of Penza.

Pochitaev. *Dead Souls.* A landowner who lived near the inn where Chichikov stopped on his way to Sobakevich's.

Podkharzhevskii. *The Underground Man.* A wealthy society figure. The Underground Man's former classmates talked about Podkharzhevskii's wealth during their drunken party at the restaurant.

Podkolesin. *The Idiot.* The hero of Gogol's comic play *The Marriage* (1842). Dostoevskii remarked that Podkolesin was an exaggerated type but that such a type did exist.

Podkumov. *The Idiot.* A student whom Prince Myshkin saved from deportation to Siberia.

Podvysotski, Pan. *The Brothers Karamazov.* The man mentioned by one of Grushen'ka's Polish friends at Mokroe. The Pole maintained that Pan Podvysotski received a million roubles from a bank on a bet. Kalganov called the Pole a liar.

Pogodin, Mikhail Petrovich (1800-1875). *The Idiot* (1, 3). The medievalist and author of *Forms of Ancient Slavic-Russian Writings* (1840) (*Obratsy slaviano-russkogo drevlepisaniia*), in which forty-four forms of Russian script from the ninth to the eighteenth centuries were studied.

Pogorel'tsev, Aleksandr Pavlovich. *The Eternal Husband.* The fifty-five-year-old father of eight children who agreed to rear Vel'chanikov's daughter Liza. Pogorel'tsev had a large house, and he and his family tried to make Liza happy; but she died soon after joining them. He buried her when her legal father Trusotskii did not come to the funeral.

Pogorel'tseva, Klavdia Petrovna. *The Eternal Husband.* The wife of Pogorel'tsev. Klavdia was once courted by Vel'chaninov, but they remained good friends after her marriage. She was the only one he confided in. She was happy to bring Liza, Vel'chaninov's daughter, into her household.

Pogozhev. *The Devils* (2, 10, 3). A literary figure in a work by Karmazinov. The author said that he showed up all the faults of the
Slavophiles in Pogozhev's character. Dostoevskii was actually
panning I. S. Turgenev, who said he showed up the Slavophiles
in his book *A Gentry Nest* (1859) in the character of Lavretskii.
Poins. *The Devils* (1, 2, 1). The companion of Sir John Falstaff in
Shakespeare's *King Henry IV, Parts I and II*. Verkhovenskii likened
Nikolai Stavrogin's antics in St. Petersburg to the merrymaking
of Shakespearean characters in Henry IV. Varvara Stavrogina
read the play but did not agree with Shakespeare.
Pokorev. *Crime and Punishment*. The fellow student who gave
Raskol'nikov the address of the old pawnbroker Alena Ivanov-
na.
Pokrovskii, Petr Zakharovich (Petinka). *Poor Folk*. Anna Fedorovna's
boarder who taught Varvara and Sasha.
Pokorvskii, Zakhar Petrovich. *Poor Folk*. The man whose son stayed at
Anna Fedorovna's. He and Varvara bought a collection of
Pushkin's works for his son Petr's birthday. Varvara allowed
Zakhar to tell Petr that he himself had purchased the volumes.
She felt sorry for Zakhar because he was ill. He did die soon
afterwards.
Pokrysha. "Taras Bul'ba," in *Mirgorod*. A Cossack chief who chose to go
fight the Tartars instead of fighting the Poles.
Pole. *Crime and Punishment*. An unfortunate who happened to be
stranded at Madame Lippevekhzel's when Marmeladov died.
The Pole helped Katerina Ivanovna set up the funeral dinner.
Polenov, Efim Petrovich. *The Brothers Karamazov*. A marshal of the
nobility who supervised the education of Alesha and Ivan
Karamazov after the death of the general's widow, who had
taken the children from their father Fedor. Polenov educated
both boys at his own expense.
Polezhaev. *Dead Souls*. The man whose name came from the verb "to lie
down for a nap" ("polezhat"). When news of Chichikov's buying
of dead souls spread through the town of N--, people who never
stirred came to life, even Polezhaev.
Poliakov, Samuel Solomonovich (1837-1888). *The Adolescent* (1, 5, 2). A
Russian financier in the nineteenth century. Arkadii Dolgorukii was sure he could be as wealthy as Poliakov.
Polignac, Jules de (1780-1847). "Notes of a Madman," in *Arabesques*. A
reference was made to the French reactionary political figure.

Policarp. *Dead Souls.* The village priest who, it was expected, would find Pliushkin's money in bureau drawers after the miser had departed from the earth.

Polina. *The Precipice.* See Kritskaia, Polina.

Polina Aleksandrovna. *The Gambler.* See Praskov'ia Aleksandrovna.

Polinka. See Sachs, Polinka.

Polkan. *Oblomov* (1, 9). A Russian epic hero. When Oblomov was a child, his nurse told him stories about Polkan.

Polonius. *The Brothers Karamazov* (2, 5, 4). A character in Shakespeare's *Hamlet.* Ivan Karamazov told his brother Alesha that he had the knack of turning a phrase just like Shakespeare's character.

Polosukhin, Petr Kus'mich. *The Eternal Husband.* An acquaintance of Trusotskii. When Vel'chanikov's moaning from his painful illness awakened him, Trusotskii told his sick friend that an acquaintance Polusukhin had used compresses for a similar disease.

Polovitsin. *The Village of Stepanchikogo.* A figure in Russian society. Anfisa Petrovna Obnoskina claimed a General Polovitsin as one of her close friends in St. Petersburg.

Pompey (Gnaeus Pompeius Magnus) (106-48 B.C.). *The Devils* (3, 1, 3). The Roman general who organized the First Triumvirate with Julius Caesar and Crassus in 60 B. C. In a long and ridiculous introduction at the literary fete, Karmazinov mentioned that a couple was sitting in Germany beholding Pompey in battle.

Ponomarev. *Dead Souls.* A store owner who usually cheated his customers, but at the village fair he gave Nozdrev and some officers an excellent wine.

Pope. *The Underground Man* (2, 2). Mentioned by Dostoevskii, who was referring to the conflict between Napoleon I and Pope Pius VII in which Napoleon was excommunicated from the church in 1809 and the Pope was a prisoner of the French Emperor for five years.

Poplevin. *Dead Souls.* The unknown who was playing the part of Rollo in the play by Kotzebue. See Kotzebue.

Popov. *Dead Souls.* Pliushkin's runaway serf whom Chichikov considered a very cunning peasant. "Ivan Ivanovich and Ivan Nikiforovich," in *Mirgorod.* An early nineteenth century publisher of popular literature for the semi-literate. *The Precipice.* The governor who expected Berezhkova to call on him first; but since she never did, he never visited her.

Popovich, Demic. "Taras Bul'ba," in *Mirgorod*. A thick-set man who was once captured and tortured. He returned with his head all blackened and singed.

Poprishchin, Aksentii Ivanovich. "Notes of a Madman," in *Arabesques*. The hero of the story who suddenly discovered that he was the King of Spain even though others did not agree with him and escorted him to a mental hospital.

Porfirii. *The Brothers Karamazov*. A novice who helped Father Zosima. Porfirii was fearful that Father Zosima loved Alesha Karamazov more than he loved him, but Zosima assured him that he loved them both. *Dead Souls*. Nozdrev's servant.

Porfirii Petrovich. *Crime and Punishment*. The chief of the criminal investigation department who was about thirty-five-years-old. He was highly intelligent, perceptive, and clever. He had a large round head with a rather snub-nosed face. He had compassion for Raskol'nikov and allowed him two days to confess to his crime before an official deputation would be made.

Porthos. *The Idiot* (1, 8). One of *The Three Musketeers* (1844) by Alexandre Dumas *père* (1802-1870). He was mentioned by General Ivolgin when thinking about his old friends General Epanchin and Prince Nikolai Myshkin. Ivolgin considered Epanchin to be like Porthos.

Pospelov. *A Common Story*. Aleksandr Aduev's friend who rode 150 miles to say goodbye to Aleksandr.

Postumia. *The Precipice* (2, 7). A name by which Kozlov sometimes called his wife. Postumia is an ancient road in northern Italy constructed in 148 by the consul Spurius Albinua.

Potanchikov, Lieutenant. *Crime and Punishment*. A deceased friend of Raskil'nikov's deceased father. Potanchikov fell into a well and was not pulled out until the next day.

Potapych. *The Gambler*. Tarasevicheva's butler who was a white-haired old man with a bald pink pate. He was not allowed in the gambling room with his mistress.

Potchinkov. *Crime and Punishment*. An acquaintance of Razumikhin. After talking with Zametov in a restaurant, Raskov'nikov met Razumikhin, who invited him to a housewarming at Potchinkov's house. Raskol'nikov refused.

Potemkin, Grigorii Aleksandrovich (1774-1776). *The Brothers Karamazov* (1, 2, 2). The Russian general and favorite of Ekaterina II; mentioned by Fedor Karamazov.

Potiphar's wife. "Vii," in *Mirgorod*. In the Old Testament (Gen. 39), she was the wife of Joseph's master in Egypt. When Joseph fled her advances and left his coat behind, she accused him of evil deeds and had him cast into prison. One of the most popular plays at the Kiev monastery was about her.

Potocki, Nikolai. "Taras Bul'ba," in *Mirgord*. The Polish leader who was captured by the Cossacks but was freed when the priests of the Russian Church asked them to liberate him. Taras opposed freeing a treacherous Pole and left the Cossack army when they did. Later Potocki captured Taras and burned him at the stake.

Potseikin. *Notes from a Dead House*. The prisoner who played the part of Kedril in the play *Kedril the Gluttonous*. See Kedril. He was supposed to be a better actor than the convict Bakluskin, to the sorrow of the latter.

Potseluev. *Dead Souls*. An officer who was at the fair with Nozdrev.

Poulet. *A Common Story*. The French teacher who was hired to teach Tafaeva French literature.

Praskov'ia. *The Devils*. A nun who used to ask Mary Lebiatkina to tell her fortune in cards without letting the mother superior know about it.

Praskov'ia Fedorovna. *Dead Souls*. The woman who thought that the checks in the design of the material of Sof'ia Ivanovna's dress were too large for the dress of a lady.

Praskov'ia (Polina) Aleksandrovna. *The Gambler*. The stepdaughter of the general.

Praskov'ia Il'inichna. *The Village of Stepanchikogo*. The narrator's maiden aunt who was the daughter of Madam Krakhotina by her first marriage. Praskov'ia was meek and simple-hearted. The general was spiteful toward her and pulled her hair when she leaned over his deathbed.

Praskov'ia Pavlovna (Pashen'ka). *Crime and Punishment*. Raskol'nikov's landlady and the mother of Natal'ia Egorovna. Raskol'nikov had once planned to marry Natal'ia.

Praskushaka. *Dead Souls*. A diminutive for the name Praskov'ia. Gogol' wrote that clerks found it different to turn down bribes when their wives presented them yearly with extra mouths to feed, like some infant Praskushka.

Praxiteles (390?-330) B.C.) *A Common Story* (2, 6). The Greek sculptor who, Petr Aduev was sure, would not find suitable models for his statues in St. Petersburg. *The Precipice* (5, 23). Raiskii wanted to be a sculptor like Praxiteles.

Predishchev. *Dead Souls*. The landowner with whom Koshkarev had a law suit over the village Gurmikovkii.

Predposylov. *The Eternal Husband*. The man who had a drink with Lobov and Trusotskii at a train station.

Prilukov. *Crime and Punishment*. An acquaintance of Svidrigailov. During a visit with Raskol'nikov in St. Petersburg, Svidrigailov mentioned that he had known interesting personages, mentioning a Madame Prilukov.

Pripukhlov. *The Devils*. A merchant who played cards with Petr Verkhovenskii on the train when Petr made his escape.

Prokhor. *The Brothers Karamazov*. The nephew of Nazar Ivanovich. Prokhor told Dmitrii Karamazov that Grushen'ka had gone to Mokroe. *The Precipice*. A groom on Raiskii's estate who remembered the master when he returned after a long absence.

Prokhorych. *The Brothers Karamazov*. The person to whom Samsonov's servant was running in the dark, the night of Fedor Karamazov's murder. *The Devils*. The club chef.

Prokhorov, Antip. *Dead Souls*. The church bell-ringer to whom Popov said he gave the passport.

Prokhorova. *The Brothers Karamazov*. A widow who came to Father Zosima for help in finding her son. His advice was later proclaimed a miracle.

Prokofii Astaf'ich. *A Common Story*. The man who gave Anton Ivanovich a birch-tea cure. Anton wanted to give the cure to Aleksandr Aduev when he was ill.

Prokofii Ivanovich. *Poor Folk*. A character in a literary work by Rataziaev which Makar Devushkin praised as humorous. Prokofii bit a piece out of the leg of Zheltopuz.

Prometheus. *Dead Souls*. (1, 3). The famous Greek mythological character who stole fire from the gods and brought it to mankind. The fire has become a symbol for wisdom in literature. Gogol' mentioned that Russians can look like Prometheus, but in front of a superior they shake like a leaf. *Oblomov* (4, 8). When Ol'ga Il'inskaia said that sorrow had been added to her happiness, Sholtz said it was payment for Prometheus's fire. *The Precipice* (2, 5). Kozlov preferred the Prometheus legend to the Faust legend.

Proserpine. *The Brothers Karamazov* (1, 3, 3). The Greek goddess of seasonal changes who was mentioned by Dmitrii Karamazov when he recited Schiller's poem "Hymn to Joy" ("*An die Freude*," 1786).

Proshka. *A Common Story*. A servant at the Aduevs' who chased women. *Dead Souls*. The servant boy whom Pliushkin ordered to ready the samovar.

Prostakova, Mashka. *The Eternal Husband.* An acquaintance of Trusotskii. When Vel'chanikov was looking for Trusotskii after Liza's death, he was told by a woman of dubious reputation that Trusotskii spent his time with Prostakova ("simple"). The woman added that Prostakova should really be called Prokhvostova ("scoundrel").

Protushin, Sergi. *The Idiot.* The acquaintance from whom Parfen Ragozhin borrowed twenty roubles in order to take the train for Pskov to escape his father's wrath.

Proudhon, Pierre Joseph (1809-1865). *The Brothers Karamazov* (1, 1, 2). The French philosophical anarchist who wrote *What Is Property?* (1840). He answered the question with "Property is theft." Petr Miusov knew Proudhon personally in Paris. *The Devils* (2, 7, 2). When Shigalov presented his plan for the future organization of mankind, Petr Verkhovenskii called it rotten. However, it was defended by others who felt socialists, for example, Proudhon, had worked out worse systems. *The Idiot* (2, 10). Radomskii pointed out in a conversation at Pavlovsk that Proudhon had shown that "right is might."

Prutkov, Koz'ma. *The Village of Stepanchikogo* (2, 3). The pseudonym of A. K. Tolstoi and his cousins the Zhemchuzhnikov brothers. They wrote many popular poems in the 1860's under this name, including the poem which Il'iusha Rostanev read in Foma Fomich Opiskin's honor.

Prutkova, Tat'iana Pavlovna. *The Adolescent.* Versilov's friend who managed her own estate efficiently. Prutkova approved the marriage of the fifty-year-old Makar Dolgorukii to the eighteen-year-old Sof'ia.

Pshenitsyn, Vania. *Oblomov.* Pshenitsyna's son, whom Oblomov liked to have read and write for him.

Pshenitsyna, Agaf'ia Matveevna. *Oblomov.* The widow of a collegiate secretary and the owner of an apartment which Oblomov rented. She tended to all of his needs and was his maid, mother, landlady, and finally his wife. He was the great love in her life even though she had been married before. When he died, she felt that she had lived to serve his gentle soul.

Pshenitsyna, Masha. *Oblomov.* The daughter of Oblomov's landlady. Masha sometimes tried to sell Oblomov mushrooms and other things.

Psyche. "The Portrait," in *Arabesques.* A beautiful maiden beloved by Cupid. When Chertkov put his painting of Psyche on his easel,

Annette thought it was her portrait and would not believe otherwise.

Ptitsyn, Ivan Petrovich. *The Idiot.* A money lender who married Varia Ivolgina. Her family went to live with him after the marriage.

Ptitsyna, Varvara Ardalionovna. *The Idiot.* Varvara (Varia) Ivolgina's name after her marriage.

Ptolemy (2nd cent.). *The Precipice* (2, 10). The astronomer who stated that the sun revolves around the earth. His theory is known as the Ptolemaic system. Raiskii asked Marfen'ka if she remembered Ptolemy's system of the world.

Pugachev, Emel'ian Ivanovich (1744-1775). *The Precipice* (1, 6). The leader of a famous Cossack revolt. Raiskii liked to listen to an old man tell about the famous mutineer. (3, 23). Volokhov told Vera that his name was feared as much as Pugachev's in the town. *The Village of Stepanchikogo* (1, 7). Gavrila claimed that his grandfather helped hang the rebel Pugachev on an aspen tree.

Pukhivochka, Dorosh Tarasovich. "Ivan Ivanovich and Ivan Nikoforovich," in *Mirgorod.* The Poltava commissar who always visited Ivan Ivanovich when visiting Mirgorod.

Pushkin, Aleksandr Sergeevich (1799-1837). *The Adolescent* (1, 5, 3). The famous Russian writer. Arkadii Dolgorukii quoted from Pushkin's short play *The Miserly Knight* (1830). Arkadii claimed that the greatest thought Pushkin ever wrote was contained in that play: "money is power and that's enough to know" (1, 8, 2). Stebelkov quoted a line of Pushkin's. (2, 3, 2). Arkadii Dolgorukii referred to Pushkin's *Queen of Spades* (1833). (2, 8, 2). Old Prince Sokolskii referred to the perfection of Pushkin's poetry. (3, 8, 1). Versilov mentioned Pushkin's *Eugene Onegin* as a work painful to recall. (Epilogue,3). Pushkin was credited with having pointed out the legitimate themes for the Russian novel in *Evgenii Onegin. The Brothers Karamazov* (1, 2, 7). Rakitan mentioned Pushkin as the poet of women's feet. Pushkin referred to women's feet several times in *Evgenii Onegin.* (3, 8, 3). Pushkin's comments on *Othello* were reflected on by Dmitrii Karamazov. See Othello. (4, 11, 4). In a poem, Perkhotin mentioned Pushkin's numerous references to women's feet. *Crime and Punishment* (1, 5). Dostoevskii wrote that the sick dreamer sees such monstrous images that even if he were Pushkin, he could not recreate them while awake. (5, 1). In and argument with Luzhin, Lebeziatnikov expressed a common theme of the socialists of the period: that work of an honorable nature was better than Pushkin's efforts because it was more useful. *The Devils* (1, 1, 6). Stepan Verkhovenskii was booed until he cried during the literary fete after he mentioned that boots were less important than Pushkin. (1, 3, 2). Dostoevskii stated that Pushkin said something original and was not forgotten after one generation like most Russian writers. (2, 1, 5). Pushkin's letter to Baron Heckeren before the fatal duel with Georges d'Anthes was mentioned by Kirilov. *The Double* (4). Dostoevskii wrote that only a talent such as Pushkin's could attempt to describe the wonders of Olsufii Berendeev's birthday party for his daughter Klara. *The Idiot* (2, 7). Aglaia Epanchina recited Pushkin's poem *Lived a Poor Knight Once, Poor and Plain* (1829) at a gathering at Pavlovsk. (3, 1). Prince S—— said that in Russian literature there was nothing Russian except for Lomonsov, Pushkin, and Gogol'. (3, 3). The Prince discussed the duel in which Pushkin lost his life. (4, 7). Prince Myshkin read Pushkin together with Rogozhin. "Nevskii Prospect," in *Arabesques*. A reference was made to Pushkin. "Notes of a Madman," in *Arabesques*. After seeing the director's daughter, Poprishchin went home and copied a poem which he thought sounded like Pushkin. *Oblomov* (4, 9). Oblomov wanted to know why Pushkin was not named by Alekseev as one of Russia's best authors. The latter did not know why. *Poor Folk* (Part II, June 1). Varvara and Pakrovskii bought a set of Pushkin for his son. See Pakrovskii. *The Precipice* (2, 3). Marfen'ka read *Poltava* (1828) by Pushkin but did not like it because she felt sorry for the heroine of the poem. *The Underground Man* (2, 5). The Underground Man knew that he was acting in a romantic vein, like Silvio in Pushkin's short story "The Shot" (1830). *The Village of Stepanchikogo* (1, 1). Pushkin was supposed to have told a tale about a father who impressed his son by saying "the tsar loves your papa." Foma Fomich Opiskin talked the same way with the peasants. (1, 7). Foma Fomich wondered why Pushkin had not written more poems of a moral nature to help the peasants.

Puzino, Policarp Ivanovich (1781-1866). *A Common Story* (1, 2). An author of medical books and works on superstitions and prejudices. Gorbatova asked Petr Aduev for a book by this writer.

Pygmalion. *Oblomov* (2, 9). In Greek mythology, a sculptor who fell in love with a statue he made. *The Precipice* (3, 20). Raiskii told Vera that Belovodova was a beautiful cold statue that only Pygmalion could love.

Pykthtin. *The Village of Stepanchikogo.* The man who married Kornoukhov's sister in the tale which Egor Rostanev told and which irritated Foma Fomich Opiskin.

Pylades. *A Common Story* (2, 1). The friends of Orestes in Homeric legend. Aleksandr Aduev believed in true friendship and thought of these legendary Greeks.

Pythagoras (c. 530 B.C.). *The Village of Stepanchikogo* (1, 5). The Greek mathematician to whom was attributed the doctrine of the transmigration of souls and the forty-seventh proposition in the first book of Euclid. Foma Fomich Opiskin was supposed to have drawn Pythogoras's theorum when Ezhivikin visited him.

Quasimodo. *The Eternal Husband* (16). The hunchbacked literary figure in Victor Hugo's *Nôtre Dame de Paris* (1830). When analyzing the love which Trusotskii had expressed for him, Vel'chanikov thought of Quasimodo. Vel'chanikov decided that Trusotskii loved him because of the hatred he felt for him, hatred being the strongest of all loves. *Notes from a Dead House* (1, 5). Gorianchikov felt that A——v was a moral Quasimodo.

Queen of Festivities. *The Double.* The title given Klara Berendeeva on the day of her birthday.

Querney, Monsieur de. *The Precipice.* A French aristocrat. Belovodova remembered him as a man who had escaped the French revolution; so she knew that there had been a revolution in France.

Quickly, Mistress Nell. *The Devils* (1, 2, 1). A companion of Sir John Falstaff in Shakespeare's *Henry IV, Parts I and II.* Stepan Verkhovenskii likened Nikolai Stavrogin's antics in St. Petersburg to the merrymaking of Shakespeare's characters in *Henry IV.* Varvara Stavrogina read the play but did not agree with Stepan.

Quixote de la Mancha, Don. See Don Quixote de la Mancha.

R——. Baron. *The Adolescent.* A forty-year-old German colonel in Russian service. He was full of baronial arrogance though penniless. He went to Versilov to express Baron Bjoring's displeasure.

R——, K——. *The Precipice.* K—— R—— and his wife invited Raiskii to dinner to find out what happened between Sof'ia Belovodova and Milari. See Bellini.

Rachel. *The Brothers Karamazov* (1, 2, 3). The Biblical figure (Matt. 2, 18) mentioned by Father Zosima. *The Precipice* (2, 19). Openkin called Marfen'ka the beautiful Rachel. (4, 7). Aianov wrote to Raiskii that Koko married the girl whom he had courted for some years as the Biblical Rachel had been courted.

Rachel, Éliza Félix (1820-1858). *The Devils* (1, 1, 9). A French tragic actress who appeared in Russia. Dostoevskii mentioned her while discussing the adoration of the Russian peasant in Russian literature. He also wrote that a Russian poet had said that Rachel was worth more than all the peasants.

Racine, Jean (1639-1699). *A Common Story* (2, 3). The famous French classical writer. Tafaeva knew one of his lines by heart. *The Gambler* (17). Talking with Mr. Astley, the narrator called Racine affected but still a delight to read. Racine's subjects were derived from the classical tragedies of Euripides. *The Precipice* (1, 10). Raiskii found Racine's works in the family library and read them.

Radcliffe, Ann (1764-1823). *The Village of Stepanchikogo* (2, 3). The English writer of Gothic novels. Egor Rostanev thought that he had read about Catholic orders in Radcliffe's novels.

Radishchev, Aleksandr Nikolaievich (1749-1802). *Crime and Punishment* (2, 2). The Russian writer, political philosopher, and reactionary. Razumikhin told Raskol'nikov that someone told the bookseller Kheruvimov that Rousseau was a kind of Radishchev. Dostoevskii was referring to the socialist Chernyshevskii's remark that Rousseau was a revolutionary democrat. *The Devils* (1, 1, 5). When Stepan Verkhovenskii was compared to Radishchev in a journal, he immediately was obsessed with a desire to show his power. Varvara Stavrogina took him to St. Petersburg to investigate all avenues of expression. (3, 1, 1). The narrator mentioned that people of station suddenly began to listen to the words of worthless individuals, people like sniveling home-bred Radishchevs.

Radomskii, Evgenii Pavlovich. *The Idiot.* Prince S——'s relative who was impressed with Aglaia Epanchina and proposed marriage, but was refused. Nastas'ia Filippovna wanted to discredit Radomskii so that Prince Myshkin could marry Aglaia.

Radomskii, Kapiton Alekseich. *The Idiot.* Evgenii Pavlovich Radomskii's seventy-year-old uncle who shot himself. A large sum of money under his control in state funds was missing.

Raiskaia, Sof'ia (Sonichka) *The Precipice.* The deceased mother of Boris Raiskii, who inherited from her his artistic talent and tendency toward daydreaming.

Raiskii, Boris Pavlovich. *The Precipice.* The hero of the novel who loved art, music, and beauty. He had a changeable character and loved several women, but never married. Although he painted and wrote, he was always a dilettante.

Rakitin, Mikhail Ospovich. *The Brothers Karamazov.* A young liberal who was regarded as a most religious and devout man. He talked Alesha into going to Grushen'ka's in hopes of seeing "the downfall of the righteous." He wanted Grushen'ka to seduce Alesha Karamazov and thereby betrayed his friendship with him.

Ramin, Michel. *The Precipice.* A young man on vacation in the town where Kritskaia lived. She appropriated him as a page.

Raphael (Raffaello Sanzio) (1483-1520). *Crime and Punishment* (4, 1). The great Italian painter. On a visit to Raskol'nikov, Svidrigalov talked of his past, mentioning that he knew great personages. He could even write about Raphael's *Madonna* in Madame Prilukov's album. (5, 1). In an argument with Luzhin, Lebiziatnikov expressed a common theme of the socialists of the 1860's: that work of an honorable nature was better than the work of the artist Raphael because it was more useful. (6, 4). In a conversation with Raskol'nikov about child molestation, Svidrigailov mentioned the beauty of Raphael's *Sistine Madonna.* The face of the Madonna was the face of a young girl whom Svidrigailov once took advantage of. *The Devils* (3, 1, 4). In a long and ridiculous speech at the literary fete, Stepan Verkhavenskii mentioned that Raphael was more beautiful than petroleum and was therefore booed off the stage. *Oblomov* (2, 4). When Stoltz tried to persuade Oblomov to travel abroad, he reminded Oblomov that when they were young Oblomov had expressed a desire to see Raphael's *Madonna. The Precipice* (2, 5). Kozlov did not respect Raphael's works of art. (5, 25). Raiskii saw Marfen'ka in Raphael's paintings.

Raskol'nikov, Rodion Romanovich (Rodia). *Crime and Punishment.* A handsome, intelligent, twenty-three-year-old student who was proud and moody. At times he was kind, generous, and showed compassion to others; but at other times he was cold and withdrawn. He seemed to have a split personality. He was greatly concerned with the meaning of life, and evolved a theory of an amoral superman who had the right to be above moral and civil law. He believed that a person had the right to commit a crime if the deed had the correct aim: for instance, a

murder that would benefit mankind. He tested his theory to see
if he would have remorse. His regeneration came from Sof'ia
Marmeladova.

Raskol'nikova, Avdot'ia Romanovna (Dunia). *Crime and Punishment.* The
beautiful and intelligent sister of the protaganist. She sacrificed
her future for the sake of her family by agreeing to marry the
successful businessman Luzhin. But when he proved to be
unworthy of her, she broke the engagement. Svidrigailov's
advances were also rejected by her, and she finally married the
man she loved, Razumikhin.

Raskol'nikova, Pul'kheria Alekandrovna. *Crime and Punishment.* The
timid, kind, and well-meaning mother of the protaganist of the
story. She loved her son and deprived herself of things in order
to help him. She never accepted his troubles fully and died
without telling her innermost fears.

Rassudkin. *Crime and Punishment.* The name which Luzhin called
Razumikhin by mistake when they were discussing
Svidrigailov.

Rataziaev. *Poor Folk.* A clerk who lived at the boardinghouse where
Makar Devushkin lived. He was a writer and held literary
evenings, often inviting Makar.

Razin, Stepan Timofeevich (-1671). *The Precipice* (3, 23). The leader of a
peasant revolt. Volokhov told Vera that people feared him as
much as they used to fear Razin. *The Underground Man* (1, 7). In
disputing Buckle's theory that civilization makes man less
inclined to warfare, the Underground Man wrote that most
famous slaughterers were civilized men, not crude Cossacks
like the rebellious leader Stenka Razin.

Razumikhin, Dmitrii. *Crime and Punishment.* A loyal friend of
Raskol'nikov. Razumikhin was good-humored and good-
natured. He was a normal, uncomplicated character and quite
industrious. When Raskol'nikov deserted his family,
Razumikhin entered their lives and finally married Dunia.

Rebecca. *The Brothers Karamazov* (2, 6, 1). The Biblical wife of Isaac (Gen.
24-27), mentioned in Father Zosima's biography.

Reinhold. *Oblomov.* A friend of Sholtz's father. Sholtz refused to seek
Reinhold's help in spite of his father's encouragement.

Renan, Ernest (1823-1892). *The Devils* (3, 7, 1). A French philosopher.
When running away from Varvara Stavrogina, Stepan Verkhovenskii met a Bible saleswoman in a restaurant. He remembered that he had not read the holy book in over thirty years,
except for some parts in Renan's *Vie de Jésus* (1863).

René. *A Common Story.* A foreigner with a beard whom Tafaeva invited to her box at the ballet one evening.

Resslich. *Crime and Punishment.* A female money lender. Luzhin told Dunia and Mrs. Raskol'nikova that Svidrigalov once had relations with Resslich. A niece of the woman was found hanging in a garret, and the verdict was suicide. Later it was revealed that the child had been cruelly outraged by Svidrigailov.

Richard. *The Brothers Karamazov.* A French murderer who was mentioned by Ivan Karamazov. *The Precipice* (3, 16). In Voltaire's *Candide* (1759), Richard loved Cunégonde, but he was not allowed to marry her and was sent to America.

Rigaud, Abbé. *The Adolescent.* The priest who confirmed Lambert at Touchard's school when Arkadii Dolgorukii was a student there.

Rinaldini, Rinaldo. *Dead Souls* (1, 9). The bandit hero in a book by C. A. Vulpius (1767-1827). Rinaldo is also one of the great heroes of medieval romance, sometimes called Renault. Sof'ia Ivanovna said that Chichikov burst into Korobochka's house armed like Rinaldo Rinaldini. *The Precipice* (1, 6). As a child, Raiskii enjoyed reading about the brave Rinaldo.

Robert le Diable. *Oblomov* (1, 9). The hero, to whom reference was made, of the opera (1831) by that name by Jacob Meyerbeer (1791-1864).

Rogozhin, Parfen Semenovich. *The Idiot.* The inheritor of a huge fortune. He met Prince Myshkin on the train to St. Petersburg. Rogozhin was passionately in love with Nastas'ia Filippovna. When he brought her 100,000 roubles, she ran away with him. Although she promised to marry him, relations between them broke down several times. He finally killed her with a knife wound under her left breast. He was convicted and sentenced to fifteen years at hard labor in Siberia.

Rogozhin, Semen Parfenovich. *The Idiot.* Parfen's father, who left his son a fortune.

Rogozhin, Sen'ka Semenovich.*The Idiot.* Parfen Rogozhin's younger brother, who received the family fortune after Parfen was convicted of killing Nastas'ia Filippovna.

Rohan, Princess de. *The Idiot* (4, 10). A member of the famous French family by that name. Keller acted toward Prince Myshkin as if the prince were marrying a Rohan instead of Nastas'ia Filippovna.

Rokotov. *Oblomov*. Taran'tev's acquaintance who was planning to be married. Taran'tev asked Oblomov to lend him a dress coat for the wedding. To Zakhar's disgust, Taran'tev never returned the coat.

Roman. *Notes from a Dead House*. A one-time peasant about fifty years old who was a camp water carrier. He was taciturn and staid.

Romeo. *The Adolescent* (2, 8, 1). Shakespeare's famous lover in the play *Romeo and Juliet*. When Prutkova became mad at Arkadii Dolgorukii, she called him a "paper Romeo," but he did not understand. *Crime and Punishment* (3, 4). When Razumikhin and Raskol'nikov were on their way to Porfirii Petrovich's flat, Raskol'nikov teased Razumikhin and called him a Romeo since he had cleaned up and put pomade on his hair.

Rosa Fedorovna. *Dead Souls*. A relative of Pobedonosnov. The blonde with whom Chichikov was talking at the ball began to yawn when he told of visiting Pobedonosnov, who was being visited by Rosa Fedorovna, a second cousin of his sister-in-law.

Rose. "Notes of a Madman," in *Arabesques*. A name that the dog Madgie wished she had been named. Madgie mentioned this fact in a letter to the dog Fidele.

Rossini, Gioacchino Antonio (1792-1868). *The Precipice* (4, 7). The famous Italian opera composer. According to gossip, while Sof'ia Belovodova and Milari were playing some music by Rossini, a kiss was heard.

Rostanev, Egor Il'ich. *The Village of Stepanchikogo*. The narrator's uncle who was of heroic proportions and perfectly satisfied with everyone. When he was about forty and a widower, he retired from the army and settled in Stepanchikogo, a village he had inherited.

Rostanev, Il'ia Egorovich. *The Village of Stepanchikogo*. Egor Rostanev's eight-year-old son, whose birth took the life of his mother.

Rostaneva, Aleksandra (Sashenka) Egorovna. *The Village of Stepanchikogo*. Egor Rostanev's fifteen-year-old daughter, who was brought up in a boarding school in Moscow. She was the only one in the household who dared speak out against Foma Fomich Opiskin. She called him a liar, a mischief-maker, and a stupid bully.

Rostaneva, Katia. *The Village of Stepanchikogo*. The deceased wife of Egor Rostanev.

Rothschild, James (1792-1868). *The Adolescent* (1, 3, 2). A French financier who made millions on the London stock market by being the first to learn of Napoleon's defeat at Waterloo. Arkadii Dolgorukii was mistaken in saying that Rothschild made money by selling information on the forthcoming assassination of the Duc de Berry. See Duc de Berry. *The Idiot* (3, 5). In Ippolit Terentev's article "My Essential Explanation," the wealthy family was mentioned. *The Gambler* (2). When the narrator went to the gambling tables, he commented that what was a paltry sum to a Rothschild was a great sum to him. (4). The narrator again referred to the Rothschilds as a family that had amassed great wealth.

Rousseau, Jean Jacques (1712-1778). *The Adolescent* (1, 5, 4). The famous French philosopher. Arkadii Dolgorukii said that he hated women and referred to Rousseau's memoirs, in which the writer said that he used to expose himself to women that passed by. *Crime and Punishment* (2, 2). Razumikhin told Raskol'nikov that someone told the publisher Kheruvimov that Rousseau was a kind of Radishchev, a reference to A. N. Radishchev (1749-1802), the noted Russian radical. Dostoevskii was referring to the socialist N. G. Chernyshevskii's remark that Rousseau was a revolutionary democrat. *The Devils* (2, 7, 2). When Shigalev spoke at the Virginskiis' group meeting, he mentioned the famous philosopher as a naïve dreamer whose works were for sparrows, not humans. *The Double* (12). When Goliadkin was losing his wits, he mentioned that the times of Rousseau were past. *The Idiot* (3, 9). Kolia Ivolgin felt that Ippolit Terentev's confession was full of tremendous thought which would have been readily evident if Rousseau had written it. *Oblomov* (2, 9). Oblomov gave the works of Rousseau to two sisters he knew to improve their education. *The Underground Man* (1, 11). Heinrich Heine (1797-1856) accused Rousseau of lying in his *Confessions* because no man can tell the truth about himself. The Underground Man felt that he could tell the truth about himself because he was writing for himself, not for the public, as Rousseau had done.

Rubens, Peter Paul (1577-1640). *The Precipice* (1, 4). The celebrated Flemish painter. Raiskii said that Sof'ia Belovodova was not so perfect as the women in Ruben's pictures.

Rubenstein, Anton Grigorievich (1829-1894). *Crime and Punishment* (3, 1). The Russian composer and pianist, whom Dostoevskii knew. They both performed in a literary-musical evening in March, 1862. Dostoevskii read from his book *Notes from a Dead House*, and Rubenstein played Beethoven.

Rubini, John Batista (1795-1854). *A Common Story* (2, 6). An Italian tenor who sang in Russia. Petr Aduev obtained box seats for a Rubini performance, but Mrs. Aduev was displeased because she did not like to go out. *Oblomov* (4, 4). Oblomov left the theater early and did not hear Rubini.

Rusapetov, General. *The Village of Stepanchikogo*. Egor Rostanev's old chief who was invited to visit Stepanchikogo with his family. Foma Fomich Opiskin was insulted that Egor would invite the general. Egor's position was saved when the general turned down the invitation.

Rustan. *The Idiot* (4, 4). Napoleon's bodyguard, who was an Egyptian Mameluke captured by the Emperor on a campaign near the pyramids close to Cairo in 1798. General Ivolgin said that when he was a page of Napoleon, he knew the Mameluke Rustan.

Rutenspitz, Krestian Ivanovich. *The Double*. Goliadkin's doctor.

Ryleev, Kondratii Fedorovich (1795-1826). *The Devils* (2, 6, 4). The famed Decembrist whose *Reflections* (1823) are patriotic and historical in nature. When Blum talked of raiding Stepan Ver-khovenskii's home for forbidden books, he mentioned Ryleev's *Reflections*.

S——, Prince. *The Idiot*. A young, sincere, and modest man who came to St. Petersburg from Moscow. He was engaged to Adelaida Epanchina.

Sabaneev. *The Brothers Karamazov*. A name used by Kolia Krasotkin while teasing a clerk in the market place when Kolia was on the way to visit Il'ia Snegirev.

Sachs, Polinka. *The Adolescent* (1, 1, 5). The heroine of a novel by that name (1847) by A. V. Druzhinin (1824-1864). The theme was the rights of women, not a popular subject at the time. *The Devils* (3, 3, 3). When Petr Verkhovenskii joined Liza Tushina after the Lebiatkins had been murdered, he asked her if she had read the novel *Polinka Sachs*. In the novel, a man arrested his wife for infidelity.

Sade, Marquis de (Count Donatien de Sade) (1740-1814). The French writer and decadent. *The Brothers Karamazov* (1, 3, 8). Fedor Karamazov said that Russians have a bit of de Sade in them because of the way they thrash women. *The Devils* (2, 1, 7). Kirilov asked Nikolai Stavrogin if it were true that the noted debaucher could have taken lessons from him. *Notes from a Dead House* (2, 3). Gorianchikov wrote that some prison officials meted out punishments like a de Sade.

Safronov. *The Adolescent*. A merchant who once insulted Ol'ga Onisimovna. She considered him an uncouth clod.

Salazkin. *The Idiot*. The solicitor who wrote to Prince Myshkin in Switzerland to tell him about his inheritance.

Sallust (Gaius Sallustius Crispus) (86-34 B. C.). *The Precipice* (3, 9). An ancient historian. Volokhov said that Kozlov's students had been reading Sallust for five years.

Saltykov, Michael Evgrafovich (1826-1889). *The Underground Man* (1, 6). The writer whose pen name was N. Shchedrin. His article "Whatever You Like" was mentioned by the Underground Man and printed in *The Contemporary* in 1863.

Salzfisch. *The Devils*. The doctor who came to Stepan Verkhovenskii when he was ill in the country.

Samoila. *Oblomov*. The man who laughed at the idea of Ol'ga Il'inskaia's marrying Oblomov.

Samoilov, Petr Petrovich. *Dead Souls*. The man who was suggested as an overseer for Chichikov by the village chairman.

Samosvistov. *Dead Souls*. A friend who promised to save Chichikov from prison for thirty thousand roubles.

Samson. *The Idiot* (2, 2). The Old Testament hero (Judges 13-16). Lebedev said that Samson was the name of the executioner who dragged the Countess du Barry to the guillotine for the amusement of the French fishwives. *The Precipice* (2, 9). Openkin confused Bibical stories and stated that Samson swallowed the whale.

Samsonov, Kuz'ma Kuzmich. *The Brothers Karamazov*. The rich landowner who was known as Grushen'ka's protector. Through his influence, his relative Madame Morozova took Grushen'ka in as a lodger. Grushen'ka always spent one evening a week with him to help him with his accounts.

Sand, George (Amantine Lucile Aurore Dupin) (1804-1876). *The Devils* (1, 1, 1). The French writer known for her love affairs and novels with socialistic and humanitarian themes. Stepan Verkhovenskii managed to publish an article on the moral nobility of knights in a journal that propagated the ideas of George Sand. (1, 1, 9). Stepan Verkhovenskii stated that Christianity had failed to understand women, as "George Sand has proved in one of her remarkable novels." He was referring to Sand's novel *Lelia* (1833). (3, 1, 2). In the poem Lebiatkin read at the literary fete, there was a reference to George Sand, whom he called a reactionary. *Oblomov* (2, 6). Oblomov did not like the freedom for women supported by George Sand. He believed in a placid married life. *The Underground Man* (2, 8). A reference was made to the famous French novelist.

Sandmann, Der. *The Precipice* (2, 3). The hero of a work by E.T.A. Hoffmann (1776-1822) which Marfen'ka enjoyed reading.

Sapozhkova, Anfisa. *The Adolescent*. A housemaid at Versilov's who escaped bedding with the master. Arkadii Dolgorukii considered her a winner, not a loser.

Sappho (c. 600 B.C.). *The Brothers Karamazov* (3, 8, 7). The Greek poetess of Lesbos known as the "tenth muse." Maksimov mentioned Sappho in a quotation during Dmitrii Karamazov's wild spree at Mokroe.

Sarah. *The Brothers Karamazov* (2, 6, 1). The Biblical wife of Abraham (Gen. 12-13), mentioned in Father Zosima's biography.

Sasha. *Poor Folk*. Anna Fedorovna's orphaned relation with whom Varvara lived and studied as a child. In her letter of April 25, Varvara commented that she saw Sasha and that the girl was going to ruin. Sasha told Varvara that it was wrong for her to have close relations with Makar Devushkin since he was not a kinsman.

Sashen'ka. *A Common Story*. A name which Petr Aduev used for Naden'ka.

Savel'ev, Ivan Dmitrich. *The Idiot*. The art merchant who offered the Rogozhins five hundred roubles for a painting, for which the deceased head of the family had paid only one or two roubles. Prince Myshkin said the painting was a copy of a Hans Holbein.

Savel'ev, Petr-Neuvazhai-Koryto (Peter-No-Respect-For-The-Pig-Trough). *Dead Souls*. One of Korobochka's dead serfs.

Savelii. *The Precipice*. The new overseer on Raiskii's estate.

Savinov. *Oblomov*. The man who had open house every Thursday.

Savla. See Paul.

Savrasov. *The Precipice* The student who was first in the class when Raiskii was in school.

Savva Gavrilovich. "Ivan Ivanovich and Ivan Nikiforovich," in *Mirgorod*. A guest at the police captain's party where a reconciliation between the two warring Ivans was unsuccessfully attempted.

Say, Jean Batiste (1767-1832). *Oblomov* (2, 4).). A French economist. Sholtz reminded Oblomov of the time he brought him a translation of the works of Say.

Scheherazade. *Dead Souls* (1, 10). The daughter of the Grand Vizier of
the Indies from the *Tales of the Arabian Nights*. St. Petersburg was
referred to as a Scheherazade fairyland. *The Precipice* (10, 3).
Raiskii told Vera that nothing compares to passion, not even
the tales of Scheherazade.

Schiller, Johann Christoph Friedrich von (1759-1805). *The Adolescent* (3,
6). The German philosopher of the romantic period. Arkadii
Dolgorukii claimed that there were no pure Schillers in the
world. He felt they were only an invention. *The Brothers Karamazov* (1, 2, 8). Fedor Karamazov referred to Schiller's *The
Robbers* (1781) when creating the scandalous scene in the monastery. (4, 12, 6). Schiller was mentioned by Ippolit Kirillovich at
the trial. (4, 12, 13). Fetiukovich mentioned Schiller at Dmitrii
Karamazov's trial. *A Common Story* (1, 2). Aleksandr Aduev
translated some works by Schiller, but Petr Aduev destroyed
the translations. *Crime and Punishment* (1, 4). When Raskol'nikov
thought about his mother's hopes of help from Mr. Luzhin
after Dunia had married him, he was saddened, knowing that
Luzhin acted as if he had a Schilleresque heart, but chances
were that he did not. The reference was to the idealistic
romanticism connected to the German's name. To Dostoevskii,
the name Schiller was a symbol of ethical idealism and a
beautiful soul. (6, 3). Svidrigailov called Raskol'nikov a Schiller.
(6, 4). Svidrigailov again referred to Raskol'nikov as Schiller. (6,
5). Svidrigailov said that the Schiller in Raskol'nikov was in
revolt every moment. *The Eternal Husband* (16). When analyzing
the love which Trusotskii had expressed for him, Vel'chanikov
called him a Schiller inside and a Quasimodo outside. "Nevskii
Prospect," in *Arabesques*. A reference was made to the German
philosopher because another character in the story had the
same name as the German romantic writer. *Oblomov* (2, 4).
Oblomov gave works by Schiller to two young sisters for the
improvement of their education.

Schiller. "Nevskii Prospect," in *Arabesques*. The ironmonger and tin-
smith who was the husband of the blonde whom Pirogov
followed home.

Schlosser, Frederick (1776-1860). *The Idiot* (4, 5). The German historian
and author of *Universal History* (1844). A boy gave Kolia Ivolgin
some money to buy Schlosser's history, but he bought a
hedgehog instead. The Russian edition of Schlosser's work
appeared in 1862.

Schmertsov, Mavrikii Mavrikievich. *The Brothers Karamazov*. A police inspector at Mokroe.

Schubert, Franz Peter (1797-1828). *Oblomov* (2, 10). The Austrian composer. Hearing Ol'ga Il'inskaia sing Schubert's music, Oblomov thought that life was wonderful.

Scopets. See Skopets.

Schmidt. *The Brothers Karamazov*. A retired colonel who was supposed to have built the summer house at the Karamazov manor. *A Common Story*. Tafaeva's German teacher in the past. *The Idiot*. A companion of the Princess Belokonskaia. *The Precipice*. A jeweler at whose shop Raiskii picked up some purchases for Vera.

Schneider. *The Idiot*. The doctor whom Pavlichev met in Berlin. Prince Myshkin was sent to Schneider's clinic in Switzerland for a cure from epilepsy. After Pavlichev died and no longer sent money, Schneider continued to take care of the Prince. When Myshkin relapsed at the end of the novel, he was sent back to Schneider.

Schultz. *The Brothers Karamazov*. An official mentioned by Fedor Karamazov.

Scott, Sir Walter (1771-1832). *A Common Story* (2, 4). The Scotch poet and novelist. Aleksandr Aduev recommended that Liza read Scott instead of Byron. *Oblomov* (1, 9). The type of castles depicted in Scott's novels did not exist in the area of Oblomov's estate. *The Precipice* (1, 10). Raiskii read the novels of Scott while visiting Berezhkova.

Scribbler. *The Village of Stepanchikogo* (1, 7). The "Scribbler" is a reference to a series of letters printed in the *Contemporary* from 1849 to 1850 and written by the journalist A. V. Druzhinin (1824-1864). The letters were supposedly from a landowner who read all the news of activities in the major cities.

Selifan. *Dead Souls*. Chichikov's coachman.

Selma. *The Gambler*. The name by which Mlle. Blanche went for a while after she had lost her Italian prince.

Semechkina, Dashen'ka. *The Precipice*. Vera's friend who was continually falling in love, even with a picture of a Spanish prince.

Semele. *A Common Story* (2, 3). The daughter of Cadmus and Harmonia in Greek mythology. She was the mother of Dionysus by Zeus, and she was slain by lightning when Zeus appeared before her as the god of thunder by her request. Tafaeva liked stories from mythology.

Semen. *The Adolescent*. Lambert's pockmarked acquaintance who preferred paying for himself when he went to the restaurant with

Andreev and Arkadii Dolgroukii. *Oblomov*. A servant of the Il'inskiis. *The Precipice*. The servant who awakened Vikent'ev when he screamed during a nightmare.

Semen Arkhipych. *A Common Story*. A person who died. Anton Ivanych brought news of the death to Adueva.

Semen Iakovlevich. *The Devils*. A noted half-wit and prophet to whom many townspeople went for saintly messages. When Liza Tushina and Maurice Drozdov went to Semen, Liza whimsically insisted that Maurice kneel to the saintly man. Maurice carried out her wish and made himself appear ridiculous. Liza ran to him and made him stand up. They left immediately.

Semen Ivanich. *The Double*. The clerk who died and was replaced by Goliadkin Junior.

Semen Ivanovich. *Dead Souls*. The town official who was never called by his last name. He also became much thinner during the Chichikov affair, as did most of the other officials.

Semen Semenovych. *Oblomov*. Oblomov's former colleague who was always trying to impress others.

Semenov. *Oblomov*. A man who was as lazy as Oblomov and as disappointed with life.

Semiramis. *Dead Souls* (1, 10). The Queen of Assyria in legendary history. She supposedly built the city of Babylon and its hanging gardens. Kopeikin felt that the suspended bridges in St. Petersburg were as majestic as the ancient hanging gardens.

Sen'ka. *The Idiot*. See Rogozhin, Sen'ka Semenovich.

Senkovskii, Osip Ivanovich (1800-1858). *The Double* (7). A writer of tales and the editor of the journal *A Library for Reading* (1834-1856). He wrote under the pseudonym Baron Brambeus. Goliadkin Senior mentioned the writer while talking with Goliadkin Junior. *The Village of Stepanchikogo* (1, 1). The narrator mentioned that Foma Fomich Opiksin once wrote a novel in a style affording an agreeable butt for the wit of the Baron Brambeus.

Seraphicus, Pater. *The Brother Karamazov* (2, 5; 5). A figure in the concluding scene of Goethe's tragedy *Faust*. Ivan Karamazov called Father Zosima by this name when relating his tale of the Grand Inquisitor.

Serapion Brothers (Serapionsbrüder). *The Precipice* (2, 3). Literary figures of the German romantic E.T.A. Hoffmann (1776-1822). Marfen'ka liked Hoffmann's stories, especially the *Serapion Brothers* (1819-1821).

Serge. *The Precipice.* Belovodova's uncle who was in the War of 1812. That was the only date she remembered in history. *The Village of Stepanchikogo.* Mme. Obnoskina could not remember Sergei Aleksandrovich's name and called him Serge.

Sergei Aleksandrovich. *The Village of Stepanchikogo.* The narrator of the novel. After the death of his parents, he was reared by his uncle Egor Rostanev, whom he greatly revered. Sergei was educated well and was living in St. Petersburg when a letter from his uncle took him to Stepanchikogo for a confrontation with Foma Fomich Opiskin.

Segeir Ivanovich. *The Precipice.* Raiskii's rich uncle who was in the military service.

Sergei Mikheevich. *The Double.* A porter who brought Goliadkin a letter from Vakhrameiev.

Setochkin, Anton Antonich. *The Underground Man.* The Underground Man's superior who lent him money when the Underground Man was planning his confrontation with the officer.

Setochkin, Anton Antonovich. *The Double.* Goliadkin's immediate superior in the government service. Their desks were alongside each other.

Sevasti'anov. *The Precipice.* A fellow student in school with Raiskii.

Sebody'ianov. *The Devils.* The merchant who owned the house where Semen Iakovlevich lived.

Shablykin. *The Devils.* The name of the Hussar officer who Praskov'ia Drozdova claimed proposed to her at boarding school. Varvara Stavrogina reminded Praskov'ia that the story of the officer had been proved years ago to be a lie.

Shakespeare, William (1564-1616). *The Adolescent* (1, 5, 3). The English writer. Arkadii Dolgorukii's favorite vision was of an average man who could face the world and feel superior to Shakespeare. (3, 8, 1). Versilov stated that painful memories were like great scenes in literature which are painful to remember, for instance the final monologue of Shakespeare's *Othello. A Common Story* (1, 2). Petr Aduev named the English writer as an example of talent in literature. *Dead Souls* (2, 4). Chichikov saw a bust of the English bard in Khobuev's house. *The Devils* (2, 8, 1). When Petr Verkhovenskii criticized Shigaliev's plan for the reorganization of mankind, he stated that in such a system, a Shakespeare would be stoned. (2, 10, 3). Commenting on great writers in Russia, the narrator said that he had heard that one of the Russian Shakespeares referred to himself as "great." (3, 1, 4). In

his ridiculous speech at the literary fete, Stepan Verkhovenskii
mentioned that Shakespeare was more beautiful than a pair of
boots and was later booed off the stage. *Oblomov* (1, 2). Penkin
discerned Shakespearean style in a poem he read. *Poor Folk* (Aug.
1). Devushkin considered Shakespeare rubbish and fit only for
lampoons. *The Precipice* (1, 16). Raiskii had an old Gothic edition
of Shakespeare's works which he gave to Kozlov. Later Volkhov ruined the set. *The Underground Man* (2, 4). During the
drunken party at the restaurant, the Underground Man's former classmates spoke of Shakespeare's immortality. *The Village
of Stepanchikogo* (2, 5). Foma Fomich Opiskin advised Egor Rostanev to read Shakespeare's *Hamlet* in order to understand the
sufferings of Opiskin's soul.

Shamsharov. *Dead Souls*. The man who won the girl in whom
Chichikov had been interested years before he went to the
town of N——.

Shapkin. *Notes from a Dead House*. The prisoner with long, protruding
ears who felt that having one's ears pulled was the worst thing
that could happen to anyone.

Sharmer, I. B. *Crime and Punishment* (1, 3). A noted tailor in St. Petersburg. Razumikhin mentioned that he was wearing
Sharmer's clothes.

Shatov, Ivan. *The Devils*. The son of one of Mrs. Stavrogina's serfs. He
was reared on her generosity and given a fine education. He
became an idealist. Petr Verkhovenskii and his fellow conspirators murdered Shatov when he refused to participate in their
reactionary schemes.

Shatova, Dasha. *The Devils*. Shatov's sister, who was also reared by
Mrs. Stavrogina. Dasha agreed to marry Stepan Verkhovenskii
after her affair with Nikolai Stavrogin. The marriage plans
failed, and later Dasha expected to leave with Nikolai
Stavrogin; but his suicide again ruined her expectations.

Shatova, Mar'ia. *The Devils*. Shatov's wife, who returned to him
pregnant just before he was murdered. She also discovered
Kirilov's body and become ill. She and her newborn child died.

Shchedrin, N. *The Brothers Karamazov* (3, 8, 3). The pseudonym for M. E.
Saltykov, the noted writer, with whom Dostoevskii had dis-
agreements and literary battles. Madame Khokhlakov stated
that she wrote to Shchedrin for advice. Dostoevskii belittled
her character by such a statement. See Saltykov, M. E.

Schegol'skoi, Prince. *Crime and Punishment.* A *kammerjunker* who danced with Katerina Ivanovna Marmeladova when she was young. When he proposed, she refused.

Shelopaev, Semen Semenovich. *Crime and Punishment.* The employer of the clerk who brought Raskol'nikov news of his mother.

Sheptun. "Vii," in *Mirgorod.* The man whose wife and baby were drained of their blood by the beautiful witch.

Shigalev. *The Devils.* Mrs. Virginskii's gloomy brother, who created a socialist system for Russia. He refused to help murder Shatov.

Shil'. *Crime and Punishment.* An apartment-house owner in St. Petersburg. When the porter in the building of the murdered Alena Ivanovna asked Raskol'nikov who he was, he answered and said he lived in Shil's house. Dostoevskii actually lived in a house (1847-1849) owned by a person with that name.

Shilkin. *Notes from a Dead House.* A typical Moscow stone mason: shrewd, sly, and chary of words. He was peaceful but sometimes drunk. Unsuspectingly, he let Kulikov and A—v leave a tool shed when they tried to escape. Later his suspicions were aroused, and he reported the men missing.

Shilo. "Taras Bul'ba," in *Mirgorod.* A Cossack suggested for the position of headman of the camp; but someone remembered that Shilo had once been caught stealing, and his name was dropped.

Shishkov, Ivan Semenich. *Notes from a Dead House.* The hospital patient who told Cherevin the story of his wife Akul'ka. Gorianchikov overheard the long, sad tale. Shishkov murdered Akul'ka after he learned that she really did love Morozov, the man who had shamed her.

Shkvornev. *The Brothers Karamazov* (3, 8, 7). The person mentioned by Maksimov as the one whom Gogol' had had in mind when he created the literary figure Kuvshinikov.

Shmul. "Taras Bul'ba," in *Mirgorod.* A Jew who denied that the pillagers of churches in the Ukraine were Jews. The Cossacks refused to believe him, and threw him and his friends into the Dnieper to drown. The Cossacks laughed at the misery of the dying men.

Sholtz, Andrei Ivanovich. *Oblomov.* A friend with whom Oblomov grew up in the country. Sholtz lived near the Oblomov estate, and the two young men went to school together. When they lived in St. Petersburg, Sholtz looked after his friend, saving him from many unfortunate situations.

Sholtz, Ivan Bogdanych. *Oblomov.* Andrei's father, who started the pension where Oblomov studied.

Shtol'ts. *Oblomov.* See Sholtz.

Shultz. *Notes from a Dead House.* A middle-aged clockmaker who expressed a desire to marry Luisa, but Bakhlushkin killed him in a fit of jealousy.

Shvabrin, Aleksei Ivanovich. *The Idiot* (4, 7). The name which Dostoevskii borrowed from Pushkin's work *The Captain's Daughter* (1836).

Sibirikov, Savelii. *Dead Souls.* A Russian ironmonger. Nozdrev showed Chichikov a dagger which he insisted was Turkish even though "Made by Sibirikov" was engraved on it.

Sidor. *Dead Souls.* The priest who was supposed to wed Chichikov and the governor's daughter, according to the liar Nozdrev. *The Precipice.* A name Raiskii reflected on while writing his novel.

Sidorikha. *A Common Story.* A peasant healer whom Aleksandr Aduev found in his room and chased away.

Sidorovna. *Dead Souls.* A common name. Chichikov reasoned that clerks take bribes to buy some Sidorovna better material for a dress.

Sidorych. *The Precipice.* The watchman in the school who helped with corporal punishment.

Sikher. "The Portrait," in *Arbesques.* The woman who ran a fashionable shop in St. Petersburg. When Annette came to Chertkov to have her picture taken, Gogol' described her mentality as that of a young girl who was impatient to describe the flounces of Madame Sikher to a friend.

Silenus. *The Brothers Karamazov* (1, 3, 3). The mythical father of Bacchus, the god of wine. When suggesting a drink to Alesha Karamazov, Dmitrii Karamazov said that he was not Silenus even though he considered himself strong. He made a pun with the Russian word "strong" (silen) and the mythical name Silenus.

Silin, Frol. *The Village of Stepanchikogo.* The name of a tale (1791) by N. M. Karamzin (1766-1826). Silen was so kind that he divided his food among his peasants during a year of famine.

Silych. *The Precipice.* The legless old man to whom Marfen'ka gave a rouble in change before going away for a visit with her future mother-in-law.

Simonov. *The Underground Man.* An old schoolmate of the Underground Man.

Sinitskaia, Aleksandra. *The Adolescent.* The woman who told Lambert as a boy that he would have children the first year he was married because he said he would not have any.

Sirotkin. *Notes from a Dead House.* A very handsome, enigmatic man who was condemned to hard labor for life for the murder of Captain Gregorii Petrovich. He was twenty-three, courteous, unobtrusive, meek, and artless. He considered himself an important criminal.

Sistine Madonna. *The Adolescent* (1, 6, 1). The famous painting (1518) by Raphael. Among the valuable things left from Versilov's former wealth was an engraving of the *Sistine Madonna. The Devils* (2, 1, 2). Petr Verkhovenskii maintained that bread carts are more useful than the *Sistine Madonna. The Precipice* (5, 25). While traveling abroad, Raiskii saw the *Sistine Madonna.*

Skachin. *A Common Story.* A family in society. When Aleksandr Aduev was despondent about his love for Naden'ka, the Skachin family wondered why he had disappeared from the social scene.

Skopets. *The Idiot.* A member of a religious sect that practiced castration. Many of the sect were money changers.

Skotoboinikov, Maksim. *The Adolescent.* The merchant in one of Makar Dolgorukii's stories. He paid his employees only what he wanted and considered them as dirt.

Skuratov. *Notes from a Dead House.* One of the most lively prisoners, full of spirit. He took pleasure in amusing his graver companions.

Sloczewski. *The Devils.* An exiled Polish priest whom Liputin brought to Stepan Verkhovenskii's circle. He was accepted on principle for a time, but later avoided.

Slon'tsevskii. *The Devils.* See Sloczewski.

Smaragdov, Sergei Nikolaevich (-1871). *The Brothers Karamazov* (1, 3, 6). A historian referred to by Fedor Karamazov. (4, 10, 1). Kolia Krasotkin read his *Short Outline of General History for Primary Institutions* (1845).

Smekalov. *Notes from a Dead House.* The prison lieutenant who would sometimes give stern punishments, but still retained the prisoners' respect.

Smel'skii, Vladimir. *Poor Folk.* A character in a romantic book by Ratziaev which Makar Devushkin praised.

Smerdiakov, Pavel Fedorovich. *The Brothers Karamazov.* Fedor Karamazov's son, who grew up in the household as a servant. Fedor thought up the surname Smerdiakov because Pavel's mother was Stinking Liza. The Russian verb *smerdit'* means "to stink."

Smerdiashchaia, Lizaveta. *The Brothers Karamazov.* A deformed, mentally defective girl who was seduced by Fedor Karamazov. She

died giving birth to her child in the bathhouse on the Ka-
ramazov property. Griogrii found the dying mother and child.
Smerdiashchaia was not a family name. It was derived from the
Russian verb *smerdit'* which meant "to stink." She was called
Stinking Lizaveta because of her contemptible filth.

Smirnov. *A Common Story.* Petr Aduev's business partner.

Smurov. *The Brothers Karamazov.* One of the boys throwing stones at
Il'iusha Snegirev when Alesha Karamazov came upon them.

Snegirev. *Poor Folk.* A porter at the office who refused to brush
Devushkin's boots because they would dirty up the brush that
belonged to the government.

Snegirev, Il'iusha Nikolaevich. *The Brothers Karamazov.* The young boy
who was being stoned by his classmates when Alesha Karamazov came on the scene. Il'iusha threw a stone at Alesha and
bit his finger. When Il'iusha was dying of tuberculosis, Alesha
visited him with some of the boy's comrades.

Snegirev, Nikolai Il'ich. *The Brothers Karamazov.* The destitute father of
Il'iusha. When Alesha Karamazov took two hundred roubles to
him from Katerina Ivanovna, Nikolai at first accepted the
money because of his poverty but then refused it to save his
pride.

Snegireva, Arina Petrovna. *The Brothers Karamazov.* The impoverished
captain's wife who became mentally deranged. She was a
woman of genteel appearance whose face was thin and yellow.
Her sunken cheeks betrayed her illness.

Snegireva, Nina. *The Brothers Karamazov.* Captain Snegirev's crippled
daughter.

Snegireva, Varvara. *The Brothers Karamazov.* Captain Snegirev's daughter who was young, rather plain, with scanty red hair. She told
her father not to play the fool before Alesha Karamazov when
he came with Katerina Ivanovna's money.

Sobakevich, Mikhail Semenovich, *The Brothers Karamazov* (4, 12, 6). The
fictional character from Gogol's *Dead Souls* who was mentioned
at Dmitrii Karamazov's trial by Ippolit Kirillovich. He said that
such a hero could not be an example for the West, referring to
Gogol's aim that the book set an example for the decadent
Western world. *Dead Souls.* A huge, coarse, bear-like man who
did not exhibit social niceities. He was a prosperous landowner
and valued his serfs, treating them well.

Sobakevicha, Feoduliia Ivanovna. *Dead Souls.* Sobakevich's retiring
wife.

Sof'ia. *The Brothers Karamazov.* See Sof'ia Pavlovna. *A Common Story.*
Mar'ia Karpovna's daughter, who was in love with Aleksandr
Aduev. "Notes of a Madman," in *Arabesques.* The director's
daughter, who ridiculed Poprishchin even though he loved her.
He found out her contempt for him in the dog's letters which he
stole.

Sof'ia Aleksandrovna. *Dead Souls.* The cousin of the daughter-in-law of
Petr Varsonof'evich. The blonde with whom Chichikov was
talking at the ball began to yawn when he told of meeting Sof'ia
Aleksandrovna.

Sof'ia Antonovna. *The Devils.* An old gentlewoman who lived many
years with Mrs. Lembke.

Sof'ia Ivanovna. *Dead Souls.* A most agreeable lady who went to visit
Anna Ivanovna. They got into an argument.

Sof'ia Pavlovna. *The Brothers Karamazov.* A character from A. S. Griboedov's play *Woe from Wit* (1824) who was mentioned by
Madame Khokhlakova when she overheard Lise and Alesha
Karamazova declare their love for each other. The mother said
that her daughter was playing the role of Sof'ia in real life. *The
Precipice.* Marfen'ka thought that Sof'ia Pavlovna in Griboedov's
play was not a good person.

Sof'ia Rostislavna. *Dead Souls.* The niece of the daughter-in-law of Petr
Varsonof'evich. The blonde with whom Chichikov was talking
at the ball began to yawn when he told of meeting Sof'ia
Rostislavna.

Sohn, von. *The Adolescent* (3, 11, 2). A civil servant murdered in a
Moscow brothel in 1869. Old Prince Sokolskii asked Arkadii
Dolgorukii if he remembered the story of von Sohn. The
Brothers Karamazov (1, 2, 8). Fedor referred to Maksimov as von
Sohn, creating a scandalous scene.

Sokolov. *Notes from a Dead House.* A deserter and callous murderer. The
narrator felt that Gazin looked more repulsive than Sokolov.

Sokolovich. *The Idiot.* A Russian general whom General Ivolgin claimed
he knew. When Prince Myshkin accompanied him to the home
where Sokolovich was supposed to live, no one was there by
that name, but General Ivolgin pretended to know the people
that did reside there. Fortunately for him, the residents were
not at home.

Sokolskii, Prince Nikolai. *The Adolescent.* Arkadii Dolgorukii's old employer in St. Petersburg. Sokolskii was a very rich man and a

privy councilor. He was a widower for twenty years and had one daughter, Anna Akhmakova, the young widow of a general.

Sokolskii, Prince Sergei Petrovich. *The Adolescent*. A member of the Moscow branch of the Sokolskii family which was not nearly so wealthy as the St. Petersburg branch. Sergei befriended Arkadii Dolgorukii.

Solomon (638-599 B.C.). *The Adolescent* (2, 8, 2). Solomon was the wisest of the kings of Israel, and was the son of David and Bathsheba (I Kings 2-11). Old Prince Sokolskii referred to Solomon when speaking of the art of life, which to him was akin to poetry. *Dead Souls* (1, 11). Chichikov's school teacher preferred proper behavior to scholastic achievements and would give a boy a zero who could give advice to Solomon. *The Devils* (2, 8, 1). When Petr Verkhovenskii tried to convince Nikolai Stavrogin to become the pretender that the Russian masses would follow, he stated that Nikolai could pass on the judgments of Solomon as new truths. (3, 1, 4). After Stepan Verkhovenskii had left the speaker's stand at the literary fete in disgrace, the third speaker, Petr Aduev asked his nephew Aleksandr what he thought of a tioning that in the courts we get Solomon's judgments and jurymen take bribes to survive. "Taras Bul'ba," in *Mirgorod*. Taras looked at Mordecai as a new Solomon when the Jew told him he would help Taras free his son.

Solon (-560? B.C.). *Crime and Punishment* (3, 5). The Athenian lawgiver. Raskol'nikov maintained that men like Solon were criminals because in making new laws they broke old laws; yet he felt their crimes were justified.

Solov'ev, Sergei Mikhailovich (1820-1879). *The Idiot* (2, 3). The noted Russian historian whose *History of Russia* in twenty-nine volumes appeared between 1851 and 1879. Prince Myshkin noticed Solov'ev's works in the Rogozhin's apartment.

Sonechka. *Oblomov*. Ol'ga Il'inskaia's girl friend to whom Ol'ga turned for advice when Oblomov professed his love for her.

Sonin. *A Common Story*. An acquaintance of Aleksandr Aduev. When Petr Aduev asked his nephew Aleksandr what he thought of a person named Sonin, he answered, "Nothing good."

Sophie. See Sof'ia.

Sophocles (495-406 B.C.). *A Common Story* (1, 3). The Greek dramatist whose bust stood on the Aduevs' bookstand. The bust fell and broke into pieces because of Aleksandr's clumsiness. *The Precipice*

(2, 7). Kozlov spoke about Sophocles with the upperclassmen in his school.

Sopikov. *Dead Souls*. A name derived from the Russian verb *sopet'* meaning "to wheeze." Gogol' used the phrase "to drop in on Sopikov," which means "to sleep and snore with a wheeze."

Sossius. "The Overcoat." A name which Akakii Akakievich's mother considered for her son before settling on Akakii.

Sotskaia. *The Idiot*. A guest of the governor's wife who was attending a ball with a bouquet of camellias. She was in the tale which Totskii told at Nastas'ia Filippovna's party.

Soulie, Frederick (1800-1847) *A Common Story* (1, 4). A noted French writer. Mar'ia Mikhailovna Lubetskaia thought that Soulie's *Les Memoires du diable* (1837) was a wonderful book.

Spigulin. *The Devils*. The family that owned a factory which was kept in a deplorable condition. Petr Verkhovenskii maintained that the factory was a hotbed for cholera and that the workers were never paid their proper wages.

Spinoza, Baruch (1632-1677). *The Precipice* (1, 6). The German philosopher whose works were in the library of Raiskii's father. (1, 16). Kozlov wanted Raiskii to see his library, which included the works of Spinoza.

Spirid. "Vii," in *Mirgorod*. One of the six strong Cossacks who came for Khoma Brut when he refused to read prayers for the beautiful dead girl.

Stavrogin, Nikolai Vsevolodovich. *The Devils*. The handsome young hero who, after a progressive education, became a degenerate in St. Petersburg, where he married the cripple Mar'ia Lebiatkina as a joke. Disappointed in love and disillusioned with his political ideas, he committed suicide by hanging.

Stavrogin, Vsevolod. *The Devils*. Varvara Stavrogina's husband, who died of acute indigestion on the way to the Crimea, where he planned to join the army in the War of 1855.

Stavrogina, Varvara Petrovna. *The Devils*. A strong, determined woman who ruled Stepan Verkhovenskii and many others through her wealth and strong personality. The death of Stepan and the suicide of her son Nikolai left her a lonely old woman.

Stebelkov. *The Adolescent*. A lawyer who was Vasin's stepfather.

Stepan. *Dead Souls*. Sobakevich's dead serf who was called Stepan the Cork. *The Precipice*. A servant who sawed wood early in the morning at Raiskii's estate.

Stepan (Stepa) Dorofeich. *Notes from a Dead House.* A convict who was called a bastard by his friend at the Christmas party. Two minutes later, the friend was his old pal. They argued and made up all evening.

Stepan Dmitrievich. *Dead Souls.* The man to whom Aleksei Ivanovich asserted that Chichikov's dead souls would run away during transportation.

Stepan Ivanovich. *A Common Story.* A common Russian name. When the social season started, people like Stepan Ivanovich prepared their card tables.

Stepan Karlovich. *Poor Folk.* A clerk in Devushkin's office. When Devushkin once talked with him on a business matter, Stepan suddenly exclaimed, "Ah, poor Makar," and walked away, causing Devushkin to blush.

Stepan Varlamovich. *"The Overcoat."* The important person to whom Akakii Akakievich turned when he lost his overcoat. Stepan smugly shamed the poor clerk for his audacity.

Stepanida. *The Brothers Karamazov.* One of the girls whom Dmitrii Karamazov asked to entertain him during his spree at Mokroe. *Oblomov.* If someone had said that the peasant Stepanida was a witch, people would have believed it at Oblomovka.

Stepanida Agapovna. *Oblomov.* A distant relative of Oblomov.

Stepanida Il'inishna. *The Brothers Karamazov.* A rich merchant's wife who was mentioned to Father Zosima by Prokhorovna. Stepanida advised Prokhorovna to write her son's name down for prayer in a church as if he were dead. She maintained that the prayer would trouble his soul and that he would therefore write his mother. Father Zosima shamed her for praying for her son as if he were dead. He assured her that her son was well, and she later found it to be true.

Stepanida Mikhailovna. *The Devils.* Stavrogin's landlady in St. Petersburg and the mother of the child he molested.

Stepanov. *The Adolescent.* The man who was accused of the criminal action done by Prince Sergei Sokolskii. He wrote a letter to the military authorities and cleared Stepanov, but condemned himself. *Oblomov.* A man who wanted only peace and comfort in life, according to Oblomov.

Stepka. *The Precipice.* Berezhkova's new valet who had not been trained to stand straight.

Stinking Lizaveta. *The Brothers Karamazov.* See Smerdiashchaia, Lizaveta.

Stolbeev. *The Adolescent*. The deceased man whose will gave rise to the lawsuit between Versilov and Prince Sokolskii.

Stolbeeva, Anna. *The Adolescent*. A friend of Dar'ia. After Dar'ia's daughter Ol'ga had hanged herself, Anna took Dar'ia into her home.

Stolniakov. *The Double*. A former master of Goliadkin's servant Petrushka.

Stradella, Alessandro (c. 1645-c. 1681). *The Adolescent* (3, 5, 3). An Itlaian composer. Lambert mentioned Stradella while talking with Arkadii Dolgorukov.

Stunend'ev. *The Eternal Husband* (2). The hero of *A Provincial Lady* (1869) by I. S. Turgenev. Trusotskii was reminded of the play when discussing past relations with Vel'chanikov.

Sud'binskii. *Oblomov*. Oblomov's former colleague, who announced during a visit to Oblomov that he was now a department head.

Sue, Eugène (1804-1859). *A Common Story* (2, 3). A French novelist. Tafaeva liked the works of Sue. *Oblomov* (2, 10). Ol'ga Il'inskaia mentioned that Oblomov quoted phrases from Sue's novels which were spoken by ladies.

Sultan of Turkey. "Notes of a Madman," in *Arabesques*. A title for a former ruler of Turkey. Poprishchin claimed that he knew the barber whom a Sultan of Turkey paid to spread Mohammedanism around the world.

Sumarokov, Aleksandr Petrovich (1718-1777). *A Common Story* (2, 3). A Russian writer of classical tragedies. Tafaeva studied his works. *Oblomov* (1, 9). Oblomov's father read Sumarokov's tragedies occasionally. *The Precipice* (1, 10). Raiskii read Sumarokov's works while visiting Berezhkova.

Surikov, Ivan Fomich. *The Idiot*. An acquaintance of Ippolit Terentev. In his article "My Essential Explanation," Terentev mentioned Surikov as a man who was always complaining, not realizing that the power to change his life was within him.

Surkov. *A Common Story*. A fellow businessman of Petr Aduev. Surkov chased women, including Petr's wife.

Sushilov. *Notes from a Dead House*. A good man who posed as Goriachikov's servant by washing his linen. He was a pitifully meek man, downtrodden by nature and not very bright. He was in prison because he had changed places and identities with another man on the march across Russia to Siberia. Instead of serving his own short sentence, for a rouble and a red shirt he was serving an undefined, interminable sentence.

242   SUSLOV

Suslov, Onisim. *Oblomov*. A peasant whose hut was built on the brim of
a precipice, half of it on the ground and half hanging in the air.
Sutugova, Mar'ia Petrovna. *The Idiot*. When Gania Ivolgin confronted
his father General Ivolgin with the fact that the general had
made up the name Eropegov, the accused said that Eropegov
was married to Mar'ia Petrovna Sutugova, but no one believed
him. Later he called her Sutugina.
Suvorov, Aleksandr Vasil'evich (1730-1800). *The Adolescent* (2, 1, 2). The
distinguished military figure during the war with Prussia
(1756-1763), the First Turkish War (1768-1774) and the Second
Turkish War (1787-1791). In 1799, he commanded the Austro-
Russian armies in the war against France. When the landlord
was telling Versilov the tale about the peasant who buried a
large rock, he mentioned General Suvorov. *Dead Souls* (1, 4).
Nozdrev swore as a lieutenant would in Suvorov's army. *The
Double* (6). Goliadkin's reference to Suvorov was based on an
anecdote by Suvorov himself in which he sang like a rooster.
Svetlova, Agrafena Aleksandrovna (Grushen'ka). *The Brothers Karamazov*. A prostitute who aroused the passion and jealousy of
Fedor and Dmitrii Karamazov. She followed Dmitrii to Siberia
after his trial.
Svidrigailov, Arkadii Ivanovich. *Crime and Punishment*. A handsome,
fifty-year-old man who was well preserved and wealthy from a
fine marriage. He tried to seduce Dunia Raskol'nikova when
she was a servant in his home. He was known for his sensuality
and amorality. When Dunia rejected him, he realized that his
life held nothing but desires for physical pleasure. His self-
deceit no longer held him, and he committed suicide. Dostoevskii took the name Svidrigailov from the journal *Iskra (The
Spark)*, in which the name Svidrigailov was used to describe a
lower-class clerk.
Svidrigailova, Marfa Petrovna. *Crime and Punishment*. The wife of the
successful lawyer. When she learned of her husband's treatment of Dunia Raskol'nikova, she tried to help her. She died
after a severe beating by her husband.
Svinchatkin. *The Double*. A former master of Goliadkin's servant
Petrushka.
Svin'in. *Dead Souls*. A landowning neighbor of Korobochka.
Svinkin. *Oblomov*. Sud'binskii's colleague who lost a folder of important papers.

Svirbei, Prince. *Crime and Punishment.* A St. Petersburg aristocrat. When Svidrigailov visited Raskol'nikov, he talked of his past and mentioned that he knew important people such as Prince Svirbei.

Swift, Jonathan (1667-1745). *The Precipice* (2, 5). The English satirist whose works Marfen'ka tried to read.

Sychuga. *Oblomov.* A watchman at some closed textile complexes.

Sylphs. *A Common Story* (1, 4). Elemental spirits of air. Deceased virgins were said to become sylphs and flutter in the air. Naden'ka did not move so gracefully as a sylph.

Sylvester, St. *The Brothers Karamazov.* A holy man mentioned by a monk from the little northern monastery of Obdorsk. He talked with Father Zosima.

Sysoi Pafnut'evich. *Dead Souls.* An infrequent visitor in the town of N—— —. When the town was upset over Chichikov's purchases of dead souls, Sysoi Pafnut'evich showed up from nowhere.

T——vskii. See Tokarzewski, Simon.

Tacitus, Cornelius (55?-117? A.D.) *The Precipice* (1, 12). The Roman politician and historian. Raiskii was interested in Roman literature and read the works of Tacitus.

Tafaeva, Iulia Pavlovna (Julie). *A Common Story.* A young widow whom Surkov was courting. To oppose him, Petr Aduev asked Aleksandr Aduev to try for her affections.

Talleyrand-Périgord, Charles Maurice de (1754-1838). *The Adolescent* (1, 5, 3). The French diplomat who was minister of foreign affairs during the Napoleonic period. Arkadii Dolgorukii felt that if he were as rich as a Rothschild, such a diplomat as Talleyrand would not outshine him. *The Idiot* (4, 10). Lebedev claimed he had been born to be a Talleyrand but had always remained a Lebedev. *The Village of Stepanchikogo* (1, 3). Egor Rostanev felt he had to be as great a politician in his household as the famous Talleyrand was in relations with European countries.

Tamara. *The Precipice* (3, 12). The heroine of M. Iu. Lermontov's poem "The Demon" (1829-1839). Kozlova quoted a line from it when Raiskii scolded her for unfaithfulness to her husband.

Tamerlane (Timur) (1336-1405). *The Brothers Karamazov* (2, 5, 5). The Oriental conqueror who was mentioned by Ivan Karamazov in his philosophical poem. The Grand Inquisitor said that conquerors such as Timur were but the unconscious expression of man's craving for universal unity.

Tania. *The Idiot.* The girl to whom Vera Lebedeva referred when her father tried to scare her by stamping his feet. Only Tania, according to Vera, would be afraid of such an action.

Tantsev. *The Village of Stepanchikogo.* A name which Vidopliasov chose to exchange for his last name until the other peasants pointed out that it rhymed with an unprintable word.

Tarant'ev, Mikhei Andreevich. *Oblomov.* The morose and contemptible man who took advantage of Oblomov whenever he could. When the latter realized that Tarant'ev was trying to extort part of the Oblomov estate, he showed a rare display of courage and ordered Tarant'ev from his apartment.

Tarapygina, Avdotia. *The Devils.* The name given to a woman in a rumor that was assumed to have been started by Petr Verkhovenskii. She was supposed to have criticized a public flogging and was dealt with by the police.

Taras. *Oblomov.* The blacksmith who almost suffocated in a sauna and had to be revived with a bucket of water. *The Precipice.* Berezhkova's coachman.

Taras Bul'ba. See Bul'ba, Taras.

Taras Tikhonovich. "Ivan Ivanovich and Ivan Nikiforovich," in *Mirgorod.* The court secretary who read cases aloud even though the judge did not listen.

Tarasevicheva, Antonida Vasil'evna. *The Gambler.* The wealthy grandmother with lynx-like eyes whose death everyone was anticipating. Her arrival and her loss of her fortune at the gambling tables shocked everyone.

Tartuffe. *The Precipice* (1, 5). The hero in a comedy by that name (1664) by Molière. Tartuffe was a religious hypocrite who pretended to be religious when it suited his ulterior motives. Anna Petrovna decided that modern plays were not so intriguing as *Tartuffe*, and planned to write a play herself.

Tasso, Tarquato (1544-1595). *The Precipice* (2, 5). The famed Italian writer whose works Raiskii read.

Tat'iana. *The Adolescent* (3, 8, 1). The heroine of A. S. Pushkin's *Eugene Onegin* (1820-1830). She was mentioned by Versilov when he spoke of painful scenes in literature. He referred to Tat'iana's spurning of Onegin after he fell in love with her. *The Brothers Karamazov* (4, 10, 6). While talking with Alesha Karamazov, Kolia Krasotkin mentioned Pushkin's heroine.

Tat'iana Ivanovna. *Oblomov.* A peasant with whom Zakhar talked occasionally, comparing notes about their masters. *The Village of*

Stepanchikogo. A lady, not young, who "may be a distant relative" and who was staying at Egor Rostanev's when the narrator arrived. Foma Fomich Opiskin wanted Egor to marry her for her money.

Telemachus. *Oblomov* (2, 1). A character from Homer's *Odyssey*. He was the son of Ulysses and Penelope. Sholtz read about him. *The Precipice* (1, 6). Raiskii did not enjoy reading the French prose epic about Telemachus by François de Salignac de La Mothe-Fénelon (1651-1715). (3, 12). Mentioned by Raiskii.

Teliatnikov, Alesha. *The Devils*. The well-bred civil servant who was in the room when Nikolai Stavrogin bit the governor's ear.

Teliatnikov, Maksim. *Dead Souls*. A dead serf and former shoemaker whose soul Chichikov bought.

Tell, William. "Nevskii Prospect," in *Arabesques*. A legendary Swiss hero who was used by F. Schiller in his *Wilhelm Tell* (1804).

Teniers, David (Elder) (1582-1649). *The Precipice* (2, 5). The Flemish painter whom Kozlov preferred to Raphael.

Teniers, David (Younger) (1610-1690). *The Devils* (1, 3, 3). The noted landscape and portrait painter. Varvara Stavrogina sent her painting by Teniers to Stepan Verkhovenskii to make his place more presentable in case Karamazinov called on him.

Tentetnikov. *The Devils* (3, 1, 1). The narrator reported that people of station and dignity such as Tentetnikov can begin to heed the words of the most worthless individuals. Tentetnikov was a landowner in Gogol's *Dead Souls*.

Tentetnikov, Andrei Ivanovich. Dead Souls. A young, single landowner who was not a bad man but wasted his life away.

Tereb'eva. *Crime and Punishment*. A woman whose name Lebeziatnikov mentioned while he was talking with Luzhin. She had informed her parents that she was through with conventional marriage and had entered into a free-love liaison.

Terentev. *The Idiot*. A deceased military officer whom General Ivolgin claimed to know.

Terentev, Ippolit. *The Idiot*. Kolia Ivolgin's best friend, who was a consumptive. He wrote "My Necessary Explanation," in which he gave the reason for killing himself. He attempted suicide since he had only a few weeks to live, but the gun did not go off because he had forgotten to put the cap on it. He died at the end of the novel.

Terenteva, Lena. *The Idiot*. The daughter of Marfa Terenteva. When General Ivolgin led Prince Myshkin to Terenteva's apartment, he asked the eight-year-old daughter of the widow to bring him a pillow.

Terenteva, Marfa Borisovna. *The Idiot*. A widow. When General Ivolgin escorted Prince Myshkin to Marfa Terenteva's, a terrible scene took place in which the widow accused the general of robbing her and giving her worthless IOUs. Ivolgin gave her Myshkin's twenty-five roubles, leaving the Prince broke.

Terentii. *The Precipice*. One of the few old servants who remembered Raiskii when he returned to his estate.

Terentych. *The Idiot*. The drunk who pointed out an entrance to Ippolit Terentev when he was chasing after a man who had dropped a packet. Ippolit mentioned the incident in his article "My Essential Explanation."

Teresa. *Poor Folk*. See Fal'doni.

Teucer. *The Brothers Karamazov* (4, 10, 5). The best archer among the Greeks in the *Iliad*. He was mentioned by Kartashov as a founder of Troy.

Thedora. See Fedora.

Themis. *Dead Souls* (1, 7). The Greek goddess of justice. When Chichikov and Manilov approached the administrative offices, the incorruptible priest of Themis popped out of the window.

Theresa. See Teresa.

Thérèse-philosophe. *The Gambler* (16). A woman in society. When Mlle. Blanche set up a salon on the narrator's money, a certain woman named Hortense was called Thérèse-philosophe. The reference was to an erotic book entitled *Thérèse-philosophe, ou Memoires pour servir a l'historie de D. Dirrog et de Mlle. Eradice* (1748). It was assumed that the author was either Montigny or the Marquise d'Argens.

Thersites. *The Eternal Husband* (7). The foul-mouthed common soldier in the Grecian army who was killed by Achilles in a quarrel. The poem in the novel was "Das Siegesfest" by Schiller (1803) and was translated into Russian by V. A. Zhukovskii (1828).

Thibaut, Jules. *The Idiot*. A teacher in the school in Switzerland where Prince Myshkin lived. He was jealous of the prince.

Thomas, See Foma.

Thomas, St. *The Brothers Karamazov* (1, 1, 5). The disciple of Jesus who doubted. While talking with Alesha, Fedor Karamazov mentioned that St. Thomas did not believe until he saw for himself. However, it was not a miracle which he saw, according to Fedor; rather, he believed because he wanted to believe. (4, 11, 9). In

Ivan Karamazov's nightmare, the devil said that St. Thomas
believed because he wanted to. *The Village of Stepanchikogo* (1, 2).
Foma (Thomas) Fomich Opiskin maintained that his nameday
was the same as Il'iush Rostanev's so that he would also receive
a present.

Thucydides (460?-400? B.C.). *The Precipice* (1, 16). The most famous
historian of ancient times. Kozlov had his works and wanted
Raiskii to see how Volokhov had damaged them.

Tikhomirov. *The Adolescent.* A twenty-seven-year-old teacher with
black sideburns who participated in Dergachev's circle. The
name Tikhomirov was borrowed from the memoirs of the wife
of A. V. Dolgushin. See Dergachev.

Tikhon. *The Devils.* A priest to whom Nikolai Stavrogin confessed his
heinous conduct in St. Petersburg.

Tikhontsev, Valentin Ignatevich. *The Village of Stepanchikogo.* A man who
was made an assessor in 1841, according to Ezhevikin.

Timofei. *The Brothers Karamazov.* The driver of the carriage from
Mokroe that came for Grushen'ka.

Timofei Ivanovich. *Poor Folk.* The clerk who brought Devushkin the
document that had to be quickly copied. Devushkin left out a
whole line.

Timofei Petrovich. *The Gambler.* The man who wired the general and
his family from St. Petersburg that Tarasevecheva was ill. He
was considered a reliable source, and all hoped that his next
wire would confirm her death.

Timur. See Tamerlane.

Timoshka. *Notes from a Dead House.* The executioner who beat Luka
Kuz'mich, giving him rests to revive during the blows.

Tit Vasil'ich. *Crime and Punishment.* One of the workmen who was
amazed at Raskol'nikov's remarks when he returned to the
scene of the murder of Alena Ivanovna.

Titan. *The Idiot* (4, 4). In Greek mythology, Titans were the children of
Gaea and Uranus, who ruled before the Olympian gods. General Ivolgin called Napoleon I that "Titan in adversity" who was
allegedly not ashamed to cry before Ivolgin, the Emperor's
page. Ivolgin was lying. *Oblomov* (4, 8). Sholtz felt that he and
Ol'ga Il'inskaia were Titans. "Taras Bul'ba," in *Mirgorod*. Ostap
Bul'ba bore his tortures like a Titan as his father Taras watched
in the crowd.

Titian (Tiziano Vecelli) (1477-1576). *Oblomov* (2, 4). The famous Italian
painter. Sholtz remembered that Oblomov had once wanted to

see the paintings of Titian. *The Precipice* (5, 25). Raiskii paid respects to Titian's paintings in the Dresden Museum.

Titov. *The Devils*. The merchant to whose house Marie Shatov went and reported Kirilov's death.

Tiul'panov. *The Village of Stepanchikogo*. A name which Vidopliasov chose to exchange for his last name. But then he changed his mind.

Tiumen'ev, Prince Michel. *Oblomov*. A figure in society. Goriuev could not come to Oblomov's because he was going to Prince Tiumen'ev's.

Tiutchev, Fedor Ivanovich (1803-1873). *The Brothers Karamazov* (2, 5, 5). The Russian poet who was mentioned by Ivan Karamazov in a philosophical poem.

Tocqueville, Count Alexis Charles Henri Maurice Clérel de (1805-1859). *The Devils* (1, 1, 5). The author of the book *La démocratie en Amérique* (1840), which was translated into Russian in 1860. Stepan Verkhovenskii often carried de Tocqueville into the garden, but he usually had de Kock in his pocket.

Tokarzewski, Simon. *Notes from a Dead House* (2, 7). A member of a Polish peasants' organization that fought against serfdom. In 1907 he published a book *Seven Years of Hard Labor*.

Tokeeva, Anna Petrovna. *The Precipice*. An acquaintance of Berezhkova. In Marfen'ka's opinion, her grandmother's dislike of Tokeeva was a sin.

Tolkachenko. *The Devils*. A queer fellow about forty who was known for his great knowledge of common rogues and robbers. He was the first to announce to Virginskii's group about the return of Petr Verkhovenskii from abroad. He was also a member of the group of five who carried out Shatov's murder.

Tolstoi, Lev Nikolaivich (1828-1910). *The Brothers Karamazov* (4, 11, 9). The Russian writer mentioned by the devil in Ivan Karamazov's nightmare. The devil maintained that man sees plots in his dreams far more complicated than those which Tolstoi wrote about.

Totskii, Afanasii Ivanovich. *The Idiot*. The aristocrat who took Nastas'ia Barashkova into his home when she was a child and then seduced her. When she was mature, he asked her to marry him, but she refused. When he wanted to marry another, he made an arrangement with General Epanchin: Totskii would marry one of the general's daughters if Nastas'ia married Gania Ivolgin. The latter arrangement was broken off when Nastas'ia ran off with Rogozhin.

Touchard. *The Adolescent.* The founder of a school which Arkadii
   Dolgorukii attended. He met Lambert at Touchard's as a boy.

Tovkach, Dmitro. "Taras Bul'ba," in *Mirgorod.* Tara's old friend who
   was second in command of Taras's Cossack group.

Tovstogub, Afanasii Ivanovich. "Old-World Landowners," in
   Mirgorod. The sixty-year-old landowner who always wore a
   camlet-covered sheepskin.

Tovstoguba, Pulkheria Ivanovna. "Old-World Landowners," in
   Mirgorod. The fifty-five-year-old wife who was grave and rarely
   laughed. When her runaway cat returned, she decided it was a
   sign that death had come for her. She made preparations and
   died.

Trepakin. *Dead Souls.* A landowner neighbor of Korobochka.

Trepalov. *The Idiot.* The man who helped Rogozhin collect 100,0000
   roubles for Nastas'ia Filippovna, which she threw into the fire,
   telling Gania Ivolgin he could have them if he took them out.
   Trepalov also was in the tale which Totskii told during Nastas'ia
   Fillipovna's party.

Trifilii. "The Overcoat." A name which his mother considered for
   Akakii Akakievich before settling on the name Akakii.

Trifon Borisovich. *The Brothers Karamazov.* An innkeeper at Mokroe
   who testified at Dmitrii Karamazov's trial that Dmitrii had
   squandered three thousand roubles on an orgy at his establish-
   ment.

Trifon Nikitich. *The Brothers Karamazov.* A name used by Kolia
   Krasotkin while teasing a clerk.

Trifonov. *The Brothers Karamazov.* An old widower with a big beard who
   was the merchant to whom Katerina Ivanovna's father loaned
   money.

Trishatov. *The Adolescent.* A very pretty boy who was a friend of
   Andreev. Together they were continually trying to extort
   money from Lambert.

Trishin. *The Village of Stepanchikogo.* A person involved in a law suit who
   was mentioned by Ezhivikin. The latter claimed that Trishin
   was found guilty of not taking proper care of government
   property because his niece had run off with an officer the year
   before.

Trishka. *Dead Souls.* A tailor. At the Khlobuev estate, Trishka's kaftan
   system was followed: the cuffs were cut off to fix a hole at the
   elbow.

Trojan. *The Devils* (3, 5, 4). A *brave homme* of Troy in Homer's *Iliad*. When Mrs. Virginskaia helped deliver Marie Shatova's baby, she worked like a Trojan, meaning with the courage and spirit of the ancient Trojans.

Tros. *The Brothers Karamazov.* A name mentioned by Kartashov as one of the founders of Troy.

Trudoliubov. *The Underground Man.* A military lad, remarkable in no way, who was a former classmate of the Underground Man.

Trukhachevskii. *Dead Souls.* The man whom Sobakevich suggested for a witness of the purchase deeds when Chichikov was buying dead souls.

Trusotskaia, Natal'ia Vasil'evna. *The Eternal Husband.* Trustoskii's deceased wife, who had had an adulterous affair for a year with Vel'chaninov. She was passionate, cruel, and sensual. She hated depravity; yet she herself was depraved. She considered her affairs no concern of her husband, and she cast Vel'chaninov off like an old shoe.

Trusotskaia, Olimpiada Semenovna (Lipochka). *The Eternal Husband.* The second wife of Trusotskii. She was a priest's daughter and was very attractive. She met Vel'chaninov accidentally at a train station, causing Trusotskii much embarrassment.

Trusotskii, Pavel Pavlovich. *The Eternal Husband.* A confused, middle-aged man. Mourning for his deceased wife Natal'ia, he went to St. Petersburg to transfer to another post. An ulterior motive in his move was to see his wife's former lover Vel'chaninov, whom he had secretly loved for years. He confessed his feelings to Vel'chaninov and tried to kill him, not fully understanding why. Later Trusotskii remarried and forgot his depraved feelings for his friend.

Tsimmerman. *Crime and Punishment.* See Zimmerman.

Turgenev, Ivan Sergeevich (1818-1883). *The Adolescent* (1, 6, 3). The famous Russian writer. Arkadii Dolgorukii enjoyed reading Turgenev's *Hunter's Sketches* (1852) aloud. *The Brothers Karamazov* (3, 8, 3). When Dmitrii Karamazov went to beg money from Madame Khokhlakova, she agreed to help him and talked about the change in her own personal philosophy. She claimed to be a realist, cured of romanticism, and shouted, "Enough!", referring to Turgenev's work "Enough" (1865). *The Devils* (2, 1, 2). Peter Verkhovenskii said that he did not understand Turgenev's nihilist Bazarov in *Fathers and Sons* (1862) and felt that the literary hero was a mixture of Byron and Gogol's

Nozdrev. *The Eternal Husband* (3). Trusotskii told Vel'chaninov that his first visit in the country in the old days had been like a scene from a Turgenev play because of the warm hospitality. *The Idiot* (4, 9). When Dostoevskii commented on modern nihilism à la Turgenev, he was referring to *Fathers and Sons* (1862).

Tushara. *The Adolescent* (1, 2, 3). A former landlord of a pension where Arkadii Dolgorukii stayed in Moscow.

Tushin. *The Devils.* The deceased father of Liza. He left her a fortune of 200,000 roubles.

Tushin, Ivan Ivanovich. *The Precipice.* The landowner who lived in a forest. Berezhkova wanted him as a husband for Vera. He was very positive and accomplished whatever he planned.

Tushina. *The Devils.* Praskov'ia Drozdova's name during her first marriage.

Tushina, Anna Ivanovna. *The Precipice.* A friend of Berezhkova.

Tushina, Liza. *The Devils.* The heiress who was taught by Stepan Verkhovenskii until she was eleven. She then lived abroad and met Nikolai Stavrogin in Paris. In love with him, she was tormented by his indecision. When she went to see the murder victims at the fire scene, she was attacked and killed by the mob for her association with Nikolai.

Tuzikov. *The Brothers Karamazov.* A boy whom Kolia Krasotkin envied for being taller than he was.

Tychkov, Nil Andreevich. *The Precipice.* The president of the Chamber of Deputies whom Raiskii visited with Berezhkova.

Ulanov. *The Village of Stepanchikogo.* A name which Vidoplaisov chose to exchange for his own last name until the other servants said it rhymed with Bulianov (blockhead).

Ul'iana. *Poor Folk.* Varvara's old nurse.

Ulita. *The Precipice.* One of the few servants who remembered Raiskii on his return to his estate.

Ulitina, Sof'ia Matveevna. *The Devils.* A young religious widow who befriended and nursed Stepan Verkhovenskii in the country. She went to live with Mrs. Stavrogina after Stepan's death.

Ulysses. *The Brothers Karamazov* (3, 8, 5) The Roman name for the Greek Homeric figure Odysseus. When Dmitrii Karamazov bought back his pistols from Perkhotin the night of the murder of Fedor Karamazov, Dmitrii said that he agreed with Ulysses that women are fickle. *Oblomov* (1, 9). Oblomov heard stories about Ulysses from his boyhood nurse.

Underground Man. *The Underground Man.* A spineless clerk who went underground for twenty years. His memoirs present one of the greatest philosophical polemics in literature: man in the state of apostasy.

Ustiantsev. *Notes from a Dead House.* A convict in the hospital who had a lung disease from having drunk a mug of vodka infused with tobacco. He had done the rash act while in terror of flogging.

Ustin'ia. *The Precipice.* The cook for Kozlova when she kept a boarding-house for students.

V——, Countess. *Poor Folk.* A social lioness. Rataziaev went to her receptions and said that she was a woman of great intellect and wit.

V——, Prince. *The Adolescent.* The friend of Versilov Junior with whom Versilov was staying when Arkadii Dolgorukii came to receive the money old Prince Sokolskii had sent him.

V——, I——. *The Precipice.* A politician. Aianov mentioned in his letter to Raiskii that I—— V—— was a candidate for the position of minister.

Vagengeim. *The Underground Man* (1, 4). A dentist. In the *General Address Book of St. Petersburg* in the 1860's, eight dentists were listed with the name Vagengeim. Their advertisements were spread all over the city. The Underground Man referred to them as if to all dentists.

Vakhrameev, Nestor Ignatievich. *The Double.* Goliadkin's colleague who was duty secretary the day Goliadkin sent a letter via Petrushka to Goliadkin Junior.

Vakhramei. *Dead Souls.* The name which Nozdrev used when he called Chichikov's servant Petrushka.

Vakhrushkin, Afanasii Ivanovich. *Crime and Punishment.* The merchant from whom Mrs. Raskol'nikova borrowed fifteen roubles to send her son. There was a wealthy, well-known merchant in Moscow by this name during Dostoevskii's life.

Vakhtissi. "The Overcoat." A name which Akakii Akakievich's mother thought of naming her son before settling on the name Akaii.

Valoniev. *The Adolescent.* When Arkadii Dolgorukii went to Lambert's to find out why Dar'ia had given him his address, two young male guests were amused at how Russian names were transliterated in the paper *Indépendance.* It was remarked that a name like Valoniev would come out as Wallonieff in the French paper.

Vania. *Dead Souls.* A diminutive of Ivan. Uncle Mikhei called Stepan the
     Cork by this name. *The Village of Stepanchikogo.* Mr. Bakhcheev
     used the name Vania for Foma Fomich Opiskin when referring
     to his rise in status from servant to master.

Vaniukha. *The Underground Man.* The name of a grave digger in the tale
     which the Underground Man told Liza the night they met.

Van'ka. *The Brothers Karamazov.* A diminutive of Ivan. When Ivan
     Karamazov was going to Smerdiakov's for a talk, he ran into a
     drunken peasant singing a song about a Van'ka. *Oblomov.* An
     Oblomov servant who was always called to help little Il'aia
     when he tried to do something by himself.

Van'ka-Tan'ka. *Notes from a Dead House.* The wench who was probably in
     on Kulikov's escape plan. According to A. F. Brangel', Dos-
     toevskii met such a woman with such a name in Siberia.

Varadat. "The Overcoat." A name suggested to Akakii Akakievich's
     mother for her son, but she settled on Akakii.

Varakhasii. "The Overcoat." A name which Akakii Akakievich's moth-
     er considered for her son before settling on Akakii.

Varen'ka. *A Common Story.* The name which Petr Aduev sometimes
     called Naden'ka.

Varents. *Crime and Punishment.* A woman who abandoned her family.
     While talking with Luzhin, Lebeziatnikov recalled Madame
     Varents, who had informed her husband that she was finished
     with her marriage, and then abandoned him and their two
     children.

Varlamov. *Notes from a Dead House.* A braggart who had a beggar for a
     girl friend. Bulkin attached himself to Varlamov even though
     they had nothing in common.

Varsonofii. *The Brothers Karamazov.* A former elder at the monastery
     who was revered as a crazy saint. He was remembered during
     Father Zosima's funeral because Varsonofii's body did not
     decompose so quickly as did Zosima's.

Varukh. "The Overcoat." A name suggested to Akaii Akakievich's
     mother for her son, but she settled on Akakii.

Varvara. *The Brothers Karamazov.* A holy martyr mentioned by Madame
     Khokhkakhova.

Varvara Alekseevna. *Poor Folk.* The heroine of the story who has a long
     friendship through correspondence with the despondent clerk
     Makar Devushkin. Varvara married to better her position, not
     for love.

Varvara Aleksandrovna. *The Brothers Karamazov*. The owner of the dog
which Dmitrii Karamazov noticed at Plotnikov's.

Varvara Nikolaievna. *The Precipice*. Raiskii's aunt who he thought was
like Armidas. See Armidas.

Varvinskii. *The Brothers Karamazov*. The district doctor who testified at
the trial about Dmitrii Karamazov's mental condition. Ivan
Karamazov remembered that Varvinskii had said Dmitrii
would end in madness. Varvinskii also asserted that Smerdiakov's epileptic fit was genuine.

Vasen'ka. *The Brothers Karamazov*. The missing son of Prokhorovna, the
old woman who came to Father Zosima seeking aid. The
incident was based on one from Dostoevskii's life. The nurse of
his children asked the writer for help when her son had not
written from Siberia. He assured her that she would soon hear
from him, and she did.

Vashti. *The Brothers Karamazov* (2, 6, 1). The Queen of King Ahasuerus in
the Old Testament (Esther 1, 10-19). When the king ordered her
to appear at a party to show her beauty, she refused and he
divorced her. Father Zosima mentioned her in his memoirs.

Vasia. *The Double*. A name used by Dostoevskii to refer to a typically
fine young man at the birthday party for Klara Berendeeva.
Notes from a Dead House. The younger brother of Akul'ka.

Vasil'ev. *Oblomov*. Oblomov's former colleague who was transferred to
Poland. *The Precipice*. The man who Berezhkova knew was
named Popov; but because he did not call on her, she called him
Vasil'ev. *The village of Stepanchikogo*. The drunken man who fell
asleep in an abandoned, broken-down carriage and could not
get out when he sobered up because the door had been nailed
shut as a joke. Vasil'ev got drunk because his master Egor
Rostanev was signing him over to Foma Fomich Opiskin.

Vasil'ev, Anton. *Notes from a Dead House*. The convict who was pressing
Sushilov for payment of a debt, forcing the latter, much to his
embarrassment, to ask Gorianchikov for a loan.

Vasil'ev, Stepan. *The Precipice*. The village elder whom Berezhkova
called by his full name as a matter of respect.

Vasilii. *A Common Story*. Petr Aduev's servant. *The Precipice*. The coachman of Natal'ia Ivanovna. Also, Father Vasilii was a priest
whom Marfen'ka listened to seriously.

Vasilii Fomich. *Oblomov*. Mar'ia Onisimovna's deceased husband.

Vasilii Nikitich. *The Precipice*. Raiskii's teacher of geography in school.

Vasilisa. *Oblomov.* A servant of the Il'inskiis. *The Precipice.* Berezhkova's servant who was trustworthy and very neat. She alone was allowed to handle her mistress's shawl.

Vasin. *The Adolescent.* Arkadii Dolgorukii's school friend.

Vas'ka. *Oblomov.* A runaway serf from the Oblomov estate. Another serf by that name was ordered to clear away the debris from the fallen balcony at the estate. *The Precipice.* A serf who was reprimanded for predicting Mot'ka's death.

Vasiukov. *The Precipice.* The man who was admired by Raiskii because he played the violin well and Raiskii loved music.

Vatrukhin. *The Precipice.* The man who sold home-made Madeira which Openkin preferred to Italian wines.

Vatutin, Tit Nikonych. *The Precipice.* Berezhkova's old friend and adviser who daily visited her and often brought small gifts.

Velazquez, Diego Rodriguez de Silva (1599-1660). *The Precipice* (5, 25). The great Spanish painter. In Europe, Raiskii saw his grandmother's image in the paintings of Valazquez.

Vel'chaninov, Aleksei Ivanovich. *The Eternal Husband.* A handsome, well-built man about thirty-eight who had doubtful morals and who had lived a full and grand life. His health was failing. He was terribly confused about his relationship with Trusotskii, whom he considered a degenerate. When Vel'chaninov learned that he had a daughter by Trusotskii's wife, he took care of the child till it died.

Velichkovskii, Paisii (1722-1794). *The Brothers Karamazov* (1, 1, 5). A great ascetic noted for his translations of the works of the church fathers into the Moldavian language. His life was published in a Moscow journal in 1845. Dostoevskii mentioned him in a discussion about the institution of elders in the Russian Orthodox Church.

Venus. *A Common Story* (2, 3). The Roman goddess of love. Tafaeva liked comedies about ancient gods. *The Idiot* (1, 15). A statue of Venus stood in Nastas'ia Filippovna's apartment.

Venus de Milo. *The Precipice* (1, 4). A famous statue (400? B.C.) of the goddess of love. Raiskii told Sof'ia that she was perfect, but not so perfect as the Venus de Milo.

Vera (Verochka). *The Precipice.* Berezhkova's young relative who called her grandmother. Vera was attractive and mature, but confided her thoughts to no one. She was educated, determined, and quiet.

Verigina. *The Adolescent*. An aristocratic hostess. When Arkadii Dolgorukii met Darzan, he told him that he was sure that they had
met the year before at Countess Verigina's.

Vernyi. *The Village of Stepanchikogo*. A name (meaning "truthful") which
Vidopliasov choose to exchange for his last name until his
fellow peasants rhymed it with *skvernyi* (the nasty one). Dostoevskii borrowed the play with words from a historical incident. During the Decembrist revolution, I. V. Shervud
(1798-1867) turned informer for the crown, whereupon the
tsar ordered that the term *"vernyi"* be added to his name.
However, his activities were so well known in society that he
was called *skvernyi*.

Verkhishin, *The Devils*. A name mentioned by the woman who visited
the so-called saintly monk Semen Iakovlevich. The monk had
the woman shown out.

Verkhovenskii, Petr Stepanovich. *The Devils*. Stepan's son who was
educated abroad. He returned to his home town and created a
revolutionary conspiracy which caused chaos in the town and
brought about the murder of Shatov.

Verkhovenskii, Stepan Trofimovich. *The Devils*. A disillusioned intellectual who slavishly attended Varvara Stavrogina for twenty
years. In a final attempt to break away from her, he became ill
and died after being rescued by her.

Verochka. *A Common Story*. A name which Petr Aduev called Naden'ka
by mistake. *The Precipice*. See Vera.

Veronese, Paolo (1528-1588). *The Precipice* (5, 25). The noted painter
whose works Rasikii admired in Dresden.

Versilov. *The Adolescent*. The legal son of Andrei Versilov and the half-
brother of Arkadii Dolgorukii. The younger Versilov was tall
and good-looking, but was extremely rude to Arkadii when
they met.

Versilov, Andrei Petrovich. *The Adolescent*. The master of Sof'ia Dolgorukaia, whom he seduced, thereafter remorsefully confessing to the husband. The son born of his union with Sof'ia was
named Arkadii. Versilov ran through three fortunes amount-
ing to 400,000 roubles.

Versilova, Anna Andreevna. *The Adolescent*. Arkadii Dolgorukii's stepsister who was tall and slender, with an oval and strikingly pale
face, and luxuriant black hair. She was twenty-two years old.

Vertykhvist. "Taras Bul'ba," in *Mirgorod*. A Cossack troop chief who
chose to stay and fight the Poles when others went to fight
Tartars.

Véry, Constant (1778-1845). *The Idiot* (4, 4). Napoleon I's valet. According to General Ivolgin, when he served as a page to Napoleon I he inspired the Emperor to write to the Empress Josephine a letter which was delivered by Véry.

Vesta. *A Common Story* (1, 5). The Roman goddess of the hearth. Aleksandr Aduev wanted Naden'ka to be the Vesta of his home. *Oblomov* (1, 9). As Vesta worshiped an eternal flame, the Oblomovs worshiped the norm of life they had inherited from their ancestors.

Viasnikov. *Oblomov*. The man who had dinners every Saturday for his friends.

Viazovkin, Timofei Fedorovich. *The Idiot*. A distant relative of Pavlishchev from whom Garila Ivolgin obtained letters which helped prove that Burdovskii was not Pavlishchev's son.

Vidopliasov, Gregorii. *The Village of Stepanchikogo*. Egor Rostanev's footman who Foma Fomich Opiskin decided was a poet. Foma therefore taught him how to write. Egor Rostanev was persuaded to publish *The Plaints of Vidopliasov* with a preface by Foma.

Viken'tev, Nikolaii Andreich (Nikolka). *The Precipice*. The twenty-three-year-old man who Marfen'ka decided was the best prospect for a husband she could find; so she married him.

Vikent'eva, Mar'ia Egorovna. *The Precipice*. Berezhkova's friend who felt that Marfen'ka was the best choice for her son. She and Berezhkova were not surprised when they heard of the plans for marriage.

Viktor. *The Precipice*. The proprietor of an inn. Nini ordered dinner at Viktor's farm, and no one could persuade her to change the date to another time.

Vilkin. *The Idiot*. A drunken person to whom Ferdyshchenko went to spend the night, but Vilgin was asleep and could not be aroused.

Villèle, Count Joseph (1773-1854). *The Double* (4). A French royalist who was in the cabinet of Louis XVIII from 1821 to 1827. While standing at the backdoor of Berendeev's, Goliadkin thought of a phrase by Villèle to the effect that all comes in due season to him who waits.

Virgil (Publius Virgilius Maro) (70-19 B.C.). *Dead Souls* (1, 7). The Roman writer. Gogol' wrote that Virgil served Dante as a collegiate registrar served his guard. (2, 3). Koshkarev wanted his peasants to read Virgil's poem about the glory of agricultural work.

Virginia. *The Precipice.* See Paul.

Virginskaia, Miss. *The Devils.* Virginskii's sister, who was a student and a nihilist. Her prototype in history was A. Dement'eva-Tkacheva, who financed the publications of the revolutionaries led by Sergei Nechaev (1847-1883).

Virginskaia, Mrs. *The Devils.* Virginskii's wife, who was a professional midwife. She kept her lover Lebiatkin in her home and made her husband support him. She attended the birth of Marie Shatova's baby.

Virginskii. *The Devils.* A local official called "half-baked" by Stepan Verkhovenskii. A member of Stepan's circle and Petr's group, Virginskii participated in the murder of Shatov, but screamed in horror during the affair.

Vishnepokromova, Varvara Nikolaevna. *Dead Souls.* A neighbor of Tentetnikov. Becoming tired of visits from his neighbors, Tentetnikov told a servant to tell Vishnepokromova that the master was not at home, even though he was standing in a window looking out.

Vitali, Ivan Petrovich (1794-1855). *The Precipice* (5, 25). The Russian sculptor and portraitist whose work Raiskii admired in the Cathedral of St. Isaac.

Vitovtova, Aleksandra. *The Adolescent.* The owner of a private theater where Versilov saw a performance of A. S. Griboedov's play *Woe from Wit* (1824).

Vladimir Semenovich. *The Double.* Andrei Filippovich's nephew.

Vlas. *The Precipice.* Berezhkova's servant.

Vlonskaia. *The Village of Stepanchikogo.* A fictional character. Foma Fomich Opiskin was writing a novel about a Countess Vlonskaia. Such light, aristocratic novels were popular in the 1830's.

Vogt, Karl (1817-1895). *The Devils* (2, 6, 2). A popular writer among liberals in the 1860's. In a district where Petr Verkhovenskii had been spending time, a lieutenant of the police went mad and bit his superior while receiving a reprimand. In the lieutenant's quarters, a candle was burning before Vogt's works.

Volkov. *Oblomov.* A young man who was a friend of Oblomov.

Volochkov. *A Common Story.* A man whom Aleksandr Aduev considered to be a mean nonentity.

Volokhov, Mark Ivanych (Markushka). *The Precipice.* The man who was so uncouth that he lighted his cigars with pages from the books in Raiskii's library. He was a revolutionary and loved Vera, but did not want to marry her.

Volokita, Anton. *Dead Souls*. Pliushkin's runaway serf, whom Chichikov bought.

Volokita, Nikita. *Dead Souls*. Anton's father, who was also a runaway.

Voltaire (François Marie Arouet) (1694-1778). *The Brothers Karamazov* (2, 5, 3). The famous French philosopher. When Ivan Karamazov said that some French philosopher remarked that "if there were no God, man would have to invent him," he was referring to Voltaire. *A Common Story* (3, 2). Tafaeva could not remember which works were Voltaire's and which were Chateaubriand's. *The Devils* (1, 3, 2). Dostoevskii stated that most Russian writers are forgotten and neglected after one generation, unlike Voltaire, who had something original to say. (2, 5, 2). The saintly Semen Iakovlevich sat in a shabby Voltaire chair when people came for an audience. (2, 10, 1). When von Lembke was waiting for a carriage, he picked up a book and read the famous line from Voltaire's *Candide* (1759): "Tout est pour le mieux dans le meilleur des mondes possible." His own agitation made him throw the book down. *The Idiot* (3, 9). Kolia Ivolgin that felt Ippolit Terentev's confession was full of tremendous thought which would have readily evident if Voltaire had written it. *The Precipice* (1, 6). Raiskii found Voltaire's works in his father's library and read them. *The Village of Stepanchikogo* (2, 3). Ezhevikin maintained that all authors are Voltairian and that the plague should take them all.

Vorkhovskii, Petia. *The Idiot*. The man who was desperately in love with Ordynseva and tried to obtain camellias for her. When Totskii tricked him and procured the flowers for the lady before Vorkhovskii could, the latter went to war and was killed in the Crimea.

Vorkhovskii, Stepen. *The Idiot*. A figure in the tale which Totskii told at Nastas'ia Filippovna's party. Stepan was the brother of Petia, who wanted to find camellias for his beloved.

Vovtuzenko. "Taras Bul'ba," in *Mirgorod*. A Cossack chieftain who rushed to Taras during the siege of the Polish city. He reported the deaths of several chieftains.

Vrazumikhin. *Crime and Punishment*. The name by which Razumikhin presented himself to the clerk from the merchant Shelopaev. The clerk brought Raskol'nikov money after his illness.

Vrublevskii. *The Brothers Karamazov*. The companion of Mussialovich during the orgy at Mokroe.

Vulcan. *A Common Story* (2, 3). The old Roman god of fire. Tafaeva liked comedies about ancient gods like Vulcan.

Vygoretskii, Prince. *The Idiot.* An aristocrat whom General Ivolgin claimed he had known in the military service. The prince was supposed to have been his captain at one time.

Vyrin, Samson. *Poor Folk.* A character in the story *The Stationmaster* (1830) by A. S. Pushkin (1799-1837). Devushkin referred to the work.

Vysatskii, Stepan. *The Devils.* The man who spread the news about the duel between Antemii Gaganov and Nikolai Stavrogin.

Vytiagushkin. *Oblomov.* Oblomov's overseer, who wrote him that the income on the estate had dropped.

Wagner, Adolf (1835-1917). *Crime and Punishment* (5, 3). The German economist whose work *General Conclusions on a Positive Method* was translated into Russian in 1866 by N. Nekhliudov. At Marmeladov's funeral dinner, Lebeziatnikov came late because he had taken an article by Wagner to an acquaintance.

Wallonieff. *The Adolescent.* See Valoniev.

Watt, James (1735-1819). *A Common Story* (1, 2). The inventer of the steam engine. Peter Aduev considered Watt a great man.

Weise, Christian Felix (1726-1804). *A Common Story* (2, 3). The creator of a book of children's stories which a teacher found for Tafaeva.

Wellington. "Notes of a Madman," in *Arabesques.* Poprishkin reported that an English chemist by this name had discovered that the earth would soon mount the moon. In his mental state, Poprishkin probably associated the famous English name with a chemist because it was the first name that come to mind. The first Duke of Wellington was Arthur Wellesley Wellington (1769-1852).

Werther. *Dead Souls* (1, 7). The hero of Goethe's *The Sorrows of Werther* (1774). Chichikov referred to Werther while talking with Sobakevich at a party. *Oblomov* (4, 8). When Sholtz thought about love, Werther came to his mind. *The Precipice* (2, 21). Vera told Raiskii that they were old enough to be beyond sentiment like Werther's.

Wieland, Christoph Martin (1733-1813). *Oblomov* (2, 1). The German writer whom Oblomov as a child read aloud to his father.

Wilhelm Meister. The Precipice (2, 5). A novel (1795-1796) by Goethe which Kozlov did not like.

Williams, Caleb. *Oblomov* (1, 7). The hero of a novel of the same name
(1794) by William Godwin (1756-1836). Zakhar was not so
blindly devoted to his master Oblomov as the Caleb Williamses
of the old time were to their masters.

Wurmerhelm, Baron von. *The Gambler.* The German aristocrat who
demanded that the general reprimand the narrator for insult-
ing the baroness. The baron was tall and lean, taut and covered
with a thousand wrinkles.

Wurmerhelm, Baroness von. *The Gambeler.* The German aristocrat
whom the narrator insulted to honor Polina's whim. He said to
her, "I have the honor of being your slave." She was a short,
stout, ugly woman with a double chin.

Xenophon (445-391 B.C.). *The Precipice* (3, 9). The Greek historian.
Volokhov felt that the brains of Kozlov's students must become
insipid after reading so much history.

Yorick. *The Brothers Karamazov* (3, 8, 5). The deceased jester Yorick
whose skull was apostrophized by Shakespeare's Hamlet.
Dmitrii Karamazov mentioned Yorick.

Young, Edward (1683-1765). *Dead Souls* (1, 8). The English poet whose
poems were popular with the postmaster in the town of N——.

Zadorozhnyi. "Taras Bul'ba," in *Mirgorod.* A Cossack who was killed
during the siege for the Polish city.

Zaezzhalov, Vasilii Tikhonych. *A Common Story.* The man who sent
Petr Aduev a request for help in straightening out some matters in the senate.

Zagoretskii. *A Common Story* (2, 3). A character from the play *Woe from
Wit* (1824) by A. S. Griboedov (1795-1829). Surkov quoted a line
from the play to Tafaeva.

Zagorianskii. *The Gambler.* One name by which Mlle. Blanche approxi-
mated her new surname after she had married the general. She
also thought the name might be Zagozianskii.

Zagoskin, Mikhail Nikolaivich (1789-1852). *A Common Story* (1, 2). A
popular writer in the 1830's. Gorbatova asked Petr Aduev to
send her books by Zagoskin.

Zagozianskii. *The Gambler.* See Zagorianskii.

Zakhar Profof'evich. "Ivan Ivanovich and Ivan Nikiforovich," in
Mirgorod. The man who told the judge that a blackbird would
sing if you pricked the little pimple that grows under its throat.

Zakhar Trofimych (Zakharka). *Oblomov.* Oblomov's servant who was as lazy as his master and hardly ever cleaned the apartment or picked things up. He loved his master. After Oblomov's death, Sholtz found Zakhar begging on the streets of Moscow and gave him help.

Zakhlebinin, Feodosii Petrovich. *The Eternal Husband.* The civil counselor who was the father of the fifteen-year-old girl Trustskii wanted to marry. Zakhlebinin had eight daughters and worried about their future. Consequently, he consented to the marriage.

Zakhlebinina. *The Eternal Husband.* Zakhlebinin's wife, who had an abundant figure and tired eyes.

Zakhlebinina, Katerina Fedosevna. *The Eternal Husband.* The twenty-four-year-old daughter of Zakhlebinin. She was distinguished from her seven sisters by her dress and luxuriant hair, and by her sweet face and gentle character. It was assumed that Vel'chaninov was interested in her when he visited.

Zakhlebinina, Nadezhda Fedosevna. *The Eternal Husband.* The most charming of the eight girls in the Zakhlebinin family. She was a brunette with blazing eyes and wonderful lips. While she was only fifteen, Trusotskii wanted to marry her. Nadezhda loved Aleksandr Lobov and refused Trusotskii.

Zalezhev. *The Idiot.* A member of Ragozhin's gang.

Zametov, Aleksandr Grigorievich. *Crime and Punishment.* A head clerk at the police station. Raskol'nikov half-jokingly confessed to the murder of the old pawnbroker during a conversation in a restaurant with Zametov.

Zapol'skii. *Poor Folk* (June 1st). The writer of a French grammar published in 1817. Varvara considered it a terrible book.

Zaraiskii. *A Common Story.* The name of the family that gave a ball which Aleksandr Aduev attended. When he later disappeared from society because of his despair over a lost love, the family asked his uncle Petr Aduev about him.

Zarnitzin. *The Idiot.* A man who, according to Terentev, was supposed to have allowed himself to die of hunger even though he was young.

Zatertyi, Isai Fomich. *Oblomov.* The man, who, Ivan Matveich advised Oblomov, could best settle the problems on the Oblomov estate.

Zavadskii. *Oblomov.* The name of the family where Ol'ga Il'inskaia often met a young man whom her aunt did not find suitable for her.

Zavalishin. *Dead Souls.* A man in the town of N—— whose name came from the Russian verb *zavalit'sia* ("to lay oneself down"). When the news of Chichikov's buying of dead souls spread through the town, people who had never stirred came to life, for instance, Zavalishin.

Zavialov. *The Adolescent.* The Russian to whom the English were supposed to have offered a million roubles for not putting his trademark on his products.

Zavialov, Fomka. *The Devils.* A man who was often drunk. When the "five" gathered at Erkel's house after the fire and the murder of the Lebiatkins, Tolkachenko was accused of urging Zavialov to set the fire. Tolkachenko denied it, maintaining that Zavialov was too drunk to have participated in the crime.

Zavilevskii. *The Eternal Husband.* An aristocrat who neglected his estates. When Aleksandr Lobov asked Trusotskii to forget Nadezhda Zakhlebinina, he mentioned that he was planning to help manage the count's estates.

Zeidler. *The Idiot.* The money lender whom Lebedev defended in court, to the outrage of his nephew. He claimed that his uncle had made an ass of himself in court.

Zemfira. *The Precipice* (2, 14). The gypsy heroine in A. S. Pushkin's poem "The Gypsies" (1824). Raiskii called Marina a Zemfira when he caught her at night with a man.

Zershchikov. *The Adolescent.* The owner of a gambling saloon which Arkadii Dolgorukii habituated.

Zeus. *Crime and Punishment* (1, 4). The King of the Greek gods. When Raskol'nikov pondered the fate of his mother and Dunia, he realized that he must save them from their debtors. He considered his own life and realized that he was thinking of himself as a future millionaire Zeus who would save them all. *Dead Souls* (1, 7). A town official had the power to advance or dismiss people like Zeus.

Zh——ki. See Zochowski, Josef.

Zheltopuz, Ivan Prokof'evich. *Poor Folk.* A character in a literary work by Rataziaev which Makar Devushkin praised as humorous.

Zhemarin. *The Idiot.* The name of a family that was murdered. Lebedev claimed that his nephew was capable of such a crime. In *Golos (Voice)* on March 10, 1868, Dosteovskii read a report from Tambov about the murder of a merchant named Zhemarin. Dostoevskii called the murderer Gorskii a typical youth of the 1860's who was influenced by the nihilists of that period. See Gorskii.

Zhemtiuzhnikov. *The Idiot.* The man with whom Ragozhin claimed
Nastas'ia Filippovna had shamed herself in Moscow.

Zherebiatnikov. *Notes from a Dead House.* An official who took morbid
pleasure in administering pain to the prisoners. He was thought
of as a monster by both prisoners and fellow officials. He was a
tall, fat man with puffy red cheeks, flashing teeth, and a hearty
guffaw.

Zhibelskii. *The Adolescent.* An attorney's clerk.

Zhileiko. *The Adolescent.* The actor who performed the role of Chatskii
in A. S. Griboedov's play *Woe from Wit* (1824) which was performed at Vitovtova's.

Zhukvskii, Vasilii Andreevich (1783-1852). *Dead Souls* (1, 8). A noted
romantic poet. The chairman of the administration office of the
town of N—— knew Zhukovskii's "Luidmila" (1808) by heart
and recited it well. *Oblomov* (4, 9). Alekseev told Oblomov that
Zhukovskii was the best Russian poet. *The Precipice* (2, 3).
Marfen'ka told Raiskii that she had read Zhukovskii's works.

Ziablova. *Dead Souls.* The unknown actress who played the role of Cora
in the Kotzebue play that was being presented when Chichikov
came to the town of N——.

Zibert. *Notes from a Dead House.* The officer who Skuratov said drank
forty glasses of water a day. A prisoner reflected that he must
have tadpoles in his belly.

Zimmerman. *Crime and Punishment* (1, 1). The owner of a noted hat store
on the Nevskii Prospect in St. Petersburg. Dostoevskii bought a
hat for himself in the store.

Zinaida. *Poor Folk.* A character in a book by Rataziaev.

Zinaida Mikhailovna. *Oblomov.* Ol'ga Il'inskaia told Oblomov that she
felt Sholtz loved her more than he did Zinaida because he talked
with Zinaida as he would a daughter.

Ziuleika. *Poor Folk.* The daughter of Kuchum in a story by Rataziaev.

Zochowski, Josef. *Notes from a Dead House* (2, 8). A history and natural-
science teacher who was sentenced for participation in the 1848
Warsaw uprising. He died in the Omsk convict prison in 1851.

Zolotukha, *Dead Souls.* The public prosecutor in the town of N——.
Sobakevich wanted him for a witness for the purchase deeds
even though he knew he was a shyster and bribe-taker.

Zon, von. See Sohn, von.

Zosima, Father. *The Brothers Karamazov.* The celebrated monastery elder
whose teachings became the basic philosophical concepts of the
novel. He was the spiritual guardian of Alesha Karamazov, and
Zosima's death caused the young man much sorrow. When the

father's body was laid out for viewing, the smell of decomposition became apparent all too soon. Never in the history of the monastery had a corpse smelled so putrid so quickly; the unbelievers rejoiced, and the believers were left with great disappointment and grave doubts. *The Devils*. A holy hermit referred to by Captain Lebiatkin.

Zosimov. *Crime and Punishment*. A friend of Razumikhin. He was a doctor and a student of mental diseases who took a great interest in Raskol'nikov's illness after the later had killed Alena Ivanovna.

Zubkova, Mar'ia Petrovna. *The Idiot*. A woman in the tale which Totskii told at Nastas'ia Filippovna's party. Totskii met Verkhovskii at Zubkova's and found out about the location of some camellias, which were in demand for a ball. See Verkhovskii.

Zubova, Vera Aleksandrovna. *The Idiot*. A widow and landowner from whom Garvila Ivolgin obtained a letter that helped prove Burdovskii was not Pavlishchev's son.

Zuia. *The Village of Stepanchikogo*. The peasant who had the chisel needed by Vasil'ev to get out of the carriage in which he was locked.

Zverev, Efim. *The Adolescent*. Arkadii Dolgorukii's old school friend from high school When Arkadii met him later at a technical college in St. Petersburg, they became friends. Arkadii asked him if he intended to go to America, a popular runaway place for young people in the 1870's.

Zverkov. *Notes from a Dead House*. The man at whose place Chekunda, considered the dirtiest female in the world, was accused of stopping off before proceeding to the prison. "Notes of a Madman," in *Arabesques*. The owners of the house to which the madman followed the lady with the talking dog Madgie. *The Underground Man*. A good-natured, well-mannered, and vulgar former schoolmate of the Underground Man. It was in Zverkov's honor that the schoolmates held the party to which the Underground Man invited himself. On that occasion, the Underground Man acted like a fool and was ignored by his companions. *The Village of Stepanchikogo*. The cavalry officer who ran away with the actress Kuropatkina before the performance she had been giving was completed. Egor Rostanev told the story to the annoyance of Foma Fomich Opiskin.

Zvonskii. *Dead Souls*. A name used by Gogol' in a comparison. Chichikov was speechless before the governor's daughter at the ball like some character with the name Zvonskii in a popular novel. The novels of A. A. Bestuzhev-Marlinskii (1797-1837) were very popular at that time.